From STEM To STEW

Finally Fixing Math Education By Turning It Upside Down

Marla Weiss

Copyright © 2017 Marla Weiss. All rights reserved.

No part of this book may be reproduced, stored in a retrieval system, or transmitted by any means without the written permission of the author.

First published October 23, 2017

ISBN–13: 978-1977803283
ISBN–10: 1977803288

Library of Congress Control Number: 2017915522
CreateSpace Independent Publishing Platform, North Charleston, SC

Because of the dynamic nature of the Internet, web addresses contained in this book may have changed since publication and may no longer be valid.

In memory of my father, one of the country's leading New Math teachers, who gave me both the gift and love of mathematics, who raised me in a home full of math, and who regularly asked me how I would fix math education

The author's father (standing left) is seen with Max Beberman (standing right and pointing), founder and leader of the University of Illinois Committee on School Mathematics (UICSM), one of the leading Sputnik New Math groups. The photo was taken at the University of Illinois in the late 1950s. Seated are three math teachers from Massachusetts learning the New Math curriculum and methods.

ACKNOWLEDGMENTS

With deepest appreciation to—

• my friend, Ellen, a college math major, who read an early draft, provided continual encouragement, and made a valuable suggestion for the organization of Chapter 18;

• my friend, Dorothy, who eloquently expressed that this book is a collection and culmination of decades of my work in varying aspects of math education;

• my friends, Bunny and Karen, who invited me to give pre-publication talks on this book, thereby helping me to organize the material and gain first-hand feedback from the attendees;

• my friend, Gwen, who made insightful comments relating the National Assessment of Educational Progress to Common Core Math;

• my remarkable, talented, former female students—Avila, Francesca, Geena, Jaclyn, Liz, Lynn, Sarah, and Stephanie—who provided quotes for the back cover; and

• all of my students who taught me more than I taught them about what students want and need to understand and enjoy math.

Acknowledgments

With sincere gratitude for the following permissions—

• Excerpts from THE EDUCATED CHILD by William J. Bennett, Chester E. Finn, Jr. and John T. E. Cribb, Jr. Copyright © 1999 by William J. Bennett, Chester E. Finn, Jr. and John T. E. Cribb, Jr. Reprinted with the permission of The Free Press, a division of Simon & Schuster, Inc. All rights reserved.

• Excerpts from THE DISCIPLINED MIND: What All Students Should Understand by Howard Gardner. Copyright © 1999 by Howard Gardner. Reprinted with the permission of Simon & Schuster, Inc. All rights reserved.

• Quotations (659 words) from SCHOOLS WITHOUT FAILURE by WILLIAM GLASSER, M.D. Copyright © 1969 by William Glasser. Reprinted by permission of HarperCollins Publishers.

• Quotations (1336 words) from THE CONSPIRACY OF IGNORANCE: THE FAILURE OF AMERICAN PUBLIC SCHOOLS by MARTIN L. GROSS. Copyright © 1999 by Martin L. Gross. Reprinted by permission of HarperCollins Publishers.

• Excerpts from THE SCHOOLS WE NEED AND WHY WE DON'T HAVE THEM by E. D. Hirsch, Jr., copyright © 1995 by E. D. Hirsch, Jr. Used by permission of Doubleday, an imprint of the Knopf Doubleday Publishing Group, a division of Penguin Random House LLC. All rights reserved.

• Excerpts from THE SMARTEST KIDS IN THE WORLD by Amanda Ripley. Copyright © 2013 by Amanda Ripley. Reprinted with the permission of Simon & Schuster, Inc. All rights reserved.

• Excerpts reprinted by permission of the Publisher. From William H. Schmidt and Curtis McKnight, *Inequality for All: The Challenge of Unequal Opportunity in American Schools*, New York: Teachers College Press. Copyright © 2012 by Teachers College, Columbia University. All rights reserved.

• Excerpts from THE LEARNING GAP: WHY OUR SCHOOLS ARE FAILING AND WHAT WE CAN LEARN FROM JAPANESE AND CHINESE EDUCATION by Harold W. Stevenson and James W. Stigler. Copyright © 1992 by Harold W. Stevenson and James W. Stigler. Reprinted with the permission of Simon & Schuster, Inc. All rights reserved.

• Excerpts from THE TEACHING GAP: Best Ideas From the World's Teachers for Improving Education in the Classroom by James W. Stigler and James Hiebert. Copyright © 1999 by James W. Stigler and James Hiebert. Reprinted with the permission of The Free Press, a division of Simon & Schuster, Inc. All rights reserved.

Acknowledgments

With sincere gratitude for the following courtesies—

• Excerpts from *Educational Wastelands: The Retreat From Learning in Our Public Schools* by Arthur Bestor, University of Illinois Press, under Fair Use.

• Excerpts from THE PROCESS OF EDUCATION by Jerome S. Bruner, Cambridge, Mass.: Harvard University Press, Copyright © 1960, 1977 by the President and Fellows of Harvard College.

• Excerpts from TOWARD A THEORY OF INSTRUCTION by Jerome S. Bruner, Cambridge, Mass.: The Belknap Press of Harvard University Press, Copyright © 1966 by the President and Fellows of Harvard College.

• Excerpts from *Why Knowledge Matters: Rescuing Our Children From Failed Educational Theories* by E. D. Hirsch Jr., Harvard Education Press.

• Excerpts from *The Death and Life of the Great American School System: How Testing and Choice Are Undermining Education* by Diane Ravitch, Basic Books, Hatchette Book Group, under Fair Use.

• Excerpts from REIGN OF ERROR: THE HOAX OF THE PRIVATIZATION MOVEMENT AND THE DANGER TO AMERICA'S PUBLIC SCHOOLS by Diane Ravitch, copyright © by Diane Ravitch. Used by permission of Alfred A. Knopf, an imprint of the Knopf Doubleday Publishing Group, a division of Penguin Random House LLC. All rights reserved.

• Excerpts from *The Technology of Teaching*, courtesy of the B. F. Skinner Foundation.

OTHER BOOKS
By Marla Weiss

Available at most online bookstores and AuthorHouse.com

Novels

School Scandalle
(debut)
School Scoundrelle
(sequel)

Math Workbooks

MAVA Math: Number Sense
MAVA Math: Number Sense Solutions
MAVA Math: Grade Reviews
MAVA Math: Grade Reviews Solutions
MAVA Math: Middle Reviews
MAVA Math: Middle Reviews Solutions
MAVA Math: Enhanced Skills
MAVA Math: Enhanced Skills Solutions

Available from Terrapin Software at www.terrapinlogo.com

Computer Programming Workbooks

Go, Logo!
Go, Logo! Solutions

For future books by Marla Weiss and additional information, please visit her website: www.mavabooks.com

CONTENTS

ACRONYMS	xv
Chapter 1. Selecting Breadth and Depth	1
Chapter 2. Specifying the Scope	5
Chapter 3. Ridiculing Mathematics	7
Chapter 4. Detailing the Problem	9
Chapter 5. Establishing the Framework	17
Chapter 6. Bolstering Societal Wellness and National Security	29
Chapter 7. Testing Poorly Nationally	35
Chapter 8. Testing Poorly Internationally	45
TIMSS	46
PISA	51
Chapter 9. Interceding Presidentially	57
President Harry Truman (April, 1945—January, 1953)	57
President Dwight Eisenhower (January, 1953—January, 1961)	58
President John Kennedy (January, 1961—November, 1963)	59
President Lyndon Johnson (November, 1963—January, 1969)	59
President Richard Nixon (January, 1969—August, 1974)	60
President Gerald Ford (August, 1974—January, 1977)	61
President Jimmy Carter (January, 1977—January, 1981)	61
President Ronald Reagan (January, 1981—January, 1989)	62
President George H. W. Bush (January, 1989—January, 1993)	64
President Bill Clinton (January, 1993—January, 2001)	65
President George W. Bush (January, 2001—January, 2009)	67
President Barack Obama (January, 2009—January, 2017)	70
President Donald Trump (January, 2017—Publication Date)	72

xii Contents

Chapter 10. Chasing Reforms	73
Math Reform 1. Sputnik New Math	75
Math Reform 2. Back to Basics	84
Math Reform 3. Constructivism	85
Math Reform 4. Math Wars	91
Math Reform 5. Common Core State Standards Math (CCSSM)	99
Chapter 11. Hindering Solutions	109
Obstacle 1. In-field Teachers	110
Obstacle 2. Colleges of Education	116
Obstacle 3. Out-of-field Teachers	125
Obstacle 4. Math Teacher Pay	128
Obstacle 5. Foundational Structure of Math	130
Obstacle 6. Vocabulary and Symbols	131
Peculiar Terminology, Duplicate Definitions, Related Symbols, Key Words, Nonexistent Terms, Confused Terms, Modified Lies, Modernized Terms, English Translation, Ambiguous Definitions	
Obstacle 7. Absences	136
Obstacle 8. Math Anxiety	136
Obstacle 9. Parents	139
Obstacle 10. Curriculum	141
Obstacle 11. Drill	152
Obstacle 12. Fractions	153
Obstacle 13. Algebra	154
Obstacle 14. Ability Grouping	161
Obstacle 15. Inequality	165
Curricular Tracking, Teacher Decisions	
Obstacle 16. Textbook Publishers	169
Obstacle 17. State Policies	179
Obstacle 18. School Boards	182
Obstacle 19. School Administrators	183
Obstacle 20. Teacher Unions	184
Obstacle 21. Classroom Structure	188
Obstacle 22. Time Management	190
Obstacle 23. Classroom Size	192
Obstacle 24. Cumulative Review	195

Contents

Obstacle 25. Homework	196
Obstacle 26. Summers	201
Obstacle 27. Tutoring	203
Obstacle 28. Homeschooling	204
Obstacle 29. Charter, Independent, Magnet, Religious, and Virtual Schooling	205
Obstacle 30. Grade Inflation	205
Obstacle 31. Report Cards	208
Obstacle 32. Transparency	211
Obstacle 33. Standardized Testing—School Assessment	212
Obstacle 34. Standardized Testing—University Admission	219
Obstacle 35. Associations of Math Education	221
Obstacle 36. Education Organizations	226
Obstacle 37. Research	229
Obstacle 38. Misguided Experts	231
Obstacle 39. Media	232
Obstacle 40. Technology	235
False Hopes, Misuses, Naysayers	
Obstacle 41. Computer Science	240
Obstacle 42. Fads	242
Notebook Quizzes, Problem of the Day, Classroom Games, Popular Games, Multiplication Arrays, Box-and-Whisker Plots, Household Math, Mile Wide/Inch Deep, STEM, Math Writing, Cooperative Learning, Singapore Math	
Obstacle 43. Attitude	250
Obstacle 44. Motivation	253
Obstacle 45. Sports	253
Obstacle 46. Myth: Girls vs. Math	254
Obstacle 47. United States Government	258
Obstacle 48. United States Supreme Court	261
Obstacle 49. Bandage Approaches	264
Independent Thinking, Pilot Program Expansion, Student Transfers, Math Teacher Coaches, Math Specialists, Alternative Certification	
Obstacle 50. Individuality vs. Replication	268
Chapter 12. Learning Mathematics	271

Contents

Chapter 13. Using Technology	279
Chapter 14. Organizing the Curriculum	287
1. Objectives	289
2. Structure	289
3. Foundation (Background)	290
4. Content (Rigor)	292
5. Sequence	293
6. Spiraling (Review)	294
7. Integration	296
8. Coherence	296
9. Episodes	298
10. Themes	299
Chapter 15. Training Teachers, Changing Teaching	301
Chapter 16. Understanding Programmed Instruction	315
Chapter 17. Shrieking "Eureka!"	321
Chapter 18. Revealing the Plan	323
Chapter 19. Demanding Improvement	341
Scant Solutions	341
Contradictions	345
Realities	348
Chapter 20. Speaking Personally	355
BIBLIOGRAPHY	359
BIBLIOGRAPHY—PAGE NUMBER CROSS REFERENCES	387
WEBSITES ONLY	391
INDEX (Not in CONTENTS or BIBLIOGRAPHY)	401

ACRONYMS

ACT	American College Test
AFT	American Federation of Teachers
AMS	American Mathematical Society
ANAR	*A Nation At Risk*
AP	Associated Press
ASCD	Association for Supervision and Curriculum Development
CAI	Computer Assisted Instruction
CCSS	Common Core State Standards
CCSSM	Common Core State Standards Math
CEEB	College Entrance Examination Board
COM	Commission on Mathematics
CS	Computer Science
DAT	Dental Admission Test
DoDEA	Department of Defense Education Activity
DPMA	Distributive Property of Multiplication over Addition
DRT	Distance-Rate-Time
DSM	The Diagnostic and Statistical Manual of Mental Disorders
ED	United States Department of Education
ESEA	Elementary and Secondary Education Act
ESSA	Every Student Succeeds Act
ETS	Educational Testing Service
FIMS	First International Mathematics Study
GMAT	Graduate Management Admission Test
GRE	Graduate Record Examination
HSLDA	Homeschool Legal Defense Association
IEA	International Association for the Evaluation of Educational Achievement
ISTE	International Society for Technology in Education
MAA	Mathematical Association of America
MARS	Mathematics Anxiety Rating Scale
NACOME	National Advisory Committee on Mathematical Education
NAEP	National Assessment of Educational Progress
NAGB	National Assessment Governing Board
NAS	National Academy of Sciences

NBPTS	National Board for Professional Teaching Standards
NCEE	National Commission on Excellence in Education
NCES	National Center for Education Statistics
NCLB	No Child Left Behind Act
NCMR	National Committee on Mathematical Requirements
NCTAF	National Commission on Teaching & America's Future
NCTM	National Council of Teachers of Mathematics
NCTQ	National Council on Teacher Quality
NDEA	National Defense Education Act
NEA	National Education Association
NETP	National Education Technology Plan
NGA	National Governors Association
NMAP	National Mathematics Advisory Panel
NRC	National Research Council
NSB	National Science Board
NSF	National Science Foundation
OECD	Organisation for Economic Co-operation and Development
PCAT	Pharmacy College Admission Test
PISA	Programme for International Student Assessment
PRISM	Priorities in School Mathematics
PROM/SE	Promoting Rigorous Outcomes in Mathematics/Science Education
SAT	Scholastic Assessment Test
SAT–M	Scholastic Assessment Test Mathematics Sections
SIMS	Second International Mathematics Study
SMPY	Study of Mathematically Precocious Youth
SMSG	School Mathematics Study Group
SOTU	State of the Union
SSTP	Secondary Science Training Program
STEM	Science, Technology, Engineering, and Mathematics
TEDS-M	Teacher Education Study in Mathematics
TIP	Talent Identification Program
TFA	Teach For America
TIMSS	Trends in International Mathematics and Science Study
UICSM	University of Illinois Committee on School Mathematics
USGPO	United States Government Printing Office

1
Selecting Breadth and Depth

It has been said that an education is what survives when a man has forgotten all he has been taught.
B. F. Skinner [S17, p. 89]

How much math should children learn? One valuable technique in mathematical problem solving is "make a simpler problem." Answering a narrower question provides insight into answering a more complicated one. Thus, ask first: How much math should children learn about averages? Based on the straightforward computation of an average, that question might appear silly; but it's not.

Prior to the "redesign" of the SAT in March, 2016, College Board typically asked at least one *average* question on every exam. The following discussion uses a sampling of old, authentic, multiple choice SAT questions with the five answer choices omitted. A calculator was not permitted.

Should students know how to compute an average using the basic definition?

1. *A gymnast competed in a meet and received the following scores for three events: 9.5 for bars, 8.7 for balance beam, and 8.8 for floor routine. What is the average (arithmetic mean) of these three scores?* [C12, p. 42, #2]

Should students know how to compute an average of fractions?

2. *What is the average of 1/5 and 1/7?* (horizontal fraction lines in original) [C10, p. 263, #6]

Should students understand that knowing the sum of the numbers is often as helpful mathematically as knowing the actual numbers?

3. *If the sum of p and r is 18 and if s = 12, what is the average (arithmetic mean) of p, r, and s?* [C13, p. 263, #10]

Should students be able to find a missing number that yields a given average?

4. *The average (arithmetic mean) of a student's scores on four tests was 78. If she received a score of 70 on each of the first two tests and 84 on the third, what was her score on the fourth test?* [C10, p. 132, #10]

Should students be able to find a partial average?

5. *If the average (arithmetic mean) of four numbers is 37 and the average of two of these numbers is 33, what is the average of the other two numbers?* [C13, p. 235, #5]

Should students be able to compute additional numbers needed to convert from an original average to a new average?

6. *In a certain basketball league, a player has an average (arithmetic mean) of 22 points per game for 8 games. What is the total number of points this player must score in the next 2 games in order to have an average of 20 points per game for 10 games?* [C15, p. 315, #7]

Should students be able to compute the average of numbers removed from an original average?

7. *The average of 10 students' test scores is 72. When the 2 highest and 2 lowest scores are eliminated, the average of the remaining scores is 68. What is the average (arithmetic mean) of those eliminated?* [C10, p. 212, #24]

Should students be able to compute a range of values that yields an average?

Selecting Breadth and Depth

8. *A teacher gave a test to 30 students and the average score was x. Scores on the test ranged from 0 to 90, inclusive. If the average score for the first 10 papers graded was 60, what is the difference between the greatest and least <u>possible</u> values of x?* [C10, p. 273, #21]

Should students be able to compute an average when a percent, rather than the number of numbers, is given?

9. *On a biology quiz, the average score for a class was 80. If 20 per cent of the class scored 90 and 30 per cent scored 70, what was the average score for the remainder of the class?* [C13, p. 214, #34]

Should students be able to apply the definition of an average to a system of equations?

10. *The average (arithmetic mean) age of Dave, Emily, and Frank is 12. The average age of Dave and Emily is 11, and the average age of Emily and Frank is 10. What is the average age of Dave and Frank?* [C10, p. 82, #23]

The topic of averages is a microcosm of general mathematical thinking. The math writers at College Board believed that students should be able to handle these kinds of questions at a pace of roughly one question per minute—that correctly answering questions about a familiar topic (averages) in unfamiliar settings (turning the basic definition inside out and upside down) showed mathematical insight worthy of succeeding in numeric situations in college courses.

In speaking to groups of parents (sometimes homeschooling) and teachers (sometimes at independent schools), I have used this sequence of questions to explore the breadth and depth of mathematical thinking desired, to reveal the ambiguity and incompleteness of state standards and local curricula, and to show the path and option of enriching math education horizontally (within grade level) rather than vertically (rushing toward calculus).

For decades starting in the 1950s, College Board conducted numerous scientific studies examining short-term coaching effects on SAT math scores, declaring that the best way to achieve a high score was years of solid, vivid math education. With my tutored students I proved that high-quality, short-term preparation yielded improved results; yet with my classroom students I established that daily, rigorous math lessons produced high scores without extra help. Unfortunately, current trends in math education have reduced this essential breadth and depth.

Perhaps educators are right when they say that delivering this richness of math—especially for every topic, not just averages—is impossible within a normal classroom setting. But in my professional opinion, omitting that splendor is equivalent to eliminating the essence of math itself. Students learn some subject containing numbers, but it is not mathematics. If true mathematics cannot be taught within the traditional framework, then society needs a new approach. That new system of math education, as *From STEM To STEW* reveals, can be found at the intersection of noted psychology, modern technology, and rigorous mathematics.

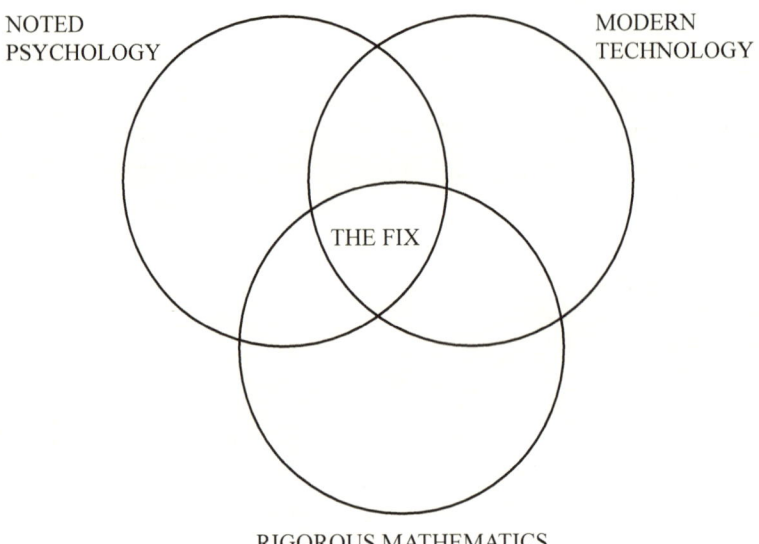

The answers to the 10 questions are: (1) 9.0, (2) 6/35, (3) 10, (4) 88, (5) 41, (6) 24, (7) 78, (8) 60, (9) 82, and (10) 15.

2

Specifying the Scope

Books serve to show a man that those original thoughts of his aren't very new after all.
Abraham Lincoln

Ordering the chapters of this book to make the clearest, strongest case was challenging. Ultimately, I rejected pure chronology in favor of separate categories. Ordering the material within chapters was equally demanding. Like mathematics itself, the chapters and their sections contain intrinsic overlap. Wanting to avoid repetition, I focused on readability, thereby keeping the entire length manageable and making the specific topics accessible.

Because many concerns in this book could be books themselves, I had to narrow both scope and content. *From STEM To STEW* is not a history of math curricula, not a compendium of math reforms, not a summary of math reports, not a survey of math exams, not a prescription for math teaching, and not an analysis of math learning. The goal is not to make points as lengthy as possible. Rather, the quantities of all discussions should fit together harmoniously, providing the necessary background, context, and perspective for readers to understand my solution.

People wishing more information on any specific matter may explore further. For example, instinctively we know that students forget math over the summer. Five citations make the point; fifty references drown the message. I apologize if I omitted anyone's favorite article or book.

In search of completeness, one may ask: When is research done? One answer is when references circle back, citing writings already found. I was fortunate to experience many such arcs.

While researching, I read many fascinating books by mathematicians, educators, historians, psychologists, and professors. Many of these authors used math to illustrate their points. Ironically, while the public deems math as having a dearth of understandable concepts, writers view math as possessing a wealth of germane examples.

I quoted extensively from other authors for two equally important reasons—in both regards intentionally presenting multiple viewpoints. First, I wished to give credibility to my arguments. Please do not assume that I agree with any authors just because I cited them, nor that they, unaware of any citations, agree with me. Moreover, I refrained from criticizing other authors, as found in some sources. Second, I wanted to provide background for my readers—for their personal understanding and for their publicly-aired comments. Discussion is stronger when pro and con critiques are from informed people. Overall, the main purpose of this book—to present my plan to improve math education—demanded the substantial justification that only a literature review can deliver.

Many citations included both "science" and "math," as if the two words were inseparable. As a non-scientist, I limited my scope to math education, sometimes using an ellipsis within quotations to remove the science aspect. Although math is an important tool in science, math and science are different subjects; and one must understand math before applying it.

To save space on the overall length, citations in square brackets give the matching reference in the bibliography, followed by the page number.

Surely, I will find more I wish I had added—such is the nature of writing. But children have one chance at an education, so the time is now.

3

Ridiculing Mathematics

A Conversation Between Two Math Symbols (illustrated in original)
i to π: "Be Rational."
π to i: "Get Real."
Math Jokes—If you get them, you probably don't have any friends.
G. J. Caulkins

In the 1960s Tom Lehrer, both mathematician and satirical lyricist/composer, poked fun at the subtraction algorithm using the problem 342 minus 173 in his song "New Math." Upon making an error he joked, "But the idea is the important thing." Then later in the song, he admonished, "Base eight is just like base ten really if you're missing two fingers." I admit that at the time, I laughed; I am not laughing now. (Versions of the song are on YouTube.)

Enter "images for math jokes" into a computer search engine, and numerous cartoon drawings will appear. Perhaps you have received some of these visuals as email forwards.

For example, "Find x in the given equation if $y = 2$" shortens the problem "What is the value of x in the given equation if $y = 2$?" by replacing the five initial words in interrogative format with the one word *find* in imperative format. Inanely, this concise sentence structure common in mathematics is a catalyst for humor in which jokesters treat the variable x as a person or object—something to physically *find*.

In 1994 *The American Mathematical Monthly* published the following joke about the change in math education through the decades. [A6] The journal confirmed to me by email that the source of the joke is unknown. Many variations of the joke now appear online with the wording changed from potatoes to rain forests, stock options, capital gains, search engines, and e-mails, depending on the current in-thing.

"1960s: A peasant sells a bag of potatoes for $10. His costs amount to 4/5 of his selling price. What is his profit?

1970s: A farmer sells a bag of potatoes for $10. His costs amount to 4/5 of his selling price, that is, $8. What is his profit?

1970s (New Math): A farmer exchanges a set P of potatoes with set M of money. The cardinality of the set M is equal to 10, and each element of M is worth $1. Draw ten big dots representing the elements of M. The set C of production costs is composed of two big dots less than the set M. Represent C as a subset of M and give the answer to the question: What is the cardinality of the set of profits?

1980s: A farmer sells a bag of potatoes for $10. His production costs are $8, and his profit is $2. Underline the word "potatoes" and discuss with your classmates.

1990s: A farmer sells a bag of potatoes for $10. His or her production costs are 0.80 of his or her revenue. On your calculator, graph revenue vs. costs. Run the POTATO program to determine the profit. Discuss the result with students in your group. Write a brief essay that analyzes this example in the real world of economics."

My point in emphasizing this "decades joke" is not to chuckle but to cry. What will the additions be for the decades 2000s, 2010s, 2020s, 2030s, 2040s, and 2050s? When will the joke stop? When and how will the United States finally teach math correctly? When will Americans stop ridiculing math? Are foreign competitors laughing?

4
Detailing the Problem

Pure mathematics is, in its way, the poetry of logical ideas.
Albert Einstein

"Any teacher who can be replaced by a computer, should be," affirmed Joe Crosswhite in 1986, then President of the National Council of Teachers of Mathematics. [C23, p. 574] Certainly, he was not advocating for replacing all math teachers with computers. In schools at that time, desktop computers were appearing; their use, purpose, and future were unclear and alarming. Crosswhite was comforting capable math teachers—that they should fear nothing—while chiding incompetent math teachers—that they should leave regardless. Thirty-one years later, I agree with Crosswhite's eerily predictive words. My solution for fixing math education involves judicious, not indiscriminate, replacement of math teachers with technology.

During the process of writing this book, a friend who is both a scientist and marketer told me that to affect change I should exaggerate, making the state of math education as dire as possible. Only impending doom will motivate parents, educators, and politicians to act, he implied. But I don't need to embellish my words; in my opinion, the situation is dreadful on its own.

I am aware of pockets of excellence in math education across this country. Superb math teaching and learning occur in various public, private, and charter schools, as well as in education colleges, homeschooling, and supplementary programs. I am neither ignoring nor discounting that great work. But I am making a larger argument—that bad math overpowers good education, that superficial math hinders deep understanding, that weak math precludes strong intellect, and that vacuous math hurts developing children. This country must create a system that eliminates ineffective math teachers, removes befuddled math explanations, and shuns shallow math textbooks. All students should have access to proper math education.

Quality math education opens doors to success. Certainly, high math performance is desirable on college admission exams (SAT and ACT). Moreover, many professional school entrance exams such as the DAT (dentistry), GRE (academics), GMAT (business), LSAT (law), and PCAT (pharmacy) contain a math or logic section; and the MCAT (medicine) requires math in its science sections. Knowing math also boosts scores on civil service and real estate exams as well as on various certification tests. With growing concern about police relations, one promising piece of a multi-faceted solution is having more young adults enter police academies in their home communities. I have wondered how these candidates will pass the math on law enforcement entrance exams, which require algebra, averages, percents, proportions, and rates in problems such as elapsed time, bank account balances, speed rates, stopping distance, and bail bonds.

Beyond testing, math knowledge positively influences logical thought and notable accomplishment in a broad range of careers. From my observations, math success would be more common than currently documented if students were taught properly. Math talent can surface when not a family trait, as hundreds of my students have demonstrated. Wasting this math ability, regardless of its degree, limits professional options individually and jeopardizes necessary growth nationally. Society should want great math education.

In 1978 *The Science Teacher* published a significant article by sociologist Lucy Sells. She described girls at the University of California at Berkeley who had ended high school math with Algebra II. They later learned that pre-calculus (the next course) was mandatory for college statistics, which in turn was required for essentially all soft-science majors such as psychology and sociology. The article stated that while 57 percent of entering male freshmen had taken four years of high school math, only 8 percent of the females had the same amount of preparation.

Because of their lack of math, 92 percent of females were excluded from 10 out of 12 divisions and 22 out of 44 majors. [S12]

Trouble in math education has existed for over a century. Many people do not know the long history of reforms, other than the Sputnik-era New Math (due to the scare of Soviet supremacy), the Bush-era No Child Left Behind (due to the onslaught of high-risk testing), and the present-day Common Core State Standards (due to the political debate). Parents gain cognizance when their children navigate daily math struggles. Others develop awareness when they view television ads or read magazine articles depicting the relative low performance of United States students on international math exams compared to youth of other industrialized nations. Recognition increases during presidential election cycles, when education news becomes more prominent.

Despite a growing presence of both STEM projects in school and STEM jobs in industry, many people maintain a bad attitude toward math, partly due to their own math anxiety. Unfortunately, some with this affliction are elementary school teachers who transmit fear to their students, thereby perpetuating the situation. Additional concerns include a plethora of the following: certified math teachers who are inadequately prepared; uncertified "math" teachers who teach out-of-field; math-ignorant state legislators who mandate education policies; math curriculum that is inadequate or inequitable; and for-profit publishing houses that create unsound, non-rigorous textbooks. Furthermore, successful citizens boast about never needing the school math taught to them, such as the quadratic formula. But how many students know at age 13 that they will definitely study law or literature?

Both locally and nationwide, I enjoy conversing with people I meet about their children's math education. Regarding Common Core, I recently heard a public school mother say, "I'm only one more moronic math homework assignment away from finding a private school." Translation: The teacher requires young children to do every simple word problem four different ways. Moreover, I have heard a middle school mother say, "My son's math teacher does not *teach*; she *assigns*." Translation: The teacher posts problem numbers on the board, orders students to work quietly at their desks, and answers questions by saying to look at the examples in the book.

Yet when teachers do interact with students, often the math is trivial; students cannot learn math if they are not taught math. Researchers James Stigler and James Hiebert made this point in the following anecdote: "In the fall of 1994, after several months of watching [TIMSS Video Study] tapes, the project staff met to present some preliminary impressions and interpretations. . . . One of the participants, a professor of mathematics education, had been relatively silent throughout the day." When asked to share his observations, he said that he could "summarize the main difference among the teaching styles of the three countries [United States, Japan, and Germany]. . . . In U.S. lessons, there are the students and there is the teacher. *I have trouble finding the mathematics* [emphasis added]; I just see interactions between students and teachers." [S26, pp. 25–26]

From my decades of teaching math, I have untold, frightening, firsthand tales. I relate nine here, but I suspect that countless readers have their own math horror stories.

1. In speaking with a woman transferring her 8th grade son from one top-notch Manhattan private school to another, I learned that the boy had flunked the math high school entrance exam, thus needing extensive private tutoring. The mother was surprised when I correctly guessed the name of the math series that the boy had used in grades K–7. The widely used book is one in which *I have trouble finding the mathematics*.

2. In helping a 5th grader, whose mother described her as hopelessly confused about fraction operations, I discovered that her teacher had used diagonal (instead of horizontal) fraction lines. Clear visibility of numerators and denominators is essential.

3. In helping a 5th grader with a multi-step word problem, she was exhausted upon reaching the last step: 600 divided by 4. Instead of simply using number sense to cut 600 in half twice (300, then 150), she became entangled in long division. She lacked useful mental math skills.

4. In helping a 6th grader, I asked, "What is 1 divided by 7?" The student began long division, rather than replying 1/7—an answer showing the power and meaning of fractions.

5. In asking a 6th grader to divide 3/4 by 1/2, the student converted the fractions to decimals and used tedious long division instead of simple fraction division.

6. In helping an 8th grader prepare for an algebra mid-term exam, I discovered that his teacher had skipped all of the classic word problems (age, coin, distance-rate-time, interest, mixture, uniform motion, work, and so on). Thus, the teacher had covered skills without applications.

7. In assessing a 7th grader who visited my former independent school as part of the application process, my colleague chose to give the guest an easy question as the oral participation requirement. Part of a longer problem, the area of a rectangle was needed. But the visitor replied, "I can't answer that. We're working on algebra now in my school."

8. In consoling a mother, panicked that her A math daughter now had a C grade, I reviewed the girl's papers. I saw that the teacher's parent volunteer who graded homework and quizzes had marked numerous problems wrong that were actually right. The textbook, in its first year of use at the school, included many open-ended questions such as, "Name a two-digit prime number." The parent-grader had ignored the caution in the answer book: "11; answers may vary."

9. In consulting with a headmaster concerned about declining standardized test scores in his school, I discovered his failure to discern that among the lower school head, the grade 4–5 math teacher, and the math specialist, not one had formally studied math.

Discussing Abraham Maslow's research on the hierarchy of human needs, Grace Burton wrote: ". . . one should not expect a hungry child to attend to the lesson on place value, or be surprised when the child who is physically abused at home or in the schoolyard fails to care about finding the least common denominator of two fractions." [B25, p. 249]

Decades later in 2013, foremost on Diane Ravitch's list to fix the ills of education was ending poverty. She stated succinctly, "Poverty matters." [R7, p. 93] Among others, Melissa Harris-Perry also argued that poverty comes first in addressing education: "If you're hungry, it's more difficult to learn math." [L3] However, human needs are not within the purview of this book. Fixing math education, purely and directly, is the goal.

How ironic—most people, including math jokesters and math education faux fixers, don't know what math really is. Of course, they have taken math in school. But they have neither experienced nor studied math; they have neither engaged mathematicians in conversation nor observed them at work. They think that math resides in tidy topic categories with no overlap, that math problems result in a single solution by one method, and that math requires more memorization than thinking. They believe that the majority of elementary school math is arithmetic, that school mathematics is hard, and that the ultimate goal of math education is competency in calculus or application to science. They are wrong.

In quoting four wonderful descriptions of mathematics, I ask readers to forgo previous conceptions and to enter into an unfamiliar but authentic world, thereby grasping a truer sense of mathematics. These passages have meaning for me not from one course or one professor but from a life of math. These passages have relevance for this book not for one chapter or one point but for an overall perspective. These passages should have relevance for everyone to appreciate the impact that mathematics has on society.

Description 1. Donovan Johnson and Gerald Rising

"Mathematics is a creation of the human mind, concerned primarily with ideas, processes, and reasoning. Thus, mathematics is much more than arithmetic, the science of numbers and computation; more than algebra, the language of symbols and relations; more than geometry, the study of shape, size, and space. It is greater than numerical trigonometry, which measures distances to stars and analyzes oscillations. It encompasses more than statistics, the science of interpreting data and graphs; more than calculus, the study of change, infinity, and limits.

"Primarily, *mathematics is a way of thinking*, a way of organizing a logical proof. ... *Mathematics is also a language*, a language that uses carefully defined terms and concise symbolic representations, which add precision to communication. ... *Mathematics is an organized structure of knowledge* in which each proposition is deduced logically from previously proved propositions or assumptions. ... *Mathematics is also the study of patterns*—that is of any kind of regularity in form or idea. ... *Mathematics is finally an art*. As is any other art, beauty in mathematics consists in order and inner harmony." [J7, pp. 3–4]

Description 2. G. H. Hardy

"A mathematician, like a painter or a poet, is a maker of patterns. If his patterns are more permanent than theirs, it is because they are made with *ideas*. A painter makes patterns with shapes and colours, a poet with words. ... The mathematician's patterns, like the painter's or the poet's, must be *beautiful*; the ideas, like the colours or the words, must fit together in a harmonious way. Beauty is the first test: there is no permanent place in the world for ugly mathematics." [H4, pp. 24–25]

Description 3. Paul Lockhart

"The first thing to understand is that mathematics is an art. The difference between math and the other arts, such as music and painting, is that our culture does not recognize it as such. Everyone understands that poets, painters, and musicians create works of art, and are expressing themselves in word, image, and sound. In fact, our society is rather generous when it comes to creative expression; architects, chefs, and even television directors are considered to be working artists. So why not mathematicians?

"Part of the problem is that nobody has the faintest idea what it is that mathematicians do. The common perception seems to be that mathematicians are somehow connected with science—perhaps they help the scientists with their formulas, or feed big numbers into computers for some reason or other. There is no question that if the world had to be divided into the 'poetic dreamers' and the 'rational thinkers' most people would place mathematicians in the latter category.

"Nevertheless, the fact is that there is nothing as dreamy and poetic, nothing as radical, subversive, and psychedelic, as mathematics. It is every bit as mind-blowing as cosmology or physics (mathematicians *conceived* of black holes long before astronomers actually found any), and allows more freedom of expression than poetry, art, or music (which depend heavily on properties of the physical universe). Mathematics is the purest of the arts, as well as the most misunderstood." [L10, p. 22–23]

Description 4. Ivars Peterson

"To most outsiders, modern mathematics is unknown territory. Its borders are protected by dense thickets of technical terms; its landscapes are a mass of indecipherable equations and incomprehensible concepts. Few realize that the world of modern mathematics is rich with vivid images and provocative ideas.

"Mathematics itself is changing. The field shows a renewed emphasis on applications, a return to concrete images, and an increasing role for mathematical experiments. These changes are making mathematics generally more accessible to outsiders than before.

"Gazing into mathland, one may now catch the glint of a fractal tower poking through the mist or feel the subtle pull of a swirling strange attractor. Sometimes the air murmurs with fragments of wondrous tales about mathematicians tangling with knots, poking into higher dimensions, pursuing digital prey, playing with soap bubbles, or wandering in labyrinths." [P8, pp. xiii–xiv]

5
Establishing the Framework

Neglect of mathematics works injury to all knowledge, since he who is ignorant of it cannot know the other sciences or the things of the world.
Roger Bacon

The following eleven cornerstones form a foundation for this book. The purpose of the many quotes that follow each, always in chronological order, is to substantiate the framework and to plunge the reader into educational literature, necessary for full understanding of the problem and its solution. Note that each cornerstone is decades old, underscoring the lack of progress. In the first six, math is indirectly inferable; in the last five, math is directly referenced. Of particular concern is the wide range of authors who have written about the continual underperformance by both math teachers and students.

Cornerstone 1. High-quality education, called a human right, has been vastly inequitable.

In 1968 B. F. Skinner wrote: "There are more people in the world than ever before, and a far greater part of them want an education. The demand cannot be met simply by building more schools and training more teachers. Education must become more efficient. To this end curricula must be revised and simplified, and textbooks and classroom techniques improved." [S17, p. 29]

In 1996 the National Commission on Teaching and America's Future, in the Executive Summary of a two-year study funded by the Rockefeller Foundation and the Carnegie Corporation of New York, stated: "We propose an audacious goal for America's future. Within a decade—by the year 2006—we will provide every student in America with what should be his or her educational birthright: access to competent, caring, qualified teaching in schools organized for success. This is a challenging goal to put before the nation and its educational leaders. But if the goal is challenging and requires unprecedented effort, it does not require unprecedented new theory. Common sense suffices: American students are entitled to teachers who know their subjects, understand their students and what they need, and have developed the skills required to make learning come alive." [N12, p. 10]

In 2012 William Schmidt and Curtis McKnight devoted an entire book to educational inequality. In three separate passages they wrote: "The sad reality is that the American educational system does not provide equal opportunity for all but rather perpetuates vast inequalities in content coverage . . . especially true for mathematics . . . ." [S7, p. xi] "Who would want to publicly defend the notion that a topic taught around the world in 8th grade—such as the algebraic idea of a slope—should be taught to children living in one part of the United States but not children living in another part?" [S7, pp. 27–28] "In education, the 'educationally rich' get richer and the 'educationally poor' get poorer. . . . The confusing lottery of differing learning opportunities is unacceptable. If we take 'freedom' and 'equality' seriously, then such large differences in society are unacceptable." [S7, pp. 205–206]

In 2013 Amanda Ripley wrote: "In countries where people agreed that school was serious, it had to be serious for everyone. If rigor was a prerequisite for success in life, then it had to be applied evenly. Equity—a core value of fairness . . . —was a telltale sign of rigor." [R13, p. 140]

Also in 2013 Diane Ravitch declared: "Education is a basic human right. It is impossible to imagine a modern society that does not educate its children, equitably and systematically. Our goal should be to provide a good school in every community." [R7, p. 298]

Cornerstone 2. Education has been widely criticized.

In 1953 Arthur Bestor expressed: "But on almost every count there is general dissatisfaction with the results of the twelve years of education

Establishing the Framework 19

currently provided by most of our public schools." [B11, p. 4]

In 1992 Harold Stevenson and James Stigler opened their book with the sentence: "It is no secret by now that American education is in crisis." [S25, p. 13]

In 1999 Martin Gross protested: "In most ways, that [Education] Establishment is an unscholarly, anti-intellectual, anti-academic cabal which can best be described as a conspiracy of ignorance, one with false theories and low academic standards. Well conceived, internally consistent, it has been powerful enough—thus far—to fight off outside challenges and true change. All this at the expense of our schoolchildren." [G12, p. 11]

Also in 1999 James Stigler and James Hiebert wrote: "The truth, as we see it, however, is that the situation in the United States demands improvement, not just because improvement is possible but because it is needed. Our students *are* being shortchanged. They could be learning much more and much more deeply than they are learning now." [S26, pp. 4–5]

In 2001 David Elkind stated: "Our schools today suffer from the same structural problems that made our industries an easy mark for foreign competition. School systems are often top-heavy administratively and excessively hierarchical and authoritarian. The creativity and innovation of teachers is deadened by overly close ties to the uniformity of educational publishing and testing. Finally, effective change in education is often blocked by school boards whose decisions may be dictated more by concerns of personality than by those that are properly pedagogical." [E1, pp. 49–50]

In 2009 Nicholas Kristof called education "our greatest national shame." He wrote: ". . . I'm coming to think that our No. 1 priority actually must be education." [K14]

In 2010 Diane Ravitch summarized: "We have known for many years that we need to improve our schools. We keep stumbling, however, because there is widespread disagreement about what should be improved, what we mean by improvement, and who should do it." [R6, p. 223]

Cornerstone 3. Broad societal issues such as funding levels, poverty magnitude, and culture wars have affected educational policy.

In 1969 William Glasser stated: ". . . poverty is not the sole or even the main cause of their [poor children's] hopelessness and resignation toward a future of failure. . . . *If school failure does not exist*, other handicaps can be more easily overcome." [G7, p. 4]

In 1999 Martin Gross noted: "*But—and this is most important—extra money put into the present system will be to no avail.*" [G12, p. 69]

In 2010 Diane Ravitch asked: "But what about the culture wars that will surely erupt if there is any attempt to decide what will be taught and learned in any subject? We can now see, with the passage of years, that it is possible to forge a consensus in every contested subject-matter terrain if the various factions accept the necessity of working together and the futility of trying to impose their views on everyone else." [R6, p. 232]

In 2011 Michael Greenstone and Adam Looney opined: "Unfortunately, the United States is in a period of stagnating educational achievement. Despite a doubling of per-pupil expenditures and decades of education reform in the United States, student achievement has only inched forward." [G10]

Cornerstone 4. Ironies, paradoxes, and contradictions have hindered education reforms.

In 1996 E. D. Hirsch described four paradoxes:
- "To stress critical thinking while de-emphasizing knowledge *reduces* a student's capacity to think critically."
- "Giving a child constant praise to bolster self-esteem regardless of academic achievement breeds complacency, or skepticism, or both, and, ultimately, a *decline* in self-esteem."

- "For a teacher to pay significant attention to each individual child in a class of twenty to forty students means individual *neglect* for most children most of the time."
- "Schoolwork that has been called 'developmentally inappropriate' has proved to be highly appropriate to millions of students the world over, while the infantile pabulum now fed to American children *is* developmentally inappropriate (in a downward direction) and often bores them." [H12, p. 66]

In 2001 David Elkind wrote: "At a time when American industry is 'restructuring,' education is 'reforming,' which means more basics, more hours, more homework, more testing—more of everything that is creating the problem. It is a classic case of the cure being worse than the disease." [E1, p. 50]

In 2010 Diane Ravitch expressed in her book's last paragraph: "At the present time, public education is in peril. Efforts to reform public education are, ironically, diminishing its quality and endangering its very survival. We must turn our attention to improving the schools, infusing them with the substance of genuine learning and reviving the conditions that make learning possible." [R6, p. 242]

Cornerstone 5. Reform movements have generally failed.

In 1992 Harold Stevenson and James Stigler stated: "Although articles describing the educational crisis appear almost daily in the nation's press, and although the 1989 summit meeting on education between the President and the nation's governors reflects an awareness of its immense proportions, discussions of the crisis seldom go beyond sober political pronouncements and hastily drawn, simplistic solutions." [S25, p. 14]

In 1996 E. D. Hirsch wrote: "Despite much activity, American school reform has not improved the nation's K–12 education during the decade and more since publication of *A Nation at Risk*. Among those of developed nations, our public schools still rank near the bottom; and in absolute terms, our children's academic competencies have not risen significantly. One reason for this continued stasis: the difficulty of spreading reform out into the vast system of fifteen thousand independent school districts. But it is doubtful that reform movements have succeeded even within the confines of their own model projects." [H12, pp. 2–3]

In 1999 James Stigler and James Hiebert wrote: "Despite massive efforts to improve [math] teaching in the United States, and despite perceptions by many that teaching was, in fact, improving, we found no evidence that anything had changed between 1995 [1st TIMSS video study] and 1999 [2nd TIMSS video study]. Students still were spending a large amount of time during each lesson reviewing material already learned in earlier lessons, and most of the lessons were devoted to practicing mathematical procedures rather than developing conceptual understanding. Students' learning opportunities had not changed." [S26, p. 184]

In 2013 Diane Ravitch noted: "As a historian of American education, I have seen, studied, and written about waves of school reforms that came and went." [R7, p. 4]

Cornerstone 6. The education establishment's stronghold has been long-lived, but corporate reformers have attempted a takeover.

In 1953 Arthur Bestor wrote: ". . . there is evidence of the debasement which the teaching profession is undergoing at the hands of the interlocking directorate of professional educationists. Forced to undergo the humiliation of piling up credits in sterile courses in pedagogy, virtually forbidden to align himself with scholars and scientists in his chosen field, ceaselessly indoctrinated in an 'official' educational philosophy, subjected to minute control and supervision by a professional educational hierarchy, the public school teacher cannot hope to resist administrative dictation to secure a real voice in the formulation of educational policy." [B11, p. 120]

In 1995 Charles Sykes critiqued: ". . . it is becoming harder to disguise the gap between the claims of public education and its realities. No other institution could survive such a record of mediocrity and failure unless it was insulated by the traditional protections of a monopoly—a guaranteed source of funding and layers of regulations, mandates, and bureaucratic insulation from accountability. But a closed system requires protection from competition and a monopoly on information if it is to survive. Both are breaking down. ... charter schools, for-profit schools, home schooling, private tutoring, ... are already transforming the educational landscape." [S29, p. 281]

In 1996 E. D. Hirsch summarized: "In short, educationist ideas have been carried too far." [H12, p. 126]

In 1999 Martin Gross stated: "The Establishment's dangerous thrust against facts, or knowledge, is endemic in our public schools." [G12, p. 61]

Also in 1999 James Stigler and James Hiebert predicted: "Class size reductions, vouchers, and most popular efforts to improve schools will end in disappointment if they do not fundamentally improve what happens inside classrooms." [S26, p. 3]

In 2010 Diane Ravitch explained: "As I watched both movements gain momentum across the nation, I concluded that curriculum and instruction were far more important than choice and accountability." She further declared: "Our schools will not improve if we entrust them to the magical powers of the market. Markets have winners and losers." [R6, pp. 12, 227]

In 2012 William Schmidt and Curtis McKnight wrote: "To date, one basic American value [fairness for all] has taken second place to another value [decentralization]. The result of our choices is a disastrously unequal educational system . . . ." [S7, p. 216]

In 2013 Diane Ravitch noted: "The [corporate reform] remedies now promoted as cures for the teaching profession are unlikely to have a beneficial effect; they are almost certain to make the profession less attractive to those who want to make a career of teaching." [R7, p. 116]

Cornerstone 7. Math teachers have been woefully inadequate.

In 1923 the report of the National Committee on Mathematical Requirements stated: "The greater part of the failure of mathematics is due to poor teaching. Good teachers have in the past succeeded, and continue to succeed, in achieving highly satisfactory results with the traditional material; poor teachers will not succeed even with the newer and better material." [N13, p. 13; B13, p. 399]

In 1953 Arthur Bestor proposed: "The distaste of many students for mathematics . . . is a measure of the number of elementary and secondary school teachers who are frightened of the subject because they have never been required to bring their command of it up to the threshold of genuine comprehension." [B11, p. 172]

In 1966 Jerome Bruner wrote: "It takes no elaborate research to know that communicating knowledge depends in enormous measure upon one's mastery of the knowledge to be communicated. . . . It is also quite plain from recent surveys that many primary and secondary school teachers are not, in the view of various official bodies, sufficiently well trained initially to teach their subject." [B21, p. 88]

In 1973 Richard Skemp explained: "Now, to know mathematics is one thing, and to be able to teach it—to communicate it to those at a lower conceptual level—is quite another; and I believe that it is the latter which is most lacking at the moment. As a result, many people acquire at school a lifelong dislike, even fear, of mathematics." [S15, p. 36]

In 1983 *A Nation At Risk* included findings related to math teachers: (1) an emphasis on computation at the "expense of other essential skills such as comprehension, analysis, solving problems, and drawing conclusions"; (2) a lack of "experienced teachers and scholars . . . involved in writing textbooks"; (3) the preparation of teachers "weighted heavily with courses in 'educational methods' at the expense of courses in subjects to be taught"; and (4) the severe "shortage of teachers in mathematics." [N11, pp. 10, 21–23]

In 1992 Harold Stevenson and James Stigler wrote: "Lacking the training and time that are necessary to prepare lessons and the opportunities to share experiences with one another, American teachers find it difficult to organize lively, vivid, coherent lessons. Preparing well-crafted lessons takes time. Teaching them effectively requires energy. Both are in short supply for most American [math] teachers." [S25, p. 198]

In 1999 James Stigler and James Hiebert stated: "What we can see clearly is that American mathematics teaching is extremely limited, focused for the most part on a very narrow band of procedural skills. Whether students are in rows working individually or sitting in groups, whether they have access to the latest technology or are working only with paper and pencil, they spend most of their time acquiring isolated skills through repeated practice." [S26, pp. 10–11]

Also in 1999 William Bennett, Chester Finn, and John Cribb questioned: "Why has the U.S. sunk so low in mathematics? No doubt there are several reasons. In many schools, the curriculum is disorganized. Many teachers don't have adequate math training. 'Honors' students may benefit from a rich and well-taught curriculum while the majority of their classmates make do with poorly taught, dumb-downed lessons. A lack of clear, tough academic standards is a widespread problem. Some schools simply don't require students to put in the time and practice needed to learn the fundamentals." [B10, p. 283]

Cornerstone 8. Students have lacked a grasp of mathematics.

In 1927 the NCTM's 2nd annual yearbook reported the following story: "In reply to her father's question about her success in high school, Mary replied that she was getting on all right except in algebra and she did not understand that. This formula was repeated night after night for some time but finally the phrase about algebra was dropped. Her father said, 'You understand your algebra all right now, don't you?' 'Oh, no!' replied Mary, 'but you don't have to understand it. You only do it the way they show you.'" [N14, pp. 132–133]

In 1995 Charles Sykes lamented: "In the United States today, only one in five nine-year-olds can perform even basic mathematical operations." [S29, p. 20]

In 2008 Jo Boaler relayed an anecdote about stopping at children's desks when visiting classrooms. When she would ask, *What are you working on?*, the students would typically reply with their page numbers. Following up with *But what are you actually doing?*, they would offer their exercise numbers. Boaler explained: "Students . . . really do not have a clear sense of the mathematical goals they are pursuing, the ways that the exercises . . . are linked to the bigger goals . . . , or the differences between more and less important ideas." [B14, p. 98]

In 2013 Amanda Ripley explained: "Math eluded American teenagers more than any other subject. . . . Again and again, the data revealed a startling math deficiency in the United States. Like a lack of nutrition, it started when children were small and took a cumulative toll." [R13, pp. 70–71]

Cornerstone 9. Demands for full high school math programs have continued despite states' minimal math graduation requirements.

In 1899 the second of four resolutions in the *Report of the Committee of the Chicago Section of the AMS* was: "That in the secondary school the standard course in mathematics should be sufficient to admit to college; that this course should be required of all pupils, and that the instruction in this course should be the same for all pupils." [B13, p. 196]

In 1983 the National Commission on Excellence in Education stated in *ANAR*: "The minimum high school diploma should require three years of mathematics and one-half year of computer science." [N11, p. 24]

In 1999 Martin Gross wrote: "Since students are in high school for four years, we should require four years of . . . math . . . and a full year of computer science" with trigonometry. [G12, p. 195]

In 2000 the National Council of Teachers of Mathematics affirmed: "All students are expected to study mathematics each of the four years that they are enrolled in high school, whether they plan to pursue the further study of mathematics, to enter the workforce, or to pursue other post-secondary education." [N24, p. 288]

Cornerstone 10. Mathematics is an essential subject.

In 1985 the College Board stated: "Mathematics is unique in that it is both a Basic Academic Competency and a Basic Academic Subject. This dual role reflects the dual position that mathematics historically has occupied in the school curriculum. It is a 'tool' subject that provides students with a family of specialized languages and associated skills for dealing with quantitative problems from any field of endeavor, and it is simultaneously one of the liberal arts whose mastery has marked an educated person since the time of Plato." [C11, p. 15]

In 2008 the National Mathematics Advisory Panel wrote: "No longer can we accept that a rigorous mathematics education is reserved for the few who will go on to be engineers or scientists. Mathematics . . . is essential for any citizen who is to be prepared for the future." [N36, p. 5]

Also in 2008 Jo Boaler wrote: "Mathematical know-how is not only one of the most important qualities for workers to possess in the future, [but also] it is critical to successful functioning in life." [B14, p. 7]

Cornerstone 11. Radical change has been suggested in math education.

In 1893 the NEA published "Report of the Committee on Secondary School Studies—Mathematics Subcommittee" based on its December, 1892 conference. Reprinted by the National Council of Teachers of Mathematics, this report began: "The Conference was, from the beginning of its deliberations, unanimously of opinion that a radical change in the teaching of arithmetic was necessary." [B13, p. 131]

In 1959 the Commission on Mathematics stated: "This then is the case for curricular revision: Mathematics is a dynamic subject, characterized in recent years by such impressive growth and such extensive new applications that these have far outrun the curriculum. Moreover, the traditional curriculum fails to reflect adequately the spirit of contemporary mathematics, which seeks to study all possible patterns recognizable by the mind, and by so striving has tremendously increased the power of mathematics as a tool of modern life. Nor does the traditional curriculum give proper emphasis to the fact that the developments and applications of mathematics have always been not only important but [also] indispensable to human progress." [C16, p. 9]

In 1963 the report of the Cambridge Conference on School Mathematics stated: "Mathematical education, to fulfill the needs of an advanced and advancing community, must be under continual scrutiny and undergo constant change, and it is the responsibility of all mathematicians, working in university, school, or industry, to concern themselves with the problem of keeping mathematical education vital and up-to-date." [C1, p. 1]

In 1985 Zalman Usiskin wrote in the lead essay of the NCTM Yearbook: "Mathematics is too important today to the average citizen who must deal with numerical information and for the person who must use mathematical techniques on the job for us to allow them to lack sufficient mathematical know-how. For this alone, if for no other reason, we need another revolution in school mathematics." [U5, p. 19]

Now in 2017, one hundred twenty-four years after the NEA's Mathematics Subcommittee, by writing *From STEM To STEW* I also call for *radical change* and *another revolution*. Our students and our nation can wait no longer.

6
Bolstering Societal Wellness and National Security

If we take education seriously, we can no more afford to gamble our safety upon inferior intellectual training in our schools than upon inferior weapons in our armory.
Arthur Bestor [B11, p. 6]

For over half a century and still ongoing, numerous authors, committees, and organizations have stressed the importance of math for both societal wellness and national security. The purpose of the following sampling of quotes in chronological order is again to provide background for readers to understand that math education is crucial and endangered.

In 1953 Arthur Bestor wrote: "As a people we believe that education is vital to our national welfare and to the security of our democratic institutions. . . . a republican system of government requires citizens who are highly literate, accurately informed, and rigorously trained in the processes of rational and critical thought." [B11, p. 12]

In 1959 two prominent education associations, the National Education Association and National Council of Teachers of Mathematics, stated in a joint publication: "There is a demand for excellence in education of each, up to the level of his capacity—a demand which is the measure of the health of our society. . . . Indeed, this country's future and the well-being of its citizens depend in no small measure on the mathematical product of our schools." [H16, pp. 4, 43]

In 1960 Jerome Bruner wrote: "The new spirit perhaps reflects the profound scientific revolution of our times as well. The trend is accentuated by what is almost certain to be a long-range crisis in national security, a crisis whose resolution will depend upon a well-educated citizenry."

Bruner expanded: "One thing seems clear: if all students are helped to the full utilization of their intellectual powers, we will have a better chance of surviving as a democracy in an age of enormous technological and social complexity." [B21, pp. 1, 10]

In 1969 William Glasser stated: "*Unless we can provide schools where children, through a reasonable use of their capacities, can succeed, we will do little to solve the major problems of our country.*" He cited weak schooling as causing the need for more institutions—such as prisons, halfway houses, and mental hospitals—as well as more services—such as counselors, social workers, and law enforcement—to quell social disturbances and help people who cannot succeed in society on their own. Glasser continued by writing that teaching children to routinely output "predictable answers to predictable questions" would instill "into the most basic institution of democracy, the educational system, the seeds of its own destruction." [G7, pp. 6, 44]

In 1980 the NCTM stated: "Mathematics is pervasive in today's world. Mathematical competence is vital to every individual's meaningful and productive life. It is, moreover, a valuable societal resource, and the potential of our educated citizenry to make significant use of mathematics is not being fully met. The amount of time the majority of students spend on the study of mathematics in school in no way matches the importance of mathematical understanding to their lives, now or in the future." [N18, p. 17]

In 1983 the report *A Nation At Risk* gave the powerful, infamous words that have become the most well-known quote addressing the relationship between education and national security: "Our Nation is at risk. . . . If an unfriendly foreign power had attempted to impose on America the mediocre educational performance that exists today, we might well have viewed it as an act of war. As it stands, we have allowed this to happen to ourselves. We have even squandered the gains in student achievement made in the wake of the Sputnik challenge. Moreover, we have dismantled essential support systems which helped make those gains possible. We have, in effect, been committing an act of unthinking, unilateral educational disarmament." [N11, p. 5]

In 1991 a report by the Carnegie Commission on Science, Technology, and Government stated: "There are at least two reasons why the federal government should pay special attention to math and science education: the increasing demand for numeracy and problem-solving ability in tomorrow's world, and the federal government's special responsibility for assuring the nation's technical capability to address national goals for the economy, environment, health, and security." The report continued: "Inadequacies in pre-college math and science education are a chronic and serious threat to our nation's future. The national interest is strongly bound up in the ability of Americans to compete technologically. This requires not only an adequate supply of scientific and technical professionals but [also] a work force able to solve problems and use the tools of a knowledge-intensive economy." [C2, pp. 7, 15]

In 1992 Harold Stevenson and James Stigler wrote: "The current educational crisis reverberates beyond the classroom, for a poorly educated work force directly hampers a nation's productivity and economic competitiveness. . . . The very quality of life in a modern nation clearly reflects the educational level of its citizens." [S25, pp. 13–14]

In 1993 Sheila Tobias explained that *The Dictionary of Occupational Titles* published by the U.S. Department of Labor uses six codes to represent the mathematics competency required by occupations. The labels are: Levels 1 and 2—arithmetic; Level 3—beginning algebra and geometry; Level 4—intermediate algebra and geometry; Level 5—calculus, statistics, and advanced algebra; and Level 6—advanced calculus and abstract algebra. Tobias noted that people who score only at Level 1 or 2 are eliminated from countless groups of jobs. [T10, p. 35; www6–1]

In 1995 Charles Sykes wrote in a book section titled *The Cost of Dumbness*: "It is hard to put an exact number on what the dumbing down of American education costs the economy, but it is possible to make some approximations. . . . And those approximations are high." [S29, p. 23]

In 1999 Martin Gross wrote: "If we fail to eliminate the conspiracy of ignorance that is fervently supported by the Education Establishment, we will never be confident that the nation will be able to prosper in the complex twenty-first century." [G12, p. 70]

In 2000 the NCTM wrote: "A society in which only a few have the mathematical knowledge needed to fill crucial economic, political, and scientific roles is not consistent with the values of a just democratic system or its economic needs." [N24, p. 5]

In 2007 a report by the National Academies Press stated: "Although many people assume that the United States will always be a world leader in science and technology, this may not continue to be the case inasmuch as great minds and ideas exist throughout the world. We fear the abruptness with which a lead in science and technology can be lost—and the difficulty of recovering a lead once lost, if indeed it can be regained at all. . . . This nation must prepare with great urgency to preserve its strategic and economic security." [N1, pp. 3–4] Following this warning was a recommendation to increase the number and quality of math teachers.

Also in 2007 Secretary of Education Margaret Spellings said: "We know math and science skills are the common currency everyone needs to have to succeed in the increasingly competitive global economy." [www6–2]

Again in 2007 the U.S. Department of Education wrote: "Our nation is at a turning point. . . . Today we live in a technology-driven global marketplace where ideas and innovation outperform muscle and machine." [www6–3]

In 2008 the National Mathematics Advisory Panel wrote: "National policy must ensure the healthy development of a domestic technical workforce with adequate scale and top-level skill. . . . The national workforce of future years will surely have to handle quantitative concepts more fully and more deftly than at present. . . . Sound education in mathematics across the population is a national interest. Mathematics literacy is a serious problem in the United States." [N36, p. 3]

In 2009 the National Research Council started a report with the words:

"Mathematics education has risen to the top of the national policy agenda as part of the need to improve the technical and scientific literacy of the American public. The new demands of international competition in the 21st century require a workforce that is competent in and comfortable with mathematics." [N37, p. 1]

In 2010 the *National Education Technology Plan* stated: "Education is the key to America's economic growth and prosperity and to our ability to compete in the global economy. It is the path to good jobs and higher earning power for Americans. It is necessary for our democracy to work. It fosters the cross-border, cross-cultural collaboration required to solve the most challenging problems of our time." [O2, p. ix]

In 2010 Diane Ravitch wrote: "Education is the key to developing human capital. The nature of our education system—whether mediocre or excellent—will influence society far into the future. It will affect not only our economy, but also our civic and cultural life." [R6, p. 223]

In 2011 the transcript of a Brookings Institution event stated: "Over the past 10 years, growth in STEM jobs was three times as fast as growth in non-STEM jobs. STEM workers play a key role in the sustained growth and stability of the U.S. economy and are particularly important in sectors where U.S. universities and businesses are on the cutting edge of innovation and new product development. . . . If STEM jobs are more stable and STEM workers earn higher wages and are less likely to become unemployed, then producing more STEM graduates and workers means having more Americans in well paying, high-growth jobs that can support healthy communities." [www6–4, p. 5]

In 2011 a U.S. Department of Education website explained: "What do national security, military readiness, and education have in common? It turns out that national security and quality education are closely tied together. A recent study found that 75% of America's youth are NOT qualified to join the Armed Forces. This could have serious effects on America's ability to defend itself." [U4]

In 2011 a Brookings article opened: "A strong educational system and the role of teachers have never been more important for America's workforce." It concluded: "Over the last 30 years, educational attainment and achievement have stagnated and, in the face of an increasingly competitive global economy, have contributed to a decline in the earnings of many Americans. The question is not whether additional reforms to our educational system are needed, but which reforms provide the most cost-effective ways of improving student achievement." [G10]

In 2012 the Council on Foreign Relations Press published *U.S. Education Reform and National Security: Independent Task Force Report* by Joel Klein, Julia Levy, and Condoleezza Rice. The Brookings description of the book stated: "Improving America's public schools cannot be considered a purely domestic concern: the country's ability to prepare students to compete globally is integrally tied to U.S. national security." [K7]

In 2013 researchers, funded by the Eunice Kennedy Shriver National Institute of Child Health and Human Development, published a study, opening with the sentence: "One in five adults in the United States is functionally innumerate; they do not possess the mathematical competencies needed for many modern jobs." [G5]

In 2013 Amanda Ripley wrote: "Diesel mechanics needed to know geometry and the basics of physics in order to diagnose and repair modern heavy machinery. They had to be able to read blueprints and technical manuals. They had to understand percentages and ratios in order to measure the gasses found in exhaust. All jobs had gotten more complex, including blue-collar jobs." [R13, p. 143]

Despite this abundance of warnings over decades connecting strong math education to a sound economy and a formidable military, American society has adopted an almost bipolar attitude toward the academic subject. Some embrace the invention of the drone but dismiss the usefulness of the Pythagorean Theorem. Others admire the drive of the Silicon Valley millionaires but shun the prime factorization homework of their children. But then national and international testing, in the next two chapters, offer a dose of reality.

7
Testing Poorly Nationally

The roots of education are bitter, but the fruit is sweet.
Aristotle

In 1969 Congress established the National Assessment Governing Board (NAGB), a bipartisan committee to set frameworks, write exams, and conduct educational testing of America's children. This entire system of evaluation, called The National Assessment of Educational Progress (NAEP) and trademarked as The Nation's Report Card, produces a periodic document detailing the academic achievement in various subjects, including math, of U.S. students at the elementary and secondary grade levels. NAEP is administered by the National Center for Education Statistics (NCES) of the U.S. Department of Education (ED). NCES wrote: "NAEP has two major goals: 1) to discover what American students know and can do in key subject areas, and 2) to measure educational progress over long periods of time." [N6, p. 4] Because NAEP is the only nationally representative, unbiased, and continuing assessment of American students' knowledge, NAEP results are crucial to evaluating the nation's educational condition and growth.

In 1973 NAEP conducted the first assessment in mathematics. Findings were noted in scholarly publications. For example, The Phi Delta Kappa Educational Foundation reported that less than 50% of the 17-year-olds could correctly perform cost comparisons among different sized packages of food, and only 20% of 9-year-olds and 66% of 13-year-olds could make correct change for a simple purchase. [A2, pp. 18, 20]

In 1981 NAEP conducted the second assessment in mathematics. An NCTM publication reported discouraging results: "At age 13, 71 percent of the students correctly found the area of a rectangle composed of square centimeters. Only 51 percent of the students correctly answered when the same rectangle was presented without the unit squares. When no squares were included in the picture, 23 percent of the students gave the perimeter of the rectangle rather than the area." Furthermore, for a problem with an accompanying picture (without unit squares) of a right triangle 9 cm by 12 cm by 15 cm (a magnification of the most recognizable 3-4-5 right triangle) that asked for the area, the same article stated: "Only 4 percent of the 13-year-olds and 18 percent of the 17-year-olds answered this item correctly." [H15, pp. 704–705]

In 1990 NAEP began a regular schedule of mathematics assessments, reporting scores by state. Testing, always done on students in grades 4 and 8, includes 12th graders in some years in some subjects. [N6, p. 7]

NAEP uses two measures: (1) a scale score (0 to 500 for grades 4 and 8, 0 to 300 for grade 12) that reflects what students know; and (2) achievement levels—Basic, Proficient, or Advanced. By default, a fourth level is Below Basic. NAEP describes these 3 achievement levels as follows: "Basic—denotes partial mastery of the knowledge and skills that are fundamental for proficient work at a given grade.
Proficient—represents solid academic performance. . . .
Advanced—signifies superior performance." [N7, p. 2]

The results, whether scale scores or achievement levels, reflect performance on carefully constructed tests, with scientifically valid and consistent frameworks. In general, Item Distribution covers five broad Content Areas: Number Properties and Operations; Measurement; Geometry; Data Analysis, Statistics, and Probability; and Algebra. Within each of the five areas are specific skills. Then superimposed are four additional features: 3 levels of complexity—Low, Moderate, or High; 2 question types—Multiple Choice and Constructed Response; 2 question lengths—Short or Extended; and 2 question settings—Pure Math (numeric) or Contextual Math (word problem). For reliable comparison among years, only occasionally does the framework change; for example, in 2009 new objectives were instituted for grade 12 and the new subtopic "mathematical reasoning" was introduced at all three grade levels in all five content areas. [N10, pp. 3, 6, 37, 51]

Testing Poorly Nationally

In its printed reports, the NAGB publishes extensive data on NAEP testing beyond the scope of this book, including tables by race/ethnicity, free/reduced-price lunch, and gender, as well as accommodations for learning differences, a practice begun in 1996. Moreover, the NCES website includes NAEP data by state, including DC and DoDEA (Department of Defense Education Activity). The NCES also posts NAEP long-term trend reports in math, extrapolated back to 1973.

Summarized from the NCES website, NAEP mean scale scores appear in Table 1. [www7–1]

According to Diane Ravitch, the NAEP tests are not constructed like those in school where students need 90% or higher to receive an A grade.

Table 1. NAEP Math National Average Scale Scores

	Grade 4 (0–500)	Grade 8 (0–500)	Grade 12 (0–300)
1990	213	263	NA
1992	220	268	NA
1996	224	272	NA
2000	228	275	NA
2003	235	278	NA
2005	238	279	150
2007	240	281	NA
2009	240	283	153
2011	241	284	NA
2013	242	285	153
2015	240	282	152

She stated: "The maximum on the [NAEP] scale is 500, but there is no expectation that the nation will one day score 500 or that a score of 241 can be translated to mean 241/500. It is not a grade of 48 percent. It is not a passing grade or a failing grade. It is a trend line, period." [R7, p. 45] Granted that a high ceiling is necessary, the 4th grade test does not contain middle school material, nor does the 8th grade test cover high school topics. As a classroom teacher, I would have been upset if my students had scored comparably to the national averages.

Still, some viewed the NAEP scale scores as strict percentages of the total and used the numbers in Table 1 to criticize math education. Designed to soften such reactions, the three achievement levels are, according to Ravitch, "judgments set by external panels that determine what students *should* know and be able to do." Yet she stated that the levels "have not led to better understanding [of the scale scores]. Instead, the public is confused about what expectations are appropriate." In repeat fashion, critics of the public schools used the achievement levels to make a stronger case that children are failing. [R7, pp. 45–48]

Summarized from the NAEP website, national achievement level percentages appear in Tables 2, 3, and 4. [www7–2] Annual sums of 99% or 101% are due to rounding.

In 2013 Diane Ravitch wrote positively about the trends, saying that NAEP math scores in both 4th and 8th grades "improved dramatically"

Table 2. NAEP Math Grade 12 National Discrete Percentages

	Below Basic	At Basic	At Proficient	At Advanced
2005	39%	38%	21%	2%
2009	36%	38%	23%	3%
2013	35%	39%	23%	3%
2015	38%	37%	22%	3%

Table 3. NAEP Math Grade 8 National Discrete Percentages

	Below Basic	At Basic	At Proficient	At Advanced
1990	48%	37%	13%	2%
1992	42%	37%	18%	3%
1996	38%	39%	20%	4%
2000	37%	38%	21%	5%
2003	32%	39%	23%	5%
2005	31%	39%	24%	6%
2007	29%	39%	25%	7%
2009	27%	39%	26%	8%
2011	27%	39%	26%	8%
2013	26%	38%	27%	9%
2015	29%	38%	25%	8%

from 1990 to 2011. She argued that in 4th grade the percent at Proficient or Advanced increased from 13% in 1990 to 41% in 2011, while the percent at Below Basic decreased from 50% in 1990 to 18% in 2011. Similarly, in 8th grade the percent at Proficient or Advanced increased from 15% in 1990 to 34% in 2011, while the percent at Below Basic decreased from 48% in 1990 to 27% in 2011. [R7, p. 50]

However, interpretations of data vary, and negative trends also emerge. For scale scores, while improvement in 4th and 8th grades occurred from 1990 to 2003, progress is statistically insignificant since the 2005 testing. In 12th grade, the scale scores are virtually unchanged overall. For achievement levels, while improvement in 4th and 8th grades is

Table 4. NAEP Math Grade 4 National Discrete Percentages

	Below Basic	At Basic	At Proficient	At Advanced
1990	50%	37%	12%	1%
1992	41%	41%	16%	2%
1996	36%	43%	19%	2%
2000	35%	42%	21%	3%
2003	23%	45%	29%	4%
2005	20%	44%	31%	5%
2007	18%	43%	34%	6%
2009	18%	43%	33%	6%
2011	18%	42%	34%	7%
2013	17%	41%	34%	8%
2015	18%	42%	33%	7%

significant for proficient or above from 1990 to 2005, growth is less marked in years thereafter. Moreover, only 3% at the advanced level in 12th grade is a questionable figure for successful global competition.

One particularly important analysis of the data is the comparison of cohorts—for example, students in 4th grade in 2005, 8th grade in 2009, and 12th grade in 2013. Table 5 is a cohort summary of Table 1, while Table 6 is a cohort summary of Tables 2, 3, and 4 for Proficient or Above. Because of the testing's shift in years, not all cohorts may be followed. For average scale scores, all five cohorts increased from 4th to 8th grade but dropped substantially in 12th grade as a percent of the total possible score.

Table 5. NAEP Math Average Cohort Scale Scores

	Grade 4 0–500	Grade 8 0–500	Grade 12 0–300
1992 Gr 4	220	272	NA
1996 Gr 4	224	275	NA
2003 Gr 4	235	281	NA
2005 Gr 4	238	283	153
2007 Gr 4	240	284	152

Table 6. NAEP Math Average Cohort Percentages

	Grade 4 Proficient +	Grade 8 Proficient +	Grade 12 Proficient +
1992 Gr 4	18%	24%	NA
1996 Gr 4	21%	26%	NA
2003 Gr 4	33%	32%	NA
2005 Gr 4	36%	34%	26%
2007 Gr 4	40%	34%	25%

For Proficient or Above, the performance presumably needed to use math in a STEM career, the most recent cohorts showed marked decrease as the school years progressed. In 1999 Martin Gross related this decline in cohorts to attitude by describing students' negative outlook toward math as inversely proportional to NAEP scores. Thus, 4th graders have higher scores and a less negative attitude toward math, whereas 12th graders have lower scores and a more adverse attitude. [G12, p. 185]

NAEP test results became important for another reason, serving as an unbiased score with which to contrast state test scores mandated by reform movements such as No Child Left Behind and Common Core. Diane Ravitch has been outspoken about the use of NAEP as a valuable yardstick. In a 2005 Op-Ed she wrote: "The release last month of test results by the National Assessment of Educational Progress . . . vividly demonstrated why varying state standards and tests are inadequate. Almost all states report that, based on their own tests, incredibly large proportions of their students meet high standards. Yet the scores on the federal test . . . were far lower. Basically, the states have embraced low standards and grade inflation." [R4] Moreover, in her 2010 book Ravitch wrote: "NAEP monitors trends; if the state says its scores are rising but its scores on NAEP are flat, then the state reports are very likely inflated. In a choice between the state's self-reported scores and an audit test, the public should trust the audit test." [R6, p. 162]

Again in 2013, Ravitch explained that only NAEP scores can be fairly compared to those of NCLB because NAEP "is a no-stakes test." She cited that no one knows "who will take it" and "what will be on" it. She detailed that "no student takes the full test," no child or school receives a score, no test-prep exists, and no bonus or penalty is connected. Ravitch concluded: ". . . so there is no reason to cheat, to teach to the test, or to game the system." [R7, p. 125]

Tables 1 through 4 reveal that scores are slightly worse from 2013 to 2015 in the two years when Common Core State Standards had been in effect in 42 states. Indeed, Tom Loveless wrote: "The 2015 NAEP scores were a political disaster for Common Core." Still, he did not totally assign blame: "Whatever is depressing NAEP scores appears to be more general than the impact of one set of standards or another." He commented: "Maybe CCSS has already had its best years and additional gains will be difficult to attain. Major top-down reforms [like New Math and NCLB] can have their strongest effects when first adopted . . . ." [L16, pp. 14–15] My key point is: *Promised gains are not present.*

No single state has the secret to great math teaching. Massachusetts, one of the most respected states for education, has consistently scored at the top. Yet in 2005, the NCES reported a score of 247 for Massachusetts 4th graders, 3 points below the statistical mean and only one point above comparable students in Kansas and New Hampshire. Also in 2005, 43% of Massachusetts 8th graders were Proficient or Advanced, equal to Minnesota's score, but still not a majority of the students. [N7, pp. 14, 16] Moreover, comparing the 2013 to 2015 NAEP testings, Massachusetts scores dropped from 253 to 251 in 4th grade and 301 to 297 in 8th grade [www7–3]—exactly during the years, as reported on the CCSS website, when Common Core was in full implementation in MA. And Tom Loveless remarked about the 2015 NAEP scores: "None of the states are [sic] setting the world on fire." [L16, p. 15]

A good teacher indirectly prepares students for NAEP by not sticking solely to the textbook, but by providing a rich math education with exposure to a variety of question types. My students did not all enter math competitions, but Math League and MATHCOUNTS provided different, creative problems. My students did not all apply to boarding school, but SSAT practice exams offered a fresh set of exercises. NAEP sample questions now available online also offer more variety.

Students' responses to specific questions is also discouraging. The NAGB has published *Frameworks* that include old questions with performance data. More accessible is the "NAEP Questions Tool" on the NCES website. [www7–4] Rather than bemoaning low knowledge from past years, I shall focus on the current situation. Below are seven released 2013 NAEP questions (most recent available) that reflect math deficiency. All use the official NAEP code number, in which M is multiple choice and 4 or 8 is the grade level. All are marked "Easy" by NAEP.

Question 2013–4M3 #9: *2/5 + 3/5 + 4/5* (with horizontal fraction lines). Only 55% of 4th graders correctly chose 9/5.

Question 2013–4M6 #8: (A picture shows a rectangle marked 6 feet by 8 feet.) *A teacher drew this rectangle on a playground. Sam walked around the rectangle on the lines shown. How far did Sam walk?*
Only 64% of 4th graders correctly chose 28 feet as the perimeter of the rectangle.

Question 2013–4M3 #1: *4 x 50 x 9*
Only 75% of 4th graders correctly chose 1800.
(Regroup factors into 2 x 2 x 5 x 10 x 9 = 18 x 10 x 10.)

Question 2013–8M3 #3: A picture shows 4 intersecting lines (2 parallel) labeled with street names and asks for the pair that appears to be perpendicular.
Only 63% of 8th graders chose correctly.

Question 2013–8M6 #1: *The length of a photograph is 5 inches and its width is 3 inches. The photograph is enlarged proportionally. The length of the enlarged photograph is 10 inches. What is the width of the enlarged photograph?*
Only 74% of 8th graders correctly chose 6 inches.

Question 2013–8M6 #2: *A car can seat c adults. A van can seat 4 more than twice as many adults as the car can. In terms of c, how many adults can the van seat?*
Only 69% of 8th graders correctly chose 2c + 4.

Question 2013–8M7 #3: The picture shows a spinner on a circle with 6 congruent sectors—3 marked Red, 2 marked Blue, and 1 marked Green. *If the arrow is spun once, what is the probability that the arrow will land on either Red or Blue?*
Only 67% of 8th graders correctly chose 5/6.

Given percentage performance data in the C and D school-grade range on "Easy" questions, naturally scores drop on the "Medium" and "Hard" questions, as well as on the questions that require a written response. Moreover, the four 8th grade questions are actually 6th grade material from my teaching experience, making the national situation even more discouraging.

8
Testing Poorly Internationally

Mathematics knows no races or geographic boundaries;
for mathematics, the cultural world is one country.
David Hilbert

"Bad news from international comparisons of student achievement is no longer seen as esoteric by the American public; these days it is on the front page and a linchpin of many politicians' stump speeches." Like too many statements regarding math education, that one sounds current but was written in 1999 by Stigler and Hiebert. [S26, p. 1] In 2017 Tom Loveless stated: ". . . handwringing about how the U.S. does on international tests contends with baseball as a national pastime." [L17, p. 8]

U.S. students participate in two different international math exams—TIMSS and PISA. These tests vary in both content area and question style, but most importantly in the overall approach. In general, though oversimplified, TIMSS tests math skills while PISA tests math reasoning. As Amanda Ripley wrote in 2013, "The promise of PISA was that it would reveal which countries were teaching kids to think for themselves." [R13, p. 15] Unfortunately, often headlines bashing U.S. rankings fail to identify the specific exam.

The National Center for Education Statistics compares the tests as follows: "TIMSS and PISA both assess aspects of mathematical skills; however, they differ in terms of whom they assess and what they measure. TIMSS assesses 4th- and 8th-graders' knowledge of specific mathematical topics and cognitive skills that are closely linked to the curricula of the participating countries. PISA assesses 15-year-old students' *mathematics literacy* . . . . On account of these different aims, the two assessments ask students to perform different tasks." [I5, p. 16]

NCES further explains TIMSS: "TIMSS asks 4th- and 8th-graders to complete a range of multiple-choice and short constructed response questions that test their knowledge of specific mathematics topics or content domains—*numbers* (manipulating whole numbers and place values; performing addition, subtraction, multiplication, and division; and using fractions and decimals), *geometric shapes and measures*, and *data display* at grade 4; and *numbers, algebra, geometry*, and *data and chance* at grade 8." [I5, p. 16]

NCES further explains PISA: "In contrast, PISA does not focus exclusively on outcomes that can be directly linked to curricula, but instead emphasizes real world applications of mathematical knowledge. PISA's content domains are defined in terms of the manner in which mathematical knowledge is likely to be encountered in the larger world: space and shape, change and relationships, and uncertainty. Thus, PISA presents students with a variety of situations or problems in which, as young adults, they are likely to encounter numbers and mathematical concepts. . . . Most questions are multiple-choice, but there are some constructed response questions as well which could ask students to explain a mathematics principle, show their calculations, or explain their reasoning. PISA complements information obtained from studies such as TIMSS because it addresses whether students can apply what they have learned both in and out of school." [I5, p. 16]

TIMSS

The International Association for the Evaluation of Educational Achievement (IEA) oversees TIMSS. In 1964 the IEA administered the First International Mathematics Study (FIMS) in 12 countries—Australia, Belgium, England, Finland, France, Germany, Israel, Japan, Netherlands, Scotland, Sweden, and United States—to two groups—13-year-olds and pre-university students (high school seniors in the U.S.). FIMS was intended not to rank countries but to evaluate the Sputnik New Math that had spread from the U.S. across the ocean. The first key finding reported on the IEA website is: "Students who had taken courses in 'new mathematics' achieved higher scores on items in traditional mathematics than students who had not taken such courses." [www8–1]

In 1980–1982 the IEA followed FIMS with the Second International Mathematics Study (SIMS), administered to the same two age-groups but in a somewhat expanded range of countries. Topics tested at the middle school level were arithmetic, algebra, geometry, measurement, and descriptive statistics. Topics tested at the final year of secondary school were sets, relations and functions; number systems; algebra; geometry; elementary functions and calculus; probability and statistics; finite mathematics; computer science; and logic. [www8–2]

In 1995 the IEA conducted the Third International Mathematics and Science Study (TIMSS) on a growing number of countries, adding both 9-year-olds and science. [www8–3] Eventually, the age designations became grades 4 and 8, while only high school seniors in "advanced" courses participated. [www8–4]

TIMSS 1995 was a landmark in two other ways: (1) it was the first in a fixed 4-year cycle of testing; and (2) it was renamed *Trends* in International Mathematics and Science Study, so that all future exams are called TIMSS, followed by the year for identification.

Two famous quotes emerged from SIMS and TIMSS 1995: the former called U.S. math education "the underachieving curriculum," while the latter branded U.S. math education as "a mile wide and an inch deep." Of note, years prior in 1958 John Keats used those very words *a mile wide and an inch deep* in a different context. [K2, p. 68]

While TIMSS collects extensive data, for purposes here the following two tables summarize the mean scores of the top-scoring countries as well as the U.S. [www8–5; I5] Note the following from the charts. First, the consistency of those countries placing in the top five is remarkable. Second, from 2011 to 2015 in 4th grade the U.S. dropped in both mean score and ranking; in 8th grade the U.S. increased in mean score but dropped in ranking. Whether these drops are due to Common Core math is too small or early to analyze. However, CCSSM did *not* produce an improvement in 4th grade TIMSS performance as desired or predicted. The PISA scores in the next section similarly show lack of gain in the initial Common Core years. Third, note the large drop in 4th grade from

Table 7. TIMSS Math Grade 4 Mean Scores (TIMSS mean = 500)

	1995	1999	2003	2007	2011	2015
Chinese Taipei	NA		564 4th	576 3rd	591 4th	597 4th
Hong Kong	587 4th		575 2nd	607 1st	602 3rd	615 2nd
Rep of Korea	611 2nd		NA	NA	605 2nd	608 3rd
Japan	597 3rd		565 3rd	568 4th	585 5th	593 5th
Russian Federation	NA		532 9th	544 6th	542 10th	564 7th
Singapore	625 1st		594 1st	599 2nd	606 1st	618 1st
U.S.	545 12th		518 12th	529 11th	541 11th	539 14th
# countries	26		25	36	57	48

Table 8. TIMSS Math Grade 8 Mean Scores (TIMSS mean = 500)

	1995	1999	2003	2007	2011	2015
Chinese Taipei	NA	585 3rd	585 4th	598 1st	591 4th	599 3rd
Hong Kong	588 4th	582 4th	586 3rd	572 4th	602 3rd	594 4th
Rep of Korea	607 2nd	587 2nd	589 2nd	597 2nd	605 2nd	606 2nd
Japan	605 3rd	579 5th	570 5th	570 5th	585 5th	586 5th
Russian Federation	535 14th	526 12th	508 11th	512 8th	539 6th	538 6th
Singapore	643 1st	604 1st	605 1st	593 3rd	606 1st	621 1st
U.S.	500 28th	502 19th	504 15th	508 9th	509 9th	518 10th
# countries	41	38	45	48	56	37

1995 (545) to 2003 (518). If the cause of the decline is constructivism (see Chapter 10), that root was certainly not noted in the push for CCSSM, a variety of constructivism.

Fourth, the obsession of some to emulate Singapore is not substantiated by the 68-95-99 standard deviation rule. Because TIMSS is designed with a standard deviation of 100, 68% of the countries land between 400 to 600 points. While Singapore deserves credit for placing slightly above the 68% mark, why copy a country with 600-range scores? Rather, why not put time, energy, and money into designing a revised math program to score 700 at the 95% level? As Tom Loveless recently noted, "The good news is that the U.S.–Singapore eighth grade math gap has narrowed since 1995 . . . ; the bad news is that it will take, at this pace, more than 140 years to close it completely." [L17, p. 9] Grade 4 problems may be easy, medium, or hard, but they are not middle school math. Similarly, grade 8 problems may touch on high school math, but they do not include topics exclusively found in the upper grades. Thus, TIMSS math problems are ones that U.S. students should be able to do.

I have recommended administering released TIMSS questions, made available by NCES on the internet, to students as an additional gauge of achievement. However, school heads, perhaps afraid to know the results, have rarely accepted my suggestion.

Indeed, NCES wrote: "Approximately half of the items used in the TIMSS assessment are released to the public after each round of testing. These mathematics . . . items can be used by educators:
• To *inform* discussions about your schools' mathematics . . . curriculum;
• To *explore* the links between concepts you teach and ways to measure students' understanding;
• To *design* your own assessment according to your needs; and
• To *reflect* on the performance of your students in comparison to the performance of students in other countries, including the United States." [www8–6]

The following three questions from TIMSS 2003 are all ones that U.S. students should be able to answer comfortably.

Grade 4, Free Response, horizontal fraction line in original [N5, p. 55]
There are 600 balls in a box, and 1/3 of the balls are red. How many red balls are in the box?
Only 38% of U.S. 4th graders answered correctly (answer = 200).

Grade 8, Multiple Choice [N5, p. 63]
If n is a negative integer, which of these is the largest number?
(A) $3 + n$ (B) $3 \times n$ (C) $3 - n$ (D) $3 \div n$
Only 48% of U.S. 8th graders answered correctly (answer = C).

Grade 8, Free Response [N5, p. 64]
If $4(x + 5) = 80$, then $x =$
Only 57% of U.S. 8th graders received full credit (answer = 15).

What have education analysts said about TIMSS scores? Two comments follow.

Observing the 1995 TIMSS Videotape Classroom Study, Stigler and Hiebert remarked: "They [U.S. students] encounter mathematics that is at a lower level, is somewhat more superficial, and is not as fully or coherently developed as the mathematics encountered by their German or Japanese peers." They explained that, based on level of difficulty, extent of development, and coherence of presentation, "rich and challenging" content leads to greater math learning, while "fragmented and ordinary" content leads to less. [S26, pp. 66, 57]

Brookings researchers wrote in 2007: ". . . although algebra and geometry are important elements of the middle school curriculum in other TIMSS countries, U.S. middle schools tend to offer these topics to relatively few students." [K4, p. 87]

Combining TIMSS 4th and 8th grade scores by following student groups over four years, the next table discouragingly shows that all U.S. age cohorts declined in math. Brookings researchers confirmed: "These findings suggest that U.S. students do reasonably well in the primary grades, but that the longer they stay in school, the more they fall behind their peers in other countries." [M11, p. 15]

Table 9. TIMSS U.S. Math Cohort Mean Scores

	GR 4	GR 8	% decrease
Cohort grade 4 1995	545	502	8%
Cohort grade 4 1999		504	
Cohort grade 4 2003	518	508	2%
Cohort grade 4 2007	529	509	4%
Cohort grade 4 2011	541	518	4%

Currently, TIMSS administers math exams to 12th graders only if they are in advanced math courses. Those U.S. students had a mean score of 485 on TIMSS Advanced 2015, comparable to the Russian Federation. However, Russia has a further group of advanced students graduating from high school who take "intensive courses" in math—that is doubly advanced. Those Russian students placed first with a mean score of 540. One should consider the implication of the 55-point difference in scores for the future of national security and technological innovation in the U.S. versus a significant competitor. [www8-7]

PISA

The Organisation for Economic Co-operation and Development (OECD) sponsors the Programme for International Student Assessment (PISA), a series of international exams, begun in 2000 and continuing every three years, in reading literacy, mathematics literacy, and science literacy for 15-year-olds, who are in different school grades around the world. Along with the approximately 30 member countries, about 40 other countries have participated. [N8, p. iii; www8-8]

PISA, while assessing all subjects on each exam, tests one (the major area) in depth with the other two (the minor areas) to a lesser extent, on a rotating basis. For mathematics, the years are: 2000 minor, 2003 major, 2006 minor, 2009 minor, 2012 major, and 2015 minor. [N8, p. 1]

OECD defined mathematics literacy as *"an individual's capacity to identify and understand the role that mathematics plays in the world, to make well-founded judgments and to use and engage with mathematics in ways that meet the needs of that individual's life as a constructive, concerned and reflective citizen."* [N8, p. 11]

Further, "PISA uses the terminology of 'literacy' in each subject area to denote its broad focus on the application of knowledge and skills. . . . Literacy itself refers to a continuum of skills—it is not a condition that one has or does not have (i.e., literacy or illiteracy)." [N8, p. 3]

Released math items from PISA 2012 reveal a more specific meaning of mathematical literacy. The questions—all word problems—include topics such as an apartment purchase using an architectural floor plan; sales of CDs given bar graphs; sailing ships given wind rates; a Ferris wheel given circumference and rotation data; a climb up Mount Fuji given distance, rate, and time data; car sales given percentage data; and a revolving door given central angles of sectors. [www8–9]

OECD reports more than mean scores: ". . . among OECD countries, higher expenditure on education is not highly predictive of better mathematics scores in PISA. For example, the United States and the Slovak Republic . . . [each scored] 481 points in mathematics [in 2012], but the United States' cumulative expenditure per student is more than double that of the Slovak Republic." [www8–10]

For mathematical literacy, PISA ranks performance on a scale from 0 to 1,000. From those scores, PISA determines cuts to create proficiency levels on a range from 1 (lowest) to 6 (highest). "Increasing levels represent the knowledge, skills, and capabilities needed to perform tasks of increasing complexity. . . . In PISA, all students within a level are expected to answer at least half of the items from that level correctly." [N8, pp. 35, 37]

The following charts created from OECD data show select results. Because the PISA math framework was changed in 2003, some comparisons among years are flawed. [N8; www8–11]

Table 10. PISA Math Literacy Scores (0 to 1,000)

	2000	2003	2006	2009	2012	2015
Canada	533 6th	532 7th	527 7th	527 10th	518 13th	516 10th
Hong Kong–China	NA	550 1st	547 4th	555 3rd	561 3rd	548 2nd
Macao–China	NA	527 9th	525 8th	525 12th	538 6th	544 3rd
Shanghai–China	NA	NA	NA	600 1st	613 1st	NA
Chinese–Taipei	NA	NA	549 1st	543 5th	560 4th	542 4th
Finland	536 4th	544 2nd	548 2nd	541 6th	519 12th	511 13th
France	517 10th	511 16th	496 23rd	497 22nd	495 25th	493 26th
Germany	490 20th	503 19th	504 19th	513 16th	514 16th	506 16th
Japan	557 1st	534 6th	523 10th	529 9th	536 7th	532 5th
Korea, Rep of	547 2nd	542 3rd	547 3rd	546 4th	554 5th	524 7th
Poland	470 24th	490 24th	495 25th	495 25th	518 14th	504 17th
Singapore	NA	NA	NA	562 2nd	573 2nd	564 1st
Sweden	510 15th	509 17th	502 21st	494 26th	478 38th	494 24th
U.S.	493 19th	483 27th	474 35th	487 31st	481 36th	470 40th
overall mean	500	500	498	496	494	490
# countries	31	39	57	65	65	70

U.S. math performance is remarkably unimpressive on PISA. These numbers, not the TIMSS scores, are the ones that the public—often unaware of the distinction—has in mind when thinking that American students rank low in the world in math.

The U.S. means are not the only disappointing statistics; both the brightest and the lowest U.S. students fall short as well. NCES reported for 2009: "When comparing the performance of the highest achieving students—those at the 90th percentile—U.S. students scored lower (593) than the OECD average (615) on the mathematics literacy scale. Twenty-nine jurisdictions . . . had students at the 90th percentile with higher scores than the United States on the mathematics literacy scale. At the other end of the distribution, among low-achieving students at the 10th percentile, U.S. students scored lower (358) than the OECD average (379) on the mathematics literacy scale. Twenty-six jurisdictions . . . had students at the 10th percentile with higher scores than the United States on the mathematics literacy scale." [N8, p. 11]

The proficiency levels are also discouraging as reported by NCES for 2003: "In mathematics literacy, the United States had greater percentages of students below level 1 and at levels 1 and 2 than the OECD average percentages. The United States also had a lower percentage of students at levels 4, 5, and 6 than the OECD average percentages." [www8–12]

Table 10 reveals a decline in the U.S. scores from an already low start in 2000. And so criticism began. From television ads by ExxonMobil to internet images by StudentsFirst, graphics depicted America's low international standing in mathematics.

As early as 1995, Charles Sykes wrote: "American students are unable to effectively compete with the rest of the industrialized world, because our schools teach less, expect less, and settle for less than do those of other countries." [S29, p. 9]

Amanda Ripley, before writing her 2013 book, commendably took the PISA exam herself in an actual setting. Naturally, she expected her score to be higher due to "twenty-two more years of life experience than normal PISA takers, including four years of college." But she wrote: "My [high] score . . . did not bode well for teenagers in my own country. This test was not easy, but it wasn't that hard either. . . . PISA demanded fluency in problem solving and the ability to communicate; in other words, the basic skills I needed to do my job and take care of my family in a world choked with information and subject to sudden economic change. What did it mean for a country if most of its teenagers did not do well on this test? Not all of our kids had to be engineers or lawyers, but didn't all of them need to know how to *think*?" [R13, p. 23]

As Ripley pointed out, independent schools did not know the secret formula either: "Our richest kids attended some of the most well-funded, high-tech schools in the world. Yet these kids, including the ones who went to private school, still ranked eighteenth in math compared to the richest kids in other countries." [R13, p. 70]

Because U.S. teenagers could not answer word problems pertaining to real-life situations, many suggested changing school math: enter Common Core State Standards Math. But from 2012 (mean score 481) to 2015 (mean score 470) with implementation of CCSSM, the U.S. dropped eleven points—both statistically significant and educationally ominous. Moreover, Massachusetts, as a state among the highest for math, received its own PISA score. MA, which adopted CCSSM, had a score drop from 514 in 2012 to 500 in 2015. [www8–13] But PISA is given to a specific age (15-year-olds), not grade; and the growing U.S. trend is to start children in school later. Possibly, U.S. students know less math for PISA because they are in lower grades.

Any dramatic change in math curriculum without a parallel shift in societal values might be fruitless. Thus, learning from Canada might be more sensible than from an Asian country. In a Brookings seminar one participant, who had been Headmaster at the American School in Singapore, said that he was "surprised" that the "disparity between the scores of the U.S. and Singapore" was not greater because math was "immersed in the culture" in Singapore—citizens valued the subject and students took extra lessons after school and on Saturday. [www8–14] Positively, Amanda Ripley argued that based on Poland's math project, "Rigor could be cultivated. . . . Expectations could be raised. Bold leaders . . . could help to raise an entire generation of smarter kids." [R13, p. 147]

E. D. Hirsch offered interesting commentary on several countries. Germany suffered "der PISA Schock" due to its low PISA 2000 math score.

He wrote: "Reacting to the Schock, Germany began to adopt well-defined curricula." The head of PISA studies in Germany issued post-Schock curriculum guides that were "more specific grade by grade," clearly telling teachers what they had to teach and students what they had to learn. France and Sweden, in complete antithesis to Germany, started with higher scores, but declined steadily due to their introduction of looser curriculum. Hirsch wrote: "Individualism with its curricular incoherence has been a chief cause of stasis or worse in the effort to narrow the achievement gaps . . . in the United States, . . . France, and Sweden." Hirsch also noted that Asian nations rejected math constructivism. [H14, pp. 154–155, 158, 185]

Readers might be wondering if a correlation exists between the national and international exam scores. As expected, a formal analysis of the math frameworks showed that NAEP is more similar to TIMSS than to PISA. [N5, p. 101] NCES also conducted "linking" studies, creating estimated TIMSS 1995 grade 8 scores by state. [J8, p. 10–1] Over half of the states had resulting TIMSS scores below the actual U.S. TIMSS score (500) which was 28th of 41—that is the majority of the 50 states would have scored in the lowest third of all participating countries.

The 2012 Brown Center Report provided valuable insight into the pitfall of over-assessing international rankings. Mr. Loveless wrote: "International test scores receive a lot of attention, especially when first released. The press scrambles to find pundits offering instant analysis. Policy makers pour over the results to glean lessons for governments. Advocates look for evidence to bolster pre-existing arguments." But one section of the report focused on "the three most common and potentially most misleading mistakes that are made when interpreting international tests scores." [L13, p. 25] The first is "dubious causality." Multiple confounding variables can mislead cause-and-effect conclusions. The second is the intrinsic, problematic nature of rankings. Sampling errors and unequal intervals between adjacent scores can skew rankings. The third is emulation of the top-scoring country. Policies adopted by the highest ranked nation may be the same as those used by countries further down the scale, showing that variation in culture and population yield differing success. [L13, pp. 25–31]

9
Interceding Presidentially

I must study politics and war that my sons may have liberty to study mathematics and philosophy.
President John Adams

Although state and local governments assume primary responsibility for education, United States Presidents from Harry Truman to Barack Obama have addressed the issue of math education by making bold statements, setting ambitious goals, holding widespread conferences, or commissioning major reports. While no President achieved permanent success regarding math education improvement, consistent attention to the matter established its importance.

President Harry Truman (April, 1945—January, 1953)

Technological needs of World War II boosted the development of the digital computer, and more advanced mathematics accompanied that growth. Carl Allendoerfer wrote in a 1965 *Mathematics Teacher* article: "During the war [World War II] we [university mathematicians] had been aware of exciting developments in mathematics such as game theory, linear programming, new methods in statistics, and the applications of these to operations analysis. When we returned to the classroom, we found the old curriculum dull and sterile and having far too little contact with the living mathematics which we knew." [A5, p. 690]

Such was the mood in 1950 when President Truman signed the bill creating the National Science Foundation. In its first few years, the agency "was operating on the proverbial shoestring." [K13, p. 3] However, two key pieces necessary for a math education revolution were in place—professional mathematicians trained to deliver the content and a government vehicle primed to provide the funding. All that was missing was the spark, which came during the next presidency.

President Dwight Eisenhower (January, 1953—January, 1961)

In 1953 President Eisenhower signed the bill to create the new cabinet-level Department of Health, Education and Welfare. [www9–1] But a bigger event during Eisenhower's presidency was something he did not do: launch the Soviet satellite Sputnik.

While Sputnik's blast into space startled the American public, the President's advisors had been aware of an impending situation. Published by the U.S. Government Printing Office, a history of that period reported: "These [1954 budget] decisions reflected a growing concern at top governmental levels over the apparent shortage of scientists and engineers in the United States, particularly compared with indications of mounting Soviet scientific strength. For example, according to estimates made by NSF in connection with its fiscal year 1955 budget request, Russia was expected to graduate 40,000 engineers in 1955—nearly twice as many as the United States." [K13, p. 16]

On October 4, 1957 Sputnik not only incited the nation's space race but also dampened any math wrath that Americans might have harbored. Widespread discussion about the nature and importance of reforming math education boomed from the Soviet Union's surprise blast on that fateful day. NSF Director Alan Waterman described the event as "a scientific Pearl Harbor." University mathematicians began working and federal money began flowing to boost the United States from "second best, an unfamiliar and uncomfortable position." [K13, p. 27]

Moreover, in 1958 Eisenhower signed the National Defense Education Act—in essence, telling his citizens to study more math. "To help ensure that highly trained individuals would be available to help America compete with the Soviet Union in scientific and technical fields, the NDEA included support for loans to college students, the improvement of science, mathematics, and foreign language instruction in elementary and secondary schools, graduate fellowships, foreign language and area studies, and vocational-technical training." [www9-2]

President John Kennedy (January, 1961—November, 1963)

Only in office for less than three years, JFK is well known for two movements, each affecting school math but in opposite ways. His promotion of the space program required a commitment to rigorous New Math, considered elitist. However, JFK's passion for civil rights shaped a rebound to lackluster Back-to-Basics math, deemed mainstream.

Otherwise, JFK's State of the Union Addresses cited below reveal typical presidential concern for the overall inadequate state of education. Sadly, his warnings sound current, again indicating the lack of progress.

1961 SOTU: "Our classrooms contain 2 million more children than they can properly have room for, taught by 90,000 teachers not properly qualified to teach. ... We lack the scientists, the engineers and the teachers our world obligations require. ... Federal grants for both higher and public school education can no longer be delayed." [www9-3]

1962 SOTU: "If this Nation is to grow in wisdom and strength, then every able high school graduate should have the opportunity to develop his talents. ... They [our families] cannot afford such [college] costs—but this Nation cannot afford to maintain its military power and neglect its brainpower. But excellence in education must begin at the elementary level." [www9-4]

1963 SOTU: "The future of any country which is dependent upon the will and wisdom of its citizens is damaged, and irreparably damaged, whenever any of its children is not educated to the full extent of his talent, from grade school through graduate school. Today, an estimated 4 out of every 10 students in the 5th grade will not even finish high school—and that is a waste we cannot afford." [www9-5]

President Lyndon Johnson (November, 1963—January, 1969)

President Johnson was a former Texas public school teacher who saw poverty first-hand. At President Johnson's urging as part of his War on Poverty, in 1965 Congress passed the Elementary and Secondary Education Act (ESEA), called the most far-reaching and comprehensive federal education legislation at that time. The Titles of ESEA provided "financial assistance for (1) local educational agencies to educate children from low income families, (2) school library resources and instructional materials, (3) supplementary educational centers and services, (4) educational research and training, and (5) the strengthening of state departments of education." [www9–6] ESEA was reauthorized many times with modifications during future presidencies. In fact, President Bush's No Child Left Behind Act and President Obama's Every Student Succeeds Act were ESEA reauthorizations.

Combined with JFK's civil rights movement, LBJ's focus on poverty bolstered back-to basics math, viewed as more universally understandable. Moreover, some believed that tackling poverty was an essential first step to improving math learning.

Further education work during LBJ's presidency included initial plans for the National Assessment of Educational Progress. The NCES website states, "After much exploration in the early 1960s, the idea of a national assessment gained impetus in 1963. NAEP planning began in 1964, with a grant from the Carnegie Corporation to set up the Exploratory Committee for the Assessment of Progress in Education (ECAPE) in June. This was followed by the appointment of the Technical Advisory Committee (TAC) in 1965." [www9–7]

President Richard Nixon (January, 1969—August, 1974)

After planning for the NAEP during the 1960s, the first national assessment was conducted in 1969 during President Nixon's first year in office. Nixon saw the value of the NAEP even if Congress was less enthusiastic. As stated on the NAGB website, "The fiscal year 1975 budget request by President Nixon included $7 million for NAEP. Eventually, Congress appropriated $3 million." [www9–8] Other groundwork laid during the Nixon administration included the service of Terrel H. Bell as the National Commissioner of Education beginning in 1974.

President Gerald Ford (August, 1974—January, 1977)

In office less than one term and due to the circumstance of his ascendancy, President Ford understandably focused on government, rather than math, reform. Gaining more federal experience, T. H. Bell continued as the Commissioner of Education through Ford's defeat in 1976.

President Jimmy Carter (January, 1977—January, 1981)

In 1979 President Carter signed the Department of Education Organization Act, providing for a separate, cabinet-level Education agency, beginning in 1980. Christopher Cross explained: "While Jimmy Carter might be credited with creation of a cabinet-level agency, he accepted only the most anemic of versions and then lost his own reelection six months after the department came into existence, so he never used that vehicle to accomplish anything substantive." [www9–9]

However, President Carter commissioned his Secretary of Education, Shirley Hufstedler, and Acting Director of the National Science Foundation, Donald Langenberg, to examine the state of science and math education. The result was the lengthy, multi-faceted report *Science and Engineering Education for the 1980s and Beyond* published in October, 1980. Due to this document, Carter could plausibly be called the father of STEM. The following four findings sound current, reinforcing the excruciatingly slow progress in math education.

• "The role of science and technology is increasing throughout our society. In business, in government, in the military, in occupations and professions where it never before intruded, science is becoming a key to success. Today, people in a wide range of nonscientific and non-engineering occupations and professions must have a greater understanding of technology than at any time in our history. Yet our educational system does not now provide such understanding."

• "Students who take no more mathematics and science after their tenth year in school have effectively eliminated, by the age of sixteen, the possibility of science or engineering as a career. The pool from which our future scientific and engineering personnel can be drawn is therefore in danger of becoming smaller, even as the need for such personnel is increasing."

- "Education has long been the route by which upward mobility has been achieved by disadvantaged groups in our society. This verity has not changed. Increased emphasis must be given to aiding those who have been excluded, for too long, from careers in science and engineering. We stress this imperative both for reasons of equity and to increase the size of the pool of talent from which the Nation's scientists, engineers, and technicians can be drawn."

- "The declining emphasis on science and mathematics in our school systems is in marked contrast to other industrialized countries. Japan, Germany, and the Soviet Union all provide rigorous training in science and mathematics for all their citizens. We fear a loss of our competitive edge." [www9–10, p. 10]

President Ronald Reagan (January, 1981—January, 1989)

In 1981 President Reagan's Secretary of Education Terrel H. Bell created the National Commission on Excellence in Education (NCEE). In 1983 that agency published the now infamous, scathing publication *A Nation at Risk: The Imperative for Educational Reform*. One example of the blistering remarks in *ANAR* is: ". . . while we can take justifiable pride in what our schools and colleges have historically accomplished and contributed to the United States and the well-being of its people, the educational foundations of our society are presently being eroded by a rising tide of mediocrity that threatens our very future as a Nation and a people." [N11, p. 5]

Although President Reagan is remembered for Bell's work, the two men were at odds philosophically. For example, Diane Ravitch stated: "Bell was a subversive in the Reagan cabinet, a former school superintendent and a bona fide member of the education establishment." [R6, p. 24] Moreover, on a PBS website, the following three experts commented on Reagan's relationship with Bell and *ANAR*. Kenneth Wong explained that Reagan actually "entered the White House with the intention of abolishing the U.S. Department of Education." Christopher Cross wrote: "While many may cite Ronald Reagan for *A Nation at Risk*, he had nothing to do with the report or even naming the commission that wrote it. He did recognize the importance of the report and its rhetoric and did capitalize on that in his 1984 reelection campaign, but never translated that message into action." Further, Jim Guthrie stated: "*A Nation at Risk* . . . continues today as one of the nation's most significant education documents. It triggered a school reform movement that lasted three decades and still has momentum. It is still cited. Ironically, it was Terrell Bell, Reagan's Education Secretary, that initiated *A Nation at Risk*. Reagan came belatedly to use his bully pulpit to promote it, only after he saw the enormous acceptance it had with the public." [www9–11]

Now, thirty-four years later, the findings of *ANAR* are sadly unresolved.
• "Critical shortages of . . . mathematics . . . teachers exist at the secondary level."
• "The average salary of a beginning math teacher with a bachelor's degree is now only 60% of the beginning salary offered by private industry to bachelor degree candidates in mathematics."
• "Substantial numbers of unqualified persons are teaching . . . mathematics in secondary school."
• "Even certified . . . mathematics teachers at the secondary level are in need of in-service training."
• "New sequences of . . . math courses and materials are needed which match stages of intellectual development of children."
• "Elementary and secondary schools need access to microcomputers, low-cost supplies, and other resources." [www9–12; N11]

Also during Reagan's presidency, the concepts of vouchers and school choice were born. Ravitch explained that Reagan was aware of making these contentious ideas politically pleasing. Thus, he first proposed vouchers for low-performing students only, against the advice of economist Milton Friedman who wanted them universally available. Later, Reagan retreated from vouchers, promoting the milder plan of school choice instead. Bell was opposed not only to vouchers but also to Reagan's desire to rescind the U.S. ED's cabinet-level status. Bell resigned in 1985, when William Bennett became Secretary of Education. "Bennett enthusiastically embraced school choice and included it as one of his 'three C's' of education: content, character, and choice." [R6, p. 117]

Finally, as explained in Chapter 7, in 1988 during Reagan's second term, Congress created The National Assessment Governing Board (NAGB) as an independent, bipartisan group to set policy for the National Assessment of Educational Progress. The NAGB's members include governors, state legislators, local and state school officials, educators, business representatives, and members of the general public. [www9–13]

President George H. W. Bush (January, 1989—January, 1993)

In September, 1989 President George H. W. Bush held his historic meeting, called the Charlottesville Education Summit, in Virginia with the nation's governors. There, President Bush announced the six national education goals that he further developed during his State of the Union speech in January, 1990. The 4th goal was remarkably bold: "By the year 2000, U.S. students must be first in the world in math and science achievement." [V2, p. 44] Despite the help of the National Education Goals Panel, created to monitor progress, not only was the zealous goal never reached but also the striking range was never close.

In 1991 at a speech to the members of the Mathematical Sciences Education Board, President Bush revealed that the math goal was crucial to him. He stated: "Of the six national education goals, you're helping to realize one of the most important: that American students will rank first in the world in math." [D4]

Perhaps Bush should have assessed the situation prior to his assertion. Unfortunately, "The results of a prototype math test [designed for Secretary of Education Lamar Alexander], released in early June [1991], showed that 54 percent of high-school seniors couldn't do seventh-grade math. Only 5 percent were truly ready for college." [S2]

President Bush's summit and declaration are proof that proclaiming goals is easy, but achieving them is another matter. Numerous writers have commented on GHWB's well-intentioned folly—some before 2000 with blatant realism and some after 2000 with clear hindsight. Three examples follow.

In 1992 Harold Stevenson and James Stigler wrote: "Stating goals is laudable, but we are far from achieving any of these. To hear them stated so glibly with no reference to how they would be attained jars us into facing the great gap between goal and accomplishment. . . . And if we do not make profound changes in our mathematics and science curricula, the goal of becoming number one in the world in these areas is absurd. . . . Yet the public discussion that followed the governors' conference moved quickly to the question of who will pay for achieving the goals, without first deciding what would be done if money were available." [S25, p. 23]

In 1999 Martin Gross wrote: "That's exactly what a group called the National Education Goals Panel is doing—trying to establish standards so that our youngsters in 4th, 8th, and 12th grades can become educated enough to handle the twenty-first century. The group studied the question, then outlined a series of standards. Once that was done, they tested a random sample of students to see how they measured up. Again the sorry refrain. They did not." [G12, p. 28]

In 2010 Diane Ravitch wrote: "Worthy goals all, but none was attained by the year 2000. In retrospect, it seems curious that elected officials would set such ambitious targets for achieving ends over which they had so little control and for which the solutions were neither obvious nor at hand." [R6, p. 31]

President Bill Clinton (January, 1993—January, 2001)

When George H. W. Bush held his historic summit, Bill Clinton was a governor in attendance, fully embracing the goals. As Diane Ravitch wrote, ". . . he [Clinton] had drafted the language for them at the Bush summit" and "added two more for good measure." [R6, p. 149]

After becoming President, Bill Clinton furthered the work of his predecessor. While the earlier president created America 2000, the latter formulated Goals 2000: Educate America Act, signing it into law in March, 1994. Clinton's legislation stated that all students would leave grades 4, 8, and 12 with "demonstrated competency" in math and that America would become "first in the world" in math achievement. [www9–14] Goals 2000 made the new national standards voluntary but encouraged their use by linking them to federal education dollars, much in the same way that Common Core was tied to Race to the Top.

Critics were not impressed. In 1995 Charles Sykes wrote: "The flaw in Goals 2000 is fundamental: It avoids fixing what needs to be fixed, leaving intact the educational establishment's throttlehold on the school." [S29, p. 266] And in 1999 Martin Gross stated, "What have all these reforms and trillions of dollars wrought? Have they paid off in better public school performance? Absolutely not. There has been no significant improvement in the quality of public education, and under present management, there is little hope for the future. Goals 2000 has proved to be an idle dream of naive politicians and educators." [G12, pp. 9–10]

Like other modern-day presidents, Clinton's State of the Union speeches contained sections on education. For example, the 1997 speech featured a ten-point education plan that included raising standards, offering national certification of master teachers, empowering volunteers to help children read, promoting brain development from birth, fostering the right to school choice or charter schools, developing character education, building facilities, advancing two years of college with scholarships, expanding life-long learning, and elevating the power of the internet. Moreover, he called for state-wide testing: "Every state should adopt high national standards, and by 1999, every state should test every fourth grader in reading and every eighth grader in math to make sure these standards are met." [www9–15]

Clinton's 1999 SOTU referred to two problems specific to math education—international rankings and out-of-field teachers. On the former he stated: "While our fourth-graders out performed their peers in other countries in math and science, our eighth-graders are around average, and our 12th-graders rank near the bottom. We must do better." On the latter he declared: ". . . all states and school districts must be held responsible for the quality of their teachers. The great majority of our teachers do a fine job, but in too many schools teachers don't have college majors or even minors in the subjects they teach. New teachers should be required to pass performance exams, and all teachers should know the subject they're teaching." [www9-16]

President George W. Bush (January, 2001—January, 2009)

President George W. Bush is known for his signature education legislation, the No Child Left Behind Act (NCLB), passed by Congress in 2001 as a reauthorization of ESEA and signed into law in early 2002. While NCLB did not require federal standards, the law did expand the federal role in accountability, such as student testing and school grades. As Section 1 of the Legislation stated: "An Act—To close the achievement gap with accountability, flexibility, and choice, so that no child is left behind." [www9-17]

Once again, this law mandated lofty goals—two in particular—without a means of achievement.

The first unrealistic target was that every teacher of every major subject (including math) in every school would be "highly qualified" by 2005-2006. The law defined highly qualified as having a state license, a bachelor's degree, and demonstrated competence in the subject. [www9-18]

Ben Feller, Associated Press Education Writer, did extensive work on NCLB. In a 2005 article, with one school year remaining to satisfy the mandate, Feller reported that "most states say that more than 90 percent of their teachers are highly qualified." Yet Feller discussed the vague requirements that states used to define quality. He cited five organizations—the Thomas B. Fordham Foundation, The Education Trust, the Education Commission of the States, the Center on Education Policy, and The National Council on Teacher Quality—that "resoundingly" questioned the validity of the claim of teacher competence. In this same article, Feller quoted Chester Finn as saying, "It's an unkept promise. Worse yet, it's the illusion of a kept promise." [F5] Then in a 2006 article, Feller simply summarized: "None made it." [F6]

The second unfeasible aim was that every child would be proficient in reading and math by 2014 as measured by state tests. [www9–19] Yet a 2007 article in *Education Week* stated: "Because the federal law gives the states the power to define proficiency, there are 50 different definitions of the term." [H17] Diane Ravitch also wrote about this mandate: "The goal set by Congress of 100 proficiency by 2014 is an aspiration; it is akin to a declaration of belief. . . . But as a goal, it is utterly out of reach." [R6, p. 103]

Feller noted that while the unfulfilled legislation centerpiece of having highly qualified teachers was forgotten, the "CAT" tests (e.g. Florida Comprehensive Achievement Test or FCAT) took on lives of their own as the focus of continual and fervent arguments among parents, teachers, students, and politicians. Indeed, as Amanda Ripley noted, international testing was one impetus for the law: "U.S. Education Secretary Rod Paige lamented the [PISA 2000] results. 'Average is not good enough for American kids,' he said. He vowed (wrongly, as it would turn out) that No Child Left Behind, President George W. Bush's new accountability-based reform law, would improve America's standing." [R13, p. 17] As expected, opponents of excessive testing attacked NCLB. The National Center for Fair and Open Testing (FairTest) repeatedly posted online articles accusing NCLB of creating dumbed-down curricula and test-obsessed schools.

NCLB also had major unintended consequences. Five are summarized below, supported with selected comments by Diane Ravitch.

1. Emphasis on Basic Skills over Knowledge
"Whereas the authors of *A Nation At Risk* concerned themselves with the quality and breadth of the curriculum that every youngster should study, No Child Left Behind concerned itself only with basic skills. . . . In the age of NCLB, knowledge was irrelevant." [R6, p. 29]

2. Emphasis on Reading and Math over Other Subjects
"One of the unintended consequences of NCLB was the shrinkage of

time available to teach anything [such as music, art, foreign language, home economics, physical education, civics, computer science, etc.] other than reading and math." [R6, p. 107]

3. Emphasis on Test Scores over the Teaching Profession
"After the passage of NCLB, however, everything changed. Efforts to improve teacher professionalism were swept away by the law's singular focus on raising test scores." [R6, p. 178]

4. Emphasis on Corporate Involvement over Public Districts
"What began as a movement for testing and accountability has turned into a privatization movement. . . . No Child Left Behind, with its unrealistic goals, has fed the privatization frenzy." [R7, p. 6]

5. Emphasis on Test Scores over Standards
"Meanwhile the states responded to NCLB by dumbing down their standards so that they could claim to be making progress. Some states declared that between 80%–90% of their students were proficient, but on the federal test [NAEP] only a third or less were. Because the law demanded progress only in reading and math, schools were incentivized to show gains only on those subjects. Hundreds of millions of dollars were invested in test-preparation materials." [R5]

President Bush had another highly significant effect on math education—the formation in 2006 of the National Mathematics Advisory Panel, motivated by the results of the TIMSS exams. Bush received praise not only for forming a commission "to provide advice on the effectiveness of various approaches to teaching mathematics," but also for including "individuals who have been associated with both sides of the debate" [see the Math Wars in Chapter 10] and who reached "a greater degree of consensus than has been obtained in the past." [H2, p. 129] The 2008 120-page report addressed many questions, including "essential content" and its preparation, "research about how children learn mathematics," "effectiveness of instructional practices and materials," how to "recruit, prepare, and retain effective teachers of mathematics," making "assessments of mathematical knowledge more accurate and more useful," and preparation for algebra. Findings and recommendations covered Curricular Content, Learning Processes, Teachers and Teacher Education, Instructional Practices, Instructional Materials, Assessment, and Research Policies and Mechanisms. [N36, pp. xv, xvi–xxvii]

President Barack Obama (January, 2009—January, 2017)

In 2010 President Obama remarked on the U.S.'s low international ranking in math on PISA. He said that "the gap between the number of [math] teachers we have and the number of teachers we need" was growing annually. He stated that "other nations are stepping up" in addressing the importance of math education. President Obama summarized: "So make no mistake: Our future is on the line. The nation that out-educates us today is going to out-compete us tomorrow. To continue to cede our leadership in education is to cede our position in the world. That's not acceptable to me, and I know it's not acceptable to any of you. And that's why my administration has set a clear goal: to move from the middle to the top of the pack in science and math education over the next decade." [www9–20]

His speech had six proposals: (1) including money in the Recovery Act (from the Great Recession) to prevent the firing of teachers due to budget deficits; (2) awarding Department of Education grants to train teachers, whether new college graduates or scientists entering teaching as a second career; (3) creating the Race to the Top fund to reward states producing innovative programs in math and science education; (4) challenging states to improve standards, make data-driven education decisions, recruit and retain great teachers, and promote stronger curricula; (5) launching the "Educate to Innovate" campaign to encourage citizens, nonprofits, universities, and corporations to help solve the problem; and (6) hosting science events at the White House to raise awareness.

Then in a December, 2010 speech at a North Carolina college, President Obama warned of a new Sputnik moment: "In 1957 . . . the Soviet Union beat us into space by launching a satellite known as Sputnik. And that was a wake-up call that caused the United States to boost our investment in innovation and education—particularly in math and science. And as a result, once we put our minds to it, once we got focused, once we got unified, not only did we surpass the Soviets, we developed new American technologies, industries, and jobs. So 50 years later, our generation's Sputnik moment is back. This is our moment." [www9–21]

In February, 2011 one of President Obama's weekly addresses was titled "To Win the Future, America Must Win the Global Competition in Education." He stated: "Over the next ten years, nearly half of all new jobs will require education beyond high school, many requiring proficiency in math and science. And yet today we've fallen behind in math, science, and graduation rates." He commented that American scientific companies "struggle to hire American workers with the skills that fit their needs." [www9–22] The ongoing work of American immigration attorneys, tasked with securing H–1B work visas for foreigners with math skills, confirms that the problem still persists.

A 2012 press release announcing plans to increase the number of STEM teachers stated: "Today, the Obama Administration will announce the President's plan for the creation of a new, national Science, Technology, Engineering and Math (STEM) Master Teacher Corps comprised of some of the nation's finest educators in STEM subjects. The STEM Master Teacher Corps will begin with 50 exceptional STEM teachers established in 50 sites and will be expanded over 4 years to reach 10,000 Master Teachers. These selected teachers will make a multi-year commitment to the Corps and, in exchange for their expertise, leadership and service, will receive an annual stipend of up to $20,000 on top of their base salary. The Administration will launch this Teacher Corps with the $1 billion from the President's 2013 budget request currently before Congress." [www9–23]

The *Educate to Innovate* campaign was successful in dollars raised— over $240 million by 2015. [www9–24] But the STEM Master Teacher Corps Act was never passed by Congress. [www9–25] Moreover, the Race to the Top program had similarities to NCLB. As Diane Ravitch wrote, "Race to the Top was only marginally different from No Child Left Behind. In fact, it was worse, because it gave full-throated Democratic endorsement to the long-standing Republican agenda of testing, accountability, and choice." [R7, p. 15]

Meanwhile, the second unfeasible aim of NCLB—that every child would be proficient in reading and math by 2014—came due during President Obama's tenure. In 2011 Secretary Arne Duncan had no choice but to "let states off the hook," as reported in *U.S. News & World Report*, by outlining conditions for waivers: "First, show they are transitioning to college- and career-ready standards and assessments, something most have already initiated. Second, they must implement an accountability system to reward schools showing progress as well as high-achieving schools that serve low-income students, but also take action to improve low-performing schools or schools with large achievement gaps. ... Finally, states must work with local educators to find ways to evaluate and support teacher and principal effectiveness based on several proven factors, including student progress." [K5] A year later the *New York Times* reported on the waivers, "raising the question of whether the decade-old federal program has been essentially nullified." [www9–26]

In 2015 the Every Student Succeeds Act (ESSA) replaced NCLB as the new reauthorization of the Elementary and Secondary Education Act. In signing the law President Obama stated, "With this bill, we reaffirm that fundamental American ideal—that every child, regardless of race, income, background, the zip code where they live, deserves the chance to make of their lives what they will." [www9–27]

Donald Trump (January, 2017—Publication Date)

In his first eight months, President Trump has not addressed inferior math education. However, dismantling Common Core was a campaign promise, splitting the Republican Party on that matter. [B4] And the move toward more school vouchers and choice by his Secretary of Education is decades old. As early as 1997, *Time* magazine's cover story "What Makes a Good School" stated: "For the G.O.P., they [school vouchers] are a wedge issue." [T8]

On September 25, 2017 Trump signed a Presidential Memorandum, aimed at expanding access to STEM, including computer programming. Missing, however, was the recognition that strong math is a prerequisite for programming (see Chapter 11, Obstacle 41). [www9–28]

10
Chasing Reforms

As one innovation follows another, as one reform overtakes the last, teachers may be forgiven if from time to time they suffer an acute case of reform fatigue.
Diane Ravitch [R6, p. 224]

Though oversimplified, math education has had two opposing sides for almost a century. One group is called the *progressivists*, not in any way the same term *progressive*, synonymous with *liberal*, in today's politics, but rather as affiliated with John Dewey and his disciples. This faction believes in student-centered rather than teacher-centered learning, making math fun, making math relevant to the real world, relating math to students' personal experiences, working in groups, and writing about math. They also include the *constructivists* because they believe that students can and should construct or discover their own math. They believe in pedagogy above content; thus, opponents accuse constructivists of promoting anti-intellectualism.

Non-progressivists are often called *traditionalists*—a misleading term, improperly linked to simple Back-to-Basics. I prefer to coin the name *rigorists*. This faction, typically supported by university mathematicians, controlled the decade after the 1957 launching of the Soviet satellite Sputnik. Rigorists believe that having a solid foundation of math knowledge is paramount—that students must understand math before applying it.

Diane Ravitch wrote generously of the reformers' spirit: "With the best of intentions, reformers have sought to correct deficiencies by introducing new pedagogical techniques, new ways of organizing classrooms, new technologies, new tests, new incentives, and new ways to govern schools. In every instance, reformers believed that their solution was the very one that would transform the schools, make learning fun, raise test scores, and usher in an age of educational joy or educational efficiency." [R6, p. 224]

One of the earliest attempts at math education reform, written by the National Committee on Mathematical Requirements (NCMR), was *The Reorganization of Mathematics in Secondary Education*—known as *The 1923 Report* and referred to as the "major historical document of this period." [B13, p. 361] The preface to the report stated: "The National Committee on Mathematical Requirements was organized in the late summer of 1916 under the auspices of The Mathematical Association of America for the purpose of giving national expression to the movement for reform in the teaching of mathematics, which had gained considerable headway in various parts of the country, but which lacked the power that coordination and united effort alone could give." [N13, p. v] Moreover, "The influence of *The 1923 Report* continued until the report in 1959 of the Commission of Mathematics of the College Entrance Examination Board. That this influence did not create a corresponding change in practice was due mainly to the traditional inertia in educational practice and the depression of the 1930s." [B13, p. 361]

In 1935 the MAA and NCTM formed a joint commission "to study the problems of secondary mathematics." Similar to the NCMR, this new organization lacked funding, suffered from "wide geographical distribution" of members who found travel difficult, and ultimately lost members recruited to help on World War II efforts. [N15, p. ix; N13, p. viii]

Most reform attempts prior to Sputnik were incomplete and impermanent, consisting only of committee reports, conference proceedings, position papers, and the like. Essentially, no studies were conducted nor were accompanying textbooks written—certainly not on a large scale. Because funding was minimal, so was the effect—specifying what math should be taught, as well as how and to whom it should be taught, did not make change happen. The lack of results from these committees was recognized by the NCTM in retrospect: "In the past many committee reports have not led to new developments so much as they have revealed beliefs that were already generally accepted." [N17, p. 462]

Moreover, as William Betz wrote in a 1950 *Mathematics Teacher* article, "But after surveying the record of the pioneering reformers, with due appreciation and gratitude, we must admit that while they accomplished some genuine improvements within the traditional framework of academic mathematics, they did not actually come to grips with the main job confronting them. As their critics pointed out relentlessly, they did not really 'make out a constructive case' for the educational significance of mathematics; this is, they did not create a compelling type of motivation. Above all, their attempts to produce a continuous curriculum were regularly frustrated by the apparently impregnable organization of the four-year high school with its universal endorsement of sixteen more or less haphazard 'units' as a basis for graduation." [B12, p. 602]

A more detailed examination of five reforms—starting in the 1950s—is essential background for understanding the thesis of this book.

Math Reform 1. Sputnik New Math

Worry over the nation's security started immediately as Sputnik spun around the earth. Reaction to the Soviet satellite transformed the history of math education. As stated in a ten-year retrospective article in the *Mathematics Teacher*, "Frankly, without this unexpected, though admittedly questionable, incentive, many of the curriculum visionaries . . . would probably still be weak voices crying in the wilderness. Certainly, we would not be as far along as we are today." [M10, pp. 696–697]

In short, "The New Math" refers to the curriculum change in mathematics education that occurred in the Sputnik era during the late 1950s and early 1960s. The movement shifted emphasis from memorization to understanding. University mathematicians not only dominated school mathematics but also wrote new textbooks. The two best known programs were the University of Illinois Committee on School Mathematics (UICSM) and the School Mathematics Study Group (SMSG).

Was the term "New Math" new?

In 1830 Warren Colburn, a teacher, manufacturer, and lecturer who was

Harvard educated in math, spoke before the American Institute of Instruction in Boston. His address, "Teaching of Arithmetic," was so significant that it was reprinted in 1912 in the *Elementary School Teacher* and reprinted again in 1970 in a history of math education book. Eerily predictive of replacing "old math" with "new math" in the Sputnik era, Colburn wrote [emphasis added]: "By the *old* system the learner was presented with a rule which told him how to perform certain operations on figures, and when these were done he would have the proper result. But no reason was given for a single step. . . . By the *new* system the learner commences with practical examples on which the numbers are so small that he can easily reason upon them." [B13, p. 26]

In 1927 the NCTM 2nd annual yearbook used the same term: "Those who are about to teach the *new* [emphasis added] mathematics should have first of all a broad vision of what elementary mathematics is, what it does for modern civilization, and what it should be expected to do for the pupil." [N14, p. 125] And NCTM cited a reference to *The 1923 Report* as containing inspiring "new math." [N17, p. 208]

What was the state of math education prior to Sputnik?

Again in 1950, Betz cited the following conditions: "In a large number of our states, not a single hour of mathematics is now required for graduation from high school. The educational policy-makers are still pressing their demand for ever more reduced programs, for easier courses, for 'functional mathematics' devoid of algebra and geometry. Everywhere the teachers of mathematics cry out in despair that they cannot build on a vacuum. And the end is not yet. The colleges have found it impossible or inexpedient to counteract these trends. Instead, they do not hesitate to admit students without a semblance of mathematical preparation; they are offering 'remedial' or introductory courses in arithmetic and secondary mathematics; and it is reported that not infrequently they even give credit for this belated kind of training." Betz later continued: "The war years furnished dramatic evidence of the widespread collapse of mathematics as a school subject. Very many of the men taking the selective examinations given by the armed forces lacked even a rudimentary acquaintance with fractions and decimals." [B12, pp. 600, 606]

NCTM confirmed: "The induction testing for World War II presented evidence that many youths were incompetent in mathematics. ... [Worry] extended beyond military needs to encompass the employment and training problems of increasingly technical industries." [N17, p. 231]

Max Beberman, founder of UICSM, actually started revamping math education five years before Sputnik. In 1958 he wrote, "In 1952, a few of us at the University of Illinois asked ourselves: Can able mathematicians together with skillful teachers develop materials of instruction and train high school teachers in their use so that the products of the program are enthusiastic students who understand mathematics? An affirmative answer could be justified only by a constructive existence proof, and we set ourselves the task of furnishing such a proof." [B5, p. 1]

In 1960 Jerome Bruner reflected upon the widespread practice in which teachers stressed skills over cognition: "Much teaching of mathematics is of this sort. The child learns not to understand mathematical order but rather to apply certain devices or recipes without understanding their significance and connectedness. They are not translated into his way of thinking. Given this inappropriate start, he is easily led to believe that the important thing is for him to be 'accurate'—though accuracy has less to do with mathematics than with computation." [B21, pp. 38–39]

A 1961 issue of *Time* described Yale's math professor Edward Begle, founder of SMSG and a father of seven, as one who " ... once spent his days hammering topology into graduate students and his nights wrestling with juvenile homework. The nights were worse than the days. When Daughter Sally bogged down in percentages, Papa Begle blew up. Sally's math book explained percentages three ways without touching on the common principle. 'It was dull, terrible, uninteresting,' growls Begle. 'It was so revolting that I had to do something.'" [T7]

In 1973, again in retrospect, Morris Kline wrote: "There was a general agreement in the early 1950s and even before that date that the teaching of mathematics had been unsuccessful. Student grades in mathematics were far lower than in other subjects. Student dislike and even dread of mathematics were widespread." [K8, p. 15]

What was the reaction after Sputnik was launched?

While the launch of Sputnik did not completely begin the math reform movement, the Russian satellite certainly hastened its growth.

At a 1958 National Education Association conference on gifted students, the President of the National Merit Scholarship Corporation began his address with the following remarks: "On October 4, 1957 the Russians put an earth satellite, Sputnik I, into orbit. This dramatic event was immediately noted around the world. The feeble and uninspiring beep-beep emitted by that 184-pound ball caught the ear of more people than the blast of the H-bomb. . . . One of the quick responses of the American public has been that we do something about our educational system." [S22, p. 18]

The cooperation of secondary math teachers and university professors was also notable at that time: "In the spring of 1958, after consulting with the President of the National Council of Teachers of Mathematics and the Mathematical Association of America, the President of the American Mathematical Society appointed a small committee of educators and university mathematicians to organize a School Mathematics Study Group whose objective would be the improvement of the teaching of mathematics in the schools. Edward G. Begle was appointed director of the study group with headquarters at Yale University." [N16, pp. 32–33]

The Commission on Mathematics (COM), organized by the College Entrance Examination Board in 1955 two years before Sputnik, issued a report in 1959 two years after Sputnik. [www10–1] In 1965 one of the members attributed much of the widespread distribution and successful effect of the recommendations for proper college-preparatory mathematics to the launching of the Soviet satellite: "If it had not been for Sputnik I, this report might have suffered the fate of many educational documents and been filed in the archives, with little effort being made to implement it. As things turned out, the public demanded action, federal funds suddenly became available, the mathematical community organized SMSG, and the fat was in the fire." [A5, p. 691]

The Commission on Mathematics report, the first major math education document since *The 1923 Report*, was titled *Program for College Preparatory Mathematics*. It stated [emphasis added]: "In order that the school and college curricula meet the needs of mathematics itself and of its applications, there must be a change. A *new* program, oriented to the needs of the second half of the twentieth century and based on a dynamic conception of mathematics, is required. The national need for mathematical manpower, and a general feeling of dissatisfaction with the present state of affairs, support the early introduction of such a *new* curriculum." [C16, p. 9]

In 1960 Jerome Bruner echoed the common feeling: "Unquestionably, there has also been a surge of awareness born of our sense of imperiled national security." [B21, p. 74]

The feeling that high-quality math was a national imperative continued into the early 1960s. In 1963 an NCTM report stated: "The world today demands more mathematical knowledge on the part of more people than the world of yesterday, and the world of tomorrow will make still greater demands. The number of our citizens skilled in mathematics must be greatly increased. An understanding of the role of mathematics in our society is now a prerequisite for intelligent citizenship. Since no one can predict with certainty his future profession, much less foretell which mathematical skills will be required in the future by a given profession, it is important that mathematics be so taught that students will be able in later life to learn the new mathematical skills which the future will surely demand of many of them." [N16, p. 33]

What distinguished the New Math?

The New Math had four distinguishing characteristics: (1) curriculum created by university mathematicians rather than school teachers; (2) textbooks written by academic groups rather than for-profit publishers; (3) math presented with accurate and rigorous guidelines rather than wobbly and superficial appeals; and (4) organization beginning with set theory rather than arithmetic. Math anxiety expert Sheila Tobias wrote: "The New Math curriculum was developed with the best intentions by some of the finest mathematicians and math educators in the country." [T9, p. 32]

The use of set theory as the starting point for all mathematics has a fascinating history. Described in a book by Amir Aczel, in 1934 some European mathematicians formed a group and collectively gave themselves the name of a single person: Nicolas Bourbaki. Aczel wrote: "The charge of that [first] generation [of Bourbaki] was to redo mathematics and to completely rewrite the way mathematics should be pursued and taught." [A1, pp. 83, 117–118]

Aczel further explained: "Set theory is viewed as the foundation of all of mathematics, and it was Bourbaki's great idea to devote the first book produced by the group [in 1936] to this key foundational topic. André Weil, in fact, invented for this book the universal notation we use today for the empty set: Ø [now a slashed zero]. This symbol comes from the Norwegian alphabet, which Weil had encountered on his travels. The Bourbaki text on set theory thus introduced this new mathematical symbol. It also introduced a whole new way of thinking about mathematics: placing sets and operations on sets at the base of all of mathematics. This would lead to the New Math that schools throughout the world began to teach in the 1950s." [A1, p. 93]

A second and third generation of Bourbaki followed, with far-reaching influence: "Nicolas Bourbaki was the greatest mathematician of the twentieth century. Since his appearance on the world stage in the 1930s, and until his declining years as the century drew to a close, Bourbaki has changed the way we think about mathematics and, through it, about the world around us. Nicolas Bourbaki is responsible for the emergence of the 'New Math' that swept through American education in the middle of the century as well as the educational systems of other nations; he is credited with the introduction of rigor into mathematics; and he was the originator for the modern concept of a mathematical proof. . . . It can be said that no working mathematician in the world today is free of the influence of the seminal work of Nicolas Bourbaki." [A1, p. 2]

Why did the New Math thrive?

The New Math had contemporary respect. A 1956 *Time* magazine article stated: "Many mathematicians regard Beberman's new method as the most important reform in nearly a century . . . ." [T4]

The New Math had participation from the best mathematicians in the nation. At a symposium titled "Reflecting on Sputnik: Linking the Past, Present, and Future of Educational Reform" hosted by the National Academy of Sciences (NAS), one presented paper stated: "Perhaps the most distinctive feature of the Sputnik-driven reforms was the extensive participation of the university research scholars in the reform effort. For a brief period between the mid-1950s to the early 1970s some of the nation's most distinguished academics left their libraries and laboratories to spend time in pre-college classrooms." [D8]

The New Math had substantial funding. Citing an actual dollar amount would not have appropriate impact due to inflation as well as the monetary needs of modern technology innovation. But the dollar values were unprecedented at the time. The report of the same NAS symposium stated: "By 1960 the programs of the Education Directorate represented 42% of the NSF annual budget." [D8]

The New Math had promise of placing the U.S. ahead of Russia. The 1991 Carnegie Commission report stated retrospectively: "The crisis in math and science education was first recognized . . . when the Soviet Sputnik could be seen crossing American skies every 96 minutes, reminding us not to take our technical excellence for granted. At that time government was primarily concerned about the adequacy of the number and quality of professional scientists, engineers, and mathematicians needed to assure our freedom from a Soviet threat." [C2, p. 18]

Why did the New Math fail?

Sociologists have spent careers writing volumes about society's reaction, specifically resistance, to social change. As Robert Laurer explained, " . . . people are always changing their ways, but . . . they will resist change under three circumstances: when the change is perceived to be a threat to basic securities; when the change is not understood; and when the change is imposed upon them. Much of the supposed trauma of change can be accounted for in these terms." [L1, p. 10] The Sputnik New Math had all three aspects of this struggle: jeopardizing math teachers' stability; confusing almost everyone from teachers to parents to administrators; and declaring that math, from teacher workshops to student textbooks, would be done the new way.

Teachers had felt isolated, as noted by CEEB in 1985: "The last big wave of curriculum reform in mathematics, in the 1950s and 1960s, came down from above. Teachers were not truly involved in the process of change; by and large, they were expected to do what someone else had decided. That kind of change does not always get implemented in the classroom, and when it does, it is short-lived." [C11, p. 2]

The previously cited symposium paper confirmed: "Perhaps the greatest flaw in the Sputnik reforms was the 'top down' model for change that characterized their implementation." [D8]

My father was one of the fortunate math teachers brought into UICSM at the development stage and later charged with re-training countless other classroom teachers. The brilliance of the materials written by math professors and the millions of dollars poured into the project by the federal government were often irrelevant to his trainees. My father relayed one story to me in particular: at a school workshop he gave, a group of teachers sat stone-faced the entire time. Not one person reacted in any way—verbally, visually, physically. At the end, without one comment, question, or thank-you from the teachers, my father's only conclusion was that the teachers had pre-arranged their absolute silence.

In other situations where teachers tried to be cooperative, the existing level of their education was often inadequate for successful retraining. As William Glasser wrote in 1969, "Lack of relevance to teachers causes the failure of many new approaches. The 'new math' is an excellent example of a new approach that teachers don't understand and often teach poorly because they doubt its value." [G7, p. 116]

The result of either refusal or inability to change teaching methods was noted in *The Teaching Gap*. Because most math teachers are very dependent on textbooks and because emphasis during the New Math reform was on providing new textbooks, the logical conclusion would be that updated textbooks would yield updated teaching. But a study showed otherwise. In 1975 the National Advisory Committee on Mathematical Education summarized that at the elementary level, "Teachers are essentially teaching the same way they were taught in school. Almost none of the concepts, methods, or big ideas of modern mathematics have appeared." [N2, p. 77] *The Teaching Gap* authors concluded: "Even textbooks can get swamped by the system." [S26, p. 98]

And thus, discomfort among teachers became denial. Futurist Marilyn Ferguson commented: "Denial is a way of life. More accurately, it is a way of diminishing life, of making it seem more manageable. Denial is the alternative to transformation." [F9, p. 74]

Parents shared teachers' discomfort and anxiety. Sheila Tobias confirmed: "Anyone who brought up a child in this period knows one thing for sure: the New Math helped aggravate the generation gap. . . . Mysterious as math had always been, it became even more so." [T9, p. 33]

Popular magazines published cartoons that stoked the unsettled emotions of teachers and parents. In a Peanuts cartoon, Linus asked, "How can you do 'NEW MATH' problems with an 'OLD MATH' mind?" [S10] And a *Newsweek* article titled "New Math—Does It Really Add Up?" included a cartoon showing a typical family of four at a restaurant table with the son saying, "Dad, you can't expect to pick up the basics of the new math in a simple dinner-table conversation." [N43, p. 112] And a 1965 book on the New Math showed a cartoon of a man wiping sweat off his head and saying to his wife, "It's happened, Alice—fractions." [R16, p. 74]

Like other institutions threatening the status-quo, nicknames emerged for the two top programs. UICSM was dubbed "Ugh, I Can't Stand Math," while SMSG was branded "Some Math, Some Garbage."

Was the New Math effective?

Nationally, success of the New Math on a broad scale was dubious: "For instance, NACOME conjectured that despite formal changes in the school syllabi and classroom texts of the 'new math' era, the actual mathematics experience of elementary school students during the 1960s reflected few of the reformers' intentions." [F10, p. 417] Globally, as quoted in the section on TIMSS, the results of FIMS indicated that the New Math had been effective in raising test scores.

All combined, though, negative pressures defeated positive forces. Thus, in the words of William Wooten describing SMSG, "Like Alice's Cheshire cat, the scientists faded from the secondary scene until nothing remained but a grin." [W11, p. 3]

Math Reform 2. Back to Basics

When rigorous math failed, the natural swing was in the opposite direction—as elementary as possible. Moreover, social conditions—namely the civil rights era—double-downed on the removal of anything supposedly elitist, as discussed in the section on President Kennedy. And thus the next math reform movement was Back to Basics, with a heavy dose of the four whole number operations and a complete absence of anything viewed as abstruse.

Charles Sykes described this period as follows: "The Civil Rights movement shifted the focus of attention to the relationship between schools and poverty, inequality, and segregation. The Elementary and Secondary Education Act of 1965 (ESEA) deployed the considerable weight of the federal government behind the movement to place schools in the vanguard of the movement toward social, economic, and political equality." [S29, p. 220]

Jerome Bruner similarly wrote: "In America, particularly, the issue of curriculum as a means of cultivating intellect was very soon swamped by another matter. By the mid-1960s deep social forces were producing unforeseen turmoil in the American school. They seemed to come out of a common source: a striving for a new equality, for a fresh definition of the nature of society." [B21, p. xi]

Math Reform 3. Constructivism

Filling the vacuum resulting from the end of the New Math, Back to Basics was uninspired and incomplete, allowing a resurgence of progressivism and constructivism, carried forward by followers of Dewey.

Yet progressivism lingered prior to Sputnik, not only as evidenced by Dewey's lifespan, but also as referenced in later writings. For example, in discussing the retreat from rigorous academics pre-Sputnik to the reversal post-Sputnik, David Elkind noted: "How did this radical turnabout in attitudes happen? There are probably many reasons, but a major one was the attack on 'progressive' education that occurred in the 1950s and that found much education material dated." [E1, p. 7]

What is constructivism?

Diane Ravitch offered this explanation: "Constructivism is a theory that students construct their own knowledge; in its extreme forms, constructivism eschews direct instruction, focusing instead on activities, processes, and social interaction among students." [R6, pp. 40–41]

In his description, E. D. Hirsch referenced an earlier form of constructivism: "The goal of present-day educational reformers is to produce students with 'higher-order skills' who are able to think independently about the unfamiliar problems they will encounter in the information age, who have become 'problem solvers' and have 'learned how to learn,' and who are on their way to becoming 'critical thinkers' and 'lifelong learners.' The method advocated for achieving these 'higher-order skills' is 'discovery learning,' by which students solve problems and make decisions on their own through 'inquiry' and 'independent analysis' of 'real-world' projects. What Kilpatrick in the 1920s called the 'project method' is now called 'discovery learning.'" [H12, p. 129]

William Bennett, Chester Finn, and John Cribb offered this description: "This new approach to math embraces what educators call the 'constructivist' philosophy. Rather than accepting, internalizing, and using knowledge and skills developed by others over the centuries and transmitted by teachers, children are encouraged to try to figure things out for themselves, 'constructing' their own meanings and understandings. Teachers thus become 'facilitators of learning.' Rather than systematically imparting the knowledge they possess, they are supposed to create stimulating environments, encourage youngsters to explore, and guide students as they discover math. Less stress is placed on using deductive logic. Instead, trial-and-error investigations and the 'intuitive insights' of children are emphasized. Real-life, practical applications are heralded over math's abstract nature." [B10, pp. 320–321]

What was the appeal of constructivism?

The nature and size of mathematics, with its hierarchical structure yet overlap of countless concepts, suited constructivism. As math educator Jarkko Leino wrote, "Of course, the bulk of mathematical knowledge is huge and so are the problems of mathematical education too. The mathematical structures in the forms that have been developed and condensed by mathematicians are not accessible to pupils. Mathematical information cannot be assimilated in abstract forms. It must be meaningfully constructed by pupils, piece by piece, on the basis of earlier experiences and conceptions that are both basically contextual in nature and work on their criteria of meaningfulness and truth. We are now within the concepts of constructivism." [L4, p. 42]

Did the New Math embrace constructivism?

As with math itself, these reforms overlapped in philosophy—the New Math did contain some discovery method. But, as Bruner wrote, the New Math was a blend: UICSM members have "emphasized the importance of discovery as an aid to teaching. They have been active in devising methods that permit a student to discover for himself the generalization that lies behind a particular mathematical operation, and they contrast this approach with the 'method of assertion and proof' . . . by the teacher . . . . It has also been pointed out by the Illinois group that the method of discovery would be too time-consuming for presenting all of what a student must cover in mathematics. The proper balance between the two is anything but plain . . . ." [B21, p. 21]

Max Beberman wrote about the distinction between the prior and new versions of discovery: "A premature verbalization is, almost by definition . . . imprecise and, thus, not a faithful rendering of what the student actually believes, or is coming to believe. The teacher's acceptance of an imprecise verbalization is a signal to the student that he has completed the process of searching for a generalization. And even a precise verbalization from the student is not a sure sign that he is aware of the class of instances of the generalization, for he may regard the generalization itself as just another 'instance.' . . . This technique of delaying the verbalization of important discoveries is characteristic of the UICSM program, and differentiates our discovery method from other methods which are also called 'discovery methods' . . . ." [B5, pp. 27–28]

Are teachers capable of constructivism?

Howard Gardner, favoring inquiry over articulation, wrote: ". . . questions are more important than answers; knowledge and . . . understanding should evolve from the constant probing of such questions." Further, regarding algorithms, he stated: ". . . it makes sense to create a situation in which students must think like the mathematician who developed the formula, and see whether they can themselves progress toward an appropriate formula." [G3, pp. 24, 127] As one example, he suggested that guiding students to discover the formula distance = rate x time is a valuable classroom activity. But how many teachers can lead that exercise without sacrificing classroom focus or reaching wrong conclusions? How many schools can provide math teachers with adequate time to conduct discovery and still meet pacing guidelines? How many students can advance from one point to the next with limited background?

Perhaps the most significant opponent to constructivism, especially as relevant to *From STEM To STEW*, was B. F. Skinner. In his 1968 book he attacked the lack of content in constructivism: "Efforts to teach creativity have sacrificed the teaching of subject matter." He also astutely pointed out a dilemma for the teacher: "The position of the teacher who encourages discovery is ambiguous. Is he to pretend that he himself does not know? . . . Or, for the sake of encouraging a joint venture in discovery, is the teacher to choose to teach only those things which he himself has not learned? Or is he frankly to say, 'I know, but you must find out' and accept the consequences for his relations with his students?" [S17, pp. 89, 111]

Perhaps constructivism attracts underprepared math teachers, happy to hide in the play-world of pretending not to know. Master math teachers understand this biting comment by Skinner: "Only a teacher who is unaware of his effects on his students can believe that children actually discover mathematics . . . ." [S17, p. 110]

Are students capable of constructivism?

In pure constructivism, students learn math by inventing their own math. But would I as a 13-year-old have been able to uncover the Pythagorean Theorem when others had studied and practiced mathematics for decades prior to making such a remarkable discovery? And in conducting an exercise on a smaller scale, would a revelation by one class genius serve to motivate or discourage other students?

Many mathematicians, educators, and psychologists believe that further math can be discovered only after essential math has been acquired—that students need to know enough math before solving substantive problems. Four such comments follow.

Alan Schoenfeld pinpointed students' lack of formal logic: "Thus mathematical argument becomes a tool in the dialectic between what the mathematician suspects to be true and what the mathematician knows to be true. In short, deduction becomes a tool of discovery. This is hardly the experience of most students." [S9, p. 173]

Jerome Bruner cautioned about visionless discovery: "For exploration to have direction, in short, the goal of the task must be known in some approximate fashion, and the testing of alternatives must yield information as to where one stands with respect to it." [B22, p. 44]

Charles Sykes emphasized the importance of prerequisite knowledge: "Eventually, of course, a student who is versed in the essentials of mathematics will learn to 'think mathematically.' But . . . you cannot 'think' your way to the solution of an algebra problem without knowing algebra, however much math educators may enthuse over 'mathematical thinking.'" [S29, p. 121]

Co-authors William Bennett, Chester Finn, and John Cribb issued two specific warnings: "Several problems arise when this philosophy [constructivism] occupies the center of elementary school math. When you rely on children to 'construct' knowledge or skills—rather than systematically introducing material to them—learning can become a disorganized and time-consuming process. Mathematics is a highly structured body of knowledge and does not lend itself to haphazard learning." They continued: "Perhaps the biggest problem with discovery learning in math is that most theorems, conventions, terms, and operations are not 'natural' occurrences. . . . It is not a process that we can expect young children to develop, 'construct,' or 'discover' on their own. In fact, many mathematical conventions initially puzzle youngsters because they run counter to their natural intuitions—such as [unit] fractions getting smaller as the bottom number gets bigger." [B10, p. 328]

What are weaknesses of constructivism?

The singular goal of learning has been written about by many educators. Four examples are:
1. "Surely the most important single goal of all instruction is to teach how to learn independently." [J7, p. 298]
2. "The ultimate goal of the educational system is to shift to the individual the burden of pursuing his own education." [www10–2]
3. "The ultimate goal of teaching is that students acquire a set of meaningful concepts that they can use effectively to solve problems." [F4, pp. 21–22]
4. "Instruction is a provisional state that has as its object to make the learner or problem solver self-sufficient. . . . Otherwise the result of instruction is to create a form of mastery that is contingent upon the perpetual presence of a teacher." [B22, p. 53]

Certainly, education has failed if adults cannot continue to learn effectively on their own; but constructivists took statements of this nature and carried them too far. When substantial classroom time is spent on exploration, something has to go. When teachers are not adequately trained to lead discovery and advance curriculum concurrently, students are not sufficiently taught to demonstrate math knowledge on standardized exams and in future courses. One cannot learn how to learn if one does not have a knowledge base. As E. D. Hirsch wrote, "We must not accept the claim that knowing how to learn (which is an abstract skill that does not even exist) is more important than having a broad foundation of factual knowledge that really does enable further learning." [H12, p. 216]

Moreover, Hirsch warned that educational psychology does not support the practice of constructivism: "Discovery learning must, in the end, be justified by its observed effectiveness, and on that score, the results emphatically do not justify an extreme or exclusive reliance on what is currently called 'constructivist' practice. . . . In short, the term 'constructivism' has become a kind of magical incantation used to defend discovery learning, which is no more sanctioned by psychological theory than any other form of constructed learning. To pretend that it is so sanctioned illustrates what I mean by the 'selective use of research.' Despite the enthusiastic invocations of the term 'constructivism,' neither discovery learning nor any other form of pedagogy is specially singled out and sanctioned by modern psychology." [H12, p. 135]

Jarkko Leino also advised of the incomplete development of this teaching method: "Because of the lack of relevant theories, constructivism may often be regarded by educational practitioners, as well as researchers, only as a general framework, an approach, a paradigm, or meta-theory." [L4, p. 46]

Ultimately, the progressivism/constructivism movement's full-throttled embrace of discovery minus rigor cascaded into the next math reform. As Charles Sykes commented, "The gains of the earlier back-to-basics movements had been wiped out, but by the early 1980s the failures of the revived progressivism were so glaring that they were about to set off another round of reform and retrenchment. It too would fail." [S29, p. 222]

Math Reform 4. Math Wars

"The math wars are raging." So wrote William Bennett, Chester Finn, and John Cribb in their 1999 book. But these authors did not coin the widely used term *Math Wars* to describe the debate that constructivism had placed front and center—free thinking versus factual delivery. They explained: "What's all the fuss about? It's called reform math, 'new New Math' (a swipe at the ill-fated New Math movement of the 1960s and 1970s), 'whole math' (a pejorative reference to 'whole language' reading instruction), or 'NCTM math' (after the National Council of Teachers of Mathematics, which has propagated it). You may also hear it called 'fuzzy math,' 'feel-good math,' even 'rain forest math.' With education fads, there's usually a high correlation between the number of nicknames and the level of controversy." [B10, pp. 319–320]

What started the Math Wars?

NCTM's *Curriculum and Evaluation Standards for School Mathematics* [N20], embracing constructivism by encouraging a delay of performing the whole-number algorithms until children understood them, is recognized as the impetus for the Math Wars—the battle by traditionalists (or rigorists, as I prefer) to end constructivism. Though published in 1989, this document's development over the eight prior years is proof that constructivists never quit—merely freshened their image.

In 1995 Charles Sykes described the inciting incident: "As researchers sift through the rubble of innumerate America, they will likely recognize 1989 as a turning point. In that year, the National Council of Teachers of Mathematics (NCTM) launched the new New Math revolution by issuing a comprehensive set of new standards for teaching math. The new standards describe 'a vision' for school mathematics that insists that the nation's schools embrace a curriculum for teaching mathematics 'that capitalizes on children's intuitive insights and language' and that is guided not by the standards of a recognized discipline but by the 'children's intellectual, social, and emotional development.'" [S29, p. 117]

A *Time* magazine article agreed: "It all started in 1989, when the National Council of Teachers of Mathematics, in response to the consistently poor math scores of U.S. children, issued new standards overhauling math education. Out went the stalwarts of traditional math: the rote memorization drills, the droning chalkboard lectures. In came the cool stuff: calculators and geoboards, hands-on, open-ended problems, exercises that encourage kids to discover their own route to the right answer." [R1, pp. 66–67]

Lynne Cheney also wrote about the origin: "The saga of whole math began in earnest in 1989, when the National Council of Teachers of Mathematics published standards that denounced a 'longstanding preoccupation with computation and other traditional skills.' According to the council, stressing addition, subtraction and, worst of all, memorization made students into 'passive receivers of rules and procedures rather than active participants in creating knowledge.' . . . The standards recommended that students get together with peers in cooperative learning groups to 'construct' strategies for solving math problems, rather than sit in class with teachers instructing them. Calculators were a necessity from kindergarten on, the council said, because students liberated from 'computational algorithms' could pursue higher-order activities, like inventing personal methods of long division." [C7]

What was the essence of the 1989 NCTM Standards?

Standards are only a framework of educational goals—curricula supply the specifics, and textbooks offer the vehicle. Due to the ambitious nature of the 1989 Standards, NCTM followed in 1991 with the publication of *Professional Standards for Teaching Mathematics*—a 200-page attempt to help floundering math teachers enact the new goals. The first of the six teaching standards conveys the gist of the actual standards.

"Standard 1: Worthwhile Mathematical Tasks
The teacher of mathematics should pose tasks that are based on—
• sound and significant mathematics;
• knowledge of students' understandings, interests, and experiences;
• knowledge of the range of ways that diverse students learn mathematics; and that

- engage students' intellect;
- develop students' mathematical understandings and skills;
- stimulate students to make connections and develop a coherent framework for mathematical ideas;
- call for problem formulation, problem solving, and mathematical reasoning;
- promote communication about mathematics;
- represent mathematics as an ongoing human activity;
- display sensitivity to, and draw on, students' diverse background experiences and dispositions;
- promote the development of all students' dispositions to do mathematics." [N21, p. 25]

As with other math reforms, many teachers did not have the mathematical knowledge to succeed with such a challenge. Moreover, writing about math, relating math to the real world, and promoting ethno-math emerged as heavy components—perhaps because these required the least amount of mathematical knowledge from the teachers.

Did optimism exist over the 1989 NCTM Standards?

In 1993 Sheila Tobias wrote excitedly about introducing children to the NCTM *Standards*, stating that the plan called for "the teaching of how to think for ourselves, group work at all levels of math education, efficient use of technology, the teaching of paper-and-pencil estimation, more statistics and probability in the early grades, less computational drill and practice, the use of concrete materials in teaching, and more realistic problems." In her opinion, the *Standards* promised "to present mathematics . . . as a thinking and decision-making tool" that would "reward thinking and originality in place of mindless memorization." [T10, pp. 38–40]

What was some criticism of the reform movement during the Math Wars?

In 1995 Charles Sykes wrote against the reform, using the double *new New*, as others had: "Proponents of the new methods argue that they are encouraging children to 'value' mathematics, and they are emphasizing *how* children learn, rather than *what* they learn. All of which, they insist, will make children more confident 'problem solvers' who can 'communicate mathematically' and can 'reason mathematically.' . . . In the new New Math classes children dive straight into 'real-life' problems without being taught the basic disciplines . . . . The idea is that children will somehow learn the basic skills along the way—that the skills will somehow come to them 'by doing' and do not therefore need to be taught first. . . . the full impact of the new New Math probably will not be felt for a decade or so, when the tsunami of mathematical illiteracy will hit higher education and the national economy full force." [S29, p. 116]

Marianne Jennings—Arizona State University professor of Legal and Ethical Studies, public school mother, and strong math reform opponent—wrote articles such as "Rain Forest Algebra Course Teaches Everything but Algebra," "X + Y = F: Mesa's algebra textbooks flunk examination," "Rain-Forest Algebra and MTV Geometry," "MTV Math Doesn't Add Up," and "Why Our Kids Can't Do Math." [J2, J3, J4, J5, J6]

In "To sum up new math, 2 + 2 = 4ish" published in 1995 in *The Arizona Republic*, Jennings pummeled the experimental algebra program named "Rain Forest Math," stating sarcastically, ". . . it's always a good idea to try new, unresearched techniques in a class that is the foundation of all math . . . ." With clever stories, she eviscerated cooperative learning—"bunk" that "takes the work right out of learning" and "takes out the learning" as well. From algebra classes of one student doing all the work while the other students took off, to all students spending the entire period measuring their wingspans, she rebuked her daughter's teacher who assured Jennings that she didn't "understand the dramatic impact these techniques have on learning." [J1]

In his 1996 book, E. D. Hirsch attacked the reform movement: ". . . the mistaken assumption [is] that the wished-for 'higher order skills' are independent of a broad grounding in specific facts and information." Further, the Pythagorean Theorem is a good example that ". . . illustrates the implausibility of the claim that school-based information quickly grows outdated." [H12, pp. 144, 154]

In her 1997 *New York Times* Op-Ed, after citing research and testing to debunk the reform, Lynne Cheney noted an "immense paradox": "In a field distinguished by reliance on proof, an unproven approach is being taken in thousands of schools." She affirmed: "In the face of strong evidence that constructivist mathematics does not help and even hurts, they should consider closing down the whole-math experiment. If we want our children to be mathematically competent and creative, we must give them a base of knowledge upon which they can build." [C7]

In 1999 Martin Gross criticized one reformer by knocking the concept of "... seeking new ways to do old problems that were once easily solved" (a reappearing paradox in CCSSM) and calling the method of acquiring math reasoning "through personal and social experiences and even in groups" ... "highly unlikely." Gross further attacked the reformer: "(He fails to mention that many students do poorly on tests because they have never been taught the material.) Instead, he believes that more emphasis should be put on the *portfolio*, a collection of student- and teacher-selected work that reflects the child's supposed success in math—a kind of carefully prepared scrapbook that invites good assessments even when the student is mathematically tone-deaf." [G12, pp. 110, 112]

What was the media coverage during the Math Wars?

A 1997 *Newsweek* article tells the story of a second grade math teacher who asked her students if a box of 24 candles would be enough to light three birthday cakes next year for children who are now ages 3, 6, and 11. The article stated that the teacher was not satisfied with the students' realization that while $11 + 6 + 3 = 20$, 3 more candles would be needed for next year—so 24 were enough, unless each cake needed one candle for good luck. No—in reform math, this teacher wanted to see the students' "math strategies," having them write "all possible routes to the solution." [K1] If you are wondering about *what* other methods, you understand parents' and students' frustration with reform math.

Time magazine's article "This Is Math?" accurately quoted the opponents' use of pejorative terms such as "whole math" for the reform but then confused the two sides with negative language about serious math:

"Another is 'new-new-math,' recalling the ill-fated New Math fad of the 1960s and '70s, which introduced millions of students to math arcana like set theory and congruences." [R1, p. 66]

In their 1999 book, Bennett, Finn, and Cribb referred to a quote of one reform advocate in the "This Is Math?" article: "We knew there needed to be a fair amount of research and teacher training. We knew it would take 20 or 25 years to pull this off." [R1, p. 67] The three authors commented: "Those are not soothing words to a parent's ears." [B10, p. 322]

Did common ground exist between the two sides of the Math Wars?

Though barely recognized, competing sides in the Math Wars did share some overlapping beliefs. Laura Hamilton and José Martínez expressed the situation clearly: "Despite the often rancorous environment that characterizes the debate, the two approaches do not necessarily operate in opposition to one another. Moreover, the notion that 'reform' and 'traditional' approaches can be easily distinguished from one another is simplistic. Most of those who espouse the traditional viewpoint do not believe that students should engage in mindless drills or that higher-order reasoning is unimportant, and the idea that the reform-oriented instruction shuns computation in favor of purely 'fuzzy' activities that put the students in charge does not consider the ways in which many NCTM-aligned curricula incorporate a variety of activities including computation practice and teacher-led instruction." [H2, p. 129]

Moreover, Stanford professor Jo Boaler, though a proponent of constructivism, said that the math wars were fought over "two imaginary poles" of traditional and reform. She recognized that traditional teachers who prefer lecturing and having "students work individually" can "also ask students great questions, engage them in interesting mathematical inquiries, and give students opportunities to solve problems, not just rehearse standard methods." [B14, p. 40]

Had earlier educators issued warnings, ignored during the Math Wars?

Lessons from previous decades, showing that concepts and skills must be intertwined, were seemingly overlooked in the intense Math Wars. As early as 1953 Arthur Bestor cautioned: "In the long run, anti-intellectualism is bound to be self-defeating. But if powerful interests promote and sustain it, the run can be long and dangerous indeed." [B11, p. 101] Moreover, as written by Morris Kline, Max Beberman reportedly confessed at a 1964 NCTM meeting: "We're in danger of raising a generation of kids who can't do computational arithmetic." [K8, p. 110]

What caused the Math Wars to subside?

John Hechinger, in a 2006 *Wall Street Journal* front-page-left, above-the-fold article titled "New Report Urges Return to Basics In Teaching Math," wrote that NCTM had back-peddled. [H6] Then, as discussed in Chapter 9, President Bush's National Mathematics Advisory Panel helped to end the Math Wars. Hechinger covered the Panel's work in his 2008 article "Education Panel Lays Out Truce In Math Wars." [H7]

Comprehensively and informatively, the 2006 article stated: "The nation's math teachers, on the front lines of a 17-year curriculum war, are getting some new marching orders: Make sure students learn the basics. In a report . . . the National Council of Teachers of Mathematics . . . will give ammunition to traditionalists who believe schools should focus heavily and early on teaching such fundamentals as multiplication tables and long division. The council's advice is striking because in 1989 it touched off the so-called math wars by promoting open-ended problem solving over drilling. Back then, it recommended that students as young as those in kindergarten use calculators in class. Those recommendations horrified many educators, especially college math professors alarmed by a rising tide of freshmen needing remediation. The council's 1989 report influenced textbooks and led to what are commonly called 'reform math' programs, which are used in school systems across the country." Citing 120 divided by 40 as an easy problem taught with "fuzzy math," Hechinger said that the new methods "puzzled many parents," who "launched a countermovement." He added that the NCTM claimed "its earlier views had been widely misunderstood," not designed to prevent students from learning "fundamentals." Still, he quoted a math professor as calling NCTM's new suggestions "a remarkable reversal, and it's about time." [H6, pp. A1]

What were unintended consequences of the Math Wars?

Students who did not learn math adequately were the greatest casualties in the battle. But the profession of mathematics teaching also suffered. Jo Boaler explained: "One outcome of the math wars is that good teachers have been driven out of the teaching profession after years of bullying by extremists." [B14, p. 31] Interestingly, Boaler later revealed that she had been professionally attacked by two mathematicians (one, James Milgram—a colleague and objector to CCSSM). [www10–3]

Were the Math Wars new?

As early as 1975 NACOME had labeled the polarization between the constructivists and rigorists counterproductive. The report stated that school mathematics suffered because of acceding to the numerous following false dichotomies: "the old and the new in mathematics; skill and concepts; the concrete and the abstract; intuition and formalism; structure and problem solving; induction and deduction." [N2, p. 136]

Did the Math Wars end?

In 2010 Diane Ravitch optimistically wrote: "In mathematics, the wars of the 1990s between traditionalists and constructivists have also subsided, although they flare up from time to time when parents discover that their children can't add or subtract." She noted that the NCTM, which had initiated the emphasis on social discovery in learning, as well as school districts favoring constructivism, had moderated their positions to include more basic computation, problem solving, and critical thinking. In sum, she said: "A consensus is possible." [R6, p. 233]

But 2010 is the year in which many states adopted Common Core math. [www10–4] People who asked "What was the battle about anyway?" would soon be reminded. The Math Wars reform—what in 2008 Boaler called ". . . a series of unproductive and heated exchanges between advocates of different mathematics approaches" [B14, p. 31]—was reborn with different terminology but similar issues.

Math Reform 5. Common Core State Standards Math (CCSSM)

Misinformation about Common Core is rampant. While many opposed to CCSSM are anti federal overreach and pro states' rights, the irony of their position is that Common Core was created by the states—namely, by the National Governors Association (NGA) and the Council of Chief State School Officers (CCSSO). [www10–5] With good intentions, these two organizations wanted to raise the level of math education in under-performing states. The only federal involvement was that Secretary of Education Arne Duncan tied his Race to the Top program to Common Core. [B4; R7, p. 14]

CCSSM is yet another opportunity for constructivists to seize control, and the debate between the two sides of math education continues. Ironically, some opposed to CCSSM favor *Singapore Math* but do not realize that Singapore "has a strong national ministry that regulates the nation's content coverage." [S7, p. 83]

Interestingly, Howard Gardner, in *The Disciplined Mind*, stated his moderate comfort with the concept of national standards: "On most days, I could live with a national curriculum. I believe that there are many things that every child should know and be able to do; I believe that the American system could benefit from the coherence and rigor of a national curriculum; and I doubt that most of America's two and a half million-plus teachers desire, or are in a position, to create curricula and assessments that make as much sense as those drafted by expert teams of scholars and master teachers." Yet, Gardner had an important condition: "I would favor a national curriculum and national standards *only* if I—or others of like mind—could play a substantial role in their creation. When I consider how I would feel if the national curriculum or tests were placed in the hands of individuals with whom I have no ideological or educational commonality, I become an opponent of attempts to create national or federal standards." [G3, pp. 222–223]

Supporting national standards, Harold Stevenson and James Stigler wrote in 1992: "Despite their shortcomings, national standards would go a long way toward bringing order to our present chaotic curricula. Children would no longer be rewarded or penalized for moving, teachers would have clear frameworks for organizing their lessons, publishers could plan better texts with assurance of their acceptability, and parents would be able to evaluate their children's progress with less guesswork. Adopting national guidelines and standards does not necessarily mean relinquishing local control. School districts could still decide the manner in which they would follow the guidelines and attempt to meet these standards." [S25, p. 202]

I am in favor of national math standards if they reflect the breadth, depth, richness, and beauty of the subject. Common Core does not, in my professional opinion. Relevant, though, is Diane Ravitch's description of all educational standards as "not science," but rather "human judgment, subject to error and bias." [R7, p. 47]

Confusion over the value of national standards is understandable given different positions over time. As Ravitch explained, "Whereas *A Nation At Risk* encouraged demands for voluntary national standards, No Child Left Behind sidestepped the need for any standards." [R6, p. 30] Moreover, in the absence of national standards, other entities such as textbooks and college entrance exams become de facto standards, shaping curriculum. [R6, p. 232] And CCSSM is not the first movement in the history of math education to include methods—the Sputnik New Math did that as well. But CCSSM may be the first to have a website created by the lead writers to help teachers use those methods. [www10–6]

The involvement of governors dates well before CCSS, including President George H. W. Bush's Charlottesville Summit. Moreover, a 1996 report by the NCTAF revealed: "On March 26, 1996, the nation's governors and President Clinton joined business leaders and educators in a National Education Summit to reaffirm their commitment to achieving higher academic standards for America's schools and students. The governors pledged to develop internationally competitive academic standards and assessments in each state within the next two years and to reallocate funds to provide the professional development, infrastructure, and new technologies needed to meet these goals. . . . All the participants pledged to roll up their sleeves and get down to work immediately to respond to the urgent need for schools to improve so that all graduates have higher levels of skills and knowledge." [N12, pp. 2–3]

Yet when left to their own devices, states did not succeed, as described by Diane Ravitch: "The Clinton administration's Goals 2000 program gave the states federal money to write their own academic standards, but most of the state standards were vague when it came to any curriculum content. . . . Most state standards [one exception was Massachusetts] were windy rhetoric, devoid of concrete descriptions of what students should be expected to know and be able to do." [R6, p. 19]

Frustrated parents and grandparents often incorrectly refer to CCSSM as *New Math*. As discussed, New Math occurred in the Sputnik era, while New New Math was the term given to reform math during the Math Wars. Moreover, nothing is *new* about the imbedded constructivism.

Unfortunately, many opponents of Common Core would not comprehend the math standards, even if they read them—and probably, they have not. To understand the deficiencies of Common Core math, note that the CCSS website cites three "Key Shifts in Mathematics"—*focus, coherence,* and *rigor*. [www10–7]

Shift 1. Greater focus on fewer topics.

Common Core supporters, including the NCTM, are proud of their determination to fix a criticism of U.S. math education that was first reported by analysis of the international exam TIMSS 1995—that U.S. math is "a mile wide and an inch deep." But the notion that children will learn more math by covering fewer topics is patently absurd. Moreover, the irony of the wavering positions is staggering. The 2000 NCTM *Principles and Standards* stated: "To ensure that students will have a wide range of career and educational choices, the secondary school mathematics program must be both broad and deep." [N24, p. 287]

The media has enjoyed the humor in this "key shift." For example, a

2008 *USA Today* article was titled "A solution to how to teach math: Subtract." Its opening sentences were: "Wondering why your child isn't learning enough math in school? Her textbook may be too thick." [T12] I would prefer removing silly clipart and pointless photos than real math.

Shift 2. Coherence: Linking topics and thinking across grades.

This plan sounds good but does not happen in reality. For example, concerning factors, one standard appears in 4th grade, but none is in 5th grade, and then one appears in 6th.

Shift 3. Rigor: Pursue conceptual understanding, procedural skills and fluency, and application with equal intensity.

The balancing of concepts, skills, and application is *not* the definition of rigor. The word rigor means serious thoroughness. Moreover, careful examination shows the lack of equal intensity—concepts and applications overshadow skills. The Common Core notion that one can apply what one does not know is preposterous. Students must learn math skills before they can use them successfully in real-world examples.

In their true meanings, focus, coherence, and rigor are not shifts at all, but have always been the bedrock of solid math. The words *focus, coherence*, and *proficiency* were used in 2008 in the *Final Report of the National Mathematics Advisory Panel.* [N36, p. xvii] Common Core has hijacked and redefined these three essential features to actually become—in my professional opinion—delay, removal, and obfuscation.

Delayed topics include fraction operations, exponents, circles, functions, coordinate plane, integers, order of operations, greatest common factor, least common multiple, the Pythagorean Theorem, and probability.

Consider probability. The category "Statistics & Probability" does not appear until 6th grade, while no 6th grade standard actually mentions probability. Then in 7th grade massive catch-up begins with the goals of: (1) learning that a probability is certain, likely, unlikely, or impossible (3rd grade work); (2) learning that a probability is a number from

0 to 1 (4th grade work); (3) calculating a simplified probability (5th grade work); (4) calculating a simple compound probability (6th grade work); and (5) calculating a more complex compound probability (finally, 7th grade work). Delaying topics burdens middle school teachers, hinders high school readiness, bores capable students, and ultimately confuses students by undermining the developmental process essential to mastering math.

Removed topics in the elementary and middle grades include sectors of circles, divisibility rules, and except for a tiny mention in 4th grade, prime numbers—perhaps the most egregious of omissions because primes are the building blocks of all numbers.

And as for obfuscation, one 7th grade standard states: "Approximate the probability of a chance event by collecting data on the chance process that produces it and observing its long-run relative frequency, and predict the approximate relative frequency given the probability." [www10–8] Translation: spend, namely waste, valuable time conducting the simple experiment of tossing a standard die 400 times and recording the results to learn the obvious fact that the probability of a 2 landing face up is 1/6 because a die has 6 congruent faces.

Obfuscation exists even in first grade. Three birds are sitting on a branch. Two more birds fly over and join them. How many birds are now sitting on the branch? Decades ago, we all wrote the answer 5 in a few seconds and moved on. But not so fast with Common Core. Students must do the problem four different ways—draw a picture, write an equation, show counting on a number line, and write a sentence.

Even the recommended use of multiple methods for a single problem is a recycled idea, yet again as described in this book. In 1899 the *Report of the Committee of the Chicago Section of the American Mathematical Society* stated: ". . . the presentation by the pupils of other proofs which they may have found for the same proposition, or different methods of attaining the result of some exercise, and the discussion of these in class, is of great value. More may often be gained by proving one proposition in three different ways than by proving three propositions in the same way." [B13, p. 197]

Jo Boaler acknowledged but dismissed math's "reputation for being a subject of single methods." She wrote: "Part of the beauty of mathematical problems is that they can be seen . . . in different ways and, although many have one answer, they can be answered using different approaches." [B14, p. 157]

But math has a time for multiple methods—problems that deserve dwelling—and a time for singular efficiency—problems that demand speed. Students who learn to continually perseverate will never finish the ACT or SAT on time and will not recognize when to use problem solving techniques correctly. A first grader could do the birds-on-the-branch problem four ways but should not do months of this work. In reality, clever children use the same techniques repeatedly, defeating and mocking the entire concept of creating new methods. Sadly, other children frustrate themselves and their parents with each homework assignment by trying to invent ways that simply don't exist for such simple problems.

One well known fight between the two sides of CCSSM concerns when and how to use the standard algorithms for the four whole number operations. At one extreme, I have heard of an otherwise excellent teacher who insisted that her third graders take a pledge never to use an algorithm the entire year. Professors Alice Crary and Stephen Wilson explain the imprudence of omitting algorithms: "Students in this program [CCSSM] . . . are not asked to regard it [the standard algorithm] as a privileged method. . . . They [reformers] insist that the point of math classes should be to get children to reason independently, and in their own styles, about numbers and numerical concepts. The standard algorithms should be avoided because, reformists claim, mastering them is a merely mechanical exercise that threatens individual growth. . . . But it's not clear that these trends [avoiding standard algorithms for the four whole number operations] are defensible. They only seem laudable if we assume that facts don't contribute to a person's grasp of the logical space in which reason operates. . . . It is important to teach them [standard algorithms] because, as we already noted, they are also the most elegant and powerful methods for specific operations. This means that they are our best representations of connections among mathematical concepts. Math instruction that does not teach both that these algorithms work and why they do is denying students insight into the very discipline it is supposed to be about. ... The upshot is that it would be naïve to assume that we can somehow promote original thinking in specific areas simply by calling for subject-related creative reasoning. If we are to be good progressivists, we cannot be shy about calling for rigorous discipline and training." [C21]

Another ironic folly, in the attempt to have *fewer topics*, is the omission of Pólya's classic problem solving techniques: Make an organized list, table, or chart; Act it out; Draw a picture; Solve a related problem; Solve a simpler problem; Look for a pattern and generalize; Guess and check; Work backwards; Write an equation; Use logic and deduction. These valuable methods from *How To Solve It* [P10] were typically found in elementary texts decades ago. Now in an entrepreneurial but inequitable American spirit, numerous online companies have launched, filling the void for fortunate students whose schools or parents choose to supplement.

But offering Pólya's techniques is only one example of a business idea to profit from CCSSM. Diane Ravitch wrote that the widespread adoption of CCSS by the majority of states ushered the path for publishing, technology, and consulting companies to create new products and services aligned with the standards. She remarked that due to CCSS, "... there appeared to be many exciting opportunities to make money in the emerging education marketplace." [R7, p. 17]

The articles written for and against Common Core are voluminous. One homeschool site has links to dozens for further reading. [www10–9] The following is just a small amount of the lengthy discussion.

Jo Boaler wrote as a supporter of CCSSM: "We need to change the way we teach math in the U.S. ... The new curriculum standards ... do not incorporate all the changes that this country needs, by any means, but they are a necessary step in the right direction. ... All of my research studies have shown that when mathematics is opened up and broader math is taught—math that includes problem solving, reasoning, representing ideas in multiple forms, and question asking—students perform at higher levels, more students take advanced mathematics, and achievement is more equitable." [B15] Opponents would probably agree with what she wrote, but they would argue that CCSSM does not accomplish those goals.

The three authors of *The Educated Child* (Bennett, Finn, and Cribb) wrote a more moderate opinion: "The approach includes some good ideas that can usefully be *added* to traditional direct instruction in math, but not *substituted*. . . . The problem with the new approach—when it's substituted, rather than added, to time-honored methods of direct instruction—is that it shortchanges students in some very important lessons. These include the need for lots of practice in math; the value of memorization; an emphasis on gradually building basic skills; and proper attention to exactness in answers." [B10, p. 321] They further stated that while self-exploration has value, expecting "young children to rediscover the concepts, relationships, and formulas established by brilliant mathematicians over many centuries" is unrealistic and "cannot be the main avenue of teaching math. . . . To get the job done, math teachers must *teach*." [B10, pp. 328–329]

And for worriers, an article in *The Hechinger Report* quoted Jason Zimba, "a lead writer of the [CCSSM] math standards," as admitting: "If you want to take calculus your freshman year in college, you will need to take more mathematics than is in the Common Core." [C3]

Further caution is found in an article published in the *American Journal of Physics*, titled "School math books, nonsense, and the National Science Foundation," by David Klein, professor at California State, who wrote that Harvard mathematician Wilfried Schmid evaluated a popular constructivist CCSSM series and concluded that by the end of 5th grade, students were roughly two years behind. [K6]

As with many math reforms and programs, the bottom line is the teacher. Robert Rothman, in a Harvard Education Press book, cited a discouraging survey: "The bad news was that 80 percent of the teachers [who read CCSSM] considered the Standards 'pretty much the same' as their state standards. The fact is that the Standards in many ways call for substantial departures from current practice. For example, they propose . . . a balance between [*sic*] procedural knowledge, conceptual understanding, and problem solving in mathematics." [R18, p. vii]

Although from a different period, Stigler and Hiebert expounded on teachers' behavior by extensively studying the TIMSS videos and the accompanying written surveys, in which teachers did say that they were aware of reforms. The authors cautioned: "But this is where the good news ends. When we looked at the videos, we found little evidence of reform, at least as intended by those who had proposed the reforms." Moreover, they added: "When we examined the places in the video that teachers referred to as examples of reform, we saw a disturbing confirmation of the suspicion . . . that reform teaching, as interpreted by some teachers, might actually be worse than what they were doing previously in their classrooms." They continued: "Teachers can misinterpret reform and change surface features—for example, they include more group work; use more manipulatives, calculators, and real-world problem scenarios; or include writing in the math lesson—but fail to alter their basic approach to teaching mathematics." Frighteningly, they concluded: "But the TIMSS videotapes reveal that the problem [misapplication of reform] is national in scope." [S26, pp. 105–108] No compelling reason exists to believe that teachers in the CCSSM era are any different.

Almost as important as the teachers are the textbooks. Those trying to avoid CCSSM by sending their children to independent schools may be fooled. With forty-two states adopting CCSS, finding a math book not aligned with CCSSM is difficult. Even Singapore Math follows suit, as discussed in Chapter 11, Obstacle 42, Fad 12.

One reason for the broad adoption of CCSSM is that constructivists remain strong. But another obvious rationale is the low score of the U.S. on the PISA international exam. If PISA tests real-life math, then American schools should teach real-life math—or so some thought. Indeed, the OECD website includes a statement that buys into the theory: "The analysis suggests that a successful implementation of the Common Core Standards would yield significant performance gains also in PISA." [www10–10]

However, I believe that one cannot apply math that one does not know. My opinion is confirmed, as mentioned in Chapter 8, because U.S. PISA scores fell from 481 in 2012 to 470 in 2015, a statistically significant drop in the exact years of Common Core implementation. Unfortunately, the 1986 words of NCTM President Joe Crosswhite have seemingly been ignored: "In schools, *better* mathematics must be balanced mathematics." [C23, p. 573]

11

Hindering Solutions

If the shoe doesn't fit, must we change the foot?
Gloria Steinem

Multiple times, my father asked me what I would do to fix the maladies of math education. During those conversations, I could only name sources of the problem or obstacles to the solution—but not a fix. Now, organizing those thoughts, I have identified fifty such hindrances, all of which my proposal in this book removes, despite opposing positions.

Like math itself, these sources/obstacles do not fall into tidy categories. Rather, many intertwine. Consider the following passage:

"Look carefully at the seventh- and eighth-grade mathematics curriculum. More importantly, visit the seventh- and eighth-grade classrooms. What's going on? With few exceptions, the textbooks look like the sixth-grade text. The topics covered are essentially review and more practice on the same material covered in grades K–6. The content of seventh- and eighth-grade mathematics programs provides for review, practice, and mastery of all those skills previously taught. True, there are some new topics in the texts and state guidelines such as probability, more geometry, an introduction to trigonometry, and a bit of algebra. But then observe the classrooms. What students actually get is drill and practice on computational skills. In fact, sixth grade teachers often hear, 'Oh, I remember we did this last year.' Then in seventh grade, students are doing the same thing again and in eighth grade, yet again. Why? There's little doubt that many of our less-prepared students need this practice in basic skills." [S21, p. 136]

Into which obstacle would that reference best fit? Curriculum? Drill?

Textbooks? In-field teachers? Many of these obstacles converge: *school administrators* might be unaware when *in-field teachers*, who are deficient in math due to *colleges of education*, skip around in *textbooks* to cover what is on *standardized tests*. Thus, the following fifty sections, though categorized for attempted clarity, have recognized overlap.

Obstacle 1: In-field Teachers

The importance of the quality of the teacher has been stated in various settings over numerous decades.

In 1953 two math educators wrote these wise words in an NCTM Yearbook: "We learn that mathematics which we are taught. The teacher is the primary agent and force in the learning that takes place. The teacher is all important." [C9, p. 348]

In 1959 a College Board report stated: "The role of the teacher is vital: curricular change must be accompanied by effective, meaningful teaching, directed toward the development of mathematical power and understanding." [C16, p. 15]

In 1970 psychologist Lewis Aiken wrote: ". . . the teacher, rather than the curriculum, still appears to be the more influential variable as far as attitudes are concerned." [A3, p. 581]

In 1996 the National Commission on Teaching and America's Future stated as the first of three premises: "What teachers know and can do is the most important influence on what students learn." [N12, p. 10]

In 2008 at a Brookings forum, NCTM President Francis Fennell commented: ". . . United States students do not do well on items that involve the extension of a pattern if the item requires that they explicitly produce, describe, or represent a relationship rather than simply find the next terms in a sequence." He added that taking a pattern in "different directions" depends on the teacher's background and guidance—maximizing the pattern via its "potential for richness" or minimizing the pattern by "seeing it in a very limited way." [www11–1]

At a 2009 Town Hall, President Obama remarked: ". . . the single-biggest ingredient is the quality of our teachers; single most important factor—(applause)—single most important factor in the classroom is the quality of the person standing at the front of the classroom." [www11–2]

In 2012 William Schmidt and Curtis McKnight echoed the same theme: "The potential effect of both textbooks and tests on content coverage is contingent on the decision-making process of the teacher." [S7, p. 164]

Also in 2012 Diane Ravitch quoted Education Secretary Arne Duncan: "Three great teachers in a row, and the average child will be a year and a half to two grade levels ahead. Three bad teachers in a row, and that average child might be so far behind they may never catch up." [R7, p. 101]

Sadly, I have witnessed math teachers, both in public and private schools, making the following variety of errors:

1. Using the jingle "do the same to the top as to the bottom" regarding fractions. This inaccuracy causes students to add or subtract a constant to both the numerator and denominator, changing the fraction's value.

2. Changing every minus sign to "plus minus." This practice not only adds time, but also causes future confusion in Algebra II when students learn template equations that use minus signs, as for a circle.

3. Insisting on labeling every answer with units. Consider two related questions: How far is Jane's house from her school? How many blocks is Jane's house from her school? The answer to the first question requires a label. One cannot say "10" because the response could mean 10 miles, 10 blocks, or 10 turtle steps. The answer to the second question may be "10" because the unit measure is built into the question. The prevalent habit of requiring a label for every answer is not only incorrect but also annoying. MATHCOUNTS, the premier high-quality math nonprofit organization, builds the labels into the questions, precisely because the math, not the spelling and the writing, is what is important. Yet in MATHCOUNTS, students still need to understand the distinctions and conversions among linear, square, and cubic units.

4. Drawing nets (flattened images) always before computing the surface area of a cylinder or rectangular solid. This habit slows work once the concept is understood.

5. Insisting on using a textbook's formal terminology of *independent* and *dependent* events in probability problems when pulling objects. Substituting the terms "with replacement" and "without replacement" as used by College Board and MATHCOUNTS makes the topic clearer.

6. Avoiding mental math in simple problems like $5x + 1 = 11$ or 11% of 200 (add 10% and 1%). Tediousness curtails number sense.

7. Insisting on one method to calculate the slope of a line given two points, thus teaching mechanically. This demand misses the valuable lesson that $(y2 - y1)/(x2 - x1)$ is the same as $(y1 - y2)/(x1 - x2)$ because the fraction has been multiplied by 1 in the form of $(-1)/(-1)$.

8. Insisting on only one method in problems of the type "5 is what percent of 60?" This problem-type is one that permits exploration of multiple methods such as "Follow the English," "Form an is-over-of fraction," or "Write a Proportion."

9. Requiring the changing of all improper fractions to mixed numbers. In algebra the improper fraction is the form that is easily inserted back into an equation to check the answer.

10. Teaching the invalid term "cross-cancel" when multiplying two fractions. Then when multiplying three fractions, students do not think to simplify the numerator of the first with the denominator of the third.

11. Teaching bogus "crossing out" as a valid mathematical technique in fraction simplification. Then students never learn that crossing out is actually the elimination of extra multiplications by 1.

12. Insisting in an early grade that 9 minus 2 is 7 but that 2 minus 7 cannot be done. Whoever teaches that 2 minus 7 is –5 is indirectly calling a prior teacher a liar. Teachers in the same school should have consistent

techniques—in listing divisors, creating prime factorizations, and solving classic problem types—while recognizing that the richness of math allows for multiple approaches to solve problems and to help students. Teachers should never have to undo what a colleague previously taught.

13. Stressing decimals as preferable to fractions. In fact, using fractions often obtains the exact, not approximate, answer with less work.

14. Removing the standard whole-number algorithms from lessons. While students must understand the math behind the algorithms and develop number sense, algorithms remain one of many effective tools.

15. Skipping valuable problems or progressing too slowly through the textbook. Wanting students to earn better grades is a distressing reason for omitting important curriculum.

16. Ignoring questions, such as a 1st grader asking about negative numbers. Only misguided teachers reply that students shouldn't make those kinds of inquiries at young ages.

17. Using incorrect vocabulary. The points discussed in Obstacle 6 can all lead to significant confusion.

18. Not directly talking to students. Imagine a student confused by long division, only wanting an explanation of why the algorithm starts at the left when adding, subtracting, and multiplying start at the right.

19. Introducing tricks without explaining why. For example, the acronym FOIL (first, outside, inside, last) to multiply 2 binomials must be explained by using the distributive property and/or splitting a rectangle into 4 rectangular areas.

20. Interviewing brilliantly but collapsing personally once employed. Tiredness and disorganization are not excuses for a teacher's wasting class time talking about his/her recent vacation or spouse's illness.

21. Falling for fads. Using something new, cute, and worthless proposed

at a conference is not a substitute for quality teaching.

22. Mutilating problems. Questions of the type 63 x 42 = 54 x N should not be done by multiplying 63 and 42, and then dividing by 54. Students should think first and multiply last. Because the left side of the equation is 9 x 7 x 7 x 6 and the right side is 9 x 6 x N, N must be 7 x 7 or 49.

23. Dismissing meaningful methods by saying defensively, "Oh, you could do it that way." When listing the factors of a number, middle schoolers often skip some inadvertently. They could know how many factors a number has by creating its prime factorization, adding 1 to each exponent, and multiplying the resulting values. Teachers dismissing such techniques as too esoteric are close-minded and math-phobic.

24. Requiring verbatim memorization of geometry theorems. While theorems' concepts are universal in math, their language and numbering are not. Symbols for reasons in proofs can also be as clear as words.

For every teacher error I have seen, I fear that countless more have occurred. How else could national and international scores be so low? How else could so many students fear and dislike math? For students who know their teachers are wrong, incorrect presentations erode the students' necessary respect for teachers. For students who do not know their teachers are wrong, incorrect presentations damage the students' fragile understanding of math. Both paths threaten serious math growth.

The following five examples exemplify teachers' math deficiencies.

In 1956 a *Time* article asserted: "In a survey of 211 prospective elementary teachers, 150 reported a 'long-standing hatred of arithmetic.' In an examination of 370 teacher candidates, half flubbed the question: *The height of a letter in a certain size of print is 1/4 inch. If the following are the heights (in inches) of this letter in other sizes of print, which one is the next larger size?* a.) 5/16   b.) 1/2   c.) 3/16   d.) 3/8   e.) 7/16" [T3]

In 1982 an article in the NCTM Yearbook stated: "They [middle school math teachers] are not prepared to handle both a different treatment of familiar content and a treatment of content intrinsically satisfying to mathematicians." [W8, p. 4]

Also in 1982 the President of the NCTM asked: "Have elementary teachers been allowed to muddle through math?" His reply was: "Indications are they have!" [S18, p. 84]

In 1999 Stigler and Hiebert wrote: "Many U.S. teachers also seem to believe that learning terms and practicing skills is [*sic*] not very exciting. We have watched them [on TIMSS videotape study] trying to jazz up the lesson and increase students' interest in nonmathematical ways: by being entertaining, by interrupting the lesson to talk about other things (last night's local rock concert, for example), or by setting the mathematics problem in a real-life or intriguing context—for example, measuring the circumference of a basketball. Teachers act as if student interest will be generated only by diversions outside of mathematics." They continued: "Japanese teachers also act as if mathematics is inherently interesting and students will be interested in exploring it by developing new methods for solving problems. They seem less concerned about motivating the topics in nonmathematical ways." [S26, pp. 89–90]

In 2009 The Brookings Institution conducted a panel discussion with Secretary of Education Arne Duncan. He commented: "And when you get to sixth, seventh, and eighth grade, we see lots of students start to lose interest in math and science. And guess why? It's because they're taught by teachers [who] don't know math and science. And so it's hard to really instill a passion, a love of learning, when you're struggling with the content yourself." [D9, pp. 11–12]

Two suggestions for better in-field math teachers are: (1) recruit capable math teachers; and (2) require teachers to pass a subject-area exam.

Regarding the first remedy, in 1996 the NCTAF featured as the second of three premises: "Recruiting, preparing, and retaining good teachers is the central strategy for improving our schools." [N12, p. 10]

In 2004 the NCTQ reported: "Great teachers make a profound difference in the lives of children. Each of us can remember the personal qualities of a great teacher whose influence stretches into our adulthood—or who gave our own children a solid start in life. But these elusive qualities are hard to measure. It's even harder to use them to predict who will become a great teacher." [W2, p. 1]

Moreover, in 2010 Diane Ravitch commented that the replacement of poor math teachers with strong ones was actually a conundrum: ". . . it was difficult to know how to recruit good teachers when the determination of their effectiveness required several years of classroom data." [R6, p. 182]

Regarding the second remedy, in 2005 AP reporter Ben Feller quoted Tom Blanford, then a "teacher quality leader" at the NEA, as saying with regard to forcing teachers to pass a subject-area exam, "The number of take-this-job-and-shove-it notices that school districts would receive would be staggering." [F5]

I dismiss these two suggestions as unworkable. In my professional opinion, no amount of in-service, self-study, workshops, conferences, online resources, and courses are enough to finally fix math education. The operating premise of *From STEM To STEW* is that the country has not had the right number of proper math teachers for over a century and never will in the existing system.

Obstacle 2. Colleges of Education

I once wrote a math question: "Which number . . . ?" The answer was zero. One capable teacher commented that the question was not correctly phrased because she had been taught in education school that zero is a place holder, not a number. I was horrified. Zero, as the identity element for addition, is an extremely important number.

One cannot teach what one does not know, and many teachers don't know math because they were not taught the subject properly in colleges of education. Labeling these institutions, rather than the teachers, as the root cause of poor math teaching has been noted by some.

In 1992 the authors of *The Learning Gap* wrote: "It is easy to blame teachers for the problems confronting American education, as the American public is prone to do. The accusation is unfair. We do not provide adequate training and yet we expect that on their own they will become innovative teachers . . . ." [S25, pp. 171–172]

In 2012 the authors of *Inequality for All* discussed the responsibility for elementary and middle school math teachers' lack of academic readiness to teach required mathematics. They stated that while "blaming" the teachers was "tempting," the position was a "mistake." Their reason was: "Because teachers prepare themselves according to the standards and guidelines established by the states that certify them and the teacher preparation programs that train them." [S7, p. 162]

Still, criticism of colleges of education has been general in theme and long in years.

In 1953 the author of *Educational Wastelands* wrote: "American universities have failed, and failed most miserably, to apply even rudimentary common sense to the problem of devising a sound and useful graduate program for public school teachers." [B11, p. 138]

In 1959 CEEB's COM concluded that improved teacher preparation was a necessity to achieve its recommendations. [C16, pp. 15, 48, 58]

In 1992 the authors of *The Learning Gap* remarked: "Beginning teachers are given information that is either too general to be applied readily or so specific ["Cheerios make handy counters for teaching basic number facts"] that it has only limited usefulness." [S25, pp. 157–158]

In 1995 the author of *Dumbing Down Our Kids* expressed: "Unlike the more established disciplines of higher education, the position of education has always been shaky. Its pretensions to scholarship are, at best, questionable, and it is the one field that other academics are unanimous in regarding with disdain." [S29, p. 83]

In 1999 the author of *The Conspiracy of Ignorance* wrote that the presence of "many bright teachers does not change the documented fact that . . . the typical American teacher and teacher candidate are not smart enough or sufficiently well trained to handle the education of students." [G12, p. 41]

Also in 1999 the authors of *The Educated Child* wrote: "Once in college (or graduate school), these young people ["themselves victims of a weak elementary and secondary education"] enroll in teacher education programs that have notoriously low standards and expectations. It is no secret that, at many universities, an education major produces one of the easiest degrees. Unfortunately, that means schools of education attract some applicants who are among the least academically accomplished in their classes. . . . Instead of learning more mathematics, . . . they learn how to talk . . . about mathematics." [B10, p. 621]

In 2009 Secretary of Education Arne Duncan, calling education schools "cash cows" for universities, said: "America's university-based teacher preparation programs need revolutionary change—not evolutionary tinkering." [www11–3]

More specifically, complaints focused around the profusion of pedagogy and dearth of subject matter in colleges of education.

In 1953 Arthur Bestor explained: "Pedagogy itself . . . is a legitimate field of study. But its exact nature and its limitations need to be fully understood. . . . It tells us *how* something can be taught most effectively, but it provides no basis whatever for deciding *what* should be taught." [B11, p. 41]

Bestor also criticized pedagogy in another way, saying that professors of pedagogy "calmly extrapolate." Specifically, they use their teaching methods for children, who have undeveloped minds, on their adult teacher-candidate students, who should already possess a level of abstract reasoning. These experts in pedagogy make an unfounded assumption followed by a dangerous leap. [B11, pp. 49–50]

In 1958 John Keats explored the "teachers-college assumption that method is more important than content." [K2, p. 140]

In 1970 the NCTM Yearbook reminded readers that: "By 1875 . . . the state normal school was recognized . . . as the principal agency for the training of teachers, although city and private normal schools and liberal arts colleges and universities also provided such programs." In particular, the article stated that "the real issue that had developed" by 1875 was pedagogy versus content. [N17, pp. 304–305]

In 1983 *ANAR*, discussing the grave lack of math teachers, reported that educational methods utterly dominated subject content in teacher preparation. [N11, pp. 22–23]

In 1999 Martin Gross expressed: *"Education training focuses more on 'how' to teach than on content—the 'what' to teach—one of the grave liabilities of the present system."* [G12, p. 48]

Also in 1999 the authors of *The Educated Child* stated: "Future teachers spend relatively little time mastering the subjects they'll be teaching, but lots of time on classroom methods, the history and philosophy of education, and various theories of child development." [B10, p. 621]

In 2006 E. D. Hirsch wrote that many teachers are "ill-informed about the subjects they teach," diminishing their classroom effectiveness. The cause, he said, is not "inherent laziness or native incompetence," but exposure to "anti-fact, how-to ideas during their training." [H13, pp. 84–85]

Responding to this lack of content, experts called for increased mathematics in teacher training programs.

In 1945 NCTM's Second Report of The Commission on Post-War Plans made two recommendations: (1) "Teachers of mathematics in grades 1–8 should have special coursework relating to subject matter as well as to the teaching process." (2) "The minimum training for mathematics teachers in small high schools should be a college minor in mathematics." [C17 in B13, pp. 645–651]

In 1973 the Committee on the Undergraduate Program in Mathematics of the MAA wrote: "We recommend for all such [teacher] students a 12-semester-hour sequence that includes . . . number systems, algebra, geometry, probability, statistics, functions, mathematical systems, and the role of deductive and inductive reasoning . . . based on at least two years of high school mathematics that includes elementary algebra and geometry." [C18, p. 165]

In 1996 the NCTAF's groundbreaking report, *What Matters Most: Teaching for America's Future*, called for an "audacious goal" by 2006: "competent, caring, qualified teaching in schools organized for success"—every American child's "educational birthright." [N12, p. 10]

In 2008 the NCTQ produced *No Common Denominator: The Preparation of Elementary Teachers in Mathematics by America's Education Schools*. It stated: "Unfortunately, their mathematics preparation leaves far too many of them ill-equipped. . . . A deeper understanding of elementary mathematics, with more attention given to the foundations of algebra, must be the new 'common denominator' of our preparation programs for elementary teachers within education schools." [W4, p. 20]

Also in 2008 the National Mathematics Advisory Panel called for "strengthened" math preparation "beyond the level" of teaching assignments. [N36, p. xxi]

In 2009 the National Research Council, in *Mathematics Learning in Early Childhood: Paths Toward Excellence and Equity*, wrote as one of its recommendations: "An essential component of a coordinated national early childhood mathematics initiative is the provision of professional development to early childhood in-service teachers that helps them (a) to understand the necessary mathematics, the crucial teaching-learning paths, and the principles of intentional teaching and curriculum and (b) to learn how to implement a curriculum." [N37, pp. 3–4]

One reason for this emphasis on math pedagogy over content was the turnover of teacher cohorts. Quoting from a Columbia University professor in the 1930s and 1940s, Arthur Bestor wrote: "Few took note that many of the original cadre that led Teachers College to its heights [by the mid 1900s] were originally trained, not in education courses, but in the disciplines. Fewer still could believe that the problem of replacement of this illustrious but aging cadre would prove so difficult if not insurmountable. ... many of the younger generation slipped deeper into the quagmire of educationist jargon." [B11, pp. 236–237] Indeed, several of my father's colleagues were math majors at Harvard and pleased to get a teaching job given the Great Depression and World War II.

As E. D. Hirsch discussed, a second explanation for the rise of pedagogy was education schools' desire to establish their reputations. Because "content was already the domain of other academic departments," they were left with "only pedagogy as a topic." But by reducing "both intellectual content and intellectual interaction with the rest of the university," this approach backfired: "Whence the paradox: the decline of intellectual substance, which was instituted to create a special, separate discipline, thereby defeated the very goals being aimed at—institutional prestige and an imposing institutional identity." [H12, p. 117]

The state of math training in education colleges is frighteningly low overall, as documented in NCTQ's *No Common Denominator*. The following are the findings in the Executive Summary.

"FINDING 1: Few education schools cover the mathematics content that elementary teachers need. In fact, the education schools in our sample are remarkable for having achieved little consensus about what teachers need. There is one unfortunate area of agreement: a widespread inattention to algebra." [W4, p. 6]
"FINDING 2: States contribute to the chaos. While most state education agencies issue guidelines for the mathematics preparation of elementary teachers, states do not appear to know what is needed." [W4, p. 9]
"FINDING 3: Most education schools use mathematics textbooks that are inadequate. The mathematics textbooks in the sample varied enormously in quality. Unfortunately, two-thirds of the courses use no textbook or a textbook that is inadequate in one or more of the four critical areas of mathematics. Again, algebra is shortchanged, with no textbook providing the strongest possible support." [W4, p. 10]

"FINDING 4: Almost anyone can get in. Compared to the admissions standards in other countries, American education schools set exceedingly low expectations for the mathematics knowledge that aspiring teachers must demonstrate." [W4, p. 11]

"FINDING 5: Almost anyone can get out. The standards used to determine successful completion of education schools' elementary teacher preparation programs are essentially no different than the low standards used to enter those programs." [W4, p. 12]

"FINDING 6: The *elementary mathematics* in mathematics methods coursework is too often relegated to the sidelines. In particular, any practice teaching that may occur fails to emphasize the need to capably convey mathematics content to children." [W4, p. 13]

"FINDING 7: Too often, the person assigned to teach mathematics to elementary teacher candidates is not professionally equipped to do so. Commendably, most elementary content courses are taught within mathematics departments, although the issue of just who is best qualified and motivated to impart the content of elementary mathematics to teachers remains a conundrum." [W4, p. 14]

"FINDING 8: Almost anyone can do the work. Elementary mathematics courses are neither demanding in their content nor their expectations of students." [W4, p. 14]

This problem of weak math in education schools has been reported in the media—but not nearly enough.

In 2006 the Associated Press published "Study Says Teacher Training Is Chaotic" by Ben Feller. He wrote: "Aspiring teachers emerge from college woefully unprepared for their jobs, according to a study that depicts most teacher education programs as deeply flawed. The damning review comes from Arthur Levine, former president of Teachers College at Columbia University. His report . . . comes as public schools are under federal orders to have a qualified teacher for every class. It casts doubts on the most basic aspects of how teachers are taught. Teacher quality has a huge influence on whether students pass or fail." [F8]

Three concepts help explain the lack of math improvement within education schools. First, is the chicken-or-egg paradox. Given their weak math backgrounds, neither the students (future teachers) nor their professors understand the math, creating an unbreakable cycle. As John Keats wrote, "Another uncomfortable thought is that the higher we put our standards of qualitative performance—the more we emphasize intellectuality in our school—the more we reduce the chance of finding people competent to teach what we want to offer." [K2, p. 134]

Second is the lure of power. Hirsch explained: "Both critics and defenders of education schools agree that professors of education in these institutions are held in low esteem as a group by their colleagues. ... But the plight of education schools in the universities is counterbalanced by their enormous importance in the sphere of teacher certification and by their huge ideological influence in the nation's schools. It is never a healthy circumstance when people who are held in low esteem exercise dominant influence in an important sphere. The conjunction of power with resentment is deadly." [H12, pp. 115–116]

Third is the adage *follow the money*. In 2001 Vartan Gregorian, former President of Brown University, the New York Public Library, and the Carnegie Corporation of New York, wrote in a *New York Times* Op-Ed, "We lack a critical mass of very good schools of education. Many colleges and universities marginalized their schools of education, treating them as revenue generators. Survival for many of these schools has often meant increasing enrollments and reducing educational quality." [G11]

Suggestions for improvement vary. *No Common Denominator* offered "Five Standards for the Mathematics Preparation of Elementary Teachers": (1) acquire deep knowledge of math beyond procedures; (2) develop higher entry standards to education schools; (3) create higher standards for licensure; (4) coordinate math content and methods courses; and (5) assign responsibility to math departments. [W4, p. 2]

Amanda Ripley proposed modeling our system after that of another country. She wrote: "In Finland, *all* education schools were selective. Getting into a teacher-training program there was as prestigious as getting into medical school in the United States." She further stated: "Of course [in Finland] people respected teachers; their jobs were complex and demanding, and they had to work hard to get there. One thing led to another. Highly educated teachers also chose material that was more rigorous, and they had the fluency to teach it." [R13, pp. 85, 116]

Another recommendation is to improve the rigor in teacher certification exams. The Educational Testing Service's Praxis II (subject assessments) in mathematics has 56 questions that are a mix of free response and multiple choice. The 85-minute test provides "an on-screen calculator to help ensure that questions are testing mathematical reasoning by reducing the chance that a candidate's wrong response comes from a simple arithmetic error." A look at the Praxis Core Math Guide reveals basic math questions. [www11-4] Moreover, each state, rather than ETS, sets the passing score. [www11-5]

NCTQ prepared two sample tests *Exit with Expertise: Do Ed Schools Prepare Elementary Teachers to Pass This Test?* and *Exit With Expertise: Are You Qualified To Teach Elementary School Math?* with overlapping questions. Posted on the internet, these tests contain more rigorous concepts and skills than on Praxis, such as sets and functions; number theory; integer, rational, and real numbers; exponents; fractions, decimals, and percents; plane and space geometry; and probability. [N30, N31] While some colleges offer "Mathematics For Elementary Teachers," merely taking one course is inadequate to internalize the material. Teachers must know math well beyond the topics that they teach.

Most likely the NCTQ tests are not widely used as a goal because each annual *State Teacher Policy Yearbook* published by the NCTQ shows little progress in improving the math education of teachers. [N28, N29, N32, N33] The 1999 comment by Martin Gross appears valid: " . . . *the typical teacher certification test has traditionally had very low standards. And there is great resistance in the Establishment to raising them.*" [G12, p. 95]

Still another suggestion was made by Gross without mincing words: "CLOSE ALL UNDERGRADUATE SCHOOLS OF EDUCATION." He proposed that all teachers first earn a BA or BS in their content area, and second—if they have at least a 3.0 undergrad average—complete a one-year year masters degree in teaching methods including student teaching. Gross claimed that this approach would yield "a smarter, more mature brand of teacher." [G12, p. 249]

The 2006 Michigan State University study "Promoting Rigorous Outcomes in Mathematics/Science Education" included 4000 teachers who reported in large percentages that they felt under-prepared in an array of math topics from number theory to fractions. Concerning these findings, the authors of *Inequality for All* gave an easy explanation for elementary and middle school math teachers: "They felt ill prepared because if we examine the coursework they studied during their teacher preparation, they *were* ill prepared." [S7, p. 158]

Sending teachers to graduate rather than undergraduate schools of education won't work either. In *Incoherent by Design*, the NCTQ researchers found that "elementary content math," which most college graduates do not know because it must be "specifically geared to elementary teaching," is "rarely required in graduate programs." [G9, pp. 5, 7]

Obstacle 3. Out-of-field Teachers

The excessive number of out-of-field math teachers is an ongoing problem. The following citations are only a sampling of articles and reports written on the matter.

The *1923 Report* stated: "The United States is far behind Europe in the scientific and professional training required of its secondary school teachers." [N13, p. 13; B13, p. 399]

In 1984 Edwin Moise wrote: "In the next decade, excellence will not prevail in the teaching of school mathematics. The number of under-qualified teachers is enormous, and it cannot be reduced soon." [M6, p. 35]

A 1996 editorial in the *Boston Globe*, referring to the report by the National Commission on Teaching and America's Future, stated: "The problem is gravest at the high school level, where nearly one-fourth of all teachers do not have even a college minor in their main teaching field. In Massachusetts, almost 38 percent of high school math teachers fall into that category." [B19; N12]

Also in 1996 the National Center for Education Statistics published *Out-of-Field Teaching and Educational Equality* based on data from the *1990-91 Schools and Staffing Survey*. The report presented data about the large number of students in the nation's secondary schools whose teachers lacked basic training in their assigned teaching fields. [N3]

Richard Ingersoll, a sociologist at the University of Georgia, analyzed U.S. ED data. He found that large numbers of teachers taught classes for which they lacked even the equivalent of a college minor. Nationwide, he found that about 28 percent of high school math teachers had neither a major nor a minor in math. Georgia used a "broad field" middle-grades certificate—a credential requiring teachers to have college concentrations in two of four areas (English, math, social studies, or science) but permitting teaching any of those subjects. Under the regulations, a social studies major who minored in English could teach math.

In 1997 in *Education Week*, Ingersoll wrote: "Out-of-field teaching is not simply an emergency condition, but a common practice in the majority of secondary schools in this country." [I1]

In 1998 Ingersoll continued his work, publishing "The Problem of Out-of-Field Teaching" in *Phi Delta Kappan* [I2] and "Why So Many Under-qualified High School Teachers?" in *Education Week* [I3].

In January, 1999 President Clinton lambasted the practice in his SOTU Address, declaring that "... in too many schools, teachers don't have college majors or even minors in the subjects they teach." [www11–6]

In February, 1999 a *Washington Post* article titled "Right Teacher, Wrong Class" described a teacher who spent the half-hour before school started each day at his desk prepping because he "teaches math, but he doesn't know much math" and who "begged for a no-math schedule." [P7]

In March, 1999 Ingersoll published "The Problem of Underqualified

Teachers in American Secondary Schools," stating as one consequence: "But one can easily imagine the limitations imposed by a lack of subject background on a teacher's ability to teach for critical thinking and to engage the students' interest in the subject—the kinds of learning probably not well captured by standardized examinations." [I4, p. 29]

In March, 1999 journalist Jeff Archer, citing U.S. ED state-by-state data on both newly hired and veteran teachers without college majors or minors in their assigned subjects, wrote "Out-of-Field Teaching Is Hard To Curb." Archer stated: "Out-of-field teaching, many national education experts agree, is a problem that defies simple solutions." [A9]

Also in 1999 Martin Gross cited the NCES Schools and Staffing Survey, reporting that 34% of 1st assignment math teachers had neither a major or minor in math, while 71% of 2nd assignment math teachers had no math training. [G12, p. 108] Moreover, Gross wrote: "So overall, almost half the math . . . teachers are what are called 'out-of-field' instructors, doing an uninformed, ad hoc job in one of the most vital of all educational tasks." [G12, p. 191] Gross's reason for the inferiority was that math teachers were paid the same as 1st grade teachers.

In 2001 a *Business Week* article offered an answer to the problem: "One-third of secondary school math teachers . . . didn't major or minor in the subject they teach. . . . The appalling shortage of quality [math] teachers stems in part from chronically low pay. . . . The solution: Pay teachers more, and scrap single salaries for a system that rewards teachers for what they contribute to student learning." [S30, pp. 69–70]

In 2011 a *U.S. News & World Report* article stated: "According to the NCES study, which surveyed high school teachers during the 2007–2008 school year, fewer than . . . a quarter of math teachers don't hold math degrees." [K10]

In 2013 Amanda Ripley told the story of a young man: "At the education college, . . . [he] discovered that he didn't have to major in math to become a high-school math teacher. So he didn't. Nationwide, less than half of American high-school math teachers majored in math. Almost a third did not even minor in math." [R13, p. 93]

Obstacle 4. Math Teacher Pay

Some have called for salary increases for all teachers.

In 1923 the Report of the NCMR stated: ". . . the recognized position of the teacher in the community must be such as to attract men and women of the highest ability into the profession. This means not only higher salaries but smaller classes and more leisure for continued study and professional advancement." [N13, p. 13; B13, p. 399]

Seventy-eight years later, in 2001 the cover story of *Business Week* titled "How to Fix America's Schools: Here are 7 ideas that work" listed the first idea as "Pay Teachers for Performance." [S30, p. 67]

In 2006 the syndicated columnist Morton Kondracke wrote a piece in *Roll Call* titled "A Better-Schools Deal: Pay Teachers More And Demand Results." The article concluded with the sentence, "Clearly, teachers ought to be paid more—and get fired if they don't perform, just like people in other professions." [K12]

Some have advocated for greater salaries for math teachers. The rationale is twofold: a national shortage of math teachers and the fact that people knowledgeable in math can work in industry for more money.

In 1983 a report by the National Science Board Commission stated: "Incentives of all types need to be studied to *attract* and *retain* qualified teachers of mathematics. Financial incentives should be given special attention . . . . Examples of possible incentives . . . include the following: . . . High entry level salaries for special expertise. . . . Salary differentials by discipline." [N38, pp. 15–16]

In 1999 Richard Ingersoll wrote in *Educational Researcher*: "Well-paid, well-respected occupations that offer good working conditions rarely have difficulties with recruitment or retention. . . . If we treated teaching as a highly valued profession, one requiring expertise and skill, . . .

Hindering Solutions

there would be little problem ensuring that all classrooms were staffed with qualified teachers." [I4, p. 35] In other words, pay math-talented people appropriately, and they will teach.

Also in 1999 Martin Gross wrote: "Most people don't realize it, but the Establishment insists on paying a physics [or math] teacher in high school the same salary as an instructor guiding finger painting in kindergarten—a reflection of the disdain for scholarship that permeates the American public school system." [G12, p. 190]

Again in 1999 the authors of *The Educated Child* stated: "When principals try to recruit people with solid math backgrounds, they find themselves competing against headhunters from high-tech industries. . . . It's an ironic situation: a healthy demand for math knowledge in the marketplace siphons off the very people we depend upon to impart that knowledge to the next generation." [B10, p. 332]

In 2001 Vartan Gregorian wrote in a *New York Times* Op-Ed, "Unions and management must also confront market realities: there is considerable competition for teachers in certain academic specialties, like math, and teachers in these fields have to be paid more." [G11]

In 2009 Secretary of Education Arne Duncan said at a Brookings Institution conference: "I think we need to pay math and science teachers more money. I think we've had a shortage of math and science teachers for 25, 30 years, for a couple of decades. Let's stop talking about it. Let's pay them more money." [D9, p. 13]

In 2011 a Brookings Institution opinion piece stated: "A primary challenge to improving teaching quality is continuing to recruit and retain the best and the brightest in our workforce to become teachers. While no one pursues a teaching career solely for the financial rewards, compensation does matter for attracting and keeping teachers with outside options and who must support their own families. Continuing to attract a broad pool of applicants has become harder over time in part because teaching salaries—the most visible form of compensation for new teachers—have declined relative to salaries in other professions." [G10]

Two problems have impeded the implementation of increased pay for math teachers. First is a way to separate qualified from unqualified math teachers. Second is a means to control envy among other teachers—the dispiriting effect that one subject is more valuable than others.

While "merit pay" is one plan to bridge those issues, just mentioning the two words generates heated debate among educators, parents, and politicians. Diane Ravitch has written extensively about the concept. In *Reign of Error* she described how early attempts failed over a perceived lack of fairness when the school principal determined who received bonuses. [R7, p. 118] In *The Death and Life of the Great American School System* she criticized the modern idea of attaching merit pay to test scores. If a merit-pay teacher one year were reassigned to less prepared or capable students the next year, the teacher might drop in rank, losing the bonus. Thus, based on test scores, "being an effective teacher is not necessarily a permanent, unchanging quality." [R6, p. 186]

Overall, Ravitch declared: "Merit pay is the idea that never works and never dies. . . . No matter how many times it fails, its advocates never give up. . . . Their belief in the magical power of money is unbounded. Their belief in the importance of evidence is not." [R7, pp. 122–123] She argued that forcing teachers, schools, and districts to concentrate on raising test scores causes playing the system, tapering content, evading poor-performing students, and cheating.

Obstacle 5. Foundational Structure of Math

Countless concepts and skills—both hierarchal and entwined—comprise mathematics, a discipline built upon given definitions, accepted postulates, and proven theorems. A weak math education imposes gloom and chaos over a seemingly complex foundation, while a strong math education shines light and order onto a fascinatingly logical structure.

William Bennett, Chester Finn, and John Cribb referenced the foundational structure of math in their advice: "Mathematics is a precisely structured field and its teaching should reflect this. Lessons plans should be carefully ordered so that students gradually build a base of knowledge and skills, beginning with the simplest and then moving step by step, topic by topic, to more complex ideas. . . . Consequently, math is not a subject that treats students kindly when they fail to master the early lessons." [B10, p. 285]

Amanda Ripley wrote vividly about a boy who, like other American children, went astray in middle school. Due to math's inter-connectedness, first one lesson, then the next, and continually more were unclear. Embarrassed and afraid, he didn't ask for help. He could not improve his average that low quiz scores yielded. Feeling stupid, humiliated, and hopeless, he flunked algebra the next year. [R13, p. 69] She continued: "For too long, what American kids learned had been a matter of chance. The problem with chance was that math was a hierarchy. If kids . . . missed one rung on the scaffolding, they would strain and slip and probably never get a foothold on the next rung. A child's first algebra course had lasting impact, influencing whether the student would take calculus in high school or give up on math altogether." [R13, p. 78]

Obstacle 6. Vocabulary and Symbols

Most disciplines have specific vocabulary, permitting clear communication. Ballet has the terms plié, tendu, and pirouette; music has the words adagio, fortissimo, and sonata; grammar has the names past participle, active voice, and parallel construction; poetry has the forms haiku, sonnet, and limerick; basketball has the designations dribble, dunk, and traveling. Yet, as Jerome Bruner wrote, math is special: "Mathematics is surely the most general metalanguage we have developed . . . ." [B22, p. 36] Many mathematical ideas—with no physical representations—depend on verbal expressions and symbolism. Thus, in addition to a seemingly overwhelming volume of concepts and skills, students must learn vocabulary—and how the words join to form language—as well as symbols—and how the marks fit to create notation.

For over a century, recognition of the importance of language in math appears in education literature. Consider the following ten examples.

In 1899 the *Report of the Committee of the Chicago Section of the AMS* stated: "Mathematics has a language of its own. The teacher must be unwearying in his endeavors to teach his pupils to speak the sentences of the mathematical language with intelligence, and he must be ever on the alert to check the tendency to use them as meaningless jargon. . . . Ability to think *in* the language is one of the ends aimed at, but in the language of mathematics this can be attained only by much translating [to and from English] . . . ." [B13, p. 197]

In 1958 Max Beberman wrote: "We believe that a student will come to understand mathematics when his textbook and teacher use unambiguous language and when he is enabled to discover generalizations by himself. These two desiderata—discovery, and precision in language—are closely connected, for new discoveries are crystallized in precise descriptions . . . and skill in the precise use of language enables a student to give clear expression to his discoveries." [B5, p. 4]

In 1966 Jerome Bruner wrote: "Teaching is vastly facilitated by the medium of language, which ends by being not only the medium for exchange but [also] the instrument that the learner can then use himself in bringing order into the environment." [B22, p. 6]

In 1985 College Board included the following among the mathematics that students should know: "Familiarity with the language, notation, and deductive nature of mathematics and the ability to express quantitative ideas with precision." [C11, pp. 19–20]

In 1991 an NCTM report advised teachers: "The teacher of mathematics should orchestrate discourse by . . . deciding when and how to attach mathematical notation and language to students' ideas." [N21, p. 35]

In 1993 Sheila Tobias stated: "Imagine that, instead of rote memorization of arithmetic facts, our math teachers had conveyed to us the most important truth: that mathematics is first and foremost a *language* . . . ." She continued: "Conflicts between mathematical language and common language may also account for students' distrust of their intuition. . . . This problem is not unique to mathematics, but when people already feel insecure about math, linguistic confusion increases their sense of being out of control." [T10, pp. 38, 59]

In 1999 Howard Gardner wrote: "Only with adequate exposure to these [mathematical] disciplines will students have any understanding of . . . the role of mathematical language in fixing these [mathematical] truths [such as the Pythagorean Theorem] so that all may confirm them for themselves (as opposed to arguments based on slippery language, ambiguous images, or mere authority)." [G3, p. 149]

In 2000 NCTM's major report stated that as students begin to verbalize their knowledge of math, their natural tendency is to start by using common language as a foundation. However, because "*similar, factor, area,* or *function*" and other familiar words have different definitions in math, NCTM urged teachers in the classroom to clarify the words' changed meanings and recognize their frequent use, as well as to provide ample practice opportunities to encourage their correct application and value their powerful influence in mathematical expression. [N24, p. 63]

In 2008 Jo Boaler discussed the importance of "precision" in math, calling it a "hallmark" of the field—even though precision is a feature that "both attracts and repels." She called the broad supply of vocabulary, language, symbols, notation, pictures, diagrams, and graphs the tools that permit mathematicians to be precise in every aspect of their work—in their exploration of ideas, their experimentation with extensions, their solution of problems, and their communication of results. [B14, pp. 28–29]

In 2013 Amanda Ripley wrote: "Math is a language of logic. It is a disciplined, organized way of thinking." [R13, p. 70]

Kindergarten teachers ask children to *color the circle red*. While the circle is the set of border points, asking to *color the interior of the circle red* is a confusing stretch; thus we permit the language error. But care with math words creates serious discontent in older students. The following ten issues confound the use of math vocabulary and symbols.

1. Peculiar Terminology. Nothing is *improper* about an improper fraction, *prime* about a prime number, *real* about a real number, *irrational* about an irrational number, or *imaginary* about an imaginary number. In math, *expand* does not mean widen and *function* does not mean work.

2. *Duplicate Definitions.* *Range* means the set of y-values of a function as well as the greatest minus the least value of a set of numbers. *Base* means the base of a triangle, the base (such as ten) of a number system, and the number raised to an exponent. The adjective *consecutive* refers to numbers, sequence items, or angles—all with different connotations.

3. *Related Symbols.* The capital and lowercase letter E are different variables in algebra, while the vertical flip of E means "there exists" in a proof. The three dash-like symbols for subtraction, negative, and opposite (additive inverse) operate comparably but sometimes appear longer versus shorter and higher versus mid-line when type-set.

4. *Key Words.* "John has five apples and gives three to Mary. How many apples does John have left? Then John left the room to get more apples." In the first use, *left* indicates subtraction. But in the second occurrence, *left* is a verb. Teachers who solely use the key word method—always subtract when you see the word *left*—greatly confuse students. [S9, p. 65; T10, p. 41] Other key word confusions include *and*, which does not always mean to add, and *of*, which does not always mean to multiply.

5. *Nonexistent Terms.* Teachers who lack proper math education invent false terms such as *cross-canceling* fractions (*cross-multiplying* proportions does exist), leading students to incorrectly use the technique across an equal sign or to mistakenly not use the technique across more than two multiplied fractions.

6. *Confused Terms.* Teachers who lack proper math education often interchange *expression* and *equation* (similar to confusing *phrase* with *sentence*), leading to confusion between *simplify* and *solve*.

7. *Modified Lies.* Teaching a student something and then changing its future validity is poor practice. Examples include subtracting numbers (the result is not always positive), dividing numbers (the result is not

always whole), and adding or multiplying numbers (the result is not always greater).

8. Modernized Terms. Many math vocabulary words have changed from the time of parents' education to their children's. The word *regroup*, applicable to more than subtraction, has replaced the word *borrow*. The word *simplify*, applicable to more than fractions, has replaced the word *reduce*. Yet, too many parents fight with their children, clinging to *borrow*, as if obtaining money from a commercial bank, and *reduce*, as if losing pounds from a weight-reduction program.

9. English Translation. Converting English to math does not always follow from left to right. Consider: "There are six times as many students as professors at this university." The correct math is: $S = 6P$. After all, with more students, the lesser value (the number of professors) must be multiplied by 6 to yield the greater value (the number of students). For this translation, one researcher wrote: "The error rate for first-year engineering students at the University of Massachusetts is about 37%, with virtually all incorrect answers being of the form $P = 6S$. For students not majoring in science, mathematics, or engineering, the failure rate exceeds 50%." [S9, pp. 64–65] This data is particularly worrisome because MA students score relatively high on NAEP and TIMSS exams.

10. Ambiguous Definitions. I once asked a school superintendent why the middle school math teachers were not teaching problem solving; he replied that they certainly were. My frustration was vindicated when I read the following in *The Teaching Gap*: ". . . if a teacher says she does 'problem solving' (currently a popular phrase) with her students, what, exactly, does she do? Different teachers use the same words to mean different things." [S26, p. 16] A 1997 government publication addressed this matter: ". . . a number of terms from pedagogical concerns, models of learning, and styles of teaching are also used in unclarified forms. For example, such terms as *constructivism, conceptual understanding, inquiry-based learning, activity-based learning, relevant, applied, realistic*, and *real world* have come to cloud rather than clarify what is meant. . . . many of these terms are not bad in and of themselves, but they are often used ambiguously, inconsistently, or without precise meaning and thus detract from discussion rather than furthering it." [U3, p. 39]

In writing about the uproar over a 2003 NY Regents math exam, an NYU professor distinguished between essential and esoteric math vocabulary: "One cannot function mathematically without knowing the names of some important concepts." Acceptable examples were "the distributive property in arithmetic" and "the difference between similarity and congruence in geometry." Unacceptable was "undue emphasis on purely linguistic matters that are of little import." [B20]

Obstacle 7. Absences

Students' absences were annoying to me. Because I actually *taught*, not graded homework in class nor followed a textbook in lockstep, an absence was a mutual student/teacher inconvenience. Upon each student's return, I gave individual, after-school, remedial lessons.

But numerous teachers are not as giving of their time. Sheila Tobias described absences as "The Dropped Stitch." One child told her: "The day they introduced fractions, I had the measles." [T9, p. 55] And while students who miss school, whether for a day or longer, somehow learn to spell, the effect that absences have on math education is consequential, in part due to the structural and cumulative nature of the subject.

Even if parents would agree not to take vacations during school days, children still catch viruses and family emergencies continue to occur.

Obstacle 8. Math Anxiety

The term *mathophobia* was coined in the early 1970s by Jerrold Zacharias. Though recognized before that time, the affliction had gone without an official name. [L2, p. 17]

One definition of mathophobia is: "Mathematics anxiety involves feelings of tension and anxiety that interfere with the manipulation of numbers and the solving of mathematical problems in a wide variety of ordinary life and arithmetic situations." [R9, p. 551]

Someone with true mathophobia has such an "intense emotional reaction . . . that doing math becomes extraordinarily difficult if not impossible." [K11, pp. 9–10] Such a person not only strongly dislikes the subject in school, but also carefully avoids any numbers in careers. [L2, p. 17]

Mathophobia has several notable characteristics. It: (1) strikes in varying degrees; (2) may be dormant for a period of time; (3) is independent of other anxieties; (4) is widely prevalent; (5) attacks people of all ages; and (6) is independent of intelligence. Moreover, (1) mathphobes experience classic anxiety discomforts; (2) many do not comprehend the seriousness of the affliction; (3) many admit to having mathophobia without shame, while others try to hide the malady; and (4) while a pinch of anxiety can bring focus and motivation, mathophobia is a grave disorder. [L2, pp. 16–20]

Concerning prevalence, one expert wrote: "By the time a student leaves school, the chances are good that he will have acquired mathophobia at one point or another during his education." [L2, p. 16] Even professional mathematicians are not immune: "Almost all mathematicians have difficulties with math at times and have experienced anxiety in doing it." [K11, p. 9]

While mathophobia is not listed in *The Diagnostic and Statistical Manual of Mental Disorders* (DSM), since 1972 the Mathematics Anxiety Rating Scale (MARS) has been used in clinical and research studies. MARS contains approximately 100 items or situations which the evaluated person rates on a scale from 1 (no anxiety) to 5 (high anxiety). The situations range from real-life (checking an overcharged restaurant bill) to academic (taking a pop quiz in math class). [R9, p. 552]

Why math? Indeed, society does not recognize history phobia. Dividing people into math-lovers and math-haters, similar to cat-lovers and cat-haters, is too simplistic. [S15, Foreword] Further, Jo Boaler wrote: ". . . the widespread, distinctly American idea that only some people can be 'math people' . . . has been disproved by scientific research." [B15]

Of course, its foundational structure (Obstacle 5) as well as its vocabulary and symbols (Obstacle 6) make math susceptible to such a disorder. Other confounding features of math are concurrent requirements of memory, participation, practice, logic, creativity, and confidence. [O4, pp. 29–34] Moreover, math, unlike reading and writing, is not immediately applied to the rest of the curriculum. Further, math is often "taught in an atmosphere of tension created by the emphasis on right answers and especially by the demands of timed tests." [T9, p. 31]

In exploring the origins of math anxiety, parents are a definite consideration (Obstacle 9). Yet teachers typically spend more time doing math with children than parents do. Students, capable of discerning when math confuses or scares their teachers, will respond emotionally to them.

Teachers' fear of math is well documented. Three examples follow.

In 1959 W. W. Sawyer wrote: "The fear of mathematics is a tradition handed down from the days when the majority of teachers knew . . . nothing at all about the nature of mathematics itself. What they did teach was an imitation." [S4, p. 8]

In 2008 the NCTQ reported: "Unfortunately, by a variety of measures, many American elementary teachers are weak in mathematics and are too often described, both by themselves and those who prepare them, as 'math phobic.'" [W4, p. 1]

In 2013 Amanda Ripley quoted a math department chair as saying: "A large majority of education majors are afraid of math. This fear will be passed on to their students." Another math department chair "estimated that about a quarter of teachers graduating from his or her college actively hated math and showed no interest in improving." [R13, p. 94]

To prevent the passing of math anxiety from teacher to student, one psychologist wrote sternly: "When teachers admit to disliking mathematics, they should not be permitted to teach it." [E2, p. 64] Consider the effect that decree would have on the current math teacher shortage.

When coaching students for the SAT–M, I observed a common error:

reading each problem through once first. Anxiety instantly surfaced when students realized that they had not only wasted precious, scant minutes but also possessed no concept of what they had just read. Elementary teachers initiate this time-wasting, nerve-shattering strategy when they teach word problems. Preferably, students should read and digest one bite at a time, notating concurrently. As Sheila Tobias wrote, "Word problems, sometimes called 'story problems' or 'statement problems,' are, in my opinion, at the heart of math anxiety." [T10, p. 133]

Among suggestions for prevention, Tobias wrote: "A good teacher, to allay this myth [that math ability is inborn], brings in the scratch paper he used in working out the problem, to share with the class the many false starts he had to make before solving it." [T10, p. 53] Such a practice is an anathema to teachers who only grade answers.

As comfort with math increases, mathophobia decreases. The authors of *The Educated Child* agreed: "What really makes them [children] dislike and fear math is *not understanding it*. . . . The antidote to such anxiety is greater familiarity with math." [B10, p. 325]

Obstacle 9. Parents

In 1999 the authors of *The Educated Child* wrote: "First, this subject [math] is one of the most important that children study. Second, if properly taught it is a rigorous subject, and your child will probably need your help and encouragement." [B10, p. 277]

In 2008 Jo Boaler stated: "Working with your child at home could mean that she or he has a better future with math in school and life more generally." [B14, p. 199]

In 2009 a report from the National Research Council recommended: "Early childhood education partnerships should be formed between family and community programs so that they are equipped to work together in promoting children's mathematics." [N37, p. 4]

I disagree with the above three statements. More precisely, I favor *en-*

couragement but not *help*. My rule is: *parents should stay away from math homework*.

While studies show that parental involvement boosts students' success in school, activities such as reading books, quizzing spelling words, discussing current events, and attending school sports are preferable to doing math homework because math is a subject that people forget when not used. Again from *The Educated Child*: "Unless your own work includes a lot of math, the day will likely arrive when you'll no longer be able to answer or explain all those homework problems." [B10, p. 338]

Parents in the New Math era were warned of becoming math dinosaurs. The 1963 booklet *Modern Mathematics and Your Child* published by the U.S. government stated: "Have you recently heard your youngster speak of 'sets,' 'the binary number system,' 'structural patterns,' 'inverse operations,' or one of many other mathematical-sounding words or phrases? If you have, don't be alarmed. He isn't cultivating a new teenage lingo; he is talking about modern mathematics. If you are not yet one of the parents who have [sic] experienced this, you may as well prepare yourself now!" [K9, p. 1]

Frustration can lead parents to declare that they had no math talent or to lament that they had poor math teachers. The ill-effects can be far-reaching and long-lasting. As Sheila Tobias wrote, "Parents, especially parents of girls, often expect their children to be non-mathematical. If the parents are poor at math, they had their own sudden-death experience; if math was easy for them, they do not know how it feels to be slow. In either case, they will unwittingly foster the idea that a mathematical mind is something one either has or does not have." [T10, p. 53]

Parents may introduce errors. Among my experiences, a highly educated father, coaching his fifth grade son for a contest, incorrectly said that zero is not even. The child cried, sadly and ironically, when the one problem that bumped him from first place involved that very topic. Another father, too eager to do homework, forced his son to give decimal approximations by calculator for lengths of arcs and areas of sectors of circles when I required precise answers using fraction multiplication.

Confusion with math language, vocabulary, and symbols as well as lack of math knowledge all exacerbate child-parent tension. As Sheila Tobias wrote, "How can you help a child who talks about 'sets' when you have never heard of them and the child says *you* don't know what the teacher is doing?" [T9, pp. 33–34]

The authors of *The Educated Child* warned: "Parent-child math sessions can occasionally get rough." If experiencing "math-induced tears," "textbooks slamming," or cries that parents "just don't get it," they advised: "Cool down. Go to your respective corners and try again later." Overall, they cautioned: "Don't go to bed math-mad." [B10, p. 337]

Some parents actually want to be able to do their children's math homework—although the homework is not theirs. These parents should enroll in their own math courses. Some say that they want their children to learn real math but balk at the first homework assignment that they don't understand. If widespread, such an attitude can sink an entire program. As David Elkind wrote, "These new curricula . . . [Sputnik New Math] were given up because they were too difficult for the age groups to whom they were presented—not to mention for the parents who had to help with the homework!" [E1, p. 71]

A summation by Diane Ravitch underscored the need to finally fix math education: "Put another way, students learn language and vocabulary at home and in school; they learn mathematics in school." [R7, p. 53]

Obstacle 10. Curriculum

John Keats, parent turned education-researcher, wrote: "A school is not a child, a teacher and a building. A school is essentially what it teaches, and our first emphasis must be on content, on purpose, on individual quality performance. If the school teaches nothing, it is nothing. No curriculum, no school." [K2, p. 8]

The word curriculum is sometimes confused with other education jargon. William Schmidt and Curtis McKnight explained: "Almost all nations specify in some form the knowledge and skills to be transmitted through schooling—that which is intended to be learned. These often go by names such as *curriculum standards, learning goals, framework, syllabus,* or *national curriculum.*" [S7, p. 12] Some private schools skip writing formal curriculum, creating *scope and sequence* lists instead.

Jerome Bruner also cautioned: *Curriculum* "is perhaps a wrong word. A curriculum should involve the mastery of skills that in turn lead to the mastery of still more powerful ones, the establishment of self-reward sequences." [B22, p. 35]

Most public schools have an orderly 3-step process: states set standards (framework) from which school systems write curriculum (content) and then adopt textbooks (materials). An ED report agreed: "Although there are a variety of definitions of a curriculum framework, there is general agreement that curriculum frameworks are based on standards. Standards establish what students should know and be able to do." [U3, p. 1]

Schmidt and McKnight chose the word *content*: "We use the word content . . . to refer not only to knowledge but also to skills, reasoning ability, and problem solving." [S7, p. 9] They also studied the benefit of appropriate content: ". . . content coverage resulting from formal schooling—that is, learning opportunities—does, in fact, relate to academic achievement." [S7, p. 192]

Diane Ravitch argued for the importance of a strong curriculum. "So let us begin with a vision of the education we want for our children and our society. To move toward that vision, we should attend to the quality of the curriculum—that is, what is taught. Every school should have a well-conceived coherent, sequential curriculum. A curriculum is not a script but a set of general guidelines. . . . Having a curriculum is not a silver bullet. It does not solve all our educational problems. But not having a curriculum indicates our unwillingness or inability to define what we are trying to accomplish." [R6, p. 231]

Moreover, Ravitch used lack of content to reveal pitfalls: "To have no curriculum, as is so often the case in American schools, leaves schools at the mercy of those who demand a regime of basic skills and no content at all. To have no curriculum is to leave decisions about what matters to the ubiquitous textbooks, which function as our de facto national curriculum. To have no curriculum on which assessment may be based is to tighten the grip of test-based accountability, testing only generic skills, not knowledge or comprehension." [R6, p. 237]

However, teachers do not always follow curriculum. As discussed in a Brookings Institution book, three facets exist: *intended curriculum*—what is planned; *implemented curriculum*—what is taught; and *attained curriculum*—what is learned. [M11, p. 11] These aspects, compounded by ill-prepared teachers, lead to inequality and underachievement.

Schmidt and McKnight, after investigating the actual delivery of written curriculum, also used the words *intention* and *implementation*, stating that the two often differed—that "words on paper" were not the same as "real actions in real classrooms." They wrote that curricular goals of many school districts were plainly not being achieved. In other words, the formal, printed curriculum may have equitable content, but the actual, delivered lessons did not—the equality was lost in the translation from one to the other. In sum, they stated: "The devil appears to be in the details of implementation." [S7, p. 67]

Stevenson and Stigler described consequences of deviating from curriculum. "A serious impediment to achieving equal opportunities for all children is the great variation in the content of the curriculum followed in different American classrooms. Teachers are allowed to emphasize or de-emphasize subjects, depending upon their own interests and what is demanded by parents. In mathematics, for example, teachers confess a lack of interest in the subject, parents de-emphasize its importance, and the time different teachers devote to mathematics varies widely. Large discrepancies in what children have studied may lead to severe problems when children transfer to a new school or when they are called upon to use skills that they have not been taught by a previous teacher." [S25, pp. 153–154]

Formal curriculum is often tedious to write, painful to read, and ambiguous to digest. Given that the intended curriculum may be neither implemented nor attained, the money spent on full, formal curriculum writing may be staggeringly imprudent.

Unfortunately, the because-it's-always-been-that-way syndrome also affects curriculum. For example, adding fractions typically occurs before multiplying, although finding a lowest common denominator is much more difficult than simplifying. In particular, math curriculum is bound by deep roots. As Thomas Romberg, Director of the former National Center for Research in Mathematical Sciences Education, is quoted as saying in a 1991 *New York Times* article, American teachers are teaching "eight years of 15th century arithmetic, eight years of 17th century algebra and one year of 3d century B.C. geometry." [D4]

Math curriculum and family mobility are dependent. Suppose Sue and Bob took Algebra I as freshmen and geometry as sophomores. Both had planned to take Algebra II as juniors, but their families moved. Bob's new school offered math in the order Algebra I, Algebra II, geometry. Bob, who had to take math with sophomores rather than his junior classmates, was adversely affected both academically and socially by his scheduling in other subjects. Sue's new school offered three years of integrated math: Algebra I, geometry, and Algebra II intertwined. Joining her classmates, Sue fluctuated from flagrantly bored to hopelessly lost.

Now consider these scenarios from the schools' viewpoints. Imagine the demands on teachers who need to do their best for these misplaced transfer students. The end result is that many schools revert to the typical Algebra I, geometry, Algebra II sequence—rather than what is the best curriculum—to avoid the frustrating imposition of family mobility.

Indeed, Jeremy Kilpatrick gave the math sequence a societal rather than an academic context: "Our particular characteristic with this layered approach of a year of algebra, a year of geometry, another year of algebra and so on is a product of our history. It comes about because the college entrance requirements were first of all a year of algebra to get into college, then algebra plus geometry, and so as these college entrance requirements were laid down in the last century, the courses become layered in the same way sort of like geological strata." [www11-7]

Two educators wrote about this mobility problem. In 1960 Jerome Bruner stated: "Americans are a changing people; their geographical mobility makes imperative some degree of uniformity among high schools and primary schools. Yet the diversity of American communities and of American life in general makes equally imperative some degree of variety in curricula." [B21, p. 9]

In 1996 E. D. Hirsch expressed: "A country that lacks nationwide curricular standards can produce high average results when each of its schools has a good common curriculum and when mobility rates between schools are low, keeping the student body stable, so that each child receives a coherent education." But he noted about Americans: "We are also a people that continues to migrate within the nation's borders." [H12, pp. 42, 34]

Six of the various curricular themes in math education follow, all unresolved over time, although the study of data and graphs (Theme 5) constitutes perhaps the strongest aspect of CCSSM.

Theme 1. Teach algebra and geometry concurrently.

In 1893 NEA members stated "that the study of demonstrative geometry should begin at the end of the first year's study of algebra, and be carried on by the side of algebra for the next two years." [B13, p. 132]

In 1899 an NEA report recommended the joint study of algebra (including trigonometry in the upper grades) and geometry (including reviews) from grades seven through twelve. [B13, p. 193]

In 1911 *Mathematics in the Public and Private Secondary Schools of the United States* by the International Commission on the Teaching of Mathematics stated: "The different branches of high-school mathematics are not in general correlated with each other, but are pursued one after the other with such differences of method and point of view that algebra is often forgotten by the time geometry is completed. . . . The customary independence of these mathematical subjects is restricted almost everywhere by the requirement that a pupil must have 'passed algebra' before he is permitted to begin geometry." As a remedy, the report recommended "a six-year curriculum, to begin at the end of the present sixth grade." [A8 in B13, pp. 331–332, 358]

In 1963 the Cambridge Conference suggested "as its principal aspect" of reorganization "the parallel development of geometry and arithmetic (or algebra in later years) from kindergarten on." [C1, p. 8]

In 2000 the NCTM's *Principles and Standards for School Mathematics* noted that of all the various branches of math, algebra and geometry are "highly interconnected." The report recommended that the interdependence should be solidly written into the curriculum, fully present in the textbook, and clearly demonstrated in the teaching. As examples of the connection between algebra and geometry, NCTM cited two concepts from middle school math: the slope of a line and the Pythagorean Theorem. [N24, pp. 15, 212] Indeed, slope may be calculated by an algebraic formula; but whether it is positive, negative, zero, or undefined may be determined visually. And while the Pythagorean Theorem is an equation, perhaps its most elegant proof shows the sectioning of a square into two squares and two rectangles.

In 2007 Brookings authors, analyzing international tests, noted: "The college-preparatory high school curriculum in the United States is virtually unique in devoting two or three yearlong courses to algebra, with geometry given a separate year of its own. In other countries, students are taught algebra and geometry (and other areas of mathematics) simultaneously, in either integrated mathematics or parallel strands." They further commented on geometry's separation: "Despite repeated efforts to combine algebra, geometry, and other mathematics topics into integrated courses, the U.S. first course in algebra—like the yearlong course in geometry—has kept its title and much of its form." [K4, pp. 86–87]

In 2009 Paul Lockhart bemoaned high school geometry, calling it "isolated from the rest of the curriculum." He said: "Why Geometry occurs in between Algebra I and its sequel remains a mystery." [L10, p. 85]

Theme 2. Introduce geometry in elementary school.

In 1893 the NEA's Report stated: "... a course of instruction in concrete geometry, ... [must] be introduced into the grammar school. The object of this course would be to familiarize the pupil with the facts of plane and solid geometry, and with those geometrical conceptions to be subsequently employed in abstract reasoning." [B13, p. 132]

In 2000 the NCTM wrote in *Principles and Standards for School Mathematics*: "With well-designed activities, appropriate tools, and teachers' support, students can make and explore conjectures about geometry and can learn to reason carefully about geometric ideas from the earliest years of schooling." [N24, p. 41]

In 2009 the opening summary of a book written by the National Research Council stated: "There is expert consensus that two areas of mathematics are particularly important for young children to learn: (1) number, which includes whole number, operations, and relations; and (2) geometry, spatial thinking, and measurement. A rich body of research provides insight into how children's proficiency develops in both areas and the instruction needed to support it." [N37, p. 2]

In 2012 Schmidt and McKnight confirmed that geometry is typically not well taught in American schools: "TIMSS indicated that this area [geometry] was among the United States' weakest in terms of student achievement. ... given how central geometry is to modern mathematics and its uses, this is lower than desirable." [S7, p. 49]

Theme 3. Incorporate more problem solving.

The 1893 NEA Mathematics Subcommittee recommended: "... that the course in arithmetic be at the same time abridged and enriched; abridged by omitting entirely those subjects which ... exhaust the pupil without affording any really valuable mental discipline, and enriched ... in the solution of concrete problems." [B13, p. 131]

In 1938 the Progressive Education Association stated: "... the major role of mathematics in developing desirable characteristics of personality lies in the contribution it can make to growth in the abilities involved in reflective thinking, or problem-solving. ... mathematics can be made to throw the problem-solving process into sharp relief, and so offers opportunity to improve students' thinking in all fields." [B13, p. 556]

In 1968 Howard Fehr wrote in an NEA publication: "The organization of mathematics around concrete problem situations works best in the junior high school." [F4, p. 20]

In 1980 NCTM's *Agenda for Action* began: "Recommendation 1: PROBLEM SOLVING MUST BE THE FOCUS OF SCHOOL MATHEMATICS IN THE 1980s." [N18, p. 2]

In 1991 (as previously noted on pages 92–93) NCTM's *Professional Standards for Teaching Mathematics* stated: "The teacher of mathematics should pose tasks that ... call for problem formulation, problem solving, and mathematical reasoning." [N21, p. 25]

In 1992 Stevenson and Stigler wrote: "In mathematics, the weakness is not limited to inadequate mastery of routine operations, but reflects a poor understanding of how to use mathematics in solving meaningful problems." [S25, p. 50]

In 2000 NCTM's *Principles and Standards* declared: "Problem solving is an integral part of all mathematics learning, and so it should not be an isolated part of the mathematics program." [N24, p. 52]

Theme 4. Teach unifying concepts such as function, sets, operation, induction, probability, and logic—topics of Discrete Mathematics.

In 1920 J. W. A. Young's landmark book stated: "Mathematics in the synthetic finished form is deductive; mathematics in the making is inductive. ... but it is one of the chief glories of mathematics that it can take its theorems from the realm of inductive probability into that of deductive certainty." [Y1 in B13, p. 264]

In 1923 the *Report of the National Committee on Mathematical Requirements* emphasized functions ("thinking in terms of relationships" or "dependence") and logic (developing "logical structure; precision of statement and of thought; logical reasoning . . . ; discrimination between the true and the false, etc.") as two valuable skills. Moreover, the *1923 Report* stated about secondary math: "The one great idea which is best adapted to unify the course is that of the functional relation." [N13, pp. 8, 10; also B13 and N17]

In 1938 the report of the Progressive Education Association suggested reforming math by stressing major concepts—approximation, function, operation, proof, and symbolism. [B13, pp. 556–558]

In 1959 the Commission on Mathematics of the College Entrance Examination Board issued "Program for College Preparatory Mathematics." Of nine major proposals, the fourth was: "4. Judicious use of unifying ideas—sets, variables, functions, and relations." [C16, pp. 33–34]

In 1963 the Cambridge Conference members emphasized the importance of the structure of the real number system as well as concepts "like set, function, transformation group, and isomorphism," including their introduction "in rudimentary form to very young children." [C1, p. 10]

In 1983 the National Science Foundation published the ambitious report *Educating Americans for the 21st Century: A plan of action for improving mathematics, science and technology education for all American elementary and secondary students so that their achievement is the best in the world by 1995*. The document stated: "Function concepts including dynamic models of increasing or decreasing phenomena should be taught. . . . The concepts of sets and some of the language of sets are naturally useful in various mathematical settings and should be used where appropriate." Further, the report affirmed: "Careful study is needed of what is and what is not fundamental in the current curriculum. Our belief is that a number of topics should be introduced into the secondary school curriculum and that all of these are more important than, say, what is now taught in trigonometry beyond the definition of the trigonometric functions themselves. These topics include discrete mathematics (e.g., basic combinatorics, graph theory and discrete probability), elementary statistics (e.g., data analysis, interpretation of tables, graphs, surveys, sampling) and computer science (e.g., programming, introduction to algorithms, iteration)." [N38, pp. 7, 11]

In 2000 NCTM's *Principles and Standards for School Mathematics* stated: "Foundational ideas like place value, equivalence, proportionality, function, and rate of change should have a prominent place in the mathematics curriculum because they enable students to understand other mathematical ideas and connect ideas across different areas of mathematics." [N24, p. 15]

In 2007 Kilpatrick, Mesa, and Sloane wrote: "The profile of U.S. students' performance on these [TIMSS algebra] items suggests they have encountered a school mathematics curriculum that treats algebra as generalized arithmetic only, rather than one that adopts a function-oriented approach common in other countries and recently advocated in the United States." [K4, p. 85]

Theme 5. Teach graphs and statistics.

The *1923 Report* stated as one aim: "The ability to understand and interpret correctly *graphic representations* of various kinds, such as nowadays abound in popular discussions of current scientific, social, industrial, and political problems." [B13, pp. 391–392]

In 1983 *A Nation At Risk* stated that the teaching of mathematics in high school should equip graduates to . . . "understand elementary probability and statistics." [N11, p. 25]

In 1985 College Board stated, in discussing what mathematics people should know: "Familiarity with the basic concepts of statistics and statistical reasoning." [C11, pp. 19–20]

Theme 6. Teach mathematical proofs.

In 1899 the *Report of the Committee of the Chicago Section of the American Mathematical Society* emphasized: " . . . *Not to learn proofs, but to prove*, must be his task." [A7 in B13, p. 196]

In 1985 Alan Schoenfeld characterized the flawed way proof is taught: "In geometry, students' perspectives regarding the utility of mathematical argumentation (loosely speaking, 'proof') will be based on the way proof has been used in the classroom. In the experience of most students, mathematical derivation is used only to verify propositions put forth by the teacher, propositions already known (by authority) to be true. Such experience is abstracted as part of the students' mathematical world view as follows: Mathematical argumentation only serves to verify established knowledge, and argumentation (proof) has nothing to do with the process of discovery or understanding. As a result, students who are perfectly capable of deriving the answers to given problems do not do so, because it does not occur to them that this kind of approach would be of value. Such students may fail to see that 'proof problems' that they have already solved provide the answers to related 'discovery problems' that they are now trying to solve." [S9, pp. 185–186]

In 1991 NCTM's *Professional Standards for Teaching Mathematics* encouraged a broad exploration of proof: "The teacher of mathematics should promote classroom discourse in which students . . . initiate problems and questions; make conjectures and present solutions; explore examples and counterexamples to investigate a conjecture; try to convince themselves and one another of the validity of particular representations, solutions, conjectures, and answers; rely on mathematical evidence and argument to determine validity." [N21, p. 45]

In 2000 NCTM's *Principles and Standards for School Mathematics* recommended: "Reasoning and proof cannot simply be taught in a single unit on logic, for example, or by 'doing proofs' in geometry. . . . Reasoning and proof should be a consistent part of students' mathematical experience in pre-kindergarten through grade 12." [N24, p. 56]

In 2009 Paul Lockhart attacked the teaching of proof in high school geometry: "A beautiful proof should explain . . . clearly, deeply, and elegantly. A well-written, well-crafted argument should . . . be a beacon of light—it should refresh the spirit and illuminate the mind. And it should be *charming*. There is nothing charming about what passes for proof in geometry class." [L10, pp. 68–69]

Obstacle 11. Drill

Drill is a much debated, often maligned, word in math education. Literature is replete with examples calling for teachers to avoid rote, exhausting, pointless drill, replacing it with purposeful practice.

The *1923 Report* stated: "Drill in algebraic manipulation . . . must be conceived throughout as a means to an end, not as an end in itself." [N13, p. 9; B13, p. 395]

In 1945 the NCTM's Board of Directors created the Commission on Post-War Plans. Its *Second Report* outlined and discussed thirty-four "theses" for the improvement of school mathematics. Thesis 7 was: "We must learn to administer drill (repetitive practice) much more wisely." [C17 in B13, pp. 618–637]

In 1958 Max Beberman emphasized the dual importance of drilling and understanding: "The close ties maintained between the manipulation of expressions and the basic principles do not enable us to eliminate drill in manipulation. The student needs to practice using his short cuts in order to attain proficiency in their use. But during this practice the students knows that the algorithms he is using have a foundation in the basic principles and are not fortuitous procedures which seem to produce the right answers because the 'book said so.'" [B5, pp. 30–31]

In 1960 Jerome Bruner concurred: ". . . drill need not be rote and . . . [moreover] emphasis on understanding may lead the student to a certain verbal glibness." He referenced SMSG members who had experienced "that computational practice may be a necessary step toward conceptual ideas in mathematics." [B21, p. 29]

In 1963 The Cambridge Conference on School Mathematics reported: "We propose . . . the virtually total abandonment of drill for drill's sake, replacing the unmotivated drill of classical arithmetic by problems which illustrate new mathematical concepts." [C1, p. 7]

In 1999 Bennett, Finn, and Cribb similarly underscored the twofold nature of drill: "Requiring children to work a particular type of problem many times is considered 'drill'—a dirty word in education circles these days. Drill, it is said, takes joy away from learning and thus contributes to failure in math. That is certainly true of *too much* drill, but it's also true that, in many cases, it's *lack of drill* that produces poor math grades." [B10, p. 334]

Just as younger children polish arithmetic facts, older students should practice other basics such as square root simplification: for example, root 98 is 7 root 2, and root 48 is 4 root 3. While students must always grasp why and be able to revert to using definitions or properties, knowing fundamentals via drill speeds the tedious part of a math problem, revealing its essence.

Obstacle 12. Fractions

Fractions—perhaps because they are widely taught incorrectly—cause fear among students and parents alike. Even mathematician and satirist Tom Lehrer concluded his song *New Math* with the line: "Come back tomorrow night. We're gonna do fractions."

Yet fractions are extremely important. One cannot operate 1/x + 1/y without first understanding how to add 1/2 + 1/3. I use diagonal fraction lines here only for typing; sadly, sometimes teachers use them for math, confusing their students. Fraction operations require clearly seeing numerators and denominators, only accomplished with horizontal lines.

Often 5th and 6th graders prefer decimals over fractions, despite the difference in amount of work. What is 28% of 75? Many would multiply (.28)(75), rather than computing 28% = 28/100 = 7/25 and (7/25)(75) = 21. What is 1/4 ÷ 1/5? Many would convert both fractions and do decimal long division, rather than answering 5/4 by fraction division. Ultimately, students can't understand fractions when their teachers don't.

The 2008 *Final Report of the National Mathematics Advisory Panel* (commissioned by President Bush to end the Math Wars) called for more study of fractions. The Executive Summary stated: "A major goal for K–8 mathematics education should be proficiency with fractions . . . for such proficiency is foundational for algebra and, at the present time, seems to be severely underdeveloped." [N36, p. xvii]

Also in 2008 at the Brookings Institution, Tom Loveless conducted a forum on misplaced students in algebra. One of his recommendations was: ". . . to teach and assess prerequisite skills leading up to algebra. Let's make sure, for instance, they [students] know fractions. And let's make sure that that's taught and that we assess whether or not that knowledge has been gained." [www11–8]

In 2009 The Brookings Institution sponsored "A Discussion With Secretary of Education Arne Duncan." In the transcript, Jerome Dancis, a retired mathematics professor, commented: "From my perspective, the biggest problem in education is that . . . many of the middle school math teachers are not fluent in fractions . . . ." [D9, p. 11]

Unfortunately, Common Core interpreted (misinterpreted, in my professional opinion) all of this sage advice by delaying fractions study (except for a cursory overview) from elementary to middle school. For example, modeling fraction multiplication by sectioning rectangles occurs in 6th grade in CCSSM instead of in 5th as was previously taught. As Amanda Ripley commented about Common Core, "Kids would no longer have to dabble in fractions for eight years; they would dispense with the subject in five years, starting a couple years later than before but going into more depth." [R13, p. 75]

Obstacle 13. Algebra

Although algebra is a gatekeeper—the entrance for all future high school math and science courses—arguments persist in the teaching of the subject: at what grade, to whom, and how much. For such an established area of math, algebra is not clearly understood. Even math teachers disagree about the subject. For example, one 2000 edition of NCTM's *Mathematics Education Dialogues* was titled "Algebra? A Gate! A Barrier! A Mystery!" Members' comments ranged from calling algebra "a civil right" to espousing the old argument that "one does need to know how to build a car to drive one." [N25, pp. 1, 9]

Yet for over a century, educators have written that algebraic concepts should begin in elementary school. The 1893 NEA Report stated: "While the systematic study of algebra should not begin until the completion of the course in arithmetic, . . . some familiarity with algebraic expressions and symbols, including the methods of solving simple equations, should be acquired in connection with the course in arithmetic." [B13, p. 132]

The 2000 NCTM *Principles and Standards for School Mathematics* suggested: "By viewing algebra as a strand in the curriculum from pre-kindergarten on, teachers can help students build a solid foundation of understanding and experience as a preparation for more-sophisticated work in algebra in the middle grades and high school." [N24, p. 37]

Moreover, reports have called for algebra to be both rigorously and universally taught. The 1893 NEA Report stated: ". . . up to the completion of the first year's work in algebra, the course should be the same, whether the pupils are preparing for college, for scientific schools, or intend their systematic education to end with the high school." [B13, p. 133]

The *1899 Report of the Committee of the Chicago Section of the AMS* had as its 2nd resolution: "That in the secondary school the standard course in mathematics should be sufficient to admit to college; that this course should be required of all pupils, and that the instruction in this course should be the same for all pupils." [A7 in B13, p. 196]

The *1923 Report* called for "an understanding of the language of algebra and the ability to use this language intelligently and readily . . . ." [N13, p. 5; B13, p. 391]

In 2000 NCTM's major report directly stated: "All students should learn algebra." [N24, p. 37]

In 2012 Schmidt and McKnight stressed: ". . . there should be no debate about whether Algebra I or Geometry should be similar courses for all students." [S7, p. 93]

Some have even named specific algebraic skills that should be required. In 2007 Kilpatrick, Mesa, and Sloane wrote: "The algebra they [U.S. students] study in school should enable them not simply to manipulate expressions and solve equations but also to formulate problems using algebraic notation, fit functions to data, manipulate those functions to understand phenomena, visualize functional relations, and interpret properties of functions." [K4, pp. 122–123]

In 2012 Schmidt and McKnight stated: "These topics—which include slope, quadratic equations, systems of equations, and linear functions—define the internationally benchmarked core of a first algebra course, whether or not it is called algebra." [S7, p. 96]

Another debate is whether algebra should be taught in 7th, 8th, or 9th grade. In 1893 the NEA Conference Report stated: "From the age of fourteen, systematic algebra should be commenced . . . ." [B13, p. 132]

In 1983 the National Science Board Commission on Precollege Education in Mathematics, Science and Technology wrote: "Based on motivation from arithmetic, algebraic symbolism and techniques should be encouraged, particularly in grades 7 and 8." [N38, p. 7]

In 2008 the annual Brookings Brown Center report's title, *The Misplaced Math Student: Lost in Eighth-Grade Algebra*, summed its message clearly, explaining that previously, "Algebra in eighth grade was once reserved for the mathematically gifted student." After a thorough analysis of the national trend to place 8th graders in algebra (16% in 1990, 31% in 2007), despite their lack of preparation, author Tom Loveless stated: "Mandating algebra in eighth grade is the equivalent of mandating, by policy, that all buildings immediately erect a fiftieth floor—regardless of their current height." He concluded: "Two groups of students pay a price. The misplaced eighth graders waste a year of mathematics, lost in a curriculum of advanced math when they have not yet learned elementary arithmetic. . . . Their classmates also lose—students who are good at math and ready for algebra." [L12, pp. 2, 12, 13]

In 2012 Schmidt and McKnight broadened the discussion: "The choice of which first algebra course to take and when to take it conditions all future choices in mathematics through high school and even college." [S7, p. 114] For example, a mathematically talented 7th grader might take honors algebra, with the negative consequences of skipping horizontal enrichment, running out of math courses by reaching calculus too fast, and/or experiencing difficulty by encountering abstract concepts such as limits at too young an age. Also, taking non-honors 8th grade algebra might lock a student out of future honors-level math courses.

Then in 2016, the Brown Center report noted that CCSSM supports universal 8th grade algebra "by delineating a single eighth grade math course for all students." [L16, p. 10] Although this stance addresses equality, readiness remains an issue. One could say that rushing to algebra has replaced rushing to calculus. Perhaps in a perfect K–7 math system, all students would be prepared for honors algebra in 8th grade.

Did higher enrollment in 8th grade algebra improve NAEP scores? Tom Loveless studied this question and answered no. The 2013 Brown Center report stated: "States that increased the percentage of students taking algebra or geometry in eighth grade were no more likely to post NAEP gains than states with decreased enrollments in those two courses." [L14, p. 28] Why? Loveless said that algebra success not "course completion" should be the goal—that placing underprepared students in algebra classes with math teachers who are "less experienced, less credentialed, and less well prepared in mathematics training than the typical teacher of advanced math students in eighth grade" is not "educationally sound." [www11–9]

Did higher enrollment in 8th grade algebra improve TIMSS scores? The answer again is no. In 2007 an article in a Brookings book stated: "Beyond tracking, another source of poor performance in algebra [on TIMSS exams] may be that U.S. eighth-grade teachers spend considerable time reviewing topics already taught; almost 30 percent of their lessons are devoted entirely to review." [K4, p. 122]

Watered-down content is another issue with algebra. In 2012 Schmidt and McKnight stated that pre-algebra courses labeled algebra are "veritable phantoms as far as real algebra study goes" and "will not serve students well in the long run." [S7, p. 115–116]

Most states require algebra. But when I taught Algebra I at Duke University's TIP in 1992, my comprehensive final exam and North Carolina's state assessment were vastly apart in content. The NC exam was so minimal that the pass rate had no real meaning—except sadly for those who failed. Simple state algebra exams might be common. At a 2008 Brookings forum on misplaced algebra students, one attendee stated: "States and the federal government encourage pretend math instruction when they give extremely easy exams, like . . . the Maryland algebra test." Moreover, in 2013 Amanda Ripley cited another state's high school math test, which she said "wasn't very hard." [R13, p. 143]

At this same Brookings forum, Tom Loveless commented: "If you have a fake algebra class and you graduate those kids from a fake algebra class, then you have to create a fake algebra 2 [*sic*] class and a fake geometry class because they keep going, and a fake calculus class. So this problem does compound itself as those kids go up through the system." Moreover, participant Kati Haycock, then President of the Education Trust, declared: "And . . . since the burden of teaching high-level mathematics to low-level students falls on teachers, any of us who advocate that strategy must hate or at least be indifferent to teachers." [www11–10]

The range of both content and rigor is underscored by Jeremy Kilpatrick at another 2008 Brookings forum: "I am going to continue this discussion of curriculum by focusing our attention on algebra in an international context because for those in mathematics education, it is not the case that . . . an algebra test is an algebra test is an algebra test. We are interested in looking below that surface and saying what is it that the test designers for example decided was algebra." [www11–11]

In particular, I have seen teachers omit classic word problems: distance-rate-time (DRT), age, mixture, work, coin, and so on. Perhaps teachers skip word problems because these will lower students' grades, yielding more parent conferences. Or perhaps teachers don't understand the problems.

Some math educators have labeled these problems silly. For example, in 2008 Jo Boaler wrote: ". . . trains travel toward each other on the same tracks and people paint houses at identical speeds all day long. Water fills tubs at the same rate each minute, and people run around tracks at the same distance from the edge. . . . [children must] suspend reality and accept the ridiculous . . . ." [B14, p. 51]

But these problems are not all contrived. A farmer told me that he regularly created and solved his own mixture problems concerning the right amount of ingredients for animal feed. And, until the system changes, these problems are on both college and graduate school admission tests.

Math anxiety expert Sheila Tobias discussed one "work" problem in length: "If I can paint a room in 4 hours and my friend can paint the same room in 2 hours, how long will it take us to paint the room together?" [T10, p. 137] She wrote: "This problem seems difficult to do because it *is* difficult. . . . complex ideas [are] just beneath the surface." [T10, p. 140] Actually, this problem *is not* difficult—it can be read and solved (the answer is 1 hour and 20 minutes) in under a minute—for someone who has had proper algebra instruction.

Tobias also offered a classic DRT problem (extraneous details removed): "A ship goes in one direction . . . at 20 . . . miles per hour and . . . makes the return trip at 30 . . . miles per hour. What is its average speed?" [T10, p. 140] Discussing a variety of methods via this problem is fine for initial instructional purposes, but ultimately students need their "go-to" method to reach the answer of 24 mph—again in under a minute. Note that the answer is not 25 because the ship travels more time at the slower speed. Of course, both work and DRT problems can be complicated, requiring substantially more time.

In analyzing low algebra scores in a *Harvard Education Letter*, Laura Pappano cited abstraction, not word problems: "In districts across the country, failure rates for Algebra I vary but run as high as 40 or 50 percent, raising questions about how students are prepared—and how the subject is taught." She speculated: "Why is algebra so hard? For many students, math experts say, it is a dramatic leap to go from the concrete world of computation-focused grade school math to the abstract world of algebra, which requires work with variables and changing quantitative relationships. It is not just the shock of seeing letters where numbers have been but also the type of thinking those letters represent." [P4]

This attitude of algebra as a *hard* subject was underscored by Kilpatrick, Mesa, and Sloane in studying international exams. They asserted: "The United States . . . is one [country] in which too many people have assumed for too long that most students cannot learn, use, or value algebra." [K4, p. 123]

The following are two examples of writings that advocate for the important practicality of algebra.

In 1993 Sheila Tobias wrote: "People who study the link between mathematics and vocational opportunities believe that knowledge of algebra and geometry divides the unskilled and clerical jobs from the better-paying, upwardly mobile positions available to high school graduates." She argued that algebra alone can not only yield a higher score "on most standardized entry-level tests for civil service, federal service, industry, and the armed services" but also translate into recognition "for on-the-job training." [T10, p. 34]

In 1996 E. D. Hirsch stated: "Today, it is no longer possible to assert that learning algebra is inferior to learning how to select an occupation. With the nature of jobs shifting every few years, it has become obvious that algebra is in fact the more practical study." [H12, p. 110]

But the debate continued. In 2012 the *New York Times* published an opinion piece titled "Is Algebra Necessary?" It began: "A typical American school day finds some six million high school students and two million college freshmen struggling with algebra. In both high school and college, all too many students are expected to fail. Why do we subject American students to this ordeal? I've found myself moving toward the strong view that we shouldn't." [H1]

But also in 2012 Laura Pappano quoted Harvard education professor

Jon Star as saying that asking why one should learn algebra is like asking why one should read literature. He called algebra neither computation nor calculation, but "students' first exposure" to real math. [P4]

Obstacle 14. Ability Grouping

Ability grouping, a dominant method of meeting individual needs, has deep roots. As one education historian discussed, social factors dating back to the early 1920s such as heterogeneous urbanization, child labor and compulsory school attendance laws, and the advent of intelligence tests all contributed to the practice of ability grouping. [M7, p. 7]

The technique was and is a hot-button issue. In the Sputnik era, educators wrote, "If, in education today, there is a less comfortable topic to write about, we do not know what it is." [W9, p. 410] In particular, critics of ability grouping use the charged word *elitist* to describe the practice. [S29, p. 66; B10, p. 612]

For ability grouping, it facilitates: (1) special lessons, whether enrichment, acceleration, or remediation; (2) steadier presentations without boring some students or losing others; (3) increased class participation, with students feeling similar to their classmates, neither too smart nor too dumb; and (4) greater subject growth by meeting students' needs, regardless of level.

Against ability grouping, it creates: (1) further groups by different measures, removing learning how to work with student peers of other ethnic or socio-economic classes; (2) artificial boundaries, inhibiting growth by treating each grouped student as if identical; (3) challenges to maintaining stable groups while changes occur continually within individuals; (4) placement errors because of intrinsic flaws in evaluation procedures; (5) negative labeling of children prematurely; (6) self-image problems ranging from inadequacy to superiority; (7) loss of valuable intellectual stimulation for lower ability children by not learning from higher ability, same-aged children; and (8) unhealthy pressure to grow up fast.

Ability grouping is not *tracking*. William Schmidt and Curtis McKnight explained the distinction: ability grouping places students according to "a judgment of how able they are to learn that subject." In theory, students in different ability groups receive similar content, but at varying paces and depth. Tracking, however, "has as its explicit goal the coverage of different topics for different groups of students." [S7, pp. 99–100] Tracking is discussed in Obstacle 15.

Unfortunately, in decades-long educational literature, ability grouping and tracking have sometimes been incorrectly used as synonyms. Even experienced William Bennett, Chester Finn, and John Cribb in 1999 wrote: "Tracking—the practice of grouping students by ability and achievement—is . . . one of the most hotly debated topics in American education." [B10, p. 612] In the following brief chronological survey of writings about ability grouping, beware of the inadvertent use of the word *tracking*.

In 1958 John Keats supported ability grouping: "If we teach a heterogeneous class at the pace of the slow learner, the average and superior students suffer. If we teach at the average level, the dunce and the genius have an equally miserable time. If we teach at the level of the gifted child, nobody else learns. Indeed, the only possible democratic behavior would seem to be to provide everyone with an equal educational opportunity, to each according to his ability and his need, and it is difficult to imagine not teaching different children at different levels if we believe in this idea." [K2, p. 100]

In 1969 William Glasser opposed ability grouping: ". . . it works in the opposite way by increasing the number of students who are failing." He criticized the practice of forming "classes, where failure breeds failure and where the failures are isolated from the successful children who might help them . . . ." He also wrote: "Teacher expectation of poor student performance that leads to actual poor performance *is* most prevalent where students are placed in" ability groups. [G7, pp. 82, 85]

In 1992 Stevenson and Stigler warned: "Tracking by ability, special education programs, and individualized instruction benefit some children, but they also produce the unintended consequence of depriving many children of opportunities to participate in normal classroom activities, thereby limiting their possibilities for learning." [S25, p. 112]

In 1999 Martin Gross embraced ability grouping: "Tracking, or grouping students by ability, triggers Establishment psychobabble about 'educational egalitarianism' and 'democratic schooling,' all part of teachers' tendency to identify with students of lower ability or performance. Tracking reminds many educators about their own schooling, when many waxed envious as smarter students were placed on a fast track, leaving them behind. The argument rages most fiercely in middle school, where the curriculum is often weak, and tracking—thus far—seems to be the only answer to a better education for bright young adolescents just coming of intellectual age." [G12, pp. 199–200]

In 2008 Jo Boaler called ability grouping "one of the most controversial topics in education." Recognizing that parents of motivated, high-achieving, gifted, and talented students favor the practice, she cautioned that more than one international study revealed inverse results. Countries as diverse as Japan and Finland that shun ability grouping lead in test scores, while nations such as America that embrace ability grouping score far below. [B14, p. 106]

The following nine points emerge from research on ability grouping.

1. An inherently wide variation exists among children.
2. Most attempts to handle pupil differences have involved ability grouping.
3. The administration of ability grouping is a complex matter.
4. The question of whether ability grouping "works" is difficult to answer.
5. Ability grouping may cause educators to lose sight of the aims of education.
6. The findings of research on ability grouping are mixed.
7. The resultant classes grouped by ability, because of innate human differences, display heterogeneous characteristics.
8. Grouping strategies vary considerably among schools.
9. Some grouping is inevitable in the education of today and the future.

Consider the third point on administration. In 1960 Jerome Bruner wrote: "Ideally, schools should allow students to go ahead in different subjects as rapidly as they can. But the administrative problems that are raised when one makes such an arrangement possible are almost inevitably beyond the resources that schools have available for dealing with them. The answer will probably lie in some modification or abolition of grade levels in some subjects, notably mathematics, along with a program of course enrichment in other subjects." [B21, p. 11]

Similarly, in 1962 an article in *The Sixty-first Yearbook of the National Society for the Study of Education* stated: " . . . the problems of organizing the school to give recognition to the range of differences in human personality" are "ineffably complicated." [S13, p. 50]

As a private school consultant balancing the needs of all students, I was cognizant of the tug-of-war between parents loving and hating ability grouping. I administered a self-written achievement test to place students in *performance* groups rather than *ability* groups, based on students' background rather than capacity, trying to stigmatize children less and please parents more. However, the intended flexibility of the plan failed when the more learned children grew faster in knowledge than the others. Moving up a performance group was welcome but onerous; moving down was unwelcome and combative.

Math ability groups may focus on enrichment or acceleration, with a combination the wisest. Both are limited by the knowledge and skills of the teachers. Programs that are purely enrichment may be glorified game-playing and puzzle-solving, not specifically developed for gifted pupils and not permitting the proper approach to problem solving, thereby not maximizing students' mathematical growth in the allotted time. Programs that are purely acceleration may become self-defeating, causing students to tackle age-inappropriate abstract concepts.

Regardless of all the positions and pitfalls, the concern for the nation's gifted children is ongoing. In 1970 NCTM's Yearbook referred to the "new concern for superior students" as one of many forces operating in the New Math period. [N17, p. 87] In 1983 *A Nation At Risk* stated:

"The Federal Government, in cooperation with States and localities, should help meet the needs of key groups of students such as the gifted and talented . . . ." [N11, p. 32] In 1999 Martin Gross wrote: ". . . another important failure of scholarship in our public schools is the inattention to gifted children, a situation that is worsening each year." [G12, p. 199] And in 2003 a *Wall Street Journal* article by Daniel Golden titled "Initiative to Leave No Child Behind Leaves Out Gifted" explained that with NCLB, spending money on children already meeting the standards was wasteful and illogical, whereas spending on lower performing children had the potential to yield big point gains, which translated into more federal dollars. Golden commented: "To abide by the law [NCLB], schools are shifting resources away from programs that help their most gifted students." [G8] The proposal in *From STEM To STEW* meets the needs of the gifted while advancing the math education of all.

Obstacle 15. Inequality

Unequal math instruction for children—whether via teacher knowledge, textbook choice, school policy, or another vehicle—has devastating long-term effects on future educational paths and career opportunities. In 2012 William Schmidt and Curtis McKnight, authors of *Inequality For All*, one of the most comprehensive books on the issue, explained: "Given that limits on learning opportunities in mathematics are cumulative, gaps multiply over time and profoundly influence what is learned." [S7, p. 77] After thorough research on the issue, they advised: "Schools must provide equal content coverage for all children of all backgrounds at least through the first 8 years of schooling." [S7, p. 211] They gave this counsel after duly noting the conflict between two great American traditions—"local control of public schools" and "equitable learning opportunities." Yet, they wrote: "It is difficult to imagine a plausible position asserting that children in one part of the United States should be expected to learn certain topics in mathematics . . . while children in other parts of the United States are not given the same opportunities or held to the same expectations." [S7, p. 27]

The two most significant instigating factors of inequality are imposed curricular tracking and intrinsic teacher decisions, both ingrained in math instruction for decades. The solution to the former should be straight-forward elimination. As Schmidt and McKnight wrote, "In the case of U.S. middle schools, the best means of improving outcomes may be to avoid tracking altogether, as is done in many other high-achieving countries." [S7, pp. 121–122] The solution to the latter is a tougher problem. Ultimately, Diane Ravitch asserted: "The U.S. Department of Education should reclaim its mantle as an agency whose fundamental mission is to promote equality of educational opportunity." [R7, p. 284]

1. Curricular Tracking

The 2016 *Brown Center Report* provided background on tracking, stating: "Since the early 20th century, curriculum differentiation occurred by assigning students to tracks that encompassed all academic subjects. The names of tracks vaguely denoted post-secondary destinations, with 'college prep,' 'vocational,' and 'general' being the most common labels. Students were assigned to tracks based on IQ tests measuring general aptitude or achievement tests measuring prior learning. By the 1970s, tracking had changed. Omnibus tracking was replaced by subject-specific assignment to courses (i.e., students simultaneously could be placed in remedial reading and a higher level math class), IQ testing fell into disfavor, and parents increasingly could override schools' initial placement and demand a different track if they wanted more or less challenge for their children than schools recommended." [L16, p. 18]

The report, noting that the anti-tracking movement of the 1990s mostly affected middle school, cited math as the one subject that "remained tracked, but with fewer levels"—typically just algebra, pre-algebra, or general eighth grade math. [L16, p. 18] While commenting that today's math offerings are similar, the report did not distinguish between tracking and ability grouping—the difference in the actual content delivered, regardless of the grade. If pre-algebra 8th graders were merely delayed a year for more practice, but then as 9th graders received the same algebra instruction as the 8th graders enrolled in algebra, no long-term harm would be done; and one could label that situation ability grouping. But if the pre-algebra 8th graders received watered-down algebra in 9th grade, they became handicapped for future education and career choices.

Further, this report examined relationships between students who were tracked in eighth grade math and students who took AP exams. The study found: (1) no association between the numbers in the two groups; (2) a positive association between those in the first group and superior scores on the AP exams; and (3) no proof or disproof "that tracking caused the heightened success on AP tests." [L16, p. 24]

Content reduction or delay has deep implications. In 2008 Jo Boaler discussed an interesting finding from research: ". . . low achievers are often thought of as *slow* learners, when in fact they are not learning the same things slowly. Rather, they are learning a *different* mathematics." [B14, p. 148] In other words, math might be harder for these students because they were not given all of the necessary tools.

In 2016 E. D. Hirsch emphasized: "Content delay in the early years is harmful to all and disastrous to the disadvantaged. . . . Momentum is gained not just by a head start but by a *sustained* start. Lacking continued momentum, a mere head start slows down and fades out." [H14, p. 165] Hirsch also attacked the concept of depriving select knowledge from certain children as both fallacious and harmful. First, in criticizing developmental inappropriateness, he wrote: "The entire idea of natural development . . . in education is incorrect, and must be vigorously rejected. It has been a cause of disadvantaged children not receiving a coherent, challenging curriculum." He called "developmentally inappropriate" a "scientifically suspect phrase whose only possible efficacy is to keep knowledge [freely given to an advanced child] from a child." [H14, p. 67]

Second, in criticizing intellectual inappropriateness, Hirsch debunked the notion that students' different "academic abilities and rates of learning"—what he acknowledged as a centuries-old, widely known fact—should affect the material they learn. He wrote: "The incoherent classrooms and curricula supported by these scientifically challenged theories of individuality have not worked to improve either academic performance or fairness." He cited PISA 2012, when the goal of narrowing achievement gaps between rich and poor students "was achieved best by systems that followed a long, multi-year arc of commonly learned subject matter in the elementary grades." [H14, pp. 71–72]

Amanda Ripley also discussed tracking in relation to PISA: ". . . the United States was one of the few countries where schools not only divided younger children by ability, but [also] actually taught different *content* to the more advanced track." Moreover, she noted that the most significant reform leading to Poland's PISA success was delayed tracking. [R13, pp. 139, 136] Regarding tracking and TIMSS, James Stigler and James Hiebert wrote that in Japan, ". . . tailoring instruction to specific students is seen as unfairly limiting and as prejudging what students are capable of learning; all students should have the opportunity to learn the same material." [S26, p. 94]

Yet calls for tracking have appeared throughout the decades. For example, NCTM's 1980 *Agenda* listed as one of its *Recommendations* that: "more mathematics study be required for all students and a flexible curriculum with a greater range of options be designed to accommodate the diverse needs of the student population." [N18, p. 1]

2. Teacher Decisions

In 2012 Schmidt and McKnight argued that the American system of determining math curriculum was "akin to a national lottery for determining content coverage." [S7, p. 34] Extensive examination of research for grades one through eight led them to conclude: ". . . intended learning opportunities are ultimately shaped into real opportunities by what goes on in the classroom." [S7, pp. 68–69] These authors emphatically repeated this point: "In general, teachers choose which topics they will teach, in what order, and for how long—regardless of state or district standards . . . ." They also noted that teachers' knowledge and understanding of math as well as their ability to explain the subject affected their decisions in those three regards. [S7, p. 147]

Further, they downplayed administrative and regulatory attempts to control content: "Because of teacher and school-level decision making, inequalities may exist among schools within the same district, and even among classrooms within the same school. State and district attempts to ensure educational equality have only a limited effect, in spite of the mechanisms of state and district standards and associated assessments." [S7, pp. 68–69] They emphasized: "Even after controlling for state and district, we found that over 80% of the total variation in content coverage among classrooms at the same grade level within schools was due to teacher decisions." [S7, p. 164–165] Finally, they labeled "this teacher content decision making" as "virtually unique to the U.S. educational system in its magnitude." [S7, p. 146] They observed: "The United States is virtually alone among the [TIMSS] countries in permitting teachers to have such a strong influence on what is actually taught." [S7, pp. 68–69]

Schmidt and McKnight offered lengthy analysis of various math topics that were inequitably taught. Perhaps one of the most egregious findings was that in their surveyed classrooms, almost one fourth of the middle school students did not learn about the slope of a line. [S7, p. 80]

Obstacle 16. Textbook Publishers

In 1990 Jarkko Leino explained that to assist with matters of content, pedagogy, and pacing, teachers "usually open the textbook" as "easy way to organize teaching." He stated: "The results are not necessarily bad." [L4, p. 43] But are they good? In 1992 Harold Stevenson and James Stigler wrote: ". . . American textbooks tend to be excessively long, repetitive, and distracting and underestimate what children can understand." [S25, p. 213]

In 2012 William Schmidt and Curtis McKnight discussed that the order, number, depth, development, flow, and interconnection of topics in textbooks influence students' overall experience—both in acquired attitude and gained knowledge. They studied textbooks, analyzing "the number of breaks (changes from one topic to another)" as a measure of effect on learning. They stated: "Large numbers of breaks indicate a pattern of short, non-continuous coverage of a topic. . . . Books with few such interruptions in their flow would indicate that they cover content more coherently." [S7, pp. 177–178] Their approximate average results for grades 4 and 8 textbooks were: TIMSS countries—50 breaks; TIMSS highest-scoring countries—25 breaks; U.S.—185 breaks. They explained that with more breaks, making sense of the content became more difficult. They concluded: "U.S. [math] textbooks appear to offer the worst of all worlds." [S7, p. 180]

The following fourteen points summarize the hurdles that textbooks and their publishers present in the quest for strong math education.

Point 1. Math textbooks can be a de facto curriculum.

While curriculum writing is supposed to occur first, with textbook selection following to match, often the textbook becomes the curriculum. Educators have written about this practice. In 2010 Diane Ravitch expressed: "Teachers continued to rely on their textbooks to determine what to teach and test. The tests and textbooks, written for students across the nation, provided a low-level sort of national standard." [R6, p. 20] In 2012 William Schmidt and Curtis McKnight described a scenario in which texts "serve as *de facto* curriculum," especially "for busy, overworked teachers." [S7, p. 18] They noted that in general, "it is much easier to leave something out that a textbook covers than it is to add something else." [S7, p. 165] However, this situation is not necessarily inferior for the students, as in the case of a strong high school math book.

Point 2. Math textbook publishers seize authority without permission.

In 1992 Stevenson and Stigler wrote: "We must decide who should control the curriculum. Are Americans willing to abdicate this function to textbook publishers, who follow the demands of a few powerful state adoption committees?" [S25, p. 202]

In 2003 Diane Ravitch asked: "Who gave the schools and the publishers the right to decide how the next generation's minds should be molded?" She continued: "In a perfect world, teachers would be so well educated that they wouldn't rely on textbooks. It is not a perfect world, however, and there will continue to be a need for textbooks to help teachers organize their courses." [R2, pp. 160, 169]

Point 3. Math textbook publishers, following state standards, are for profit first, thus by default, for children second.

To maintain school accreditation, many states as well as state independent school associations require that math textbooks have a copyright date within five or ten years, as if math and children change substantially in that period. Instead of doing small, valid tweaks or corrections, publishers have discarded strong curriculum and methods for inferior content and presentations. Why change great math books? One reason is the continual movement of state standards, which need not shift every five years either. As Diane Ravitch wrote, "These firms make sure that each text is aligned with the curriculum standards of the states where the publisher is hoping to win adoption or make a sale." She also commented that the five-year-old copyright cutoff "makes textbooks very expensive to produce and minimizes competition by raising the cost of doing business." [R2, pp. 103–104] This financial squeeze paired with the publishers' mandatory profit margin result in passing the monetary burden to school systems, both in purchasing books and retraining teachers.

In 1992 Harold Stevenson and James Stigler commented that the "open market" in the U.S. publishing industry has caused "a profusion of textbooks" with companies of all sizes competing "fiercely to get their textbooks adopted." They added that due to broadly varying content, arguments often erupt among teachers, boards, and states. [S25, p. 139] But, as Diane Ravitch remarked, the marketplace is actually a "procurement system," not technically "wide-open" because the "ultimate consumers"—the students—have no say. [R2, pp. 102–103]

In 1995 Charles Sykes explained that with $2 billion spent annually on K–12 textbooks, "competition is intense." If a large state adopted a book, the publisher would "have a reliable cash cow for years." Thus, he wrote: "The modern textbook is the product of economics, politics, educational theory, and big business." [S29, p. 132]

In 2003 Diane Ravitch wrote about the large financial commitment that educational publishers make to create a new textbook series. She remarked that in the "highly regulated and politicized environment," gaining approval from Texas and California by avoiding "controversy" and following "guidelines" was the best path to success. Otherwise, publishers "must struggle to sell their books to smaller states and individual districts" to overcome the "economic blow." [R2, pp. 97–98]

Point 4. Math textbooks are often designed for easy teaching rather than rigorous learning.

The demand for powerful math textbooks is not new. In 1830 Warren Colburn stated: "This subject [math] also suggests a hint with regard to making books, and especially those for children. The author should endeavor to instruct, by furnishing the learner with occasions for thinking and exercising his own reasoning powers, and he [the author] should not endeavor to think and reason for him." [B13, p. 34]

Yet that rigor is often missing. In 1968 B. F. Skinner wrote: ". . . the textbook is often less a balanced summary of a field than a collection of topics which are easily taught." [S17, p. 234] And in 2013 Amanda Ripley conceded: "The purpose of American education was muddled in all kinds of ways. . . . There was no better metaphor for this mission confusion than the American textbook." [R13, p. 74]

Point 5. Math textbooks can be packed with worthless pictures that divert students' focus.

Coaching sixth grade students for Math League competitions, I used problems from old tests as a way of enhancing my curriculum. [www11–12] My students consistently scored very high—until 1992–1993 when FML suddenly included clipart on the exams. When I asked my students why their contest scores plummeted from their practice results, they admitted to spending time looking at the pictures.

In 1992 the authors of *The Learning Gap* wrote: "American textbooks, in contrast [to Japanese and Chinese], are thick, hard-covered volumes covering a whole year's work. There are colorful illustrations, photographs, drawings, or figures on nearly every page. This artwork, along with digressions into historical and biographical material, is introduced

Hindering Solutions 173

to engage children's interest, but may instead distract attention from the central purpose of the lesson." [S25, p. 139]

In 1993 a national publisher released a K–6 textbook series that overflowed with distracting color pictures. For Grade 6, the Contents featured a jar of jelly beans, a dog jumping, hot air balloons, a butterfly, a boy on a skateboard, a sand castle, origami birds, a pile of sneakers, a beach ball in the ocean, a surf boarder, a hot dog topped with swirly mustard, dice with board-game pieces, hands playing a keyboard, and political election buttons. Chapter 1 showed a piked diver, a girl in a flowered bathing suit, vegetables, a sundae, a roll of movie tickets, punch and chips, pie and milk, huddled football players, children jumping rope, a beach chair and umbrella, and stacks of pennies. Chapter 2 featured a crowded city street, a cake with candles, an elderly woman in polka-dot pants on roller skates, a cast on a leg, a kitten with a ball of yarn, a stack of magazines, a red sports car, the Great Wall of China, mountains along a highway, a baseball player at home plate, people reading newspapers, a boy playing a video game, children on telephones, colored marbles, zebras drinking water, a television and its remote, charge cards, and a high-top sneaker full of jelly beans. Chapter 3 included E.T., a football, a globe, King Kong, a three-scoop ice cream cone, racers at a starting line, an egg in a nest, a boat on water, a bee on a flower, a radio announcer, dry pasta in a container, an action figure, baseball cards, a radio tower, a woman running, colored leaves, an aerial view of the Pentagon, and a home's flower bed. You get the picture—pun intended.

Beyond diverting students' focus, three other consequences of these annoying pictures, which became normalized, were: decreased quality math (validated by students' low test scores), expanded physical weight (proven by students' wheeling books in carry-on luggage), and increased publishing cost (confirmed by schools' budgets). Ultimately, this excess of color photos helped drive the trend toward digital textbooks in which pictures are weightless and cost-free.

Point 6. Math textbooks can be created for "political correctness."

In 2003 Diane Ravitch wrote: "In mathematics, what matters most [at that time] is not whether textbooks effectively teach mathematics, but whether they incorporate multicultural themes and biographies into the math curriculum." [R2, p. 40] She added: "Even textbooks in . . . mathematics grew fatter as publishers added biographies of mathematicians and scientists who were women, African Americans, Hispanic Americans, Asian Americans, and people with disabilities." [R2, pp. 109–110] She cited 1991 guidelines from the National Evaluation Systems, proposing that references to minorities extend to math—such as reading a graph, not to find a typical numeric value but the number of minority people in a certain capacity. Ravitch remarked: "How patronizing to students, whatever their race, that even their mathematics tests are used to make political points." [R2, p. 58]

Thankfully, the days in which women were homemakers and men were scientists in word problems are long gone. As Ravitch explained, "Math problems do not have to include references to human beings, and therefore need not submit to a representation count for gender, ethnicity, disability, and age." [R2, p. 108]

In 2005 Ravitch wrote an opinion piece in the *Wall Street Journal*, highlighting the fallacies of an absurd educational idea, which she called *ethnomathematics*—teaching as if students best learned math when related to their ancestral culture. Ravitch cited researchers who compared a 1973 algebra book to a 1998 "contemporary mathematics" book. In the former, for the letter F the index listed "factors, factoring, fallacies, finite decimal, finite set, formulas, fractions, and functions." In the latter, the comparable section of the index included "families (in poverty data), fast food nutrition data, fat in fast food, feasibility study, feeding tours, ferris wheel, fish, fishing, flags, flight, floor plan, flower beds, food, football, Ford Mustang, franchises, and fund-raising carnival." [R3] The decades joke in Chapter 3 of this book is comparable.

In 2008 Jo Boaler stated: "If the ridiculous contexts were taken out of math books across America—be they traditional or reform—the books would probably fall in size by more than half." [B14, p. 55]

Politically correct inclusion can backfire. One of my students practiced arduously for the SAT. Due to CEEB's Question-and-Answer Service, she received a copy of the test and her answers after the scoring. Her 780 math score was the result of one wrong answer—to a question that contained her Indian name. Startled, she had lost focus on the problem. [reprinted in *The Official SAT Study Guide*, 1st ed., 2004, p. 776]

Point 7. Strong math textbooks have existed and disappeared.

Publishers have produced some excellent math books. In 1967 Houghton Mifflin published *Modern School Mathematics Structure and Method Grade 7*. [D6] The first chapter covered sets—the same starting point selected by the New Math authors. In 1992 Addison-Wesley published *Pre-Algebra: A Transition to Algebra*. [O1] This text included special right triangles, beginning trigonometry, conditional statements, Pick's Formula (found in MATHCOUNTS) for the area of an irregular shape on a geoboard, as well as the SSS, SAS, and ASA congruence postulates in geometry. Other solid math texts existed as well, but by 2000 many middle school math books began with what should have been mastered by the end of fifth grade—the four whole number arithmetic operations.

In 2013 Crary and Wilson defended older books: "Reformists sometimes try to claim as their own the idea that good math instruction shows students *why*, and not just *that*, algorithms work. This is an excellent pedagogical precept, but it is not the invention of fans of reform math. Although every decade has its bad textbooks, anyone who takes the time to look at a range of math books from the 1960s, 70s or 80s will see that it is a myth that traditional math programs routinely overlooked the importance of thoughtful pedagogy and taught by rote." [C21]

Point 8. Students can be too dependent on their math textbooks.

In 1968 Howard Fehr wrote: "We must teach students how to use books effectively, especially if we desire them to continue to gain knowledge in later life from the study and cross-reference of books." [F4, p. 5] Yet from my observations, that instruction is not happening. I have advised families to perform the following test—have their children do math from different textbooks, which have unfamiliar pages, layouts, and fonts as well as problems. This exercise, easily accomplished when visiting family in another state, has often revealed too strong a dependence on the textbook and too weak a knowledge of the math.

Point 9. Many math teachers cannot use rigorous math textbooks.

Because UICSM and SMSG of the Sputnik era were curriculum projects that produced textbooks, the goals and methods were never misinterpreted by outside publishers, as some claimed happened with NCTM's *Standards* as well as with Common Core. Yet these New Math rigorous books had their own trouble. Edwin Moise of SMSG stated, "One thing was obvious, however, as soon as the books were written and before they were tried: The improvement in intellectual content was so great that they surely would produce either an educational improvement or a collapse of classroom morale." [K8, pp. 104–105]

Weaker math books followed the New Math era. Then in 1983 a section of the recommendations in *A Nation At Risk* was devoted to texts. The report suggested: (1) "Textbooks and other tools of learning and teaching should be upgraded and updated to assure more rigorous content." (2) "States and school districts should: (a) evaluate texts . . . on their ability to present . . . challenging material clearly." (3) ". . . funds should be made available to support text development in 'thin-market' areas." (4) ". . . publishers should furnish evidence of the quality and appropriateness [and effectiveness] of textbooks." [N11, p. 28]

Point 10. Teacher editions support teachers' lack of math knowledge.

Houghton Mifflin's former K–7 series *Math Steps*, published in 2000 and developed to "remediate" bright students after squandered years of constructivism, is an example of a streamlined, clear, focused student text—workbook style; no extraneous pictures or biographies; no writing about math; only black, gray, and red colors; and reasonable length, allowing customization (time to coordinate with other material). But the teacher editions (TEs) were over-sized, colorful monstrosities that treated teachers as if they has learned nothing in education school. In general, elementary level TEs are in stark contrast to high school TEs that mostly provide the answers. The authors of *The Learning Gap* concurred, calling TEs "the core of much classroom instruction" and "simplistic in their step-by-step approach to teaching." [S25, p. 213]

Point 11. A teacher can still destroy a great textbook.

I have witnessed teachers render a great math textbook ineffective by skipping around for standardized test topics, finishing only about half of the book in a school year, and progressing at an inappropriate pace. Ultimately, the teacher is the controlling factor.

Point 12. Online programs that replace math textbooks can be minimalistic and misleading; digital textbooks still need materials for writing.

To compensate for physically heavy and mathematically weak texts, online programs have come on the market. After analysis, my professional opinion is that these tend to be digital gimmicks for parents who enjoy parroting the marketing ploy that their children are two to three years ahead, when in reality they are behind due to a dearth of material.

Traditional texts in digital form also exist to ease the burden of updating and to shrink the cost of printing. Ultimately, mathematicians work with paper and pencil; accompanying workbooks to digital texts need to have worthwhile, creative, challenging problems rather than trivial, repetitive, boring ones.

Point 13. The title does not define the math content; the labeling does not specify the grade level.

The authors of *Inequality For All* cited a content analysis, a recognized research method, of 353 math popular textbooks for grades 7 through 12, including some that received funding from the NSF. Based on TIMSS coding procedures that broke math into 44 topics, the wide-ranging results were remarkable, including that 17% of the books with Algebra I in the title did not include the topic of slope. Basic math books for 7th and 8th grades as well as geometry texts were particularly diverse in content. [S7, pp. 167–169] One conclusion was: "If the different textbooks were followed strictly by teachers, they would lead to very different content coverage and learning opportunities, even when the title of the book suggests that the material should be identical." [S7, p. 169]

The 2005 NAEP High School Transcript Study attempted to resolve the discrepancy between lower 12th grade NAEP scores and greater math credits with elevated math grades in higher math courses. To this end, the researchers examined Algebra I and geometry textbooks and found lack of agreement on what the two courses and their texts should require. Moreover, one result stated: "School course titles [such as honors] often overstated course content and challenge." [N9, pp. 1, 5]

After hearing many parents claim that their children were a grade ahead in one math series, I performed a content analysis on it. In fact, with slick marketing, the publisher had titled each typical grade level book with one number higher—e.g., 3rd grade content as 4th.

Point 14. Math textbooks reflect what society wants.

Who is ultimately responsible for poor math textbooks? The publishers who create them? The legislatures who recommend them? The school systems that buy them? The teachers who use them? Robert Sternberg wrote: "It is easy to blame the publishers. Why are they doing this to our kids? The problem is not with the publishers, however, but with the schools. The publishers publish what the schools will buy. If the schools want high-level texts, that's what the publishers will produce. If the schools want pretty colored pictures, that's what the publishers will produce. The publishers are in business to make money, and they give customers what they demand." [S24, p. 84] Perhaps, the ultimate responsibility should go to society in general.

Sternberg continued: "As a textbook author, I find I am never under pressure to raise the level of what I am writing. The pressure is always to lower the level. . . . We talk . . . about high standards, and we have produced governmental and foundation reports ad infinitum calling for their need. But we are all talk, no action. When publishers produce texts at a relatively high level, the texts don't sell. The big market is down-market, and everyone in the publishing industry knows it. When school districts buy . . . they buy easy, so that their students don't get too upset. But their students don't get much of a challenge either." [S24, p. 84]

Obstacle 17. State Policies

The website of the National Conference of State Legislatures shows a table of "Legislators' Occupations in all States" collectively for years 1976, 1986, 1993, 1995, and 2007. Of the 7,382 total legislative seats in year 2007, K–12 Educators comprised only 3.9%, down from 8.0% in 1976. In 2007 College Educators comprised 1.7% of the nation's state legislators, down from 2.0% in 1986. [www11–13]

Referencing a report in the *Chronicle of Higher Education*, a 2011 article in the *New York Times* revealed an even worse situation: "About one in four of the nearly 7,400 elected representatives across the country do not possess a four-year college degree . . . ." [H19]

These numbers beg the question: Should such a large percentage of non-educators be setting education policy—from approving textbooks to mandating the number of school days? When issues about math are considered, the situation is more frightening. Are people with zero to limited knowledge of the subject capable of making sound decisions?

Recognizing the importance of state legislatures is not new. In 1953 Arthur Bestor pleaded: "Citizens must also join scholars in urging state legislatures to review carefully and realistically the statutory requirements governing teacher training and certification." He argued that although "the powerful educational lobby" would "bitterly oppose any alteration," citizens should work to "secure the enactment of requirements that will protect the schools against incompetent teachers rather than the professors of pedagogy against losses in enrollment." [B11, p. 130]

The report of the 1990s ED-funded Eisenhower State Curriculum Frameworks Project made clear that the political bias rather than educational knowledge of state officials affected education reform: "Avoiding political shifts was beyond the control of the projects. In those states that underwent such change, there was nothing that the project leadership could do other than press ahead, modify the project if necessary, and hope that the transition period passed quickly." [U3, p. 17]

Moreover, in 1999 Martin Gross urged states to act firmly: "*To safeguard the community and public school students, the states must insist on tougher licensing exams and a test for recertification of all teachers—plus one to screen out incompetents before they begin a long teacher training process that may lead to nowhere.*" [G12, p. 103]

In 2010 Diane Ravitch warned: "Our schools will not improve if elected officials intrude into pedagogical territory and make decisions that properly should be made by professional educators. Congress and state legislatures should not tell teachers how to teach, any more than they should tell surgeons how to perform operations. Nor should the curriculum of the schools be the subject of a political negotiation among people who are neither knowledgeable about teaching nor well educated." [R6, pp. 225–226]

In 2012 Schmidt and McKnight suggested a role for legislators: "We are advocating for a level playing field in terms of content coverage. No educational system can guarantee equal outcomes, but policy can do more to encourage equal learning opportunities." [S7, p. 69]

In 2013 Ravitch commented on legislators' misguidance: "But they [American public schools] cannot improve if they are judged by flawed measures and continually at risk of closing because they do not meet an artificial goal created and imposed by legislators." [R7, p. xii]

Realizing that state governments have substantial impact on public education, in 2007 the National Council on Teacher Quality began its annual *State Teacher Policy Yearbook* project. Each lengthy report is an "encyclopedic presentation" of all policies that affect "the quality of teachers, specifically state efforts to shape teacher preparation, licensing, evaluation and compensation." The reports, displaying a voluminous number of charts that grade states separately on their performance in a myriad of concerns, include recommendations on improving policies. [N32]

Hindering Solutions 181

The Executive Summary of the 2007 NCTQ *State Policy Yearbook* listed the following ten key findings.
1. *State policies are remarkably inflexible and outdated.*
2. *States are not paying enough attention to who goes into teaching.*
3. *States do not appropriately oversee teacher preparation programs.*
4. *States use false proxies as measures of teacher quality.*
5. *States do not appreciate the dual nature of licensing tests.*
6. *States continue to neglect content preparation for teachers.*
7. *States do not ensure that special education teachers are well-prepared to teach students with disabilities.*
8. *State policies are not geared toward increasing the quality and quantity of math and science teachers.*
9. *States' alternate routes to teacher certification lack "truth in advertising."*
10. *The interests of adults frequently come before the needs of the children.* [N28, pp. 7–11]

Regarding point 6, the document declared that "18 states make no mention of geometry" in their coursework requirements for elementary teachers. [N28, p. 9]

The Executive Summary of the 2008 NCTQ *State Policy Yearbook* listed the following five key findings.
1. *States grant teachers tenure without considering whether they are effective.*
2. *States are not doing enough to help districts identify effective teachers.*
3. *States are complicit in keeping ineffective teachers in the classroom.*
4. *State policies raise barriers and offer few incentives to retain effective teachers.*
5. *State pension systems are generally inflexible and unfair to all teachers, but they particularly disadvantage teachers early in their careers.*
[N29, pp. 3–5]

While some states have A and B grades within the multitude of categories, overall the following chart shows some improvement but still paints a bleak picture. [N32, p. 5; N33, p. vii]

Average State Teacher Policy Grades

	2011	2013	2015
Delivering Well-Prepared Teachers	D	C–	C–
Expanding the Teacher Pool	C–	C–	C–
Identifying Effective Teachers	D+	C–	C–
Retaining Effective Teachers	C–	C–	C–
Exiting Ineffective Teachers	D+	D+	C–
Average Overall Grade	D+	C–	C–

The 2016 State Policy Yearbook focused on state standards for admission to teacher training programs. The report stated, "State admissions standards rose between 2011 and 2015 and fell in 2016." It also cautioned: "Lower admissions standards cannot effectively solve teacher shortages or increase teacher diversity." [N34, pp. i–ii]

Obstacle 18. School Boards

Supposedly, Mark Twain said, "In the first place, God made idiots. That was for practice. Then he made school boards." School board membership is often a thankless and frustrating job; citizens who run for office should be commended for their effort, and citizens who serve should be praised for their commitment.

However, school board members, who rarely know math, hire superintendents who also seldom understand math. The superintendents, in turn, not only hire assistants trained at education colleges where low-level math was taught, but also give these employees substantial power to control math education through curriculum design, textbook selection, and teacher training. Whether superintendents hire constructivists or rigorists affects the quality and quantity of learning.

In 1999 Martin Gross wrote critically: "The idea of democratically elected school boards is a good one. However, like district superintendents, school boards are also failing the students. Though their authority is near-total, surpassed only by the state itself, they have not provided a quality education in most communities. The reasons are many, including the fact that the boards usually represent only a small segment of the population and are often childishly naive in their trust of the hired help. Though theoretically the board members set educational policy, in reality they usually abdicate that responsibility." [G12, pp. 235–236]

Today, partisan candidates openly run in elections that should be non-partisan. They turn child-related issues into politically charged ones; and concerning math, they typically quote someone else without understanding the math themselves.

Obstacle 19. School Administrators

Sometimes school administrators operate with impure motives. At the time of the New Math, a Harvard Graduate School of Education thesis reported that a school head wanted "to introduce the new materials because other schools were doing it," thereby gaining "favorable publicity" in his first year as principal. [H10, p. 26] Potentially, this misguided practice continues; yet what is trendy is not always best.

I have witnessed both in public and private schools: (1) teachers undermining excellent textbooks by skipping around in an illogical fashion, perhaps motivated by covering topics on the state assessment; (2) algebra teachers omitting all word problems, perhaps motivated by fearing to teach, test, and grade challenging work; (3) middle school teachers covering in successive years only the first half of the books, perhaps motivated by dreading parent conferences for students who cannot succeed at the proper pace; (4) rogue teachers who do not follow their schools' math curriculum; and (5) lazy teachers who do not supplement a poorly selected textbook. These actions, unsupervised by administrators, deprived students of important topics necessary in future math courses.

School administrators—responsible for preventing these regrettable occurrences—should know that recognized textbooks may not be notable and that trained teachers may not be thorough. Great teachers should fear nothing from school heads who check pacing, delivery, and content.

School leaders typically either have a degree in administration—more like school managers—or pedagogy—more like classroom teachers. Regardless, without specific academic knowledge, mathematics suffers. Education reformers have advocated for replacing principals at low-performing schools. But new principals might know equally as little math.

Obstacle 20. Teacher Unions

Teacher Unions have a wide-ranging purview, affecting not only themselves—benefits, evaluations, grievances, lawsuits, leave, professional development, salary, tenure, termination, and transfers—but also students and learning—class size and school calendar. [W5, pp. 16–23] Understandably, some people place blame for problems in education with an organization that wields so much power.

Diane Ravitch has written positively about teacher unions. In 2010 Ravitch succinctly stated: "No one, to my knowledge, has demonstrated a clear, indisputable correlation between teacher unionism and academic achievement, either negative or positive." [R6, p. 175]

In 2013 Ravitch wrote more supporting words for unions: "Eliminating unions does not produce higher achievement, better teachers, or even higher test scores. Eliminating unions silences the most powerful advocate for public education in every state. It assures that there will be no one at the table to object when the governor or legislature wants to cut the budget for public schools." She argued that improved benefits for members, such as working conditions and salary, yield direct gains for students, such as smaller class size and stronger teacher recruitment. [R7, p. 126]

Others have criticized unions. A 1996 article in *U.S. News & World Report* titled "Why Teachers Don't Teach" was a scathing attack on unions. It argued that while the country relied on great education, ". . . teachers' unions are driving out good teachers, coddling bad ones and putting bureaucracy in the way of quality education." Citing that organizing was wise when teachers were treated unfairly, the article blamed AFT and NEA for copying policies and practices of industrial unions: "Under this ethic, good teaching is often punished, poor teaching rewarded and bureaucracy [is] placed squarely in the way of common sense . . . ." Moreover, the article, like other writings, compared the need for quality education to that of sound healthcare: "Teachers don't have to show in any serious way that they know the subject they are teaching or that they can teach it—a far cry from standards in professions like medicine." Sadly, they declared: "Teachers who want to 'go the extra mile' often find themselves unappreciated by their colleagues." [T11]

Moreover, in 1999 the authors of *The Educated Child* wrote: ". . . with happy but rare exceptions—they [teacher unions] have resisted serious efforts to reform and strengthen American education. These unions were started for legitimate reasons, but over time they have become almost completely self-serving in their actions and policy views. Partly because of them, many American schools have lost their focus, their confidence, and a clear sense of their mission." [B10, p. 623]

Also in 1999 Martin Gross stated: "The teachers' unions have fought, and are still fighting, every attempt to raise standards in their profession. They have countenanced the haphazard selection and training of teachers in inferior curriculums in inferior colleges. They have fought every attempt to tighten licensing criteria and weed out the army of incompetent teachers, who after they graduate from education colleges, enter the classroom and become members of the unions. They have done little or nothing to raise the level of curriculum and testing." Gross added: "Since states pass the ultimate legislation affecting education, unions put money behind their lobbying muscle there as well, which pays off in pro-union legislation." [G12, pp. 212, 217]

In 2006 former Secretary of Education Rod Paige published a book which was a comprehensive attack on teachers unions, although he claimed his writing was not about "bashing" but "explaining" them. He stated: "The behavior of the big, all-powerful teachers' unions is unquestionably the most significant determinant of the success or failure of most education reform efforts." And while he added that teachers "are sometimes subjected to conditions that require the assistance of appropriate union support," he felt "that teachers' union activity has gone well beyond the boundaries of appropriateness and far into the realm of excessiveness." [P1, pp. xvi, xi, xiv]

Less confrontational, in 2001 Vartan Gregorian, in a *New York Times* Op-Ed, offered suggestions for teacher unions: "To uphold the standards of teaching as a profession, unions need to push for more rigorous intellectual content in teacher education and professional development programs." He continued: "Unions must also press for reforms in the existing teacher certification system. The patchwork quilt of weak teacher certification requirements needs to be replaced with a national certification program. Not only would this increase teachers' mobility from state to state, but [also] it could provide research-based standards for what all teachers need to know and be able to do." [G11]

Tenure is a concern. In defense of teacher unions, in 2010 Diane Ravitch wrote: "Tenure is not a guarantee of lifetime employment but a protection against being terminated without due process. It does not protect teachers from being laid off in a recession, nor does it protect them from being fired for incompetence or misconduct." [R6, p. 176] Moreover, in 2013 Ravitch stated: "With tenure, the teacher is free to exercise his best professional judgment in the classroom without fear of political reprisals; with tenure, he can take the risk of being a whistle-blower if he sees administrators or other teachers abusing children or changing test scores or doing something else that is wrong." [R7, p. 128]

I have witnessed examples of Ravitch's points. At independent schools, thus without unions, I have observed cultures of fear and intimidation. Because teachers lived in angst over losing their jobs, they did not speak up when something was amiss; in many instances, students ultimately suffered.

In a 2008 NCTQ report titled "Invisible Ink in Collective Bargaining," the authors remarked that half of the states had "set forth procedures for dismissal with great specificity." Yet they wrote: "These procedures are time-intensive, often taking two to three years to complete." [W5, pp. 8–9] Comparably, Diane Ravitch stated: "The hearings should be resolved in months, not years." [R7, p. 127]

Because of delays, termination sometimes becomes transfer. Whether in a public or private setting, when an administrator moved a weak teacher to another school in lieu of firing, I called that practice *Pass the Trash*. [W6, p. 71] Other writers have called the unfortunate situation *Dance of the Lemons*. The following are two examples.

In 1999 Martin Gross wrote: "The unions claim that they only want their teachers to get a fair hearing, but contracts are usually so loaded down with protection clauses that dismissal of incompetent teachers is almost impossible. ... it's so difficult that many superintendents don't even bother. Instead, they make deals with the unions to give doubtful teachers a good rating in exchange for allowing them to be transferred elsewhere. The technique is colorfully known as the 'dance of the lemons.'" [G12, p. 221]

NCTQ's 2008 report stated: "What happens when both districts and states lack language prescribing the process for dismissal? It is not clear. In the absence of an explicit process, principals often complain that teachers end up being passed from one school to the next, though that surely happens in other districts with more explicit policies as well, in what is pejoratively referred to as the 'dance of the lemons.'" [W5, p. 9]

Classroom visitation is another thorny issue. In one school system in the mid-1980s, teacher union rules prevented principals from visiting classrooms unannounced. Moreover, scheduled visitations only occurred once a year. A reliable student reported to me that the day the principal visited was the only day that the teacher actually taught math. On the other days the teacher told personal stories, had the students trade papers to grade homework, and assigned new work.

In 1958 John Keats summarized his steps to improve schools: "Next, we visit our schools to find out in the classrooms just where we might need a little jacking up. To check ourselves as well as to gain additional perspective, we should also spend hundreds of man-hours visiting other classrooms in other school districts. These classroom visits are crucial. Only thus can we see educational philosophy put into practice; the theories in the books take on three dimensions." [K2, p. 12] Either union rules were different then, or Keats did not realize that such visitations might not be permitted.

In 1999 Martin Gross pointed out that visitation among teachers is as limited as visitation between teachers and administrators. He wrote: "At present the contact among teachers in the average school is so limited that few have ever seen another teacher teach. In addition, almost no teacher is comfortable when the principal is in her class." [G12, p. 118]

In my private school experience, the Head of School could enter any classroom at any time. Department chairs visited each teacher in his/her subject twice annually—scheduled, to permit teachers to display specific best work, and random, to verify continual strong performance.

In sum, Richard Ingersoll expressed with clarity: "Union work rules certainly have an impact on the management and administration of schools, and depending on one's viewpoint, this impact may be positive or negative, but eliminating teacher unions will not eliminate out-of-field teaching." [I4, p. 32]

Obstacle 21. Classroom Structure

The authors of *The Learning Gap* and *The Teaching Gap* have described the following four components of classroom structure.

1. *Classroom structure includes* the closed door. "Their [teachers'] closed classroom doors signal that they are in charge, and they cherish the authority they have over their schedule, curriculum, and classroom management. At the same time, the closed doors form barriers to communication, cutting teachers off from their colleagues." [S25, p. 163] Certainly, a closed door keeps the room quiet; but the supervisor—whether principal, headmaster, or other—needs access quietly and randomly to verify that quality instruction is occurring.

2. *Classroom structure includes* same-school, same-grade colleagues maintaining almost identical pacing. "Teachers find it easier to share helpful tips and techniques among themselves when they are all teach-

ing the same lesson at about the same time." [S25, p. 161] Certainly, collegial sharing is valuable; but teachers should not be denied the originality and flexibility in meeting the needs of their own students.

3. *Classroom structure includes* seat-work. "Seatwork is the time when students work individually or in small groups on assigned tasks. Talk is mostly private—teacher-student or student-student." [S26, p. 67] Certainly, seat-work allows teachers to give certain students extra help or to determine if students will be able to do homework on the day's lesson; but excessive seat-work supplants valuable instructional time.

4. *Classroom structure includes* interruptions. "Irrelevant interruptions often add to children's difficulty in perceiving lessons as a coherent whole. In our American observations, the teacher interrupted the flow of the lesson with irrelevant comments or the class was interrupted by someone else in 20 percent of all first-grade lessons and 47 percent of all fifth-grade lessons. . . . the mathematics lesson in one of the American classrooms we visited was interrupted every morning by a woman from the cafeteria who polled the children about their lunch plans and collected money from those who planned to eat the hot lunch." [S25, pp. 181–182]

A further story about interruptions comes from American and Japanese colleagues viewing the TIMSS videos together. On the U.S. tape "when a voice came over the public address system" announcing a change in location where students on a certain bus number should meet, the Japanese educator was horrified and said that "such interruptions would never happen in Japan . . . because they would ruin the flow of the lesson." Authors of *The Teaching Gap* summarized: "It might not be surprising, then, that we found that almost one-third of the U.S. lessons were interrupted in some way." [S26, pp. 55, 96]

Once when I proctored a standardized test, the custodian entered, pushing a dolly full of crates of milk cartons to go into the refrigerator in the classroom's interior storage closet. Despite my trying to wave him away, students' focus was broken. Thereafter, I made sure that the room always had a "Do Not Enter" sign on its door during testing.

Obstacle 22. Time Management

In 1983 *A Nation At Risk* noted "three disturbing facts about the use that American schools and students make of time: (1) compared to other nations, American students spend much less time on school work; (2) time spent in the classroom and on homework is often used ineffectively; and (3) schools are not doing enough to help students develop either the study skills required to use time well or the willingness to spend more time on school work." Further, *ANAR* stated: "We recommend *that significantly more time be devoted to learning the New Basics. This will require more effective use of the existing school day, a longer school day, or a lengthened school year.*" [N11, pp. 21, 29]

In 1992 *The Learning Gap* authors noted that both teachers and children lose time: "One of the reasons American children received less instruction [than those in Japan or China] is that American teachers spent 13 percent of their time in the mathematics classes not working with any students . . . . American teachers have to steal class time to attend to the multitude of chores involving preparation, assessment, and administration because so little nonteaching time is available for them during the day. . . . Being in an academic class is not necessarily equivalent, however, to being involved in an academic activity. Time may be lost in many ways. The lesson may begin late or stop early, the teacher may be called out of the room, or the children may be in transition from one academic activity to another." They added: ". . . several others [teachers] never taught mathematics in the twenty randomly chosen hours when our observers visited each classroom." [S25, pp. 146–147, 150]

In 1994 the National Education Commission on Time and Learning, established by The Education Council Act of 1991 as an "independent advisory body," published its report titled *Prisoners of Time*. The Letter of Transmittal stated: "Our conclusions and recommendations speak for themselves. Time is the missing element in our great national debate about learning and the need for higher standards for all students. Our schools and the people involved with them—students, teachers, administrators, parents, and staff—are prisoners of time, captives of the school clock and calendar. We have been asking the impossible of our students—that they learn as much as their foreign peers while spending only half as much time in core academic subjects. The reform movement of the last decade is destined to founder unless it is harnessed to more time for learning." [N35]

The first recommendation in *Prisoners of Time* was: "Reinvent Schools around Learning, not Time." The report stated: "As witnesses repeatedly told the Commission, there is no point to adding more time to today's schools if it is used in the same way. We must use time in new, different, and better ways." The report also noted that the issue of time management was not new—that in 1894 the U.S. Commissioner of Education "complained" about the reduction in annual school days. [N35] A 1994 *New York Times* article quoted the report's statistic that only 41% of the secondary school day was spent on core academic subjects. [M1]

In 1997 *Time* magazine's article "This Is Math?" described one fifth grade classroom that would make readers wonder about the use of time: "The students have spent close to an hour puzzling over the question at hand: 'What if everybody here had to shake hands with everyone else? How many handshakes would that take?' While the children, seated in small groups, debate and frown and scribble notes—and devise alternatives to the dread act of actually touching classmates of the opposite sex—their teacher . . . roams the room. When the hour ends, no group has an answer. . . . The class will dive in again after lunch." [R1, p. 66]

In 2001 David Elkind commented on wasted school time: "If this process [moving from classroom to classroom and thus also desk to desk] is repeated four or five times a day, the children have spent more time in getting up and getting down than they have in learning!" [E1, p. 74] And in 2006 E.D. Hirsch opened a chapter titled "Using School Time Productively" with the words, "Time is of the essence." [H13, p. 80]

In 2007 the Brown Center report stated: "Calls for more time in school have not abated." But in analyzing international test data, the correlation between time and achievement was not as straightforward as one would guess, leading to a possible conclusion that how, not how much, time is spent is more important. [L11, pp. 21, 27]

In 2009 the National Research Council issued a report stating that "kindergarten children were exposed to mathematics an average of 11 percent of the day." [N37, p. 235]

In 2012 the authors of *Inequality For All* suggested that adequate time is an essential prerequisite: ". . . no matter what the quality of instruction, a learning opportunity will be limited if too little time is made available for the instruction of a particular topic." They also explained the importance of properly allocating the day's and week's set amount of time—that poor choices can mean either the virtual elimination or insufficient development of topics. [S7, pp. 74, 85]

In 2014 the Center for American Progress (CAP) published a report on improving education, with all seven of its recommendations involving expanded time. The report called for "redesigning schools with significantly more time for both student learning and teacher professional development." Echoing *Prisoners of Time*, the CAP document recommended that the redesign should "make certain that more time in school is used effectively to avoid simply doing 'more of the same.'" [F2]

As a school consultant asking for more math time, I was promptly told, "Impossible." Yet significant time was wasted, walking to and from homeroom for related arts classes, rather than going directly from one to the next. My simple reorganization of the daily schedule gave teachers not only longer blocks for math but also more prep time. Further, I observed a school that annually missed an entire week of math due to Grandparents' Day, field trips, and musical rehearsals. In both cases, I was shocked at the lack of basic capacity for time management.

Obstacle 23. Classroom Size

Research results on the efficacy of smaller class size are mixed. In 1986 Secretary of Education William Bennett commented in a U.S. ED report: "No clear relationship has been established between size of class and pupil achievement." [B9]

In 1992 Harold Stevenson and James Stigler expounded on factors that interact with classroom size to affect overall learning: "Large schools, large class size, and old-fashioned school buildings do not necessarily limit children's academic achievement. Large classes can be managed effectively if the teachers are not overworked, if students are attentive, and if time and energy are not wasted in inefficient transitions from one activity to another and in irrelevant activities." [S25, pp. 67–68]

Moreover, while saying that the concept of smaller-class-size yielding greater-student-achievement was "popular" with teachers, Stevenson and Stigler pondered whether the number of students present or the amount of work involved influenced that position—whether teachers would accept larger class sizes if given greater lesson-planning time, more whole-group training, and increased wide-range assistance. Further, they speculated that, with school variance considered, an ideal class size existed that balanced learning, cost, and work. [S25, p. 212]

In 1998 economist Eric Hanushek wrote, "Politicians at the national, state, and local level will frequently call for a reduction in class size, a suggestion that is a certain crowd pleaser. Unfortunately, there is no research showing that incremental reductions in class size of a few students per class will improve student achievement." [H3, p. 9]

In 1999 William Bennett, Chester Finn, and John Cribb called the benefits of smaller class size "an article of faith" among many parents and teachers. While they acknowledged the political capital and tax dollars spent on the effort to reduce class size, they wrote: "The research on this issue is truly ambiguous." Recognizing that "most teachers would rather teach small classes," the authors noted that a reduction from twenty-eight and twenty-four pupils is educationally inconsequential because "most teachers don't do anything different." And under fifteen students, benefits may occur "if teachers alter their approach and organize lessons to take advantage of the much-reduced class size"—a condition they described as *"if the teacher knows what she is doing."* [B10, pp. 613–614]

These three authors made an additional, important point: "In the debate about class size reduction, the issue of teacher quality is often overlooked. To have smaller classes, schools must hire more teachers. Many parents assume that these will all be good teachers. That's not a safe bet." [B10, p. 614] This unachievable number of great math teachers is vital to the premise of *From STEM To STEW*.

Also in 1999 Martin Gross expressed a similar sentiment, basing his remarks on 1993–1994 data from NCES's *Schools and Staffing Survey*: "Most Americans are convinced, without real facts, that the fewer children in each class the stronger the teaching. After all, what could be better than more individualized instruction? That shibboleth of smaller classes, the vaunted pupil-teacher ratio, became a national goal. . . . As the pupil-teacher ratio has gone down almost 40 percent from 1955 to 1999 and class sizes have shrunk accordingly, student achievement has not only failed to rise, but [also] has dropped, almost in inverse ratio to the size of the educational staff. . . . If we look worldwide, we find that this well-ingrained American dedication to smaller and smaller classes may well be a fallacy out of step with much of the developed world." [G12, pp. 30, 33–34]

Further, in 1999 Frederick Mosteller, Harvard Professor Emeritus of Statistics, wrote: "But the valid data needed to assess and compare [to smaller class size] many alternative strategies [teaching style, teacher quality, and ability grouping] simply don't exist." [M8, p. 35]

In 2007 in a Brookings book, Jan-Eric Gustafsson stated: "Most parents, teachers, and students expect learning to be more efficient in a smaller class than in a larger class. Furthermore, class size is one of the most important variables for determining the level of resources needed for an educational system. Many studies have been conducted on the effects of class size on achievement, but the results have tended to be inconsistent, and at least up to the early 1990s the general conclusion was that neither resources in general, nor class size in particular, have any relation to achievement." Gustafsson further explained that the STAR experiment (Student/Teacher Achievement Ratio)—started in 1985 and continued into the 1990s—showed that by the end of third grade, students assigned to small classes had a "striking advantage," with most gains in first grade. Moreover, the addition of an assistant teacher into a larger class revealed "no clear difference." He summarized from TIMSS data and other studies: "... it appears that smaller classes may have some positive effect on achievement during the first few years of schooling, but little or no effect after that. There are, however, many studies in which the results run against this generalization, so further research is necessary." [G13, pp. 52–53, 55]

In 2012 Mitt Romney, campaigning for President, commented that smaller class size in Massachusetts did not correlate with higher achievement. Critics pounced, saying that he was weak on education policy. Romney experienced backlash from honesty and accuracy. [www11–14]

In 2013 Diane Ravitch wrote as one of eleven solutions to education ills: "Reduce class sizes to improve student achievement and behavior." She explained that diversity expands within larger classes, making time demands on teachers to keep students more involved and less disorderly, with the goal of more teaching and less administration. Still, Ravitch admitted: "Reducing class size is costly." Moreover, she summarized: "The research on class size is extensive. Some researchers argue against it, but they are in a minority." [R7, pp. 242, 245]

Time, energy, money, and research expended on reducing class size obscure the other ills of math education. Could the desirable, positive, academic effect that is intuitive to smaller class size be achieved in a cost-effective way while also improving math content quality?

Obstacle 24. Cumulative Review

Too often effective cumulative review is missing from the math curriculum. Even the brightest children forget without practice. I have seen weekly, teacher-generated review that is worthless due to brevity and superficiality. Moreover, textbooks promoted as spiral-based often have another problem: the original lessons were so brief that the topics were never fully understood, rendering the ongoing cumulative review futile.

In 1996 E. D. Hirsch stressed the importance of retaining material: "The principle that children should enter a new grade already sharing the background knowledge required to understand the teacher and each other is at bottom the principle that enables the functioning of an entire community or nation." [H12, p. 233]

In 2010 Diane Ravitch cited research to underscore the fact that students forget, thus the need for cumulative review: "If these studies are right, then the gains students make each year do not remain in tact and accumulate. You can't just add up the gains of one year and multiply by three, four, or five. Teachers are very important, but students don't remember and retain everything they learn." [R6, p. 186]

Obstacle 25. Homework

For decades, parents and educators have debated the overall pros and cons of homework for each grade as well as what type and how much. Psychology professor Harris Cooper, in his book that is a detailed analysis and synthesis of approximately 120 research studies and 240 articles on homework, wrote this definition: "Homework can be defined as tasks assigned to students by schoolteachers that are intended to be carried out during non-school hours. The word *intended* is used because students may complete homework assignments during study hall, library time, or even during subsequent classes." He categorized homework according to four overlapping goals: *practice*, *preparation*, *extension*, and *integration*. Moreover, Cooper noted that homework varies in quantity assigned, skills required, individualization specified, options offered, deadlines imposed, and independence needed. [C19, pp. xi, 3–5]

Overall Cooper wrote: "Homework is a source of complaint and friction between home and school more often than any other teaching activity. Parents protest that assignments are too long or too short, too hard or too easy, too ambiguous. Teachers complain about a lack of training, a lack of time to prepare effective assignments, and a lack of support from parents and administrators. Students gripe about the time homework takes from their leisure activities, if they understand the value of the exercise at all." [C19, p. ix]

While some elementary students are in after-school programs that provide time for homework, others are busy with extracurricular activities such as sports or music. After dinner and reading, little time remains. Parents rightfully become upset when their children have math "busywork" homework while wasting time in math class. In middle school and high school, where the typical math classroom structure does not permit time for adequate practice, math homework becomes essential.

Educators, while arguing for the benefits of homework, have questioned whether teachers are capable of both planning and grading relevant, worthwhile assignments. The following two quotes illustrate this snag.

In 1969 William Glasser wrote: "Students can't take their teachers home, but they can take home and read books, thus allowing the teacher time to cover additional material and to probe the importance of the subject matter by questions and class discussions." Glasser made several positive points about homework as opportunities to change the class routine, to work at one's own speed, and to supplement with individually selected material. He summarized: "Good assignments that students understand and attempt to do conscientiously each night are valuable in education." However, he noted that the idea of homework is often different from its practice. He called assignments "often excessive and irrelevant" causing frustration, uncoordinated among classes creating sporadic severe burdens, and improperly or irregularly checked yielding students who "hand in anything to get credit." [G7, p. 73]

In 1992 Harold Stevenson and James Stigler stated: "Daily lessons cannot be mastered without review and practice, and American students cannot gain this experience as long as teachers are reluctant to increase the amount of homework and parents and children hold unfavorable views about its value. Americans have some justification for their negative attitudes; homework assignments and workbooks for American children are often criticized as shallow, boring, and repetitious. Providing children with organized and meaningful assignments takes time, and most American teachers do not have sufficient time to devote to this activity." [S25, pp. 68–69]

I had a bright student who initially added a number to one side of an equation and subtracted that number from the other side. By taking the time to grade his algebra homework, I found this easily fixable error. I attribute the countless individual and first-place team trophies that he and his classmates won partly to the large amount of quality homework that they regularly did and I carefully graded.

Curiously, many American parents, though incapable, want to help their children with math homework, as discussed in Obstacle 9. Moreover, a 1998 Associated Press article by a psychiatrist introduced another twist, due to working parents' reliance on grandparents for after-school care: "Depending upon their experience and education, the grandparents also may be unable to help the grandchild with homework." [B18]

In 1995 the U.S. ED published *Helping Your Child with Homework*, revised in 2002 and 2005. [U1] The pamphlet offered advice such as turning off the TV, balancing homework with extracurricular activities, suggesting a regular time, monitoring rather than doing homework, giving praise, encouraging good study habits, avoiding test-cramming, removing distractions, providing supplies, planning for long-term projects, and arranging a quiet, consistent, comfortable, well-lit place. Interestingly, in the Q&A section, the only subject specifically mentioned is math—how parents can help when they don't understand it.

Further, homework benefits the social realm as well as short-term and long-term academic goals. John Rosemond enumerated "The Seven Hidden Values of Homework": *responsibility, autonomy, perseverance, time-management, initiative, self-reliance,* and *resourcefulness.* [R14, pp. 21–23] Harris Cooper also noted similar nonacademic positive effects: "self-direction, self-discipline, organization, independent problem solving, inquisitiveness." Cooper's negative effects were: "1. Satiation (loss of interest, physical and emotional fatigue); 2. Denial of time for leisure or community involvement; 3. Cheating." [C19, pp. 6–9]

Cooper noted: "Throughout the 20th century, public opinion about homework wavered between support and opposition." [C19, p. 1] The following chronological examples display this cycle of comments.

In 1969 William Glasser wrote: "Often in their attempts to work alone at home, young children make the same mistake over and over, thus learning and reinforcing wrong ideas that will be hard to change." [G7, p. 73]

In 1983 *A Nation At Risk* stated: ". . . time spent in the classroom and on homework is often used ineffectively." The report also recommended: "Students in high schools should be assigned far more homework than is now the case." [N11, pp. 21, 29]

In 1987 an Associated Press article titled "Educator Says Homework Not An 'Absolute Good'" quoted David Elkind as saying: "There is absolutely no evidence . . . that homework has any superordinate educational benefits." He commented that battles over homework can mask other issues. Overall, Elkind claimed that homework is valuable if teachers have "the time, energy and commitment to read it thoughtfully and correct it. If the homework is merely checked off, then it is busywork and the young person knows it." [www11-15]

In 1991 a *Newsweek* article titled "The School Reform Fraud" expressed (based on an ED report): "Students who do homework know more than those who don't." [S2]

In 1992 another AP article titled "Homework can exert positive pressure on children" authored by physician Ian Goldberg discussed ". . . two basic groups of children—those who view homework as a positive extension into their home life and those who find it an intrusion." The "positive gratification" comes from "organizing, focusing and thinking" as a continuation of what was interesting to children earlier in the day. But the negative pressure—whether due to self doubt, family instability, or peer rebellion—can display itself in harmful ways. [www11-16]

In 1995 Charles Sykes wrote that NAEP 1994 "found that a third of American seventeen-year-olds say that they are not required to do homework on a daily basis." [S29, p. 20]

In 1998 a *Newsweek* article titled "Homework Doesn't Help" began with these tag lines: "Every night, millions of parents and kids shed blood, sweat and tears over the kitchen table. Now some researchers say these dreaded lessons are generally pointless until middle school." [B7, p. 50]

In 1999 the authors of *The Educated Child* wrote: "The reality is that teachers need most of the daily math period to introduce concepts, check students' comprehension, and help them work through new problems. Often there is little class time left for children to practice what they've learned. Well-designed math homework is the way your child consolidates the knowledge and skills first encountered at school." [B10, p. 334]

Also in 1999 Martin Gross, after mentioning different ways students behave during school instruction, explained: "But homework is the ground zero of study. In the privacy of the home, the textbook or assignment has to be focused on and mastered. It is the core discipline of scholarship, the lonely pursuit of knowledge. How much homework do Americans do? Too little." He blamed teachers for "inadequate homework assignments—a symbol of their laxity." As teachers' reasons he listed fear of students' disliking them, distaste for grading papers, disdain for rigorous academics, and recollections of their own past. [G12, pp. 196, 198]

In 2001 in discussing whether homework works, Harris Cooper concluded: "In sum, the effect of homework on the achievement of young children appears to be small, even bordering on trivial. However, for high school students the effect of homework can be impressive." He concluded his comprehensive book on homework by stating: "Teachers should avoid the extremes." [C19, pp. 23, 77]

In 2004 a *New York Times* article titled "When Homework Takes Over" named an academically prominent county in which "homework is a constant irritant, a badge of honor and a force in the family." The author quoted an elementary school principal: "Homework is a very hot topic. ... Parents sometimes have the idea that if they see more homework, the more they think the child is learning. Research shows that homework has no value in itself until fifth grade. Its only value is creating a habit for children to sit down and do homework." [R15]

In 2007 the *Brown Center Report* stated: "Countries where more homework is assigned also evidence no advantage in achievement. In fact, they score lower than nations where homework is less prevalent." Because this finding contradicted a published study while confirmed a popular book, Brookings analyzed TIMSS math data from a different approach—over several years rather than one point in time, unmasking the relationships between assignments' completion time and students' ability level. The report concluded: "The findings presented here—a neutral relationship of homework with achievement and a positive relationship for instructional time with achievement—bring the findings from international data more in line with the findings from other types of research on the impact of time on learning." [L11, pp. 21–23, 27]

In 2014 the *Brown Center Report* began its section titled "Homework in America" stating: "Homework! The topic, no, just the word itself, sparks controversy." In analyzing NAEP data from 1984 to 2012, the report concluded that homework had "remained remarkably stable," increasing somewhat for students nine years old because many had none prior to that age. Author Tom Loveless suggested that "homework horror stories" in recent years in the popular press stemmed "from the very personal discontents of a small group of parents" who tend to have "a larger set of complaints and concerns" about their children's schools, including "quality of homework" and "responsiveness of teachers." Loveless concluded: "Complaints about homework have existed for more than a century, and they show no signs of going away." [L15, p. 24]

Obstacle 26. Summers

Summers create academic regression known as "summer loss," "summer setback," or "summer slide." [S19, p. 1]

Summer Slide is real. In 2011 the Vice President for Policy for the National Summer Learning Association wrote in an Op-Ed: "Summers off are one of the most important, yet least acknowledged, causes of underachievement in our schools. Decades of research confirm that summer learning loss is real." [S19]

Summer Slide is discriminatory. A 2007 comprehensive study stated: "Researchers have found that summer academic loss is not equal for all students. The magnitude of summer loss varies by grade level, subject matter and family income." [S20, p. 2]

Summer Slide is cumulative. This same 2007 report stated: "This problem of summer academic loss ... is more grave when we recognize that many students start school behind and struggle to catch up throughout their K–12 education." [S20, p. 1] Moreover, the same 2011 Op-Ed stated: "This learning loss is cumulative, summer after summer." [S19]

Summer Slide is significant. Researchers published in *The Review of Educational Research*: "A review of 39 studies indicated that achievement test scores decline over summer vacation. ... The meta-analysis indicated that the summer loss equaled about one month on a grade-level equivalent scale .... The effect of summer break was more detrimental for math than for reading ... ." [C20]

One way to reduce summer slide is to shorten summer vacation. In 1983 *A Nation At Risk* called on school systems to lengthen the school year to 200 or 220 days—still to no avail. [N11, p. 29]

A second way to mitigate summer slide is to provide homework. While summer reading lists are plentiful whether through school systems or public libraries, offerings for math practice are rare (forgotten by the schools) or inappropriate (written for the masses). *The Learning Gap* authors addressed this concern: "It is not easy for American parents to find good workbooks. They are sometimes available near check-out counters in grocery stores and at some bookstores, but there is little variety and their content is generally dull and unimaginative." [S25, p. 56]

Even summer math camps have snags. Jo Boaler described her workshops in which students had exciting math experiences in the summer, only in the fall to return to "the same math environments that most had told us they hated ... ." [B14, p. 160] Moreover, in-person and on-line summer tutors can be lacking in rigor and inconsistent with curriculum as well as expensive and hard-to-find.

Some bright students are dispirited as their math teachers spend time reviewing material that classmates should have learned and retained. Some students try out-foxing the system by purposely not learning during the school year to avoid those boring, early months of the next fall. Yet even the most capable math students forget over the summer.

Obstacle 27. Tutoring

Math tutoring is a decades-old industry. As a child, I saw my father and his colleagues expertly tutor in math not only to help struggling students but also to subsidize low salaries. As an adult, I tutored a variety of students for a broad range of math needs at my own education center.

Perhaps overgeneralizing, reasons for continual widespread math tutoring have shifted. No longer solely to improve school performance, tutoring now exists to boost standardized test scores from boarding school entrance to college admission and more. Moreover, gifted students use tutors for enrichment and advancement. As Charles Sykes wrote, "Once stigmatized as a sign of underachievement, tutors are now often hired for high-achieving students who are not academically challenged in their regular schools. Ironically, the private tutors have become a status symbol . . . ." [S29, p. 289] Competent tutors are not only somewhat rare but also rather costly—especially on top of private school tuition. Gifted online courses offered by universities are also available.

Tutoring can be frustrating in today's climate in which students only want to learn their teachers' methods and parents only want to boost their children's grades. Moreover, tutoring has an unintended consequence—because so many non-math math teachers tutor after school for extra income, they further spread poor math instruction. Tutoring can also include online help from places as far away as India.

Less known about NCLB, as described by Diane Ravitch, was the Supplementary Educational Services program or "free after-school tutoring." She wrote that NCLB "implicitly created a 'voucher' program for tutoring companies, a marketplace where tutoring companies and school districts could compete for students." Yet the program was remarkably unsuccessful according to Ravitch, who noted that all parties involved "complained": tutoring agencies who wanted space from the public schools, tutors who balked at buying costly liability insurance, districts who criticized both the ineffectiveness and ploys of the tutoring companies, and students who "did not want a longer school day, even though they needed the extra help." [R6, pp. 100–101]

Finally, math tutoring is an ongoing problem for students entering college. In 2008 the *Final Report of the National Mathematics Advisory Panel* stated: "Consistent with the NAEP findings is the vast and growing demand for remedial mathematics education among students in four-year and community colleges across the nation." [N36, p. 4] Offered at limited facilities, these non-credit courses are often the final lifeline for young adults, eager to succeed but weak in math. [www11–17]

Obstacle 28. Homeschooling

The National Center for Education Statistics reported the following number of homeschooled students in grades K–12: 850,000 in 1999; 1,096,000 in 2003; and 1,508,000 in 2007. [www11–18] In 2012 the NCES estimate grew to almost 1,800,000. [www11–19]

Reasons for homeschooling include dissatisfaction with other options, inclusion of specific subjects, and management of special demands. In homeschooling, the parent may be the principal rather than the teacher, organizing instruction from a variety of sources such as tutors and online education. Numerous homeschool magazines and conferences provide information for families. Community college courses are also available for homeschoolers in high school.

In 1995 Charles Sykes noted a trend: "As the number of parents disillusioned by public education grows, the ranks of stay-at-home schools have swollen." Sykes attributed increased homeschooling to broader "access to computers and on-line tutorial programs." He also noted expanded respect for homeschoolers' academic achievement corresponding to their rise in "numbers and sophistication." [S29, pp. 288–289]

In 1999 Bennett, Finn, and Cribb wrote of their respect for homeschooling because of the "huge commitment." Yet they warned that it should be a choice because of specific desires, not a default due to poor schools: "In America in the twenty-first century, no family should feel it has to educate at home to educate well." [B10, p. 606]

In 2005 Ray Kurzweil commented on the internet as a force in propagating homeschooling: "The accessible, inexpensive, and increasingly high-quality courseware available on the Web is also fueling a trend toward homeschooling." [K15, p. 336]

Based on some homeschoolers whom I have evaluated in math, I would caution about underperformance in the subject. In some ways, home-taught math is only as good as available textbooks. The goal of fixing math education should include home-educated students.

Obstacle 29. Charter, Independent, Magnet, Religious, and Virtual Schooling

Children enrolled by parents in charter, independent, magnet, religious, or virtual schools deserve great math. These schools face the same problems—limited availability of superb teachers and textbooks. True, some of these schools may hire from a broader base of math people without teaching certificates; some may choose from a fuller list of math materials without state designation; and some may evaluate from a sounder selection of math tests without government restrictions. But some don't know a better hire, choice, or evaluation from a lesser.

Children vary in personalities; parents differ in priorities. School options are good up to a point, but parents must realize that children can become puppets for politicians and moneymakers for corporations. Whether due to lack of transparency or overstatements in marketing, claimed success may be illusory. Parents' difficulty in evaluating a great math program remains, no matter the type of school. A school's STEM label does not necessarily equate to quality mathematics. And drained neighborhood schools can decline in societal value, dragging down communities.

Obstacle 30. Grade Inflation

Parents believe that children with an A grade in math know math. They leave teachers alone, not requesting confrontational conferences, not demanding after-school/study-hall extra help, and not sending time-consuming emails. All is well on the surface, with neither the parents' nor teachers' lives interrupted or burdened. On school evenings both parents and teachers can have personal time. But eventually college admission tests reveal the grade inflation hoax. Countless times I was asked how a child with all A grades in honors math could score 500 on the math SAT.

In 1999 Martin Gross referenced College Board's study of the correlation between school grades and SAT scores, saying that CEEB's data "is not a small sample." He summarized the results as showing: *"That as student SAT scores decline, their school grades go up dramatically, proof positive of rampant grade inflation."* [G12, p. 26]

But to survive economically, some colleges have adjusted to students' depleted mathematical knowledge. A 1991 article in *Newsweek* by Robert Samuelson stated: "Even if the plan [education strategy by Secretary of Education Lamar Alexander] were fully adopted, it wouldn't result in better-educated Americans or improved schools. Grade inflation is the national norm: through high grades and easy college admissions, we delude students about how much they know." [S2]

In 1994 the ED issued a report on grade inflation titled "What Do Student Grades Mean? Differences Across Schools." It stated that parents used grades as a measure of educational success: "A prior Research Report on parental satisfaction with schools and the need for standards (November 1992) showed that, despite clear indications and widespread concern about low achievement, most parents express satisfaction with their children's achievement and schools. Part of the reason for their satisfaction is that parents have to rely primarily on grades to determine how much their children are learning—and according to the grades, their children are doing well." However, the 1994 report cautioned: "Given the general trend of grade inflation, however, grades may not provide students and their parents with solid feedback to show them how the students are really doing, and the situation may be especially severe for students in high poverty schools." Moreover, this warning was clear:

"Anyone who considers the 'gentleman's C' to be an average grade is seriously behind the times: today's 'average' grade is a 'B.'" And the report noted: "The 'A' students in the high poverty schools mostly closely resembled the 'D' students in the most affluent schools." [U2]

Charles Sykes addressed grades in his 1995 book: "Grade inflation is both a product and a symptom of dumbing down." Sykes continued: "Giving out ever-higher grades for ever-more mediocre work reflects the collapse of standards throughout the educational system. But the inflation of grades also exacerbates the problem, because inflated grades are so useful in covering up the root causes of the collapse. . . . High grades reassure parents that all is well with their children's education; they make students feel better about themselves, and are a symbol of the persistence of excellence to the wider community." [S29, pp. 30–31]

In the 1990s, beyond grade inflation, a push occurred for no grades. Sykes wrote: "While disputes over grades continue and are often fiercely contested, it can be argued that the fight over grades is already over, at least de facto, if not de jure. The opponents of grades have succeeded in destroying the grading system as an instrument of reward, punishment, and accountability." [S29, p. 31]

In 1996 E. D. Hirsch also criticized the non-grading movement, summarizing the philosophy: "Since in American schools every child is unique and of equal worth with every other child, academic competition, which subverts this egalitarian and individualist creed, must be discouraged. Emphasis is to be placed on the child's unique imagination and creativity, not on the lockstep learning of predetermined and inert traditions. Such individualism leads, it is said, to that independent-mindedness which has made America great. If students are to be graded at all, which subverts the principle of equal worth, the implication is clear: each child deserves to pass. . . . What has been called 'grade inflation' is perhaps more accurately called 'grade egalitarianism' or 'grade individualism.' If followed to its logical extreme, each child's unique spark, being divine, would deserve an A; but since that principle would not be publicly accepted, a policy of nongrading is currently preferred in many schools." [H12, p. 100]

Grade inflation remains a conundrum in the delivery of sound math. Picture yourself as a teacher today, dealing with your students' limited prerequisite knowledge. Might you fear awarding a D or F grade?

Obstacle 31. Report Cards

Individual grades, whether inflated or not, on quizzes, tests, homework, and classroom participation—combined by some customized formula, determined by the teacher or school—form a report card grade.

Imagine Peter who has a 97% average in math class. Peter's teacher uses a rigorous textbook, assigns extensive homework that she grades herself every evening, supplements with contest material, and gives comprehensive math tests with free-response questions. Imagine Paul who has a 93% math average at another school. Paul's teacher uses an abbreviated textbook, skips the more difficult sections, progresses at a slow pace, does not supplement, and gives short math tests with multiple-choice questions. These boys are both A students in math, but they hardly know the same amount of the subject.

The story of Peter and Paul questions the worth of high school transcripts. Homeschoolers are smart to submit the names of their textbooks and as many College Board Achievement Tests (in individual subjects) as possible, given the dubious validity of report card grades. As William Glasser stated in 1969, "Grades are the currency of education. The highest grades are worth the most in terms of honors and entrance into better schools at every level." [G7, p. 61]

In 1958 John Keats wrote: "Please bear in mind that no school has yet devised a universally acceptable report card, and that the chances are no school ever will." [K2, p. 107] Over half a century later, many today would agree with Keats's statement.

Glasser echoed the conflict in changing the five traditional report card letters: "Probably the school practice that most produces failure in students is grading. If there is one sacred part of education, revered throughout almost the entire United States as utilitarian and necessary, it is A-B-C-D-F grading. Because grades are so time honored and traditional, anyone who raises a voice against them finds himself in the center of a hurricane; the defects of grades are so obvious, however, that many prominent people have spoken out against them." [G7, p. 59]

Not wanting to "label" children, schools have adopted other schemes—for example, *Outstanding*, *Satisfactory*, and *Needs Improvement*. But teachers, feeling limited by three categories, included plus and minus signs, yielding grades O, O–, S+, S, S–, and NI, almost translatable back to the usual letter grades. To prevent the possibility of fine tuning each of the three judgments, other schools adopted the plus, check, and minus signs (plus-minus and minus-minus are awkward) but gave teachers more leeway by replacing the single word "mathematics" on the report card with skills such as addition or categories such as probability.

Alternatively, schools required teachers to write a paragraph describing each child's performance—that is until principals and headmasters discovered that too many teachers had difficulty with spelling, grammar, and punctuation as well as coherent, original thoughts. Glasser gave an example of a six-sentence report card paragraph that would surely trigger a parent-teacher conference. Each simple declarative sentence, without any subordination, started with the girl's name or the pronoun "she." Adjectives were uninspiring such as "adequate." Half of the verbs were "needs," as in "She needs," without giving any how-to or get-help advice. The math mentioned was solely the four whole-number operations without any enriched topics. [G7, p. 100] Still, Glasser's example was far better than many report card paragraphs I have seen.

Awarding report card grades can be the worst part of teaching. As Glasser wrote about grades, teachers "hate them," "believe they are harmful to education because they take away time from teaching," "believe they are inaccurate," and "believe they reduce the warm, human involvement possible and necessary between teacher and student." [G7, p. 68]

In 1996 E. D. Hirsch thoughtfully described the predicament: "Few teachers who aren't sadists are fond of grades and tests. After more than thirty years of teaching, I still view those parts of my job with a distaste that has grown rather than diminished with the years. Teachers want all of their students to be *A* students, each in his or her own way. They want them to work hard without the extrinsic motivations of punishment and reward, and to be motivated entirely by intrinsic interest in the subject matter at hand and by the inherent joys of learning and accomplishment. . . . Moreover, most teachers strongly dislike disappointing a student with a bad grade. On the other hand, they also dislike the idea of giving everyone the same grade, because doing so, apart from other disadvantages, is egregiously unfair to students who do better work. Consequently, most teachers feel compelled to perform the disagreeable acts of testing and grading because they feel a sense of responsibility not only to honesty and fairness but also—and this is the critical point—to effective teaching. It has been shown convincingly that tests and grades strongly contribute to effective teaching." [H12, p. 181]

The following are six potential negative impacts of grades with supporting quotes.

1. Grades can become a replacement for education itself, with students often studying only what is on the test.

"Although grades purport to raise academic standards, there is good evidence that just the opposite is true. When grades become the substitute for learning, and when they become more important than what is learned, they tend to lower academic standards." [G7, p. 65]

2. Grades can stifle both creativity and risk-taking.

"Schools tend to be unforgiving of mistakes. When children hand in workbooks, their errors are often marked with a large and pronounced X. When they answer a question incorrectly in class, some teachers pounce on them, and their classmates snicker. . . . As a result, they become afraid to err and thus to risk the kind of independent, if sometimes flawed, thinking that can lead to the development of creative intelligence." [S24, p. 202]

3. Poor grades can close doors to further opportunities.

"Another sinister attribute of grades is that they are limiting and damning for life. In a world that sometimes judges people by their records rather than by themselves, a student with low grades has little chance to advance to high education." [G7, pp. 63–64]

4. The meaning of a C has morphed from satisfactory to poor, thereby skewing the entire scale.

"Another major flaw in the five-level system is that it is phony. That is, no one believes the formal definition of a satisfactory grade." [G7, p. 62]

5. The importance of grades could encourage students to partake in unscrupulous behavior from mis-grading a classmate's homework at one extreme to falsifying an ID for a standardized test at the other extreme.

"Grades are also bad because they encourage cheating." [G7, p. 64]

6. Schools become identified by their students' grades.

"Grades were originally conceived as an objective measure . . . of a child's progress. . . . Today, grades are the be-all and end-all of education. The only acceptable grades are good ones, and these good grades divide school successes from school failures." [G7, p. 60]

Obstacle 32. Transparency

Transparency is worse in math than in other subjects, whether parents send their children to public, private, or parochial schools. When a school says that its adopted math textbooks are excellent or that children are doing well in math, many parents accept the statements at face value. They don't know enough math to assess the situation.

In a website video called "Making technology work for education" made by the Center for Universal Education, Julia Gillard, former Prime Minister of Australia, suggested that statistics could be posted online to help parents evaluate schools. [G6] Rather than rely on dubious reputations and gossip, for example, means, medians, modes, ranges, and outliers for standardized tests per grade level, posted annually and retained, would be informative. Perhaps a school's scores were significantly higher with a previous faculty. Similarly, course pacing would help: parents might realize that having an A in algebra in November is unimpressive if they knew the class was still in chapter two of a 12-chapter book.

Indeed, Charles Sykes wrote in his 1995 book, "The lack of any reliable feedback from the schools means that many parents have a hopelessly inflated notion of their child's performance." [S29, p. 31] Sykes warned against reacting overly positively to "papers and tests festooned with gold stars." He expounded that "the lack of reliable information from the schools" to parents leads to "the nation's continuing state of denial about its educational collapse," making "it hard for parents to play their own proper role in turning the schools around." [S29, p. 291]

In 2006 former Secretary of Education Rod Paige wrote that in the NCLB education policy agenda, one of the three keys to excellence was transparency: "We have to make sure that parents and taxpayers have solid, easily accessible, accurate information in order to judge whether their schools are succeeding or not, for all children." [P1, p. 14]

Obstacle 33. Standardized Testing—School Assessment

Arthur Bestor expressed that because tests "are the universally recognized means of measuring the actual training and qualifications" of all people, regardless of age and profession, tests are a necessary evil. He wrote: "Rigorous, comprehensive examinations, which test the power to think as well as to remember, are expensive to prepare and tedious to grade. But they are not so expensive as the waste of educational and human resources that occurs without them, and they are not so tedious as is the process of pushing unprepared students through courses they are not equipped to handle." [B11, pp. 148, 157]

Jerome Bruner also commented on the dual nature of testing: "It is obvious that an examination can be bad in the sense of emphasizing trivial aspects of a subject. Such examinations can encourage teaching in a disconnected fashion and learning by rote. What is often overlooked, however, is that examinations can also be allies in the battle to improve curricula and teaching." [B21, p. 30]

E. D. Hirsch reviewed "some different functions" of tests. His examples included: (1) providing feedback on meeting educational goals; (2) assessing readiness for new goals; (3) furthering learning while studying for tests; (4) attracting students' attention and increasing their motivation; and (5) providing information on schools' overall performance. He remarked: ". . . I view the war on standardized tests as mainly a disheartened, scapegoating attempt to shoot the messenger that is bringing the bad news. Educators would hardly be so preoccupied with attacking standardized tests, and blaming them for the ineffectiveness and inequality of American schooling, if those machine-scored messengers were bringing less depressing bulletins, or if educators had workable ideas about how to make the results better." [H12, pp. 177–180]

Furthermore, a 2004 article in *Business Review*, after an analysis of all ways in which test scores could be misleading, concluded: "Despite the shortcomings of standardized test scores as a measure of school performance, there is no generally recognized substitute; test scores simply have to be used with caution." [C22, p. 13]

Standardized tests can certainly go astray. For example, outcry from parents over a June, 2003 New York Regents Math exam was so harsh that newspapers from Buffalo to New York City covered the story. An editorial in *Barron's* confirmed the exam's overly dense math vocabulary with several math experts and quoted one parent as saying, "But for the average student, this test was nothing short of child abuse." [D7]

School standardized testing existed well before NCLB. The same *Business Review* article noted that Title I of the 1965 Elementary and Secondary Education Act "required the periodic testing of students in the program to assess its effectiveness." [C22, p. 6] The lack of growth in student achievement on NAEP contributed to the accountability features of NCLB, which gave testing its negative reputation.

At a 2004 event, a high school student asked Governor Jeb Bush of Florida, a strong proponent of testing, if he could answer one of the questions from the 10th grade FCAT (the NCLB FL test): name the angles of a 3–4–5 triangle. Bush replied, "I don't know, 125, 90 and whatever remains on 180?" Mistake #1: Note that 125 plus 90 is already greater than 180. In a right triangle, the other two angles must be acute to make an angle sum of 180. (Using trigonometry, the angles are 90, 53, and 37, rounded to the nearest whole numbers.) He further said, "The fact that a 51-year-old man can't answer a question, is really not relevant. You're still going to have to take the FCAT and you're still going to have to pass it in order to get a high school degree." [S8] Mistake #2: Saying that students should keep open their career options—such as engineering—would have been more encouraging than his just-do-it advice.

Regarding NCLB, Diane Ravitch wrote: "Almost all states report that, based on their own tests, incredibly large proportions of their students meet high standards. Yet the scores on the federal test [NAEP] . . . were far lower. Basically, the states have embraced low standards and grade inflation." [R4] The argument that a comparison between NCLB and NAEP exams is unfair because students "try harder on the tests that count" is specious. [R6, p. 106] Ravitch claimed: "Many states model their testing on the national program, but still cling to lower standards for fear of alienating the public and embarrassing public officials responsible for education." [R4] This analysis begs the question: Should NAEP be expanded to replace wasteful, questionable state tests?

Common Core also requires testing. Debate is ongoing whether the new tests are better or worse. FairTest reported that CCSS tests are "yielding a new generation of testing nightmares, for students, teachers, parents and administrators." FairTest, in citing that CCSS exams "are meant to be harder to pass," also noted the irony in Arne Duncan's praising the initial bad results, quoting the Education Secretary: "Too many school systems lied to children, families and communities. . . . Finally, we are holding ourselves accountable as educators." [F1] Ideally, *harder* would mean *truer* rather than *trickier*.

If math questions seem contorted, they are written to test a specific subpoint of a standard. According to a *Harvard Education Letter*, this matching of standards and questions is improving with CCSS: "... in many states, test developers are given the standards to measure; they disappear into what we call a 'black box,' and out comes a test that supposedly measures the standards. Afterward, someone does a study that assesses the alignment between the standards and the assessment to see how well the test actually addresses the content and the intellectual demands that the standards call for. What's new is that ... alignment is built in from the beginning of test development, and the process is very transparent. So people—whether they are parents, teachers, or policy makers—if they take the time, can see what is being assessed and how." [W1]

Psychologist Robert Sternberg noted that a test has two key components: (1) Validity—"Does it measure what it is supposed to measure?" and (2) Reliability—Does it "consistently" measure what it is designed to measure? [S24, pp. 71, 75] These two points are very important because scores are now being additionally used to evaluate teachers' success—a violation of both validity (the tests' purpose) and reliability (the students' background). Diane Ravitch agreed: "The cardinal rule of psychometrics is this: a test should be used only for the purpose for which it is designed. The [state] tests are designed to measure student performance in comparison to a norm; they are not designed to measure teacher quality or teacher 'performance.'" [R7, p. 111]

Unfortunately, despite some benefits, school standardized testing has the following twelve unintended consequences.

1. Shaping the curriculum
Diane Ravitch wrote: "Tests should follow the curriculum. They should be based on the curriculum. They should not replace it or precede it." [R6, p. 16] And Jo Boaler stated: "The poorly written tests that do not assess important mathematical thinking are driving the curriculum in schools." [B14, p. 88]

2. Discouraging advanced thinking
E. D. Hirsch expressed: "It is certainly true that if students are consistently given tests that do not require or measure higher-order skills, then those tests will not encourage the teaching of higher-order skills. This

is evident to common sense, no matter what the format of the test, and independent of the fact that it is standardized . . . ." [H12, p. 198]

3. Missing teaching opportunities
Jo Boaler quoted an educator who noted: "The most engaging questions kids bring up spontaneously—'teachable moments'—become annoyances. Excitement about learning pulls in one direction; covering the material that will be on the test pulls in the other." [B14, p. 88]

4. Shifting school emphasis
David Elkind stated: "When tests become the focal point of education, they add to the pressures on children in another way. Testing is stressful at all age levels, but it adds to the pressure when test results are widely publicized in the local newspapers and on local television shows. And when teachers and administrators appreciate that student test scores are read as a measure of their competence, they concentrate on how well the students do on tests rather than on how well they learn. Under these circumstances children discover very quickly that passing tests, rather than meaningful learning, is what school is all about." [E1, p. 56]

5. Teaching to the test
William Schmidt and Curtis McKnight wrote: "Tests cannot cover all the content in an area that students are expected to learn. They sample the content on which they will test, defining only a representative sample of that content. Teaching to the test, therefore, has the potential to dilute content coverage that is not included on the test (often based on past experience with the tests). Different teachers within the same district or state are likely to interpret signals from past tests differently. . . . Both reactions [ignoring test results or using test results to shape instructional plans] exacerbate the differences in content coverage . . . ." [S7, p. 182]

Moreover, Diane Ravitch quoted a psychometrician who conducted an experiment showing "that coaching students for state tests produces test score inflation and the illusion of progress." Retesting students who "had shown impressive gains," the researcher "found that the gains disappeared when the students took a different test of similar material . . . . The skills the students had learned were specific to the test and were not generalizable to unexpected situations. The scores had gone up, but the students were not better educated." [R6, pp. 159–160]

For those who claim one can't teach to a certain test, I have successfully proved otherwise. At my education center as a tutor/coach, I taught to countless tests, including those supposedly measuring aptitude.

6. Destroying time value
Diane Ravitch wrote: "Surely, there is value in structured, disciplined learning . . . in . . . mathematics; students need to learn to study and to think; they need the skills and knowledge that are patiently acquired over time. Just as surely, there is value in the activities and projects that encourage innovation. The incessant demand for more testing and standardization advances neither." [R7, p. 73]

7. Making money off children
In 2007 *Parade* magazine's "Intelligence Report" featured "Making a Profit Off Kids," stating: "The school testing and testing services industry (which includes tutoring, test prep courses and the tests themselves) is now an estimated $2.3 billion a year enterprise, with just five big companies controlling 90% of the statewide testing revenue." [P5] In 2010 Diane Ravitch also commented: "The law [NCLB] generated huge revenues for tutoring and testing services, which became a sizable industry. Companies that offered tutoring, tests, and test-prep materials were raking in billions of dollars annually from federal, state, and local governments, but the advantages to the nation's students were not obvious." [R6, p. 101] In 2014 an *Education Week* article cited that the top few testing companies alone had received a combined total worth over $300 million awarded through state contracts with federal money. [C5]

8. Cheating
Diane Ravitch wrote: "The most reprehensible form of gaming the system is plain old-fashioned cheating. There have been many news stories about a teacher or principal who was fired for correcting students' answers before handing in the tests or leaking the questions in advance to students. In some instances, the cheating is systematic, not idiosyncratic." [R6, p. 155] And Charles Sykes stated: "Given the high stakes,

the pressures on schools to cheat on their testing may have proven irresistible to some." [S29, p. 146]

9. Misleading parents and politicians
Diane Ravitch wrote: "The problem with using tests to make important decisions about people's lives is that standardized tests are not precise instruments. Unfortunately, most elected officials do not realize this, nor does the general public. The public thinks the tests have scientific validity . . . ." [R6, p. 152]

William Schmidt and Curtis McKnight studied 4th and 8th grade math scores from fourteen states. They concluded: "The tests . . . make it impossible for parents or policymakers to know which states are doing a better job in mathematics instruction. The content of the assessments in our study varied dramatically from state to state. A child's score and official conclusions as to the child's proficiency in mathematics could well change if that child were to move to another state." [S7, pp. 181–185]

10. Discouraging good teachers
An issue of *FairTest Examiner* discussed that "to the dismay of many parents, some highly respected teachers decided to leave" the profession due to impact of testing. [F1]

11. Increasing dropout rates
Jo Boaler wrote: "The high-stakes tests also produced a number of unintended negative consequences, such as teachers leaving the profession, increased high school dropout rates, and cheating by teachers and schools." [B14, p. 89]

12. Losing long-term vision
Diane Ravitch wrote: "Test-based accountability—not standards—became our national education policy [via NCLB]. There was no underlying vision of what education should be or how one might improve schools." [R6, p. 21]

Ultimately, Jerome Bruner's wisdom prevails: "If we have a sense of what is worth measuring, we shall measure better." [B22, p. 171]

Obstacle 34. Standardized Testing—University Admission

Whether on the SAT or ACT for college or—to name just a few—on the GRE, GMAT, or DAT for graduate school, business school, or dental school, respectively, students need to know math to gain university admission. The math sections on these exams can keep students from fulfilling their dreams. As mentioned in Obstacle 30, I was often asked why A honors math grades did not translate into high standardized test scores. The answer was multi-faceted: inflated grades due to curved tests or extra credit opportunities, a non-integrated math curriculum, lack of cumulative review, calculator dependence, limited breadth and depth of important topics, excessive time on extraneous areas, and over-reliance on equations rather than other problem solving representations.

While the power of these tests cannot be underestimated, factions are working to diminish their reach. FairTest reported that 900 accredited colleges now engage in "test-optional" admissions. [www11–20]

A brief look at the background of the SAT reveals not only its co-mingled stance with curriculum development but also its fluctuating position over test content. For example, as noted by the NCTM, ". . . the committee [of the *1923 Report*] stated content requirements for college entrance which were accepted and used by the College Entrance Examination Board" for the 1926 debut of the SAT. [N17, p. 202]

In 1955 CEEB officials created the Commission on Mathematics due to an "increasing concern about the curriculum they were testing. . . . Did the tests [SAT-M] accurately reflect what the schools were teaching? If so, was this what the schools should be teaching?" [C16, p. xi]

From 1963 to 1980 the mean SAT–M score dropped 40 points. Many— including *ANAR* [N11, pp. 8–9], Arthur Bestor [B11, p. 228], and Robert Sternberg [S24, p. 83]—derided this decline. Sternberg noticed: "Until the test was renormed, what was most notable was the decline of scores in the 700s and 600s—that is near the high end of the scale."

Then in 1994, CEEB announced its re-norming of the SAT: "The 1941 test takers that were used to define the 200 to 800 College Board scale will be replaced by a new reference group from the 1990s. ... Today's seniors are very different from the class of '41, and now is the time to reflect the current population." [C14] CEEB put the average back at 500 (the midpoint of the scale) to easily permit students, parents, and colleges to compare current scores to those of previous high school students. Immediate response to this announcement was harsh in the press. For example, the *Chicago Tribune* ran an article titled "'Recentered' Scores Just Another Step Toward Mediocrity." [www11–21] Of course, one would hope that as time advances, students would become more knowledgeable, causing the re-centering to move in the other direction.

Another landmark year for the SAT was 2005. The math questions were changed somewhat in number, type, and content. Complaints remained that the test was still susceptible to high-priced coaching programs, and more colleges joined the test-optional movement. Then in 2016, an abrupt change befell the SAT—this time an alignment with Common Core. After all, CEEB influenced CCSS development. [www11–22]

With regard to the overall state of math education, consider these two points. First, only college-bound high school seniors—namely actual test-takers—were in the reference group that generated the norm. Thus, the overall math ability of America's teenagers is even lower than the SAT scores show. While college-bound students will become the country's scientists, mathematicians, and computer scientists, all students should learn enough math to have meaningful 21st century employment.

Second, despite a current trend in testing to reflect CCSSM's constructivism, ultimately students need to solidly know straight-forward math—from a high school GED to graduate school admission. For example, the DAT has a Quantitative Reasoning (math) section that includes all of the classic algebra word problems (age, averages, distance-rate-time, mixture, work) as well as wide-ranging topics—algebraic fractions, circles, equations, inequalities, percents, probability, ratios, square roots, triangles, and more. [www11–23] Assuredly, only those candidates who are strong in math can handle the 40 questions in 45 minutes, even having a pop-up calculator on the computer screen during testing.

Obstacle 35. Associations of Math Education

The American Mathematical Society (AMS) was founded in 1888 and the Mathematical Association of America (MAA) in 1915. Both organizations promote research and scholarship in math, primarily at the university level. Thus, to support K–12 math teachers, the National Council of Teachers of Mathematics (NCTM) began in 1920.

The NCTM has produced a major document almost every decade since 1980, explaining in detail what and how school math should be taught. One could consider that these reports birthed the "decades joke" included in Chapter 3. Indeed, in NCTM's own words: "Starting in 1989, the National Council of Teachers of Mathematics (NCTM) has developed and disseminated standards for curriculum, teaching, and assessment." [N24, p. xv] These substantial documents are:

1980: *An Agenda For Action: Recommendations for School Mathematics of the 1980s*
1980: *Priorities in School Mathematics (PRISM)*
1989: *Curriculum and Evaluation Standards for School Mathematics*
1991: *Professional Standards for Teaching Mathematics*
1995: *Assessment Standards for School Mathematics*
2000: *Principles and Standards for School Mathematics*
2006: *Curriculum Focal Points for Prekindergarten through Grade 8 Mathematics: A Quest for Coherence*
2009: *Focus in High School Mathematics: Reasoning and Sense Making* [N18, N19, N20, N21, N22, N24, N26, N27]

Concerning these documents collectively, NCTM stated: "Since their release, they have given focus, coherence, and new ideas to improve mathematics education." [N24, p. ix] The amount of work expended to create these reports to meet NCTM's goal of helping children learn math is laudable. However, one could argue that the opposite of consensus-building occurred. Altering the game-plan every decade is frustrating, when classroom math itself changed little in comparison. Supporting constructivist ideas and textbooks led to learning less math, in my opinion and that of other professionals. While some say that the NCTM proposals were misunderstood at times, the documents were lengthy with plentiful examples. For example, the 2000 *Principles and Standards* is 402 pages.

The 1980 *Agenda* offered sweeping change by promoting "problem solving" as "the focus of school mathematics in the 1980s." Indeed, Action 1.1 stated: *The mathematics curriculum should be organized around problem solving.* NCTM explained: "True problem-solving power requires a wide repertoire of knowledge, not only of particular skills and concepts but also of the relationships among them and the fundamental principles that unify them. Each problem cannot be treated as an isolated example." [N18, p. 2]

Concurrently with the *Agenda*, NCTM conducted and published an extensive survey of math teachers, math supervisors, math teacher educators, school principals, junior college math teachers, presidents of PTO organizations, and presidents of school boards. [N19, p. 5] NCTM wrote: "The Priorities in School Mathematics Project (PRISM) was designed . . . to collect information on current beliefs and reactions to possible mathematics curriculum changes during the 1980s. . . . Thus the data have a continuing usefulness as efforts are made to implement NCTM's *Agenda for Action* or seek other changes in the mathematics curriculum." [N19, p. 3] Why conduct a survey? Perhaps, the lesson of the New Math was alive: teachers could not cope with both radical change and sophisticated math. Organizing lessons around problem solving rather than textbook chapter topics was similarly too advanced for the majority of math teachers. Thus, 1989 brought a new document and approach, with the 1991 detailed companion guide for teachers.

With a problem solving approach, teachers needed to be master problem solvers, guiding students to choose tools and make connections. The next decade, emphasis shifted with the classroom becoming student-centered rather than teacher-centered. For example, in the 1991 document, one standard stated: "The teacher of mathematics should create a learning environment that fosters the development of each student's mathematical power by—providing and structuring the time necessary to explore sound mathematics and grapple with significant ideas and problems; ... and by consistently expecting and encouraging students to work independently or collaboratively to make sense of mathematics." [N21, p. 57] But, as discussed in Chapter 10, the approach in the 1989 and 1991 reports ignited the Math Wars.

NCTM's 2000 document attempted to right the wrongs of the previous plan. For example, the start of the report valiantly stated: "The vision for mathematics education described in *Principles and Standards for School Mathematics* is highly ambitious. Achieving it requires solid mathematics curricula, competent and knowledgeable teachers who can integrate instruction with assessment, education policies that enhance and support learning, classrooms with ready access to technology, and a commitment to both equity and excellence." [N24, p. 3]

However, one page later, as if trying to appeal to all factions (not only the strict but also the fuzzy), the 2000 report stated: "The need to understand and be able to use mathematics in everyday life and in the workplace has never been greater and will continue to increase." [N24, p. 4] The authors then described four points: *Mathematics for life*; *Mathematics as a part of cultural heritage*; *Mathematics for the workplace*; and *Mathematics for the scientific and technical community*.

The 2000 report named five *Content Standards* (Number and Operations; Algebra; Geometry; Measurement; Data Analysis and Probability) as well as five *Process Standards* (Problem Solving; Reasoning and Proof; Communication; Connections; Representation). [N24, p. 29] I argue that the three last Process Standards were sometimes carried to extremes by publishers and teachers.

Communication—
The NCTM report stated that when students have occasions and help in experiencing verbal forms of math communication—oral (speaking and listening) as well as written (reading and writing), the benefit is twofold: "they communicate to learn mathematics, and they learn to communicate mathematically." NCTM noted that through ongoing practice, cogency develops. Further, students would "acquire and recognize conventional mathematical styles of dialogue and argument." [N24, pp. 60, 62] Un-

fortunately, the younger students spent too much time writing about their feelings for math rather than actually doing math. The older students, most not planning to become professional mathematicians, only wanted to learn the math they needed, not styles of proofs absent from textbooks, standardized tests, and math competitions.

Connections—
The report correctly stated: "The notion that mathematical ideas are connected should permeate the school mathematics experience at all levels." [N24, p. 64] Then the report expanded the process standard by urging students to encounter math in other academic classes. Taking the matter a step further, the report also promoted the connection of math to "students' daily lives." [N24, pp. 65–66] In the first case, computing the area of a rectangle with fractional dimensions appropriately combines a geometry formula with fraction multiplication. In the second case, using fractions on a project in art class is valuable. And in the third case, using fractions to adapt recipes or measure shelving is essential. But math teachers must still teach math—not art and life lessons.

The Connections Standard for grades 3–5 stated: "Teachers should encourage students to look for mathematical ideas throughout the school day." Noteworthy examples included geometry in art, data in social studies, statistics in science, and logic in language arts. [N24, p. 203] Indeed, measurement, charts, and algorithmic thinking appear in a variety of areas. The problem was that publishers implemented this suggestion in both directions—not only seeking math in other subjects but also bringing other subjects into math class. Filling math books with non-math material enabled elementary teachers who neither knew nor liked math to focus on other areas during math time.

Representation—
The 2000 NCTM report made some strong statements about representation, recognizing that various forms—"diagrams, graphical displays, and symbolic expressions"—have consistently been included in school mathematics. NCTM remarked that past teaching of these representations as "ends in themselves" has been a mistake. They noted that representations can help students in several ways: organizing thoughts,

Hindering Solutions

assisting reflection, stabilizing ideas, helping visualization, illuminating complexities, clarifying relationships, and supporting arguments. The report summarized: "The importance of using multiple representations should be emphasized throughout students' mathematical education." [N24, pp. 67–69]

NCTM was not the only to address representation. In 1966 Jerome Bruner wrote: "The power of representation can also be described as its capacity, in the hands of a learner, to connect matters that, on the surface, seem quite separate. This is especially crucial in mathematics." As an example, Bruner used a list of cities as the start and end points of travel, showing paths correctly as a chart but clearer as a directed graph. [B22, pp. 46–48] Moreover, in 2002–2003, representation was the "special topic" for MATHCOUNTS. [M3, pp. 15–18]

Problems with NCTM's emphasis on representation, however, were twofold. First, younger students, perhaps merely wanting to get work done as quickly as possible, tended to use the same few representations for all problems, defeating the purpose of this process standard. Second, older students, as I observed frequently in my SAT–M coaching, would revert to trying to write an equation—familiar but often impossible—when another representation would make the problem more lucid.

More recently, the NCTM's 2006 report for PK–8 [N26] and 2009 report for high school [N27] use—both in the text and in the titles—two of the three buzz words also found in CCSSM's Key Shifts: *focus* and *coherence* (see Chapter 10).

Perhaps more concerning than *shifting approaches* over several decades is *dumbing down*. In 2007 William Schmidt and Richard Houang wrote an article in a Brookings book in which they made charts of math topics at each grade for 1989 NCTM *Standards* and 2006 NCTM *Focal Points*. The category "Exponents, roots, & radicals" first appeared in grade 5 in 1989, but grade 8 in 2006. "Percentages" first appeared in grade 5 in 1989, but grade 7 in 2006 (none in grade 8). "Number theory" occurred in grades 1 through 8 in 1989, but only grades 1, 5, and 7 in 2006. They concluded: "The results of these analyses do not bode were [*sic*] for the

United States. They predict poor levels of performance, especially in the middle grades. In fact, poor [TIMSS] performance in the middle grades has been seen repeatedly, as recently as 2003." [S6, pp. 82–84]

Obstacle 36. Education Organizations

A myriad of companies works on improving education in the U.S. Some are for-profit, others non-profit. Some are fairly recent, others decades old. Some are affiliated with universities, others with foundations. Some are government agencies, others private sector. Some train teachers, others teach students. Some focus on teacher quality, others standardized testing. Some have innocuous names, others targeted titles. Some have a universal mission, others a political bent. Some publish scheduled magazines, others research reports. Some offer math problems, others math advice. Some are ongoing, others terminated. A partial list follows.

100Kin10
Achieve the Core
American Association for the Advancement of Science
American Association of Colleges of Teacher Education
American Board for Certification of Teacher Excellence
American Educational Research Association
American Federation for Children
American Federation of Teachers
American Textbook Council
Association for Early Learning Leaders
Association for Middle Level Education
Association for Supervision and Curriculum Development
Association of Mathematics Teacher Educators
Association of State Supervisors of Mathematics
Better Education for Kids
Bill & Melinda Gates Foundation
Brown Center on Education Policy at The Brookings Institution
Carnegie Corporation of New York
Carnegie Foundation for the Advancement of Teaching
Center for Education Reform
Center for Research in Mathematics and Science Education

Center for Research on Education Outcomes
Center for the Study of Mathematics Curriculum
Center for Universal Education at The Brookings Institution
Center for Women Policy Studies
Center on Education Policy
Change the Equation
Colorado Education Initiative
Core Knowledge Foundation
Council for Exceptional Children
Education Coalition
Education Commission of the States
Education Equality Project
Education Reform Now
Education Trust
Education Week
Educational Excellence Network
EdVoice
ExcelinEd
Figure This!
Foundation for Advancements in Science and Education
Harvard Education Newsletter
Homeschool Legal Defense Association
Institute for Educational Leadership
International Assoc. for the Evaluation of Educational Achievement
International Center for Home Education Research
International Society for Technology in Education
MATHCOUNTS
Math League
Mathematical Sciences Education Board
Mathematics Education Collaborative
National Assessment Governing Board
National Association for the Education of Young Children
National Board for Professional Teaching Standards
National Center for Early Development and Learning
National Center for Education Statistics
National Center for Fair and Open Testing
National Center for Research in Mathematical Sciences Education

National Center on Performance Incentives
National Center on Time & Learning
National Citizens Council for Better Schools
National Commission on Teaching and America's Future
National Council of Supervisors of Mathematics
National Council of Teachers of Mathematics
National Council on Teacher Quality
National Education Association
National Library of Virtual Manipulatives
National Math and Science Initiative
National Museum of Mathematics
National Research Council of The National Academies
National Society for the Study of Education
National Summer Learning Association
New Leaders for New Schools
NewSchools Venture Fund
One-to-One Institute
Organisation for Economic Co-operation and Development
Parent Revolution
Project Lead The Way
Public Agenda
Stand for Children
StudentsFirst
Students for Education Reform
Success For All Foundation
Teach for America
Teach Plus
Teacher Advancement Program
TechBridge
Thomas B. Fordham Institute
Time Out From Testing

Searching "math education" on the websites of many of these organizations yields hundreds of hits with articles about what math is or how to teach it. The large number of these groups, each with substantial activity, is potentially misleading. Despite voluminous quality work, the serious situation in math education persists. These agencies will not uncover a

Hindering Solutions   229

solution to finally fix math education. Concerning education reform organizations in general, Diane Ravitch wrote: "They exist in a giant echo chamber, listening and talking only to one another, dismissing the concerns of parents, teachers, and communities." [R7, p. 22]

Obstacle 37. Research

Dozens of research centers, hundreds of professional journals, and thousands of university dissertations all give false hope that research will fix math education. The volume of material, the paths to implementation, and the means for verification are staggering. Indeed, the CCSS website states that the Common Core standards are "Research- and evidence-based." [www11–24] Opponents challenge that claim.

The following ten points are pertinent to math education research.

1. Research may be irrelevant. In a discussion of dense dissertation topics with strange titles, Charles Sykes wrote: "Because the proto-educationists must produce work that is deemed to be 'original,' they frequently explore questions that no one had ever asked before, perhaps because no one was interested in the answer." [S29, p. 86]

2. Research may be impractical and difficult to apply. The authors of *The Teaching Gap* wrote: "The same distinction between research and practice continues today [as in Dewey's time], perhaps even more strongly. A large gulf separates researchers and classroom teachers. Researchers work on better ways to teach and then hope that their findings will be applied by classroom teachers. We have pointed out . . . that this process has had little effect on standard teaching practice." [S26, pp. 173–174]

3. Research may be ignored. For example, constructivists charged forward during the Math Wars despite findings: "Several studies examining how teachers' use of reform practices is related to student achievement in large numbers of schools and classrooms have also been conducted. Together, the findings can be described as suggesting, at best, a small positive relationship between some aspects of reform-oriented instruction [pedagogy above content] and achievement, but the body of work is far from conclusive, and many of the studies also point to positive relationships with traditional practices as well." [H2, p. 131]

4. Research may be missing, including when instituting a major reform. Lynne Cheney wrote about the Math Wars: "Dr. Frank Allen, a former council [NCTM] president and whole-math opponent, has noted that as the standards were being developed, the council's research advisory committee expressed concern about the failure of the standards commission to provide research support for its recommendations. But the standards' writers were undeterred, and today their views drive the direction of curriculums and textbooks in both public and private schools." [C7]

5. Research may be non-instinctive, producing surprising or undesired results. In analyzing TIMSS data, a researcher published in a Brookings book: "For class size a fairly strong and significant positive effect was found, implying that students who attended larger classes outperformed students who attended smaller classes. This is counterintuitive and does not agree with findings in a large number of other studies . . . . For this age level [grades 7 & 8] the most well-established finding is that class size does not have any effect on achievement." [G13, pp. 42–43]

6. Research may be contradictory. Diane Ravitch cited two different studies from two different research groups but in the same year (2009) and at the same university (Stanford) that each "reached a starkly different conclusion." [R6, p. 142]

7. Research may be manipulated. Diane Ravitch noted one state that claimed 89 percent proficiency or above for its fourth graders on a section of the NCLB state-mandated test, while NAEP reported only 18 percent comparatively. Or, as she wrote referring to the twisting of statistics by charter schools, "The data wars were on!" [R6, pp. 106, 138]

8. Research may be displeasing to the researchers. Jarkko Leino wrote: "We also know very well Piaget's numerous and comprehensive studies that have been used as a basis for education. However, as practical educators we also know how very difficult it is to apply these theories in school settings in order to advance pupils' learning. Most textbooks that have been written according to Piaget's ideas did not satisfy Piaget himself. Even in the field of elementary mathematics teaching, where the most detailed results have been researched and theories developed, we have to confess that much more research is needed." [L4, p. 46]

9. Research may be faulty. E. D. Hirsch criticized ". . . the current consensus on these 'child-centered' principles for being 'progressive, developmentally appropriate, research based, and eminently teachable.' These claims . . . are not 'research based.' . . . No studies of children's learning in mainstream science support these generalizations. With respect to effective learning, the consensus . . . is that their recommendations are worst practice, not 'best practice.'" [H12, p. 173]

10. Research may be inadequate, requiring fresh study. Jerome Bruner desired "more research." He clarified: ". . . what is needed is the daring and freshness of hypotheses that do not take for granted as true what has merely become habitual. I can only hope that in pursuing a theory of instruction, we shall have the courage to recognize what we do not understand and to permit ourselves a new and innocent look." [B22, p. 171]

Obstacle 38. Misguided Experts

When notable, credentialed people take extreme, unjustifiable positions, others waste time and energy debunking the claims rather than moving forward to improve math education. One example involves the topic of fractions, established as vitally important in Obstacle 12.

A 2005 issue of *Penn Arts & Sciences,* quoted Dennis DeTurck, Dean of the College of Arts and Sciences as well as Professor of Mathematics at the University of Pennsylvania, as saying, "I have a simple suggestion when it comes to teaching fractions in elementary school: Don't." [M2, p. 13] In a 2006 "Short Talk" or "60-second Lecture" at Penn, he repeated his assertion, adding: "Despite the fact that great historical and theoretical significance has been imported to fractions and rational numbers, its study should be deferred until it's really needed and can be appreciated, which may not be until after somebody learns calculus. Premature emphasis on rational numbers is of little practical use and turns kids off to further mathematical study because it's so confusing. So I say, 'Down With Fractions!'" [D3]

Naturally, the media reported on such a stance, as seen in the 2008 *USA Today* article "Professor: Fractions should be scrapped" which stated: "DeTurck is stirring the pot again . . . ." Thankfully, journalist Maureen Milford quoted a sound expert—George Andrews, Professor of Mathematics at Pennsylvania State University and then President-elect of the AMS—who said, "All of this is absurd. No wonder mathematical achievements in the country are so abysmal." Milford also wrote about Andrews' fear that DeTurck's idea might "gain traction because of the misguided belief that math education can somehow be made easy." [M4] The back-and-forth between DeTurck and Andrews was also posted in February, 2008 on the MAA website. [www11–25]

Obstacle 39. Media

Newscasters, journalists, and pundits sometimes publicly tout a defeatist attitude toward math. On December 3, 2013 on national television when discussing Common Core, Anderson Cooper said: "Does anyone at this table know what a polynomial is? [crosstalk] I have no idea." [www11–26] Given that Cooper had a New York City private school education leading to admission to Yale, presumably Algebra I and Algebra II as well as pre-calculus were on his high school transcript. Yet his tone implied that polynomials are something strange and difficult for all rather than merely unnecessary and forgotten for him. Cooper's stance is supported by research: "Math anxiety . . . has a peculiar social acceptability. Persons otherwise proud of their educational attainments shamelessly confess to being 'no good at math.'" [R10, p. 281]

This math-phobic phenomenon in the media is especially noticeable during election years. When discussing electoral college statistics or voter category percentages, broadcasters sometimes insert the irrelevant but poisonous words that they were never good at math. Some networks even have a designated math guru, relieving others of numeric duty.

Television commentators rarely cover math—other than America's low

PISA scores every three years. Beyond a heavy dose of politics, citizens are lucky to hear something about science when news relates to global warming, outer space, or medical discovery. On October 4, 2007 reporters covered the 50th anniversary of Sputnik's initial orbit. However, on October 4, 2012 news about the first Obama-Romney debate on the prior evening substantially overshadowed the satellite's 55th anniversary.

Print media shares in influencing the public's opinion of math. For example, in 1946 an issue of *The New Yorker* included a cartoon of a small boy, surrounded by numerous adults at an information booth, asking the attendant: "If it takes John six and a half hours to paint the barn, and it takes Bill four and three-quarter hours to paint the barn, how long will it take John and Bill to paint the barn together?" [R16, p. 231]

During the Sputnik New Math, popular magazines played a role in influencing societal opinion. A 1966 *Mathematics Teacher* article discussed the plentiful articles: "Because these media [popular magazines] represent for most people the major channel of information on 'new math,' there is reason to believe that the image which they project would correlate with the public's attitude toward the subject." [M9, p. 618]

The titles of magazine articles alone, often placed on the covers, were convincing—for example, "Least Popular Subject" (*Time*, 1956). Others reflected positively on the New Math: "Math and Ticktacktoe" (*Time*, 1956), "Tryouts for Good Ideas—the Nation Stirs With New Interest in Science, New Plans for Schools" with a section called "New Patterns in Mathematics" (*Life*, 1958), "Can 'Math' Be Lively?" (*Newsweek*, 1959), "Third R a Snap?" (*Newsweek*, 1959), "Math Is Fun" (*Time*, 1960), "Captivating Key to Math" (*Life*, 1961), and "Math Made Interesting" (*Time*, 1961). [T3, T4, L7, N40, N41, T6, L8, T7]

The 1956 *Newsweek* article "Digits and Dunces" pinpointed what is still a current problem: "The current American difficulties in recruiting enough students for engineering and the sciences may well go back right to the first grade." [N39] The 1958 *Time* article "The New Mathematics" described an exercise of teaching kids and teachers together: "For many of the teachers, the course is anything but a snap. While the pupils grasp the latest teaching with ease, the teachers must first discard much of what they were taught, master such new (to them) terms as Cartesian products, null sets and strict inequalities." [T5] The 1960 *Newsweek* article "Math Made Easy" reported on a seventh grader who answered "56 1/4" immediately, with no paper and pencil, to the question 7 1/2 x 7 1/2. The result was not due to genius or tricks, but an application of the distributive property (FOIL). [N42] And a 1963 *Saturday Review* article declared: "'I just LOVE the commutative law for addition,' purrs one curly-topped first grader." [R16, p. 19]

But the 1965 *Newsweek* article "New Math—Does It Really Add Up?" changed the tone, questioning the validity of the New Math. [N43] Decades later, satirists continued using society's prevailing negativeness toward math as material, as in Dave Barry's 2003 *Miami Herald* column "Who can do the math?" [B2]

In 2005 the AP reported on a poll it conducted jointly with AOL about adult attitudes toward math. About 40% of those polled said that they hated math in school. Double the number of adults said that they hated math as those who said they hated any other subject. About 25% of respondents said that math was their favorite school subject. [L5]

In 2006 *Business Week* featured a positive cover story, teasing with the tag line: "More math geeks are calling the shots in business. Is your industry next?" The article titled "Math Will Rock Your World" encouraged students to study math: "It adds up to an era chock-full of numbers. Outfitting students with the right quantitative skills is a crucial test facing school boards and education ministries worldwide. This is especially true in America. The U.S. has long leaned on foreigners to provide math talent in universities and corporate research labs." The author concluded: "As more of the world's information is pooled into mathematics, the realm of numbers becomes an ever larger meeting ground. It's a percolating laboratory full of surprising connections, and a birthplace for new industries. Yes, it's a magnificent time to know math." [B1, pp. 60, 62]

In 2009 the *Forbes* article "East Versus West" cited research, finding that in the U.S. compared with Japan, people "preferred lawyers over

Hindering Solutions 235

engineers 41-to-1." [A4] And while that ratio reflects *attitude toward* rather than *numbers in* the two professions, a 2006 article reported that the number of annual engineering graduates in China alone to the United States is almost 10 to 1. [www11–27]

In 2010 the *New York Times* published an exciting, informative 15-part series by Steven Strogatz that illuminated the essence and brilliance of math to readers. [www11–28] In 2013 the same newspaper published the editorial "Who Says Math Has to Be Boring?" Making a pro-STEM argument, the piece stated: "The world is moving into a new age of numbers. . . . Just look at where the mathematicians are now. They're helping to map out advertising campaigns, they're changing the nature of research in newsrooms and in biology labs, and they're enabling marketers to forge new one-on-one relationships with customers. As this occurs, more of the economy falls into the realm of numbers." [T2]

Now, the *Wall Street Journal*, in cooperation with the National Museum of Mathematics, publishes a weekly math puzzle under the column heading "Varsity Math." Perhaps if more media promoted math, fewer companies would request H–1B visas for STEM professionals.

Obstacle 40. Technology

In his 1958 book, John Keats quoted involved citizens who advocated for a form of early technology: ". . . it would be useful, although of secondary importance, to have one section of blackboard in each mathematics classroom permanently graphed . . . ." [K2, p. 188] Now, few blackboards exist in classrooms, replaced by smart boards. The International Society for Technology in Education, founded in 1979, acts as a repository for standards, resources, advocacy, conferences, and more.

Chapter 13 discusses the importance of technology in fixing math education. But technology is also an obstacle for three main reasons: false hopes, misuses, and naysayers.

1. False Hopes
The following selections in chronological order exemplify the largely

unfulfilled promise of technology as years have passed.

In 1983 a report by the National Science Board Commission stated: "As a general principle, each mathematics classroom should have available computers and other related electronic technological devices to facilitate the computing and instruction required for mathematics learning and competency. ... Hand calculators should be available in mathematics classrooms (both in elementary and secondary schools) for students on the same basis that textbooks are now provided." The report compared the importance of this technology to "the availability of laboratory equipment for science instruction." [N38, p. 13]

In 1994 the *Prisoners of Time* report by National Education Commission on Time and Learning stated: "Technology is a great unrealized hope in education reform. It can transform learning by improving both the effectiveness of existing time and making more time available through self-guided instruction, both in school and out. Technology has already changed much of the rest of American society—profit and non-profit, private sector and government alike—because it makes it possible to produce more with less. A similar revolution is possible in education. At a minimum, computers and other technological aids promise to rid teachers and administrators of the mundane record keeping that is such a characteristic of school life today, permitting teachers to spend more time designing instructional programs for their students. ... But the true promise of technology lies in the classroom. Technology makes it possible for today's schools to escape the assembly-line mentality of the 'factory model' school. With emerging hardware and software, educators can personalize learning." [N35, p. 37]

In 2001 *Business Week* claimed: "Schools have embraced new technology with fervor in recent years. ... Yet so far, technology has done little to improve the national report card. ... That needs to change since no other tool offers more potential to transform our schools." [S30, p. 80]

In 2007 U.S. Secretary of Education Margaret Spellings held a series of roundtable discussions across the nation on technology in education. She included educators, businessmen, technology professionals, and other stakeholders—both supporters and critics. Her goal was not only to renew an interest in educational technology but also to explore specific, targeted actions for improving learning outcomes. [T13]

Also in 2007 a Brookings piece stated: "The newest trend and hope for education has been that of technology. Technology holds immense potential for improving student performance.... However, to be effective, educational technology has to be used appropriately. Most likely, the full potential of technology has not been reached yet." [P2, p. 221]

In 2010 the *National Education Technology Plan* presented "a model of learning powered by technology, with goals and recommendations in five essential areas: learning, assessment, teaching, infrastructure, and productivity." The report called to: "create multimedia content and share it with the world"; give students the freedom to "pursue their passions in their own way and at their own pace," including outside school; "diagnose and modify the conditions of learning and instructional practices while at the same time determining what students have learned for grading and accountability purposes"; connect both educators and classrooms; build infrastructure that is "always on, available to students, educators, and administrators regardless of their location or the time of day"; and "apply technology to implement personalized learning" based on "competence rather than seat time." However, the report cautioned: "Redesigning education in America for improved productivity is a complex challenge that will require all 50 states, the thousands of districts and schools across the country, the federal government, and other education stakeholders in the public and private sector to come together to design and implement innovative solutions." [O2, pp. x–xv]

In 2015 an article in *Education Week* stated: "Public schools now provide at least one computer for every five students. They spend more than $3 billion per year on digital content. And nearly three-fourths of high school students now say they regularly use a smartphone or tablet in the classroom. But a mountain of evidence indicates that teachers have been painfully slow to transform the ways they teach, despite that massive influx of new technology into their classrooms. The student-centered, hands-on, personalized instruction envisioned by ed-tech proponents remains the exception to the rule." [H11]

2. Misuses

In 1968 B. F. Skinner warned of the potential harm of educational technology, while tempering his caution by listing benefits: "It could well be that a technology of teaching will be unwisely used. It could destroy initiative and creativity; it could make men all alike (and not necessarily in being equally excellent); it could suppress the beneficial effect of accidents on the development of the individual and on the evolution of a culture. On the other hand, it could maximize the genetic endowment of each student; it could make him as skillful, competent, and informed as possible; it could build the greatest diversity of interests; it could lead him to make the greatest possible contributions to the survival and development of his culture." [S17, p. 91]

Mis-using initial school computers was easy—educators were unprepared for them. The size was chunky, occupying space; the speed was slow, wasting time; the memory was small, limiting capacity; the graphics were crude, affecting discernibility; and the software had bugs, causing frustrations. Now from word processing to internet research, computers are essential tools for both class and homework.

In 1998 ETS published *Does It Compute? The Relationship Between Educational Technology and Student Achievement in Mathematics*. In it, using 1996 NAEP data, Harold Wenglinsky found both positive and negative effects of technology on learning. Thus, he concluded: "All of this suggests that computers are neither cure-alls for the problems facing schools, nor mere fads that have no impact on student learning. Rather, *when they are properly used*, [emphasis added] computers may serve as important tools for improving student proficiency in mathematics, as well as the overall learning environment in the school." [W7, p. 4]

In 2007 a Brookings article referenced research in which learning decreased as technology-use increased: "The inverse relationship between technology use and student achievement found in this study is in contrast to other studies that tend to praise the use of technology and showcase its positive results. ... although technology might work exceptionally well when it is used by trained educators, it might not work as well in situations where teachers do not adopt the requisite didactical ideas for its application." [P2, p. 221] Thus, poor teachers can tarnish technology along with the rest of their lessons.

The calculator is perhaps the best and worst used of all educational devices. The same 2007 Brookings article noted: "Calculators can be considered as one of the oldest modern technological devices still being used in mathematics classes. The advent of calculator technology has influenced the teaching of mathematics in a profound way." The authors cited research showing positive experiences with graphing calculators, permitting students "to see, reflect upon, and react with several sequential inputs or outputs," as well as to gain "some understanding of inverse functions and algebraic equivalence." However, these authors cited an ETS study finding that 8th graders who treated computers similar to calculators primarily for routine drill "scored more than half a grade lower than students who did not use them in that way." [P2, pp. 207–208]

In 2013 Amanda Ripley wrote about a boy for whom calculators had been permitted in his American math classes but forbidden in his Polish courses. He observed that his Polish classmates did considerable mental math. "They had learned tricks that had become automatic, so their brains were freed up to do the harder work. It was the difference between being fluent in a language and not." [R13, p. 71]

Indeed, the suggested use of calculators in the early grades by the NCTM was one impetus for the Math Wars. Over-use of calculators impedes development of mental math and number sense. I once tutored a girl who was so dependent on her calculator that she checked -1 times -1 during ACT practice because she didn't trust herself. The launch of the re-designed College Board SAT in March, 2016—with one of the two math sections forbidding calculators—shocked many high schoolers.

3. Naysayers
Prominent educators have been partial or total technology naysayers. In 1960 Jerome Bruner could not foresee the educational technology of the future. But of the trend at the time, he wrote: "Films, audio-visual

aids, and other such devices may have the short-run effect of catching attention. In the long run, they may produce a passive person waiting for some sort of curtain to go up to arouse him." [B21, p. 72]

In 2016 E. D. Hirsch offered a modulated approach: "Those who hope to find amelioration of the 'teacher quality problem' through the use of computers and 'blended learning' may be fostering yet another skills delusion. Technological fixes haven't worked in the past." Hirsch provided some instances in which computers did help, such as in assisting teachers complete non-instructional work and in helping students practice specific routines. While citing that children need "an empathetic personal connection" which neither hardware nor software can provide, he did acknowledge that technology has an "important place" in education—but that it is "supplemental, not transformative." [H14, p. 38]

As for technology in research, Hirsch's perspective was pragmatic: "The Internet . . . mainly rewards people who already have wide knowledge and a big vocabulary. . . . Google is not an equal-opportunity fact finder; it rewards those already in the know. . . . It consolidates educational inequality. . . . it takes knowledge to gain knowledge." [H14, p. 83]

Obstacle 41. Computer Science

I was pleased but bewildered to learn of several new organizations that promote computer coding among today's youth. I say *pleased* because I have long believed that the connection between math and computer programming is exciting to teach and stimulating to learn. Many of my students could program well in three languages (Logo, BASIC, and Pascal) by the end of ninth grade. However, I say *bewildered* because coding is not only difficult but also requires math, logic, and linguistics. Then I discovered that some of these recent offerings use drag-and-drop languages with macros—single instructions that expand into dozens of lines of code in which the math, logic, and linguistics are hidden. Dragging and dropping is better than not programming at all; but without proper math, the full beauty and thrill of coding cannot be experienced.

Historically, early personal computers came with the language BASIC.

A decade later, the versions of BASIC became more sophisticated. Other computer languages, supposedly more intuitive, appeared in schools, but the majority of students still had trouble coding. When application software for databases, spreadsheets, word processing, and desktop publishing became popular, tech classes switched to teaching those, causing most coding instruction to disappear. Logo is one of the early programming languages that continues to thrive.

Of course, these new macro languages—whether in K–12 or vocational-technical schools—are better than nothing. Moreover, Barack Obama's hosting "Computer Science Tech Jams" at the White House and his becoming the first U.S. President "to write a line of computer code" are exciting. [H8] But always remember that true computer programming requires knowledge of discrete mathematics.

In 1985 a *Mathematics Teacher* article described that field of math: "In the past thirty years a number of trends in mathematics curricula have been observed: . . . new math, basic skills, problem solving, and, most recently, discrete mathematics . . . being touted by its proponents as a much needed revolution in mathematics education. . . . discrete mathematics was inspired by mathematics in relation to computers. . . . Since computers operate in a discrete, that is, countable, digital and recursive fashion, they . . . require discrete mathematics . . . [which] is usually defined by its content: mathematical logic, combinatorics, graph theory, algorithmics (the design and analysis of algorithms), abstract and linear algebra, probability, set theory, and number theory. . . . In general discrete mathematics deals with discrete objects and finite processes as opposed to the infinite limits and continuous functions that are the mainstay of calculus and classical analysis." [H5, pp. 334–335]

As described in a 2012 *Harvard Magazine* article, Dean Harry Lewis created the course "Discrete Mathematics for Computer Science" for Harvard undergraduates wanting to study computer science (CS). [L6, p. 54] Harvard is among many colleges requiring this math for its CS majors. But taking such a college course demands a proper K–12 background. The authors of *The Educated Child* wrote: ". . . math instruction is mediocre in many schools. It is ironic that in a society so dependent upon and admiring of technology, Americans often tolerate second- and third-rate mathematics education." [B10, p. 277]

Obstacle 42. Fads

In 1985 Arthur Bestor recognized fads: "Fads, in education as elsewhere, come and go." Further, he urged educators to surpass fads by saying that if his own writing were merely a critique of trivialities that had intruded into schools, "it would serve no higher purpose than as a guidebook to a museum of already faded absurdities. But educational innovation, healthful and necessary as it ever must be, raises constantly the question, What things are of unchanging value?" [B11, p. xii]

In 1995 Charles Sykes complained of pro-fad devotees: "Throughout the 1960s and 1970s, waves of successive fads would sweep over the classroom, from New Math to the Open School. As authority weakened, grades inflated and requirements were scaled back. Even so, the schools came under fire from educational radicals, who did not think the fads went far enough and who now found an enthusiastic audience for their critiques." [S29, p. 221]

In 1999 Bennett, Finn, and Cribb identified one source of fads: "Most colleges of education and graduate schools of education are staffed by professors who transmit and defend the silliest ideas, worst-conceived fads, and most dysfunctional practices in primary and secondary education." [B10, p. 621]

Also in 1999 Stigler and Hiebert warned that the quantity of fads does not equal the measure of achievement: "Reforms in the United States often are tied to particular theories of teaching or to educational fads instead of to specific learning outcomes. Because of this, success often is measured by the degree to which teachers implement recommended practices. Someone is marked as a good teacher because he or she uses cooperative groups or concrete manipulatives, instead of on the basis of his or her students' successful learning." [S26, p. 121]

In 2007 a report by the National Council on Teacher Quality addressed the burden of fads: "... in some domains education schools actually appeared to be doing harm. By pushing endless fads ... they were like anchors weighing down new teachers." [W3, pp. 3–4]

In 2010 Diane Ravitch contrasted the detriment of fads to the worth of content: "One constant has been my skepticism about pedagogical fads, enthusiasms, and movements. The other has been a deep belief in the value of a rich, coherent, school curriculum ... ." Moreover, she called corporate takeover of education a fad: "American education has a long history of infatuation with fads and ill-conceived ideas. The current obsession with making our schools work like a business may be the worst of them, for it threatens to destroy public education." [R6, pp. 2, 222]

The following are a dozen fads—some specific activities, others broad strategies, some formulated by colleges of education and textbook publishers, others at professional meetings. These math recreations might be educational fun for the Wednesday before Thanksgiving—but most schools are closed that day; or they might be productive diversions if math periods were half-days—but many classes are forty-five minutes long. As Diane Ravitch wrote, "... in education, there are no shortcuts, no utopias, and no silver bullets." [R6, p. 3] More specifically, fads do not work. They misdirect students' fragile attention and waste their limited time.

Fad 1. Notebook Quizzes

Notebook quizzes are ludicrous to the point of implausible. With this fad, teachers require students to do math homework in spiral notebooks. Students must first copy not only the page and problem number but also the wording and diagram of each question. This procedure must be followed even when questions may be done quickly by number sense. Why? These quizzes are open-notebook and closed-textbook. Giving only page and problem numbers, teachers instruct students to write the question, draw the diagram, and solve the problem. Conceived as a way for teachers to check whether students are doing their daily assignments, the quizzes undermine math education in many ways: eliminating mental math, wasting enormous time, and undercutting homework purpose.

Fad 2. Problem of the Day

Many workbooks and websites are available that feature a daily math problem. But this method for learning mathematical problem solving does not work—for two main reasons.

First, students cannot learn by doing one problem of a certain type, followed by one problem of another type, and so on repeating the chaos for dozens of problem types. By the time they finally see a repetition, they have forgotten the first exposure. They should practice numerous problems of one kind before moving on to another kind. After mastering several problem types, then the random "problem of the day" could effectively start, but only using problem varieties already learned. After students master more problem types, the collection of available problem types for the problem of the day correspondingly grows.

Second, teachers often don't understand the math in these problems. For example, consider the question with an accompanying diagram, such as a square with two diagonals: *Can you trace the picture without lifting the pencil or repeating a line?* This question type is based on the Seven Bridges of Königsberg problem that led the famous mathematician Euler in the 1700s to invent graph theory generally and Euler paths specifically. [L9, pp. 173–174]

Or consider the problem: *Sue bought some pears at 17 cents each and some oranges at 11 cents each. She spent 73 cents in total. How many of each kind of fruit did she buy?* Young students may reach the answer, 3 pears and 2 oranges, by trial and error or ones-digit analysis.

However, a teacher who wants more of these problems might randomly change the numbers, respectively, to 17¢, 7¢, and 81¢. The solution would be –162 pears and 405 oranges. Or, changing the numbers to 5¢, 35¢, and $1.21 yields a problem with no integral solution. This area of math is called Diophantine equations, in which seemingly simple problems have significant mathematical foundation.

Fad 3. Classroom Games

Hindering Solutions 245

Constructivists, supported by various NCTM publications, encouraged classroom math games. These games used dice, cards, electronics, or other means. Given a choice at home between watching mindless television or playing a math game, the latter is preferable. However, with precious classroom time, learning about order of operations, place value, or any other topic is better done through proper instruction—and I write that from first-hand experience. Often students, for whatever reason, do not make the connection from the artificial game to the actual math.

Fad 4. Popular Games

A 2006 article in the *Wall Street Journal* stated: "The Sudoku craze is getting a little out of hand. . . . Sudoku is even showing up in math classes, thanks to a growing number of Web sites that make it easy to download age-appropriate versions of the puzzle." [V1] Again, playing Sudoku is better for children than watching many TV programs. Not only does Sudoku include valuable mental math arithmetic, but also important pattern recognition. However, math classroom time, limited and precious, should be spent on real math. Facility with Sudoku not does translate to improved algebra performance or increased ACT scores.

The Rubik's Cube actually has a mathematical basis—college-level group theory. [S14] But mindlessly spinning the cube's planes is a waste of time compared to studying genuine math.

Fad 5. Multiplication Arrays

CCSSM, avoiding use of the standard algorithm (based on place value), promotes the method of rectangular arrays for whole number multiplication. For example, to multiply 36 by 45, draw a rectangle and cut it in half both vertically and horizontally, yielding 4 boxes. Outside the rectangle, label the top 30 and 6, and label the left 40 and 5. Write 1200 in the top-left box (for 40 x 30) and 240 in top-right box (for 40 x 6). Write 150 in the bottom-left box (for 5 x 30) and 30 in the bottom-right box (for 5 x 6). Then sum the 4 box entries in a column: 1200 + 240 + 150 + 30. The answer is 1620. No doubt many students are now doing this method (like FOIL, based on the distributive property) mechanically as well. As with polynomials, the method's practicality for larger problems, such as a 4-digit number times a 3-digit number, is questionable.

This CCSSM array method could also be used for 18 x 5 instead of the standard algorithm. However, if the goal is for students to truly gain insight, then all of the following five approaches should be explored.
1. 18 + 2 = 20. 20 x 5 = 100. 2 x 5 = 10. 100 – 10 = 90.
2. 10 x 5 = 50. 8 x 5 = 40. 50 + 40 = 90.
3. 15 x 5 = 75. 3 x 5 = 15. 75 + 15 = 90.
4. 18 x 5 = 9 x 2 x 5 = 9 x 10 = 90.
5. 18 x 5 = 18 x 10 ÷ 2 = 180 ÷ 2 = 90.

Fad 6. Box-and-Whisker Plots

A box-and-whisker plot is a data graph. To construct one, list the data in ascending order. Draw a number line to show the full range of the data. Next, find the median (#2). Thinking of the median as dividing the data into two sets, find the median of the lower half of the data (#1) and the median for the upper half of the data (#3). Draw vertical lines about one-half inch tall on the number line at numbers #1, #2, and #3. Connect the endpoints of those vertical lines to create a landscape-oriented rectangle; it will have a vertical line at the median of the overall data, dividing it into two smaller, attached rectangles. Now draw horizontal line segments from the middle of the vertical sides of the biggest rectangle—one from the left to the least number in the data and one from the right to the greatest. End these segments with a small, vertical segments.

I have never seen a box-and-whisker plot on any math test of significance. Yet I have observed teachers, having learned this fad at a conference, spend over a week on the topic.

Fad 7. Household Math

Sometimes to relieve students' frustration with learning math, teachers decide to do a unit on household or consumer math. The idea is that many children when grown will have to balance a checkbook more than they will need to solve a quadratic equation. But money management, which used to be taught in middle school related arts classes that are now essentially gone, can be taught in conjunction with social studies projects, rather than wasting valuable, limited math time.

Fad 8. Mile Wide/Inch Deep

I discussed the "mile wide, inch deep" expression in conjunction with TIMSS 1995 and CCSSM. Perhaps society will realize that the saying is a fad when future students do not know enough math—when too many topics have been eliminated.

Fad 9. STEM

The STEM movement is actually not new—just re-energized. Most of us attended schools that sponsored science fairs, at which some students chose math or engineering projects. Moreover, the report requested by President Carter (Chapter 9) from the NSF and U.S. ED, "Science and Engineering Education for the 1980s and Beyond," is a precursor to STEM, thirty-plus years in advance. [www11–29]

Based on STEM meetings, projects, and articles, I call STEM *scientific arts and crafts*. STEM's value is its aim to interest more students in science, hopefully leading to more college science majors and professionals. Certainly, future jobs are in the STEM fields; just do an online search for a variety of phrases such as "CBS evening news STEM jobs" or "Brookings Institution STEM jobs," and dozens of articles will pop. However, in my professional opinion, the "M" in STEM should not stand for *mathematics* but for *measurement*—essentially, the one area of math (actually, science) used in most STEM projects. Anyone believing that STEM will increase ACT or SAT math scores is deceived.

Many STEM promoters are not loyalists—they have caved to pressure, now using the acronym STEAM (Science, Technology, Engineering, Art, and Math). I am completely in favor of including art in all students' education, but I am not in favor of watering down STEM. Educators and parents wanting more art might create their own movement. After fifteen seconds of brainstorming, LAW (Literature, Art, and Writing) comes to mind, although a better acronym could be created. Of note, Jerome Bruner, in his summary book of Sputnik math and science initiatives at the Woods Hole Conference, wrote: "The theatre, the arts, music, and the humanities will need the fullest support . . . to maintain and nurture a vigorous pluralism in America." [B21, p. 80]

Fad 10. Math Writing

As discussed in Chapter 10, NCTM's 1989 *Curriculum and Evaluation Standards for School Mathematics* ignited a wave of constructivism. One of the document's five goals was learning to communicate mathematically. [N20] In the classroom, that mission translated into students' keeping math journals in which they were supposed to write about any aspect of their math experiences.

Success with math journals was mixed. Stanford professor Jo Boaler praised them, writing that the journals were for students "a safe place to communicate . . . for those who were afraid or unwilling to share ideas publicly" and for teachers a vehicle "to look for mathematical thinking . . . and to give students feedback." [B14, p. 157]

My experience was quite different. Hired by a school to determine why parents were upset, I discovered that teachers were only on chapter three in February of a twelve-chapter book because of giving students class time to play math games and write in their journals at every opportunity suggested by the textbook. Moreover, one summer when I was teaching algebra at the Duke TIP program, the math coordinator requested that students write daily in journals. After two days, I stopped the practice when students used the opportunity solely to complain.

Fad 11. Cooperative Learning

Cooperative learning is another part of constructivism. As both a student and teacher, I always viewed it as a time-waster.

In 1995 Charles Sykes described one rationale for the approach, noting students' dislike: "Supporters of cooperative learning often suggest that one of the real values of forcing students of various academic levels to work together is that gifted students will learn democratic values and humility in the process. Other educationists argue that gifted students will experience a 'higher-level processing' of material that they have to explain to other, slower students in their groups, and will therefore improve their social skills and self-esteem along the way. Students often don't see it that way." [S29, p. 78]

In 1999 Martin Gross labeled cooperative learning a "theory . . . [in which students] will work collaboratively on classroom projects and 'share responsibility' for the success or failure of the group. . . . The theme is student 'interaction' in which the smartest students are supposed to learn as they teach. . . . Rather than bringing the typical youngster up to the level of the smartest student, more than likely it will decrease the amount of knowledge gained by all." [G12, pp. 203–204]

Fad 12. Singapore Math

Various articles promote Singapore math in the eyes of the U.S. public. For example, in 2005 Thomas Friedman wrote an Op-Ed in the *New York Times* titled "Still Eating Our Lunch." [F12] In 2010 the same newspaper published an article in its education section titled "Making Math Lessons as Easy as 1, Pause, 2, Pause . . ." in which author Winnie Hu, along with descriptions of schools switching their textbook series to Singapore, stated, "Singapore math may well be a fad . . . ." [H18]

On the Singapore Math website [www11–30], clicking on FAQ followed by *Primary Math* shows three editions: U.S. Edition (U), Standards Edition (S), and Common Core Edition (C). One question on the FAQ page asks if the Common Core Edition of *Primary Mathematics* is "dumbed down." The answer is "no," stating that the book maintains the integrity of the *Primary Mathematics* curriculum. Thus, if the Common Core and Singapore Math curricula were very far apart, the authors could neither have made that statement nor created a Common Core edition.

To see the differences among the editions, I performed a content analysis of each scope and sequence. [www11–31] Of the 422 skills and concepts, 267 (63%) are identical for all editions (marked CSU); 44 (10.5%) are better for CCSSM; 44 (10.5%) are comparably good for CCSSM; and 67 (16%) are worse for CCSSM. Thus, for 84% of the skills and concepts, the Common Core edition is equal, comparable, or better. This content analysis, along with the Chapter 8 discussion of Singapore's 600 math scores out of 1000, points to a sizable fad.

Obstacle 43. Attitude

While exceptions exist, in general American society views math as a singularly hard, obtuse subject. Many people openly admit that they're not good at math and brainwash children to believe that enjoying math is unfashionable. I have seen both boys and girls try to hide their interest in math from other students for fear of teasing. One can hope that renewed interest in STEM is changing society's attitude.

The negative attitude toward math dates as far back as 1884 with the publication of *Adventures of Huckleberry Finn*. As Huck said at the opening of Chapter Four, "I had been to school most all the time and could spell and read and write just a little, and could say the multiplication table up to six times seven is thirty-five, and I don't reckon I could get any further than that if I was to live forever. I don't take no stock in mathematics anyway." [T14] Huck's brazen but honest words, still relevant, comprised the frontispiece of NCTM's 15th Yearbook in 1940. [N15]

Indeed, the National Committee on Mathematical Requirements began by fortifying math against societal pressure: "*The 1923 Report* had five major areas of impact. First, the report contained a careful attempt to define and defend the purpose of mathematics in secondary education." [N13 in N17, p. 202]

Yet in 1941, the renown mathematician G. H. Hardy was perhaps overly optimistic: "The mass of mathematical truth is obvious and imposing; its practical applications, the bridges and steam-engines and dynamos, obtrude themselves on the dullest imagination. The public does not need to be convinced that there is something in mathematics." [H4, pp. 4–5]

In 1980 NCTM's *Agenda* echoed the *1923 Report*, seeking to affect attitude: "Recommendation 8: Public support for mathematics instruction must be raised to a level commensurate with the importance of mathematical understanding to individuals and society." [N18, p. 26, all capitals in the original]

In 1985 mathematician Alan Schoenfeld identified "three typical student beliefs" about math and their "consequences, in terms of students' behavior," thus outlining the serious, negative effects that poor attitude can have toward learning math.
"*Belief 1*: Formal mathematics has little or nothing to do with real thinking or problem solving.
Consequence: In a problem that calls for discovery, formal mathematics will not be invoked.
Belief 2: Mathematics problems are always solved in less than 10 minutes, if they are solved at all (consider the typical experience of most students).
Consequence: If students cannot solve a problem in 10 minutes, they give up.
Belief 3: Only geniuses are capable of discovering or creating mathematics.
First consequence: If you (a typical student) forget something, too bad. After all, you are not a genius, and you will not be able to derive it on your own.
Second consequence: Students accept procedures at face value, and do not try to understand why they work. After all, such procedures are derived knowledge passed on 'from above.'" [S9, pp. 43–44]

In 1992 Stevenson and Stigler wrote about an "assumption" with a "destructive effect"—that "many American children are incapable of mastering the basic academic curriculum." They further acknowledged another decades-old problem concerning outlook: "Older American students often shy away from seeking distinction in their academic work because it isn't 'cool,' or because they fear they will be labeled nerds, grinds, or bookworms." [S25, pp. 94, 126]

In 1993 Sheila Tobias wrote about the need to change attitudes: "Millions of adults are blocked from professional and personal opportunities because they fear or perform poorly in mathematics. Most of these adults are capable of learning more mathematics. Theirs . . . is not a failure of intellect, but a failure of nerve. For most people, mathematics is more than a subject. It is a *relationship* between themselves and a discipline purported to be 'hard' and reserved for an elite and powerful few. . . . In the short run, these [cures for math anxiety] involve changing attitudes and exploding myths about who can do mathematics and how mathematics competence is measured; in the long run, they require changing popular perceptions about mathematics." [T10, pp. 9–10]

In 2003 humorist Dave Barry parlayed math attitude into a winning column: "Why do our children perform so poorly on standardized tests? Does the fault lie with our teachers? With our school administrators? With our political leaders? Can we, as concerned parents, sue somebody about this and obtain millions of dollars? Or maybe it's time that we parents stopped 'passing the buck' on education. Maybe instead of 'pointing the finger' at everyone else, we should take a hard look at ourselves in the mirror, and place the blame for our children's lousy test scores where it clearly belongs: on our children. They have a terrible attitude." [B2]

In 2008 Jo Boaler described a study that changed attitudes. In the control group, the children's homework was graded with just numeric scores. In the equal-sized experimental group, the children's homework was marked with "constructive feedback." The latter group "learned twice as fast as the control group students, the achievement gap between male and female students was reduced, and students' attitudes toward mathematics became significantly more positive." [B14, p. 102]

In 2013 Amanda Ripley described national attitude toward math in select countries: "Why did these countries [Korea and Finland] have this consensus around rigor? In the education superpowers, every child knew the importance of an education. These countries had experienced national failure in recent memory; they knew what an existential crisis felt like. In many U.S. schools, however, the priorities were muddled beyond recognition." [R13, p. 118]

Obstacle 44: Motivation

Motivation is an amorphous, overlooked factor in math achievement.

In 1966 Jerome Bruner explained: "For curiosity is only one of the intrinsic motives for learning. The drive to achieve competence is another. ... We get interested in what we get good at. In general, it is difficult to sustain interest in an activity unless one achieves some degree of competence." [B22, pp. 117–118]

In 2010 in discussing possible reasons for higher learning gains, Diane Ravitch stated: ". . . motivated students perform best when surrounded by other motivated students." [R6, p. 144]

In 2012 The Center on Education Policy wrote: "Motivation is a central part of a student's educational experience from preschool onward, but it is has received scant attention amid an education reform agenda focused mainly on accountability, standards and tests, teacher quality, and school management. Education reform could benefit from a robust conversation about the overlooked element of student motivation." [www11–32]

Obstacle 45. Sports

In her 2013 book studying international achievement, Amanda Ripley stated that America's obsession with sports was an obstacle not found in the highest scoring countries. She described a girl who, upon entering algebra class in the U.S., saw her teacher—not only the football coach but also a "former star football player at the same school"—talking sports with the football players in the class. Ripley asked: "Would they [math teachers in Finland] spend so much class time on ESPN.com?" Moreover, Ripley explained: "Sports were central to American students' lives and school cultures in a way in which they were not in most education superpowers." [R13, pp. 41, 118]

Ripley commented on the trade-off—acquired character rewards and physical strengths for some versus academic loss for many: "Without a doubt, sports brought many benefits, including lessons in leadership and persistence, not to mention exercise. In most U.S. high schools, however, only a minority of students actually played sports." [R13, p. 118]

Ripley's further point was financial. Given a limited budget, would a principal hire the brilliant math teacher or the average one who could also coach a sport? As Ripley wrote, "Wealth had made rigor unnecessary in the United States, historically speaking. Kids didn't need to master complex material to succeed in life—not until recently, anyway. Other things crowded in, including sports, which embedded themselves in education systems, requiring principals to hire teachers who could also coach (or vice versa). The unholy alliance between school and sports pushed student athletes to spend extreme amounts of energy and time in training before and after school." [R13, p. 119]

As long as the hiring of math teachers and sport coaches is united, great math will not prevail.

Obstacle 46. Myth: Girls vs. Math

In 1968 Rosenthal and Jacobson wrote about the problem of self-fulfilling prophecies in *Pygmalion in the Classroom*. While their discussion was multi-faceted, certainly some teachers, even if inadvertently, treated boys as more talented and successful in math. [R17]

The myth about girls' supposed lack of math ability vaulted front and center in 1971 when Julian Stanley, a psychologist at Johns Hopkins University, created the Study of Mathematically Precocious Youth. Wanting a test with a high enough ceiling, Stanley chose the SAT-M. In those years, Stanley could safely assume that students were not tutored prior to taking the exam.

Stanley was one of the first to report greater math talent for boys than girls. In 1980 his team published *Women and the Mathematical Mystique*. [F11] That same year Stanley co-authored with Camilla Benbow an article in *Science* titled "Sex Differences in Mathematical Ability: Fact or Artifact?" [B8] Sheila Tobias later wrote: "Though the authors admitted that a *liking* for mathematics might predict mathematics *achievement* in the long run, they concluded in no uncertain terms that mathematical *aptitude* is the result of 'superior male mathematical ability.'" Tobias declared that these "controversial results" set back the effort for girls to improve in math by more than a decade. [T10, pp. 92–93]

The Benbow-Stanley study ignited a firestorm of reporting in magazines and journals. These articles included: "Male superiority" in the *Chronicle of Higher Education*, Dec, 1980; "Study suggests boys may be better at math" in *Ann Arbor News*, Dec 6, 1980; "Are Boys Better At Math?" in the *New York Times*, Dec 7, 1980; "Do Males Have a Math Gene?" in *Newsweek*, Dec 15, 1980; "The Gender Factor in Math" in *Time*, Dec 15, 1980; "Boys Have Superior Math Ability, Study Says" in *Education U.S.A.*, Dec 15, 1980; and "Sex + Math = ?" in *Family Weekly*, Jan 25, 1981. [T10, p. 94]

The next landmark in girls' struggle to prove themselves in math occurred in 1992 when one of the 270 sayings (4 chosen randomly by computer per doll) of the Mattel's Teen Talk Barbie Doll was: "Math class is tough." Seeing and hearing Barbie make this brash statement is still available online. [www11–33] According to the *New York Times*, The American Association of University Women was one group that attacked the math comment. Initially, Mattel did not order a recall but offered a swap for anyone who had bought the offensive toy. Eventually, the company removed the phrase from among the selections. [T1]

In 1993 Sheila Tobias, in the second edition of her classic book on math anxiety, wrote that the view of math as a "male domain" was *perception*, not *reality*. [T10, pp. 75, 72] Yet the debate continued.

In the mid-1990s various organizations such as the National Center for Fair and Open Testing filed law suits, claiming bias in standardized tests such as the CEEB SAT. [W10] Diane Ravitch also documented this period, writing: "Feminist critics maintained that this [math test-score] gap [favoring boys] was caused entirely by sexist language or topics in the test questions." [R2, p. 51] The Center for Women Policy Studies called for an investigation into allegedly sex-biased questions on the PSAT (the qualifying test for National Merit Scholarships) and SAT. [S11]

Having examined dozens of authentic PSATs and SATs during this period, my opinion is that girls' lower math scores were due to what was happening at school or at home; the questions were pure math.

The early 2000s brought the start of debunking the female math myth. In 2002 researchers at UNC Chapel Hill published an article titled "Math gender gap doesn't add up." [www11-34]

Then in 2005, *Time* magazine featured the cover story "The Math Myth: The real truth about Women's Brains and the gender gap in Science." In her long, comprehensive piece "Who Says a Woman Can't be Einstein?" on the male versus female brain, Amanda Ripley summarized that "Expectations Matter." She wrote: "One thing we know about the brain is that it is vulnerable to the power of suggestion. There is plenty of evidence that when young women are motivated and encouraged, they excel at science." [R11, p. 59]

Thus, in 2005 when Lawrence Summers, as President of Harvard University, spoke at an economics conference from notes (not a written text), saying that "the under-representation of female scientists at elite universities may stem in part from 'innate' differences between men and women . . . ," the female faculty called for his resignation, which he tendered. Whether his comments were taken out of context (as some claimed) or whether he truly implied that women have lower math aptitude than men (as others heard), his resignation sent a clear message that females would no longer accept the old cliché. [H9] In a letter to the Harvard community, Summers apologized for his comments that "resulted in an unintended signal of discouragement to talented girls and women." [S27]

In 2006 research confirmed that, "Expectations, it turns out, really do make a difference." Reporting on the findings of a Canadian psychology professor, an Associated Press article stated: "Telling women they can't do well in math may turn out to be a self-fulfilling statement. In tests in Canada, women who were told that men and women do math equally well did much better than those who were told there is a genetic difference in math ability. And women who heard there were differences caused by environment—such as math teachers giving more attention to boys—outperformed those who were simply reminded they were females. The women who did better in the tests got nearly twice as many right answers as those in the other groups . . . ." [S5]

Again in 2006, research published in *Education Next* found that teacher-gender matters—"that learning from a teacher of the opposite gender has a detrimental effect on students' academic progress and their engagement in school." Interestingly, this conclusion excluded math for which the results were "unclear" because female math teachers were more often "assigned to lower-performing math students." [D2] This release was picked up by Ben Feller of the Associated Press who reported on at least one women's professional organization that called the conclusions "questionable and inconsistent." [F7]

The watershed year for quelling the "girls versus math" myth was 2008 when five female researchers at the University of Wisconsin and University of California–Berkeley published the article "Gender Similarities Characterize Math Performance" in *Science*. The summary simply stated: "Standardized tests in the U.S. indicate that girls now score just as well as boys in math." [H21]

In addition to publishing the original research article, *Science* followed with a piece titled "Girls = Boy at Math," exclaiming: "Zip. Zilch. Nada. There's no real difference between the scores of U.S. boys and girls on common math tests, according to a massive new study. Educators hope the finding will finally dispel lingering perceptions that girls don't measure up to boys when it comes to crunching numbers." To this end, *Science* quoted the NCTM president: "This shows there's no issue of intellectual ability—and that's a message we still need to get out to some of our parents and teachers." Moreover, *Science* relayed that the lead author said this study should be "good news" for College Board because the conclusion "means the test [SAT–M] isn't biased against girls." [www11–35]

Also in 2008, a study based at Northwestern University found that the gender gap on PISA math tests is "less pronounced in countries where women and men have similar rights and opportunities," according to an A.P. article titled "Gender-based math gap missing in some places." The news agency quoted the researcher as saying, "In more gender-neutral societies, girls are as good as boys in mathematics." [www11–36]

Unfortunately, the myth, though considerably lessened, still somewhat persisted. A 2008 *Time* article, reporting on the Wisconsin/Berkeley study, quoted the lead author as saying that "the stereotype that boys are better at math is alive and strong. Parents still believe it, and teachers still believe it." [P6] As Jo Boaler explained that same year, "Girls do well in math . . . because they are capable and conscientious, but many do so through endurance, and math classroom environments are far from being equitable." [B14, p. 139]

Sadly, as late as 2014, the myth lingered. Another article titled "Both Genders Think Women Are Bad at Basic Math" in *Science* reported on a different study by the same Northwestern researcher, stating: "Men and women employers alike revealed their prejudice against women for a perceived lack of mathematical ability." [B16]

Obstacle 47. United States Government

While superb math education is vital to the nation and deserves government spending, questions arise regarding duplication, accountability, quality, and longevity of funded work. Are projects rigorous or superficial? Have they yielded long-term progress or short-term fads? Have they shown financial value or fiscal waste? Moreover, why are countless projects needed to accomplish a united goal? Mathematics education is not like medical research, which needs multiple teams using different pathways concurrently trying to find a drug or cure a disease.

Actual federal dollars spent are cumbersome to track (due to out-dated and multiple sources) and misleading to evaluate (due to inflation). Certainly, NSF's annual budget increased dramatically after Sputnik: $3.5 million in fiscal year 1952, $4.75 million in 1953, $40 million in 1957, $40 million in 1958; and $140 million 1959. [K13, p. 27] On the NSF website's budget page, the earliest date listed is fiscal year 1997, for which the appropriation was $3.270 billion—$50 million greater than the 1996 funding level. Fast forwarding, for FY 2016 NSF's appropriation was $7.463 billion—$119 million higher than the 2015 funding level. In 2016 the National Science Board (that establishes the policies of the NSF) also received $4.37 million. [www11–37]

The following are a few examples of duplication, misuse, or waste.

• The 1958 National Defense Education Act provided states in the first four years alone with matching funds for over 47,000 math projects costing over 31 million in federal, state, or local funds. [K9, p. 23]

• During the Sputnik era government funding went not only to UICSM and SMSG but also to other groups, based at Ball State Teachers College, Boston College, Stanford University, Syracuse University, and University of Maryland, among others. [N16]

• Diane Ravitch cited a newspaper report in which "35 percent of the federal funds allocated" to one city "was spent for consultants, not for students or teachers or schools." [R7, p. 16]

• The NSF partially funded many of NCTM's projects, including the 1989 *Standards* that led to the Math Wars.

• In 2007 math professor David Klein published an article, naming a "widely used K–5 [math] series" as "one of the worst NSF funded programs." As mentioned in Chapter 10 in the discussion of CCSSM, one mathematician concluded that by the end of 5th grade, students using these NSF-funded texts were roughly two years behind in math. [K6]

• The report of the Eisenhower State Curriculum Frameworks Project stated: "In 1992, the U.S. Department of Education (ED) awarded 3-year grants to five states and the District of Columbia for the development of curriculum frameworks in mathematics or science for grades K–12, together with new approaches to teacher education, certification, and professional development. These grants averaged about $850,000 and ran through September 30, 1995. In 1993, ED awarded 3-year grants to 10 additional states." While Common Core Math has now replaced the bulk of this work, the report was overconfident in its staying power: "The impact of the projects is likely to continue as the frameworks are used by local districts and other ongoing initiatives." [U3, pp. v, 97]

- The America COMPETES Act, signed in 2007 and reauthorized in future years, provided funding to grow the number of STEM majors and to encourage professionals to become K–12 STEM teachers. While seemingly helpful, were these potential new math teachers ultimately placed into a troubled math education system that needed fixing first?

Of note, other valuable government dollars for math go toward adults. For example, the National Security Agency gives grants for unclassified research in math. "The National Security Agency Mathematical Sciences Program (MSP) was started at NSA in 1987 in response to an increasingly urgent need to support mathematics in the United States." [www11-38]

In 1991 the Carnegie Commission on Science, Technology, and Government called for an expansion of the federal government in improving math education—in its goals, number and purpose of agencies, roles of existing federal Departments (Education, Labor, Energy, Defense, and Health and Human Services), amount of funding, and vehicles for coordination, management, and congressional review. [C2, pp. 10–14]

In her 2005 Op-Ed, Diane Ravitch noted that federal money spent on the NAEP tests (math included) is essential: "The federal tests are considered the gold standard for good reason: they are the product of a long-term federal investment in research and development. Unlike the state tests, the federal program tries to align its performance standards with international education standards." [R4]

Ultimately, Amanda Ripley wrote wisely about dollars spent in education: "In essence, PISA revealed what should have been obvious but was not: that spending on education did not make kids smarter. Everything—*everything*—depended on what teachers, parents, and students *did* with those investments." [R13, pp. 17–18]

Obstacle 48: United States Supreme Court

My reply to Katie Couric's now infamous question, *Could you name a Supreme Court decision with which you disagree?*, would be Owasso Independent School District v. Falvo, 534 U.S. 426 (2002). [S28]

Kristja Falvo complained to the teachers and administrators at her children's school that her children were embarrassed or ridiculed when their grades were read aloud in class by students who graded their papers. In October 1998, after officials refused to stop the practice of trading papers, Falvo sued the Owasso, Oklahoma school district, arguing that the practice of peer grading violated her children's right to privacy according to the 1974 Family Educational Rights and Privacy Act. FERPA, also called the Buckley Amendment, prohibits schools that receive federal funds from releasing education records without parental consent.

Losing the initial case, Falvo appealed the decision to the U.S. 10th Circuit Court, which overturned the lower court in October, 2000 by ruling unanimously in her favor. The Owasso school district then appealed the second decision to the U.S. Supreme Court.

Once the Supreme Court accepted the case, some predicted that a ruling for Falvo could open a can of worms, necessitating the outlawing of posting student papers on bulletin boards, naming honor roll students, letting parent volunteers grade papers, and more. Further, in oral arguments, the attorney for the school system added mathematics to the motley collection. "In fact, chalkboard work would have to be an education record. If a teacher asks a student to come to the chalkboard, do a math problem, that's personally identifiable information." [www11–39]

On February 19, 2002, in a 9–0 ruling, the Supreme Court reversed the Circuit Court's decision. In essence, the Justices ruled that the oral reading of one student's grade by a second student is not anything "maintained" by the school district, a requirement for records protected under FERPA. [www11–40] Moreover, in the Court's written opinion, Justice Anthony Kennedy carefully stated: "Under the Court of Appeals' interpretation of FERPA, the federal power would exercise minute control over specific teaching methods and instructional dynamics in classrooms throughout the country. The Congress is not likely to have mandated this result, and we do not interpret the statute to require it."

Rather than keeping to legal issues, Justice Kennedy stepped into unwarranted, pedagogical territory. He wrote in the Opinion of the Court: "Correcting a classmate's work can be as much a part of the assignment as taking the test itself. It is a way to teach material again in a new context, and it helps show students how to assist and respect fellow pupils. By explaining the answers to the class as the students correct the papers, the teacher not only reinforces the lesson but also discovers whether the students have understood the material and are ready to move on."

With all due respect, Justice Kennedy is wrong about one of education's worst abominations. *Correcting a classmate's work* is *as much a part of the assignment* as knowing what that classmate had for breakfast. Material is not taught *again in a new context*—material is not taught, period, during this exercise. The reading of answers and marking of check or cross is as rote as counting sheep to fall asleep. The practice of trading papers neither *helps show students how to assist* others—no assistance occurs—nor does the practice encourage one to *respect fellow pupils*, as teasing throughout the day attests. Moreover, *explaining the answers* typically does not occur—the teachers simply want to get their paperwork done as quickly as possible. And even if teaching did occur, three reasons would prevent the teacher from knowing if the students *understood the material*. First, if a wrong answer is read aloud, the teacher only knows that one student had an error; no generalization could be made without interrupting the process. Second, depending on the problem, the error could be a result of a complete lack of understanding or a tiny arithmetic mistake at the end of excellent work. Third, because students cannot see their own papers, they do not know if they answered correctly or incorrectly, thereby eliminating the possibility of asking a question. A student would unlikely recall answering two, negative two, two tenths, one half, or any other number to a particular problem.

Justice Kennedy also stated in the Opinion of the Court: "Respondent's construction of the term 'education records' to cover student homework or classroom work would impose substantial burdens on teachers across the country. It would force all instructors to take time, which otherwise could be spent teaching and in preparation, to correct an assortment of daily student assignments. Respondent's view would make it much more difficult for teachers to give students immediate guidance. The interpretation respondent urges would force teachers to abandon other customary practices, such as group grading of team assignments."

Again, Justice Kennedy is mistaken. Part of a teacher's *preparation* for the next day is precisely to *correct an assortment of daily student assignments*. The notion that grading papers by teachers is unrealistic is at the core of poor math instruction. My students won countless trophies at math competitions specifically because I took the time every evening to meticulously grade their hundreds of problems. Seeing the exact nature of my students' errors, I could give them *immediate guidance*.

One might accept Justice Kennedy's reasoning that when grades are read aloud, the status of the papers is not yet "maintained," not "kept in a filing cabinet in a records room at the school or on a permanent secure database" and not even in the "teacher's grade book"—at least in the strictest terms of FERPA. Justice Scalia, without objecting to the educational theory, wrote in the Concurring Opinion: ". . . endorsement of a 'central custodian' theory of records is unnecessary for the decision of this case . . . ." Yet Justice Kennedy's opening paragraph in the Opinion of the Court, stating that the court took the case to resolve whether peer grading violated FERPA, is a stunning revelation about how widespread the practice was and might still be.

Certainly, teachers may choose not to engage in the practice of peer grading. But the Supreme Court's commentary—that peer grading is educationally sound—is a travesty of pedagogy. In my novel *School Scandalle*, the protagonist is a female, professionally passionate and overwhelmingly dedicated math teacher who called trading papers "the bane of American math education, the poisonous insult to teaching." During sleepless nights she asked herself: "Was I the only one who considered how students could learn anything by trading papers if they didn't also trade brains?" [W6, p. 24]

Obstacle 49. Bandage Approaches

Small bandage approaches have recycled through the decades, often proposed as new ideas with little knowledge of past failure. They are obstacles to an overall solution because they divert precious attention and offer flawed hope. In 1992 Harold Stevenson and James Stigler summarized the situation for one decade, though their words apply to a century: "In the 1980s, Americans debated how to reform American schools. Committees and commissions churned out countless reports, books, and other documents throughout the decade. Often they proposed simple remedies—more money, choice of schools, smaller classes, higher standards, and merit pay—all of which sounded reasonable and stimulated changes in many states. In view of the meager outcomes that these changes have generally yielded, however, we think it is unlikely that any of them, singly or in combination, can produce enough improvement to reverse the process of deterioration in American schools." [S25, p. 15]

Bandage 1. Stress thinking independently, evaluating the reasonableness of results, and relating math to other subjects and to real life.

All these ideas are has-beens that collectively have had little effect. Regarding independent thinking, the 1899 *Report of the Committee of the Chicago Section of the American Mathematical Society* stated: " . . . the aim should always be to cultivate independent thinking on the part of the pupil. A method which encourages, or even permits, rote work, or mechanical manipulations, is radically wrong. The value of the study of mathematics cannot be realized, not one of its subjects attained, unless the student himself thinks, produces." [A7 in B13, p. 196]

Regarding inspecting results, the same 1899 report stated: "The pupil should be taught to test the accuracy of his results . . . ." [B13, p. 197] A century later, in 2000 the NCTM was still pushing this bandage: ". . . students must be able to perform relatively simple mental computations as the basis for making reasonable estimates and sensible predictions and to spot potential sources of error." [N24, p. 294]

Regarding applying math, this bandage has perhaps had the most voluminous remarks, without fixing math education. The same 1899 report stated: "... the best place for a [math] topic in the course of study is where it is most closely related to other topics ... and to various sciences and the practical affairs of life." [B13, p. 196] In 1902 the MAA President said, " ... the fundamental problem is that of the unification of pure and applied mathematics." [F3, p. 415] The *1923 Report* recommended "the acquisition, in precise form, of those ideas or concepts in terms of which quantitative thinking of the world is done." [B13, p. 393] In 1959 a College Board publication stated: "Moreover, the traditional curriculum fails to reflect adequately the spirit of contemporary mathematics, which seeks to study all possible patterns recognizable by the mind, and by so striving has tremendously increased the power of mathematics as a tool of modern life. Nor does the traditional curriculum give proper emphasis to the fact that the developments and applications of mathematics have always been not only important but [also] indispensable to human progress." [C16, p. 9] In 1985 another CEEB publication clarified the math that people should know: "The ability to apply mathematical techniques in the solution of real-life problems and to recognize when to apply those techniques." [C11, pp. 19–20] In 1991 NCTM's major report emphasized: "Assessment of the teaching of mathematical concepts, procedures, and connections should provide evidence that the teacher ... emphasizes connections between mathematics and other disciplines and connections to daily living." [N21, p. 89] In 2000 NCTM's lead document stated: "The need to understand and be able to use mathematics in everyday life and in the workplace has never been greater and will continue to increase." [N24, p. 4] In 2007 Brookings researchers asserted, based on TIMSS teacher data, that U.S. eighth grade math teachers, "far more than teachers in other countries," claimed that the majority of their teaching was related to real-life. Yet their students did "relatively poorly in setting up an equation to model a real situation" because U.S. teachers, compared to their international counterparts, tended "not to use many high-complexity problems in their lessons ... ." [K4, p. 122]

Bandage 2. Expand pilot programs.

The School of One, now Teach to One, developed in New York City as a pilot was described in the *National Education Technology Plan 2010*. [O2, p. 13] This program is among those with uncertain "statistically significant effects on student achievement" and more importantly, with questionable standing as to whether it can scale up. [www11–41] Any successful school program that cannot be applied nationwide resides in isolation.

Bandage 3. Transfer students to another school.

Moving students among schools is the heart of voucher programs. But large numbers of students will remain, whether at old or new locations, with inferior math due to an inadequate number of quality teachers.

In 2011 in a *PISA IN FOCUS* publication, OECD remarked on the futility of such movement: ". . . in general, school systems that seek to cater to different students' needs by having struggling students repeat grades or by transferring them to other schools do not succeed in producing superior overall results and, in some cases, reinforce socio-economic inequities. Teachers in these systems may have fewer incentives to work with struggling students if they know there is an option of transferring those students to other schools. These school systems need to consider how to create appropriate incentives to ensure that some students are not 'discarded' by the system." [www11–42]

Bandage 4. Hire a math specialist or coach for each school.

Although staffing math specialists—not to teach students but to guide teachers—appears to be a modern idea, it's not. In 1980, in discussing "sexist attitudes" toward math, one suggestion was: "Some alternative must be provided, such as the employment of eager and competent specialists carefully trained" to help teachers. [E2, p. 64] In 1982 another, calling math anxiety "a communicable disease that is being carried by elementary teachers to generations of the student population," recommended providing "mathematics specialists in all elementary schools." [B24, p. 56] And Diane Ravitch noted that for NCLB in certain districts: "Each school was assigned . . . mathematics coaches to monitor and enforce strict implementation of the new mandates." [R6, p. 72]

Bandage 5. Have math specialists, rather than classroom teachers, teach elementary math (at least in grades 4 and 5).

This bandage, too, is decades old. *Educating Americans for the 21st Century*—the 1983 report by the National Science Board Commission on Precollege Education in Mathematics, Science and Technology—stated: "It is strongly suggested that mathematics at the elementary school level be taught by teachers who specialize in mathematics. Whether the teacher specializing in mathematics should be assigned to all grades or just to grades 4–6 (or 4–8) requires further study." [N38, pp. 16–17]

In 2008 the National Mathematics Advisory Panel recommended that "research be conducted on the use of full-time mathematics teachers in elementary school" because of "the Panel's findings about the importance of teachers' mathematical knowledge." [N36, p. 44]

Similarly since 2010, NCTM has recommended the use of Elementary Mathematics Specialists (EMS), teachers who have: "(1) deep and broad understanding of mathematical content, including the specialized knowledge needed for teaching, (2) solid knowledge of the elementary context, (3) expertise in using and helping others use effective instructional and assessment practices that are informed by knowledge of mathematical learning trajectories, (4) knowledge and skills for working with adult learners, and (5) leadership skills necessary to influence and support educational efforts to improve the teaching and learning of mathematics." NCTM said that they are needed because "most elementary teachers are generalists—that is, they study and teach all core subjects—and as a result may find it difficult to develop in-depth mathematics knowledge and expertise in teaching elementary mathematics." NCTM recognized that EMS professionals can work primarily with adults (Bandage 4) or students (Bandage 5). [www11–43]

Bandage 6. Offer Alternate Certification.

Hiring people from non-education paths is one idea to fill the math teacher shortage. In 1999 Martin Gross described one perceived hazard of alternatively prepared teachers: ". . . but much of the Establishment is still in mortal fear that alternate-route teachers will raise the bar on competence and eventually push 'regular' teachers out." [G12, p. 179]

In 2007 *Alternative Certification Isn't Alternative* by the NCTQ confirmed the threat, but acknowledged that the system absorbed it: "Alternative certification was not always such an ambiguous concept. At its inception 25 years ago, there was clear consensus about what it *should* be: a responsible way to get smart, talented individuals into the classroom without requiring them to earn a second bachelor's degree or its equivalent. Alternative certification posed an immediate threat to teacher educators, who viewed it as both irresponsible and as the potential end to their own livelihoods. They needn't have worried. A quarter century later colleges of education now operate most of the nation's alternate route programs . . . ." [W3, p. 9]

But minimizing the affront to established teachers meant diminishing the plan's effectiveness. The NCTQ authors stated that colleges of education, in self-protection mode, hijacked the potentially powerful idea to improve teaching, creating a majority of alternate route programs that have: (1) become "mirror images of traditional programs" without streamlining coursework; (2) acted "remarkably nonselective[ly]" without imposing substantial admission criteria; (3) shown "little flexibility regarding candidate background" without allowing candidates to demonstrate their knowledge in a subject area; and (4) provided "woefully inadequate training and support to their candidates" without providing initial summer practice teaching or weekly school-year mentoring. In sum: "No program [surveyed] fully meets the original intent of the alternative certification movement." [W3, p. 10]

Obstacle 50. Individuality vs. Replication

In 1999 Howard Gardner promoted individuality, stating that uniform schooling with unvarying studying and testing was "antagonistic" to his theory of multiple intelligences. [G4, p. 150]

Also in 1999, well after Sputnik New Math but long before CCSSM, an NCTM publication titled "Who Should Determine What You Teach?"

contrasted local control in the U.S. to ministers of education in foreign countries in attempting to answer the title's all-important question, acknowledging that state authorities, school boards, testing companies, professional organizations, textbooks, college-admission requirements, and math teachers all exerted influence on curriculum. [N23]

However, one must ask: Can each of the math teachers in the nation realistically create 180 coherent lessons for each of the subjects they teach? Does that approach yield the best outcome for the greatest number of students or use teachers' limited time wisely? Why not create master lessons for teachers to share?

In a chapter named "The Educational Fall of France" in his 2016 book, E. D. Hirsch attributed the significant drop of French students' test scores to the Americanization of the French curriculum with individualized programs. [H14, pp. 131–158] Hirsch explained: "For many decades the French elementary school had been the pride and the terror of the young, with every child, rich or poor, having to undergo the very same rigors under the same national curriculum." However, in 1989 (by a new law) France went from a centrally controlled school system to a decentralized one with local control. Hirsch wrote that the abrupt and total curricular change in France, documented in clear detail in France's superb education data, had an astonishing, unforeseen result: "France has thus traced its own decline in achievement and equity with remarkable precision." [H14, pp. 3, 135, 143]

As seen in Chapter 8 of *From STEM To STEW*, France's PISA scores dropped considerably starting in 2006, exactly when the students exposed to the new curriculum had reached the age of fifteen. These PISA numbers give credence to Hirsch's deduction—that the fall of test scores and the rise of individualization in France were remarkably in sync. He summarized: "Thus the intellectual origins of the French 'debacle' were largely the same theories as the ones that created 'a nation at risk' in the United States: the theory that schooling should be natural, and that the aim of schooling should be the development of individuality and critical-thinking skills." Hirsch also importantly warned that the U.S., lacking "large-scale, curriculum-related data" should learn from the French escapade. [H14, pp. 143, 146]

As described by Hirsch, in 1994 Sweden copied France, providing yet more proof of the negative consequences of individualization. The Swedish legislature adopted a "principle of equivalence" over the "common curriculum" as stated: "Education should be adapted to each pupil's circumstances and needs, based on the pupils' background, earlier experiences, language, and knowledge." Hirsch summarized: "With the new emphasis on individuality and thinking skills, the elementary curriculum in Sweden became as incoherent as the curriculum had become in France and the United States." [H14, p. 153] Sweden's drop in PISA scores is noted in Chapter 8, Table 10.

Hirsch's explanation for the new laws in the two countries is a stinging attack on educational individualization: "Why did France and Sweden, which stood at the top in equity and achievement, suddenly destroy two of the most admirable and effective large school systems in the world? It was because they intended to make their good systems even better. They were unlucky enough to believe the well-meant but misguided slogans about individualization and skills." [H14, pp. 153–154]

On September 20, 1971 *Time* magazine's cover featured a picture of B. F. Skinner with the tag line "B. F. Skinner Says: We Can't Afford Freedom." [www11–44] Although the image was startling at the time, in the 21st century across a broad range of industries, managerial experts are deciding that replication surpasses individuality. Is not the supremacy of replication equivalent to the conjecture by Skinner? As one healthcare CEO recently said, "Anybody who studies quality will tell you that variation is the absolute enemy of quality." [M5, p. 30] Of course, an octogenarian's hip is not the same as a child's brain. Yet the question remains: Does a system of math education delivery exist that can successfully balance replication of quality with individualization of needs?

12
Learning Mathematics

In mathematics the art of proposing a question must be held of higher value than solving it.
George Cantor

The question of how the human brain learns math has confounded those studying the issue—from graduate school candidates searching for dissertation topics to university level psychologists working toward breakthrough theories. The answer is not known, for if it were, many of the problems of math education would be solved.

In 1964 mathematician Z. P. Dienes stated that the question itself is bold: "It is very daring to ask ourselves to explain how mathematics is learnt. In fact it is somewhat daring to ask how anything at all is learnt, once we depart from the stimulus-response explanation, which is really no explanation at all but merely the statement of the fact that things appear to be learnt when certain conditions are satisfied." [D5, p. 17]

In 1977 educational psychologist Robert Gagné suggested that determining whether a person had learned math could be made by observing that person in the act of performing math over time: *"Learning is a change in human disposition or capability, which persists over a period of time, and which is not simply ascribable to processes of growth.* The kind of change called learning exhibits itself as a change in behavior, and the inference of learning is made by comparing what behavior was possible before the individual was placed in a 'learning situation' and what behavior can be exhibited after such treatment." [G1, p. 3]

In 1980 Edward Begle of SMSG fame reiterated that how people specifically learn math was unknown: "Although we draw from general theories of learning, we have no established theory of learning mathematics to provide a basis for our discussions. ... the curriculum projects of the 1950s and the 1960s have not improved the teaching and learning of mathematics on a broad scale. Research has developed competing explanations for partial views of learning ... but generalizations ... are limited for the explanation and prediction of learning." [B6, pp. 9, 15]

In 1996 educator E. D. Hirsch stressed the importance of layering learning: "Children's readiness for secondary processes such as ... arithmetic is not simply a matter of natural development but also one of prior relevant learning. Learning builds on learning." [H12, p. 89]

In 1999 educational psychologist Howard Gardner, having surveyed a large quantity of data, dismissed learning math by memorization. He contended that "... even the best students in our best schools do not understand very much of the [math] curricular content." He called the prevailing problem with math education "rigidly applied algorithms"—namely, memorizing formulas and plugging numbers into those formulas. Gardner explained the educational flaw: "But in the absence of some trigger that a particular formula is wanted, they [students] prove unable to marshal it. And if they forget the formula, there is little chance that they will be able to derive it from scratch, because they never actually understood it." [G3, p. 120]

Also in 1999 as part of the TIMSS 8th grade math testing, video research projects proved equivocal. The seven participants—Australia, Czech Republic, Hong Kong (treated as a country), Japan, Netherlands, Switzerland, and United States—were a few of the highest scoring countries, the U.S. not one. The 2003 official report on this study stated in its summary: *"A broad conclusion that can be drawn from these results is that no single method of teaching eighth-grade mathematics was observed in all the relatively higher achieving countries participating in this study."* [N4, p. 11]

Although a single magical method did not appear, analysis of the TIMSS videos revealed that one or more countries showed greater emphasis on: "reviewing previously learned content," "introducing new content," or "practicing new content." Other variations included "the level of procedural complexity," "the relationship between one mathematics problem and the next," and "the relationships between mathematics and real-life situations." [N4, pp. 4, 6, 7, 10] However, these comments are more categorical than pedagogical; as a math teacher, I want to know specifics. For example, did the *content* include the teaching of mixture problems? Did the *procedural complexity* compare the chart and equation methods? Did the teaching examine the *relationship between* mixture and other algebraic word problems, and did it use examples from *real-life* such as farmers who regularly compute feed mixtures for their animals?

Regardless of the difficulty, educational psychologists have spent careers studying how the human mind learns—math in particular. The frustration was that they all developed their own specific theories, with inherent overlap. If they did not, they would not have made their mark in the field. Their original theories became their emblems, similar to a mathematician's proof of a significant new theorem. In my opinion, writing a proof is harder because it must be validated using previously proven math, whereas an education theory can be concocted and left in intellectual space for others to ponder. And, even if one educational theory were "proved" true, people would argue about its conclusiveness due to the nature of soft science.

Psychologist Robert Sternberg's entwined writing about theories of intelligence and learning, confirmed my speculation: "The field has been notoriously contentious, with every theorist setting out to prove that his theory is right and everyone else's is wrong. . . . For me, the most disturbing element of these and other opposing theorists has been that while they have done reasonably well in amassing evidence to support their own point of view, they have generally failed to disprove the views of others. How could this be? After reviewing earlier theories, I came to the conclusion that the reason for this was that virtually all of them have been incomplete. Though proposed as full theories of intelligence, each has dealt with only some limited aspect. Often, too, these theories have proved to be complementary rather than contradictory, as might be expected. . . . The point to be made, then, is that often the competition among theorists has been spurious. Their theories are really theories of different aspects of intelligence." [S23, p. 58]

Four theories are of note here.

Theory 1. Although published earlier in the French language, in the 1960s Jean Piaget's theory of the stages of cognitive development—Sensorimotor, Pre-operational, Concrete Operational, and Formal Operational—took hold. As Howard Gardner wrote, "Thanks to the pioneering work of the Swiss psychologist Jean Piaget, we no longer believe that young children are just miniature or ignorant adults." [G3, p. 69]

Moreover, E. D. Hirsch commended Piaget when ". . . new evidence had caused him to revise his theory of mental development. He concluded that the stages of mental growth did not reflect a purely developmental process but were powerfully influenced by the specific content of education. He concluded that the developmental process could be speeded or delayed by as much as four years." [H14, pp. 188–189]

Theory 2. In 1960 Jerome Bruner outlined "four general claims that can be made for teaching the fundamental structure of a subject," specifically referring to the New Math in his book. These are: (1) "understanding fundamentals makes a subject more comprehensible"; (2) "the most basic thing that can be said about human memory, after a century of intensive research, is that unless detail is placed into a structured pattern, it is rapidly forgotten"; (3) "an understanding of fundamental principles and ideas . . . appears to be the main road to adequate *transfer of training*. To understand something as a specific instance of a more general case [is a] . . . model for understanding"; and (4) "by constantly reexamining material taught in elementary and secondary schools for its fundamental character, one is able to narrow the gap between 'advanced' knowledge and 'elementary' knowledge." [B21, pp. 23–26]

Theory 3. In 1985 Jeremy Kilpatrick summarized, with admitted oversimplification and overlap, the five categories in which children learned mathematical problem solving. (1) Osmosis: Immerse students "in an environment of problems, assuming thereby that techniques will be absorbed through a process seldom explicit but presumably akin to osmosis." (2) Memorization: Develop algorithms to handle different classes of problems. Train students to follow the algorithms to reach solutions. Note, however, that "students often have trouble recognizing when the algorithm is applicable." (3) Imitation: Encourage students to copy the techniques of master problem solvers (either adults or other students). (4) Cooperation: Create small group discussions to help problem solving "by getting tentative ideas out into the open, where they can be refined and defined." (5) Reflection: Allow children to learn not only by doing, but also by thinking about what they do. [K3, pp. 8–10]

Theory 4. In 1999 Howard Gardner outlined *Four Approaches to Understanding*. These are: (1) *Learning from Suggestive Institutions*; (2) *Direct Confrontations of Erroneous Conceptions*; (3) *A Framework That Facilitates Understanding*; and (4) *Multiple Entry Points to Understanding*. [G3, pp. 126–133] Examples of the four approaches could include, respectively: (1) apprenticing with a master math team coach; (2) seeing why certain fraction *canceling* is invalid; (3) learning fraction multiplication by shading parts of rectangles; and (4) answering "x is what percent of y?" by following the English into an equation, writing a proportion, or constructing a fractional part.

Regardless of the approach, memorization is not learning. Students who memorize 9+3=12 have not learned the value of *twelveness*—that 6+6 also equals 12 or that 12–3=9. Nor do students necessarily understand the concept of place value—that in the first addition problem, 1 from the 3 combines with the 9, yielding 1 in the tens place. In 1973 Richard Skemp made this distinction: "[There is] a qualitative difference between two kinds of learning which we may call habit learning, or rote-memorizing, and learning involving understanding, which is to say intelligent learning. The former can be replicated in the laboratory rat or pigeon . . . . The latter kind of learning is that in which man most excels, and in which he most differs from all other species." [S15, p. 15]

Another universal consideration is that some form of work is necessary to learn. E. D. Hirsch wrote about the importance of effort: "While there is no natural way to learn nonnatural, secondary processes, many American experts would still insist on the Romantic doctrine that having a young child learn nonnatural processes through 'drill and kill' or reward and punishment does psychological harm. Consistent pressure on young children is of course harmful and will backfire, but enticement and a little pressure are no bad thing. The idea that stress avoidance is the sum of wisdom in early education assumes that what is natural is also what is painless. But some pain, like pleasure, is an unavoidable part of the educative process, and the one is not less natural than the other. Effort and persistence are needed for almost all secondary learning." [H12, p. 89]

A further aspect is that learning is two-way, requiring active participation from the student. As Otto Bassler and John Kolb wrote, success in learning to a great extent rests with the learner: "A learner must acquire his behavior himself. His learning cannot be accomplished for him by another person, nor will his observation of another person engaging in the desired behavior guarantee his attainment of the task. A teacher must structure conditions for the learner so that he is given the time and opportunity to try to exhibit the desired behavior. To summarize . . . , just because a teacher has taught (structured the conditions or shown the learner the expected behavior) does not ensure that the learner has learned (has acquired the expected behavior)." [B3, p. 23]

Jerome Bruner reinforced this two-way process, citing an "intrinsic motive that bears closely upon the will to learn. Perhaps it should be called reciprocity. For it involves a deep human need to respond to others and to operate jointly with them toward an objective." [B22, p. 125]

Still one more concern, which has been researched extensively in mathematics, is the potentially vastly applicable concept of *transfer*. If a student learns to write a proportion in an algebraic situation—e.g. production to cost—can the same student realize to write a proportion in a geometric situation—e.g. the sides of a triangle to a similar triangle? E. D. Hirsch succinctly wrote: "Learning Latin did *not* 'teach you to think;' it just taught you Latin." [H12, p. 114] Yet a gifted math teacher can teach effectively, working toward achieving transfer using three of Howard Gardner's tools: *By Providing Powerful Points of Entry*, *By Offering Apt Analogies*, and *By Providing Multiple Representations of the Central or Core Ideas of the Topic*. [G3, pp. 186–187]

An additional consideration is that math encompasses problem solving—not just arithmetic. George Pólya, one of the greatest mathematical problem solvers, wrote: "Solving problems is the specific achievement of intelligence, and intelligence is the specific gift of mankind: solving problems can be regarded as the most characteristically human activity." [P9, p. vii] Problem solving has requirements beyond those of learning mathematical manipulation: analysis of techniques of others, awareness of prototypes and schemata, tolerance for temporary uncertainty and imperfection, involvement and active participation, discrimination and selectivity, pattern recognition, and exploration.

But all of this discussion has ignored natural talent. Jerome Bruner commented that intuition alone is insufficient: "The good intuiter may have been born with something special, but his effectiveness rests upon a solid knowledge of the subject, a familiarity that gives intuition something to work with." Bruner identified two kinds of thinking: *analytic thinking* that advances directly with complete awareness and *intuitive thinking* that proceeds indirectly with vague perceptions. He cautioned that results ". . . achieved by intuitive methods . . . should if possible be checked by analytic methods." [B21, pp. 56–58]

Can mathematical natural intuition be learned? Bruner suggested that content learning can lead to intuitive performance: "Individuals who have extensive familiarity with a subject appear more often to leap intuitively into a decision or to a solution of a problem—one which later proves to be appropriate." [B21, p. 62]

Moreover, Bruner remarked that learning intuition requires special methods: "It requires a sensitive teacher to distinguish an intuitive mistake—an interestingly wrong leap—from a stupid or ignorant mistake, and it requires a teacher who can give approval and correction simultaneously to the intuitive student. To know a subject so thoroughly that he can go easily beyond the textbook is a great deal to ask of a high school teacher. Indeed, it must happen occasionally that a student is not only more intelligent than his teacher but better informed, and develops intuitive ways of approaching problems that he cannot explain and that the teacher is simply unable to follow or re-create for himself." [B21, p. 68]

My solution to finally fixing math education incorporates the aspects of learning math discussed in this chapter: spanning time, layering levels, deriving formulae, presenting details, understanding fundamentals, imitating masters, embracing immersion, practicing reflection, confronting errors, weighing approaches, expending effort, recognizing transfer, and developing intuition. Still, learning theories are just that—often vague, impractical, or non-translatable propositions. Howard Gardner succinctly and eloquently expressed the essential aspect: "The point is that there is no direct tie between a scientific theory and a set of educational moves. ... Indeed, in an art like teaching, the proof comes down to whether an approach works; it matters little whether the theory was correct. And conversely, even if the theory is both correct and elegant, if it cannot be mobilized for concrete educational consequences, the theory matters not a whit to the educators." [G4, p. 144] Yet I believe that one theory can be *mobilized*, and it forms the foundation of the proposal in *From STEM to STEW*.

13
Using Technology

You will see more and more perfection of that—computer as servant. But the next thing is going to be computer as a guide or agent.
Steve Jobs

While Chapter 11 included technology as one of fifty obstacles, this chapter examines the recognition over the past several decades that educational technology is a necessity for the improvement of math education. Indeed, in 1960 when the word *technology* included filmstrips and the word *tablet* meant paper, Jerome Bruner ended his landmark book positively: "... the teacher's task as communicator, model, and identification figure can be supported by a wise use of a variety of devices that expand experience, clarify it, and give it personal significance. There need be no conflict between the teacher and the aids to teaching. There will be no conflict if the development of aids takes into account the aims and the requirements of teaching." [B21, p. 91]

Six years later, with educational technology still in its infancy, Jerome Bruner futuristically noted the importance of software over hardware: "What is most characteristic of any kind of tool-using is not the tools themselves, but rather the program that guides their use. It is in this broader sense that tools take on their proper meaning as amplifiers of human capacities and implementers of human activity." [B22, p. 81]

In 1980 the NCTM set off a firestorm by stating in its landmark *Agenda* report: "Recommendation 3: Mathematics programs must take full advantage of the power of calculators and computers at all grade levels." [N18, p. 8, all capitals in the original] Unfortunately, misinterpretation followed, with some concluding that using basic calculators was more important than knowing arithmetic facts.

Moreover at the time, computer graphics were coarse, rendering some software (for example, geography maps) ineffective.

Also in 1980 MIT professor Seymour Papert, creator of the language Logo, was optimistic, proclaiming: "We are at a point in the history of education when radical change is possible, and the possibility for that change is directly tied to the impact of the computer." [P3, p. 36–37]

As more computers appeared in schools, some educators warned of possible negative effects while they maintained optimism. For example, in the 1983–84 President's Report to the Harvard Board of Overseers, Derek Bok cautioned: "We know that computers can have an unwholesome, almost addictive effect on some individuals." Yet he advised: "In view of the billions spent on higher education and its growing importance to modern society, there is an evident need to work systematically at its improvement. If technology can help in encouraging such an effort, that is reason enough to welcome its appearance." [B17, pp. 34, 38]

As a private school Computer Science Department Chair during that period, I know the issues well—from stopping use of violent computer games to promoting study of creative computer languages. Thankfully, the 1990s brought a more positive tone for educational computing.

In 1990 a report by the International Society for Technology in Education stated: ". . . the United States must recognize the need for improvement in its educational system and seize the opportunities offered by technology." Suggestions were: (1) the President should declare the 1990s "The Decade of Technology in Education"; (2) Congress should enact legislation substantially increasing support for technology in education; and (3) Congress should establish "a National Educational Technology Trust Fund analogous to National Highway Fund." [I6, p. 10]

In 1994 one of eight recommendations in the report of the National Education Commission on Time and Learning was "Invest in Technology." The lead sentence of that section was: "We recommend that schools seize on the promise of new technologies to increase productivity, enhance student achievement, and expand learning time." [N35, p. 37]

In 1999 Howard Gardner titled a book chapter "Education in the Future" with one section called "Six Forces That Will Remake Schools." Citing technology as the first force, Gardner praised the creation of the computer as the "most important technological event of our time." He explained that while schools use the hardware for business and operational needs, for educational purposes the computers often "deliver the old lessons in a more convenient and efficient format." Yet he predicted that the computer would eventually become the organizing mechanism of education—for delivery of daily lessons, formation of mental habits, development of algorithmic thinking, personalization of individual needs, customization of learning style, advancement of interactive approaches, and dispersement of equitable access. [G3, pp. 42–44]

In the same book, while encouraging use of "sophisticated technologies," Gardner addressed software: "In itself, technology is neither helpful nor harmful; it is simply a tool. The most advanced and speediest computers in the world will be of little help . . . if the software is mindless and fails to engage understanding. Conversely, armed only with their minds, a few books, chalk, and a pencil, well-informed and motivated teachers can lead their students triumphantly down the road to understanding." [G3, p. 135] Because the teachers mentioned by Gardner are too few for the entire country, education needs technology.

Also in 1999 Gardner wrote with cautious optimism: "Educators have always tinkered with promising technologies. Much of the history of education chronicles the varying fates of paper, books, lecture halls, filmstrips, television, computers, ... Current technologies seem tailor-made to help bring into reality the kind of . . . approach . . . [needed]. Still, there are no guarantees. Many technologies have faded, and many others have been used superficially and unproductively." [G4, p. 180] Of course, at the time, tablets did not exist.

Continuing into the 21st century, with educational reform still sorely needed, computer power remained a hope. In 2000 the NCTM wrote in its comprehensive report: "Technology is essential in teaching and learning mathematics; it influences the mathematics that is taught and enhances students' learning." [N24, p. 11]

In 2001 an issue of *BusinessWeek*, featuring the cover story on seven ideas to fix schools, listed as #7: "Use Technology Effectively." As noted in Obstacle 40 of Chapter 11, the author observed: (1) technology to date had not improved education; and (2) that defeat needed fast remedy because no other option offered more promise. He wrote: "Most educators don't know how to use it [technology] to improve student learning, teacher cooperation, or even school administration." [S30, pp. 67, 80]

In 2003 cautious optimism remained regarding educational technology. For example, Diane Ravitch wrote: "Intelligence and reason cannot be achieved merely by skill-building and immersion in new technologies; . . . Intelligence and reason cannot be developed absent the judgment that is formed by prolonged and thoughtful study . . . ." [R2, p. 164]

In 2007 authors of a Brookings Institution book-chapter summarized the contradiction between the ills and benefits of technology: "There is plenty of evidence to indicate a positive relationship between technology and student achievement. However, most of these studies emphasize that for technology to have an effect on achievement, it must be challenging and focused on higher-order thinking skills, and the teachers must be capable of using and teaching it and have the appropriate support. . . . examining computer use or technology by itself is not enough to determine its effects on student achievement. What seems to be important, however, is the way in which technology is used." [P2, p. 208]

In 2010 one report suggested a more aggressive use of technology: "The *National Education Technology Plan 2010* calls for revolutionary transformation rather than evolutionary tinkering. . . . The plan recognizes that technology is at the core of virtually every aspect of our daily lives and work, and we must leverage it to provide engaging and powerful learning experiences and content, as well as resources and assessments that measure student achievement in more complete, authentic, and meaningful ways." [O2, p. ix]

In 2011 an Associated Press article titled "Many U.S. schools adding iPads, trimming textbooks" mentioned the notion that texts in some subjects are out-of-date by the time the books arrive at schools. Tablets could not only store textbooks, permitting continual revisions, but also act as a research tool with internet access. [R8]

In 2012 a leader at the Bill & Melinda Gates Foundation wrote in *Harvard Business Review* about the customization features of educational software, making individualized instruction possible: "A new generation of sophisticated adaptive courseware and schools that blend the best of teacher- and computer-delivered instruction are making personalized-learning approaches feasible and affordable, not as a replacement for teachers but as a way to give them the tools they need to become dramatically more effective." [C8, p. 79]

But in 2013 Diane Ravitch warned about the misuse of technology by profit-driven, corporate education reformers: "When they speak of 'innovation,' they mean replacing teachers with technology to cut staffing costs. . . . When they speak of 'personalized instruction,' they mean putting children in front of computers with algorithms that supposedly adjust content and test questions to the ability level of the student but actually sacrifice human contact with a real teacher." [R7, p. 34]

In the same book, Ravitch criticized educational technology, saying it is not a proper substitute for teachers: "Yet with all its great potential, technology can never substitute for inspired teaching. Students will respond with greater enthusiasm to a gifted teacher than to a computer with the world's best software. Electronic technology has its charms, but it can't compete with the lively interchange of ideas that happens when students discuss . . . a math problem they wrestled with . . . ." [R7, p. 180] She also reinforced her opposition to a heavy dose of technology: "There is no evidence that students learn more or better when taught on computers. Computers have many exciting uses in the classroom as a supplement to good teaching, as a vehicle for research and exploration, as a means for cooperative learning and student projects. But computers are not a satisfactory substitute for a human teacher." [R7, p. 303]

Also in 2013 in a Brookings Institution online video called "Making Technology Work For Education," Julia Gillard at the Center for Universal Education said that small children "intuitively" know how to operate an iPad, that they "grow up drenched in technology," but that technology should be used to get the learning "outcomes" desired. [G6]

On June 26, 2015 the One-to-One Institute and Education Dive both published an article titled "What's the future of iPads in schools?" that originally referred to the iPad as the "cool, sexy device" but then cited school districts evaluating the device for cost versus effectiveness, especially regarding useful software at the various grade levels—similar to the way the desktop computer entered schools. [O3; www13–1]

The Bill & Melinda Gates Foundation is investing in improving education through technology. Its website states: "Students deserve learning experiences tailored to their needs and that make the most of teachers' time with students. Ninety-five percent of 12- to 17-year-olds already go online on a regular basis. . . . Our work is focused on taking full advantage of the kinds of tools and technologies that have transformed every other aspect of life to power up and accelerate students' learning. We need to do things differently, not just better. We're investing in a new generation of courseware that adapts in sophisticated ways to students' learning needs. We're also supporting game-based learning that generates rich data about students' progress and challenges them with exactly what they need to learn next. Blending face-to-face instruction with digital tools allows students to learn independently and at their own pace, freeing up time for teachers to give students more individualized attention and to focus on more complex tasks. Allowing students to progress to new levels of learning as soon as they demonstrate mastery of a topic rather than moving forward based on the number of hours spent in a classroom provides students with customized pathways to achievement, enabling them to be successful every step of the way." [www13–2] Evaluating the thoroughness, clarity, rigor, and richness of this math is impossible without access to the lessons.

Another project of note is Khan Academy. In 2004 Salman Khan tutored his cousin in math, first in person and then on the phone. From that experience, the number of cousins grew, until in 2006 Khan created math lessons that he posted on YouTube. [www13–3] Since then, Khan Academy has grown into a significant, praiseworthy, not-for-profit online education resource, where people worldwide may study a vast number of subjects.

In a *Vanity Fair* profile on Khan, Arne Duncan wrote: "Students can pick up a new skill working alone with a video, and teachers can use class time to deepen skills and answer questions. Just as important, students who have an easy time with the material can race ahead, while those who are struggling can repeat a lesson without fear of embarrassment. It's not a silver bullet, but it's a great tool in teachers' tool kits, and it's a welcome force to shake up some old patterns." [D10, p. 160]

The Khan Academy website includes articles about schools using the Khan videos for math lessons. [www13–4] The list is not extensive despite years of availability. As of 2016, Khan Academy developed an online tutoring partnership with College Board for the re-designed SAT.

Go to the Khan Academy website and follow the selection path: Subjects|Math by grade|5th|Fractions|Multiplying fractions|Intro to multiplying 2 factions. The video shows the problem 2/3 x 4/5 (with proper horizontal fraction lines) first done by the definition of fraction multiplication (multiplying across both numerators and denominators) and then by a visual representation of sectioned rectangles to explain why. While the math is correct, children might view the graphics as crude and the talking as tedious. Moreover, with only one video example available, instruction must revert to the classroom teacher to explain many self-created examples correctly. If the teacher were capable of such a task, then the video would not be needed at all for the students. Thus, the video by default serves as a device to instruct the teacher who should but doesn't know the material or the parent who desires a refresher to help his/her child. Indeed, the detailed menu of lesson options reinforces this use of the videos as a targeted tool rather than a continuous delivery.

Now follow the same selection path but instead of the "Intro," choose "Multiplying 2 fractions: 5/6 x 2/3." The video show two methods—multiply first, simplify second and simplify first, multiply second—never stating that the former method wastes time and generates work, while the latter method creates efficiency and shows insight. Then, going back to Subjects|Math by grade|6th, fractions does not exist as a category, despite so much more to learn. The path Subjects|Math by grade|7th does yield the category "Fractions, decimals, and percentages," but the beauty and power of fraction multiplication as a problem solving method is absent. Thus, the videos cover the basics of math but not the richness.

As technology progressed, serious work remained on the computer, while "unwholesome, almost addictive" behavior cited by Derek Bok moved to the smart phone due to its convenient size and texting capability. The tablet remains in a middle, gray area. Certainly, many parents today struggle with limiting their children's game time on the family tablet. But the capacity to provide both fun and education is not a reason to doubt the device. Adults need to be smarter than children, turning a negative into a positive. The technology in my idea has a purpose. My plan does not involve handing a child a tablet and crossing one's fingers.

We must reconcile the valid concern about technology and the crucial need for progress. Children may go from the concrete to the abstract—joining 4 blocks with 3 more before writing 4+3=7. Yet that tactile, visual approach is elusive for many higher math concepts. Students rarely work hands-on past grade school. Graphing calculators help, with students altering an equation's constants to see if its graph widens, narrows, flips, or shifts. But with superb software, could the tablet assume the role of the blocks and the graphing calculator, as well as other tools not yet envisioned? If Papert could declare in 1980 that "radical change is possible" due to the computer's advent, then certainly now with the tablet's invention, that change is overdue.

14

Organizing the Curriculum

If people do not believe that mathematics is simple, it is only because they do not realize how complicated life is.
John von Neumann

Through proper organization, a great curriculum reveals the beauty and power of mathematics. But math curriculum-writing is a daunting task—where does one begin and how does one proceed? Tediously, too many textbooks start with the four whole number operations and advance in a disparate fashion, often saving important topics for the end—topics that some teachers never reach. Yet discussion about better organization of the American math curriculum dates back more than half a century.

In 1945 the Commission on Post-War Plans of the National Council of Teachers of Mathematics emphasized the importance of a curriculum. Its eleventh of thirty-four theses was: "The mathematics program of grades 7 and 8 should be so organized as to enable the pupils to achieve mathematical maturity and power." [B13, pp. 618–637]

In 1963 twenty-eight university mathematicians gathered at a conference in Cambridge, MA to design the ideal math curriculum. They boldly set aside matters of educational resources, pedagogic techniques, cognitive psychology, political accommodations, and teacher training. Their intent was to create the perfect mathematics curriculum for the future without regard to practical issues. [C1, pp. vii–ix]

In 1966 Jerome Bruner wrote extensively about math curriculum in three ways. (1) He related the overall curriculum to its smaller components: "A first and obvious conclusion is that one must take into account the issues of predisposition, structure, sequence, and reinforcement in preparing curriculum materials—whether one is concerned with writing a textbook, a lesson plan, a unit of instruction, a program, or, indeed, a conversation with didactic ends in view." (2) He connected the curriculum to both the student's knowledge and learning process: ". . . a theory of instruction seeks to take account of the fact that a curriculum reflects not only the nature of knowledge itself but also the nature of the knower and of the knowledge-getting process. It is the enterprise par excellence where the line between subject matter and method grows necessarily indistinct." (3) He underscored the importance of the math curriculum being true to the discipline: "The more elementary a course and the younger its students, the more serious must be its pedagogical aim of forming the intellectual powers of those whom it serves. It is as important that a good mathematics course be justified by the intellectual discipline it provides or the honesty it promotes as by the mathematics it transmits. Indeed, neither can be accomplished without the other." [B22, pp. 70, 72, 73]

In 1967 a report by the Association for Supervision and Curriculum Development reaffirmed the fusing of algebra and geometry as discussed in Chapter 11: "The problem of *how to organize the many diverse bits and pieces of the mathematics curriculum* will become a severe one, indeed, if a real 'mathematics revolution' ever does get started. At present, the curriculum in the United States is arranged mainly by grade-level placement of topics. . . . We can integrate the study of geometry so completely into our study of arithmetic and algebra that no dividing line will be visible and arithmetic-algebra-geometry will merge into a single unified subject, or we can keep geometry separate and clearly distinct from the rest of our mathematics. The present grade-level placement of topics in the United States provides a purely conventional answer to the question of what should go where. There is no foundation to this sequence other than simple accident." [D1, pp. 32–33]

Any serious endeavor to organize math curriculum must incorporate the following ten aspects: objectives, structure, foundation, content, sequence, spiraling, integration, coherence, episodes, and themes. My plan for turning math education upside down not only addresses but also fixes all of these features.

1. Objectives

Understanding mathematics by 12th grade—the broad objective—starts in kindergarten or earlier and happens day by day, month by month, year by year. Understanding each lesson is the narrow objective. As Jerome Bruner wrote in 1960, "In planning a curriculum, one properly distinguishes between the long-run objective one hopes to achieve and certain short-run steps that get one toward that objective." [B21, p. 69]

Moreover, proper math curriculum should not exist solely for those who are mathematically gifted or precocious, those who live within the borders of a good public school system, or those with educated parents. The overall objective is to provide a sound math education for all. Yet for a variety of reasons, too many school systems as well as private schools offer a stronger curriculum to some and a weaker curriculum to others.

As discussed in Chapter 11, William Schmidt and Curtis McKnight argued for curriculum equality as an objective. In 2012 after chronicling extensive content disparity "among classrooms, schools, and districts—differences that are so large that it makes it implausible to assert that all children receive equivalent learning opportunities in mathematics," they claimed that "the inevitable consequence" of preserving conventional authority over the curriculum was a "high price" paid by the children—the quality of their math education. They stated: "Parents and politicians should be made aware that the cost of sustaining the tradition of local control of the curriculum is diminished prospects for an entire generation of American schoolchildren." [S7, p. 141]

2. Structure

In 1960 Jerome Bruner emphasized the importance of structure in a curriculum: "Grasping the structure of a subject is understanding it in a way that permits many other things to be related to it meaningfully. To learn structure, in short, is to learn how things are related." Bruner expanded on three important results of solid structure—generalization, excitement, and retention: "Teaching specific topics or skills without making clear their context in the broader fundamental structure of a field of knowledge is uneconomical in several deep senses. In the first place, such teaching makes it exceedingly difficult for the student to generalize from what he has learned to what he will encounter later. In the second place, learning that has fallen short of a grasp of general principles has little reward in terms of intellectual excitement. The best way to create interest in a subject is to render it worth knowing, which means to make the knowledge gained usable in one's thinking beyond the situation in which the learning has occurred. Third, knowledge one has acquired without sufficient structure to tie it together is knowledge that is likely to be forgotten. An unconnected set of facts has a pitiably short half-life in memory." [B21, pp. 7, 31]

Too many students call math complex because they don't see its underlying structure. Like John von Neumann in this chapter's epigraph, Bruner wrote about simplicity—and connecting the concept to a well-structured mathematics curriculum. Bruner stated: ". . . it took the efforts of many highly talented mathematicians to discern the underlying structure of the mathematics that was to be taught. That is to say, the simplicity of a mathematics curriculum rests upon the history and development of mathematics itself." [B22, p. 71]

In 1995 Bruner united structure and simplicity. William Schmidt and Curtis McKnight quoted Bruner: ". . . to understand something well is to sense wherein it is simple, wherein it is an instance of a simpler, general case. . . . In the main, however, to understand something is to sense the simpler structure that underlies a range of instances, and this is notably true in mathematics." [B23; S7, p. 34]

3. Foundation (Background)

Mathematics must be learned step by step. Students need background—a foundation on which to build. In his 1966 book, Jerome Bruner discussed number bases as just one example: "For while many virtues have been discovered for numbers to the base 10, students cannot appreciate such virtues until they recognize that the base 10 was not handed down from the mountain by some mathematical God. It is when the student learns to work in different number bases that the base 10 is recognized for the achievement that it is." [B22, pp. 71–72]

Yet Bruner expressed his appreciation for background even more profoundly: ". . . if you wish to teach the calculus in the eighth grade, then begin it in the first grade by teaching the kinds of ideas and skills necessary for its mastery later." [B22, p. 29]

Certainly, Bruner was not advocating for teaching calculus in middle school. But he was making a point—one so central to his beliefs that he repeated it. In 1960 he wrote: "We begin with the hypothesis that any subject can be taught effectively in some intellectually honest form to any child at any stage of development." [B21, p. 33] Again in 1966 he wrote: "Any idea or problem or body of knowledge can be presented in a form simple enough so that any particular learner can understand it in a recognizable form." [B22, p. 44]

While *any subject* in its final form cannot be brought down to the earliest level, its primal seeds perhaps can: "If the understanding of number, measure, and probability is judged crucial . . . , then instruction in these subjects should begin as intellectually honestly and as early as possible in a manner consistent with the child's forms of thought. Let the topics be developed and redeveloped in later grades." [B21, pp. 53–54]

One key phrase repeated in Bruner's statements is *intellectually honestly*. Do not tell children that all numbers are either prime or composite, and then later say that 1 is neither. Do not tell children that mixed numbers are more important than improper fractions, and then later show that checking an equation's solution in improper fraction form is easier. Do not tell children that a number is either a decimal or a fraction, and then later teach that an equivalent percent exists. Do not tell children that a problem has a singular method, and then reveal more choices.

Another key phrase is *developed and redeveloped*. Consider probability. Second graders can learn beginning probability by labeling events as occurring always, sometimes, or never. Third graders can expand that concept to include certain, likely, unlikely, or impossible. Fourth graders can express a probability as a fraction between 0 and 1. Fifth graders can simplify probability fractions. Sixth graders can find simple compound probabilities. Similarly with age problems, students need not wait until high school algebra class—and then struggle—to learn how to construct charts. Elementary students can complete cells of an age chart of increasing difficulty, where the rows represent people and the columns represent years in chronological order.

Bruner emphasized that a child's carefully developed foundation on a myriad of math topics is exactly what permits abstraction to occur in the later grades: " ... the proposition [is] that the foundations of any subject may be taught to anybody at any age in some form. Though the proposition may seem startling at first, its intent is to underscore an essential point often overlooked in the planning of curricula. It is that the basic ideas that lie at the heart of all science and mathematics ... are as simple as they are powerful. To be in command of these basic ideas, to use them effectively, requires a continual deepening of one's understanding of them that comes from learning to use them in progressively more complex forms. It is only when such basic ideas are put in formalized terms as equations or elaborated verbal concepts that they are out of reach of the young child, if he has not first understood them intuitively and had a chance to try them out on his own." [B21, pp. 12–13]

E. D. Hirsch confirmed Bruner's philosophy of developing concepts early: "To follow this advice [wait to teach a concept until children can learn all of it easily such as place value] would put off a lot of basic mathematical learning until fourth grade—about age ten. It is doubtful that such a policy would contribute to [efficient teaching and learning]." [H12, p. 82]

4. Content (Rigor)

Too many math teachers teach watered-down math; then society is surprised when children don't know math. To yield math-smart students, rigorous math has no replacement; content is foremost.

In 1963 U.S. Commissioner of Education Francis Keppel advised that demands of content, not limitations of teachers, were paramount: "Most

Organizing the Curriculum

curriculum reforms, practically enough, have chosen to limit their ambitions in the light of these realities [math teacher inadequacies]. They have tended to create such new courses as existing teachers, after enjoying the benefits of brief retraining, can completely handle. . . . If the matter were to end there, the result might well be disastrous. New curricula would be frozen into the educational system that would come to possess, in time, all the deficiencies of curricula that are now being swept away." [C1, p. viii]

In 1966 E. D. Hirsch argued for strong content: "There is no substitute for this requisite domain specific content knowledge in the performance of . . . any . . . intellectual skill. It is a fallacy, then, to claim that the schools should or could teach all-purpose reading, thinking, or learning skills. But paradoxically, adequate attention to the transmission of broad general knowledge actually does lead to general intellectual skills. The paradox is quite stunning. Our emphasis on formal skills [application of a formal pattern or strategy to a new problem] has resulted in students who are deficient in formal skills, whereas an appropriate emphasis on transmitting knowledge results in students who actually possess the skills that are sought by American educators—skills such as critical thinking and learning to learn." [H12, p. 219]

In 1999 Martin Gross described content as essential but lacking in American schools: "*The concept is that knowledge builds on knowledge, which stimulates understanding, then makes it possible to absorb and understand still more knowledge . . . .*" [G12, p. 128]

5. Sequence

Too many students get lost in their math teachers' sequences, especially in light of skipping around in preparation for standardized tests. While many sequences are possible, they must be logical. Some topics must precede others—certainly, one cannot compute the area of a rectangle with fractional dimensions unless one knows how to multiply fractions. But many topics can be rearranged. As discussed in Chapter 10, the New Math mathematicians, faced with the problem of ordering all of school mathematics, decided to begin with sets. After all, whole numbers form a set, the graph of a line is a set of points, and so on.

In 1960 Jerome Bruner emphasized the importance of sequences, calling them *sequential programs*. He wrote: "There are certain orders of presentation of materials and ideas in any subject that are more likely than others to lead the student to the main idea. The courses being devised by the University of Illinois Committee on School Mathematics, the School Mathematics Study Group, . . . and others are excellent instances of the well conceived sequence designed to lead the student to an understanding of basic ideas and structures." [B21, p. 82]

In 1966 Jerome Bruner commented on the choice of sequences: "There are usually various sequences that are equivalent in their ease and difficulty for learners. There is no unique sequence for all learners, and the optimum in any particular case will depend upon a variety of factors, including past learning, stage of development, nature of the material, and individual differences." [B22, p. 49]

At the conclusion of my first summer studying at the NSF SSTP with Professor Arnold Ross, he asked his students to write a Definition-Theorem Outline of Number Theory as a review. This exercise, which took a year part-time, was exceptionally rewarding. I had all of the material, but the issues were the initial point and the path forward to reach the complete presentation of the subject in the most orderly way.

6. Spiraling (Review)

Like other math terms, the word *spiral* has different meanings for different people. Because spiraling is only one of ten important aspects of a solid curriculum, beware of textbooks that feature spiraling as the main component; circling back to previous lessons that were inadequately taught is futile. While I am a strong proponent of cumulative review—with that review then leading to extensions—students cannot review material never learned properly in the first place.

In 1963 the Cambridge Conference members used spiraling in their curriculum restructuring proposal: ". . . we want to make students familiar with part of the global structure of mathematics. This we hope to accomplish by the 'spiral' curriculum which repeatedly returns to each topic, always expanding it and showing more connections with other topics." [C1, p. 8]

In 1980 an NCTM publication discussed the countless ways of organizing a math curriculum and advocated for a spiral approach. The author James Fey wrote: "In search of more general principles of sequence, the incredible diversity of ways that mathematical topics can be structured—in the mind of the instructor and the mind of the learner—suggests that a single line of march through a fixed sequence of topics is unlikely to yield learning that produces maximum meaning, retention, and transfer for all students. Instead, the following principle seems likely: *A spiral style of sequence in which students return several times to each topic, meeting it each time at a higher level of abstraction and complexity and from a different point of view, will be more effective than a mastery sequence in which students are expected to demonstrate thorough comprehension and skill in a single topic before they move on to another.*" [F10, p. 421]

In 1992 Harold Stevenson and James Stigler discussed spiraling as an unofficial mandate in American textbooks, saying that writers know what adoption committees want—"repetition and review." Yet Stevenson and Stigler warned that teachers' decisions to skip many topics (postponing them for future teachers) because of length, causes an educational calamity: "Different topics are omitted by different teachers, thereby making it impossible for the children's later teachers to know what has been covered at earlier grades—they cannot be sure what their students know and what they do not." [S25, pp. 139–140]

The above caution is sound. When I conducted a year-long curriculum improvement project at a private school, I found that due to spiraling within a textbook series, teachers knew neither what was original in their years nor what was taught in prior years. Thus, they covered topics as initial presentations, rather than as reviews and extensions. Dispirited from boredom, too many students shut down, thinking that they would just learn the material the following year.

7. Integration

In 1963 Cambridge Conference participants advocated for integration, hoping to make all students from a young age "familiar with the structure of the real number system and the basic ideas of geometry" as well as "familiar with part of the global structure of mathematics." [C1, p. 8]

In 2000 the NCTM's *Principles and Standards* suggested integrating math topics for more proficiency—that seeing a concept from various viewpoints would generate both broader comprehension and appropriate application. The report recommended that textbook writers as well as classroom teachers should conscientiously intertwine multiple skills and concepts from a range of mathematical areas. [N24, p. 289]

In 2007 Kilpatrick, Mesa, and Sloane also advocated for integration: "In international curricula, therefore, mathematics is seen more as an integrated whole than as subject matter that can be parsed by topic area without overt integration. This curricular parsing is the same for weak and strong students in the United States. The integration is left up to the student, a task many find difficult or fail to complete on their own." Furthermore, they described this troublesomely missing integration as leading to dangerously overt compartmentalization: ". . . some of these categories [TIMSS content classifications] can be seen as equivalent mathematically; for example, writing a rule for a pattern (*Patterns*) and identifying a rule relating two variables (*Functions*) can be interpreted as essentially the same mathematical activity. Research suggests, however, that from the student's point of view, the two activities are different. Students' knowledge becomes compartmentalized in ways that render equivalent activities separate and sometimes incompatible." [K4, pp. 86, 93]

Arguably, too few math topics are skillfully integrated, whether by publishers in their textbooks or teachers in their lessons. Students cannot perform this integration on their own; the result is too many students who believe that math exists in small, discrete cubby holes.

8. Coherence

The discussion of coherence in math curriculum is not new. In 1992 Harold Stevenson and James Stigler made two important points about coherence, the first a possible reason for its paucity: "The American teachers' tendency to shift topics so frequently may be due to their desire to capitalize on variety as a means of capturing children's interest." Unfortunately, too many American teachers do not understand that the opposite is true—that teaching math properly captures students' natural interest. Their second point is a warning about teaching: "Even when a lesson is designed to be coherent, it is not necessarily perceived that way by the students. ... Coherence is lost because of the teacher's failure to interrelate the components of the lesson." [S25, pp. 182, 180–181]

In 2007 William Schmidt and Richard Houang described coherence as follows: ". . . coherence is a critical, if not the single most important, element defining high-quality content standards. Such content standards are defined in terms of the disciplines that underlie the school subject matter articulated in those standards. . . . standards are coherent if they specify topics, including the depth at which the topic is to be studied as well as the sequencing of the topics, within each grade and across grades, in a way that is consistent with the structure of the underlying discipline." [S6, p. 79]

Moreover, Schmidt and Houang underscored the importance of coherence over time: "If content standards reflect the structure of a discipline, then the 'depth' of those standards should *increase* as students move across the grades. Failure to increase in depth, sophistication, and complexity across the grades would indicate a lack of coherence. Extensive repetition of virtually the same standards across grade levels is found in the United States. This repetition runs counter to the idea of 'coherent' development, is unwarranted, and contributes to a lack of focus. Such repetition can be replaced with standards that form a trajectory by linking coverage of the topics over grades and by reducing the repetition over the same grade levels." [S6, p. 66]

In 2012 William Schmidt and Curtis McKnight similarly defined coherence: "We define content standards in the aggregate to be coherent if they are articulated over time as a sequence of topics and performances that are consistent with the logical and, if appropriate, hierarchical nature of the disciplinary content from which the subject matter derives. This is not to suggest the existence of a single coherent sequence, only that such a sequence reflect the inherent structure of the discipline." They continued: "This evolution should occur both over time within a particular grade level and as the student progresses across grades." And: "This definition of coherence implies that the particular selection and sequencing of topic-grade combinations for a hierarchical subject like mathematics should not be arbitrary." [S7, p. 36]

Schmidt and McKnight made key points about coherence—one about its dearth and two about its positive impact if present: "First, previous studies have found that the U.S. state standards and the original professional standards of the National Council of Teachers of Mathematics (NCTM) reflected a general lack of coherence in the sense described here. . . . Second, recent work has shown that coherence was positively related to achievement at 4th, 7th, and 8th grades (the only grades tested in their study)." These authors also connected coherence to sequence: "Coherence is not really just about whether states intend for educators to cover key topics. It is also about the sequence in which a state intends the topics to be covered." [S7, pp. 37, 39]

As discussed in Chapter 10, CCSSM claims coherence as a feature, though it is sometimes lacking. Moreover, whether teachers jump around in the textbook on their own or whether school systems order teachers to do so, the goal of higher scores on state exams impedes coherence.

9. Episodes

In 1960 Jerome Bruner broadened the concept of lesson learning by pinpointing three processes in a series of episodes: (1) *acquisition*—refining previous knowledge; (2) *transformation*—manipulating the knowledge to make it "fit"; and (3) *evaluation*—checking its fit. He wrote: "A learning episode can be brief or long, contain many ideas or a few." Regardless, Bruner's learning episode required a "climax in understanding." Bruner explained: "It also seems reasonable that the more one has a sense of the structure of a subject, the more densely packed and longer a learning episode one can get through without fatigue." [B21, pp. 49, 51]

A learning episode compares to a three-act play. The audience first discovers the plot and characters, second rearranges the spoken clues to assemble the story, and third confirms the meaning after reaching a culminating moment. Few publishers and math teachers seem to group daily lessons into longer episodes.

10. Themes

The concept of organizing math curriculum around broad categories is more than a half-century old. But too common with math education, important ideas cycle—suggested, ignored, shelved, and reactivated.

In 1945 NCTM's Commission on Post-War Plans formulated thirty-four theses. The tenth featured *themes*: "*The mathematics for grades 7 and 8 should be planned as a unified program and should be built around a few broad categories.*" [C17 in B13, pp. 618–637]

The 1963 Cambridge Conference underscored *themes* such as sets and functions for the purposes of structure and growth, writing that the concepts can be "repeatedly applied until a sophisticated comprehension is built up." Moreover, the conference members stated: "We believe that these concepts belong in the curriculum not because they are modern but because they are useful in organizing the material we want to present." [C1, p. 10] In fact, in the 1990s the Duke University Talent Identification Program titled a summer on-campus math course *Functions*—the one between Algebra II and calculus, traditionally known as pre-calculus.

In 2007 Jeremy Kilpatrick, Vilma Mesa, and Finbarr Sloane reflected on the set and function thematic approaches of the New Math, stating that "the function concept" was initially only a "minor influence" in the U.S. even though other countries were using it "as a basis for developing not simply algebra but the entire secondary mathematics curriculum." They explained: "Algebra as generalized arithmetic was the mainstream approach until the new math movement began to influence the U.S. curriculum in the early 1960s. Algebra was only then recast as a more abstract subject, with functions playing a central role and with definitions based on set theory." [K4, p. 88]

In 2008 Jo Boaler described this same thematic approach: ". . . the students learned the same methods, but the curriculum was organized around bigger mathematical ideas, with unifying themes such as 'What is a linear function?'" [B14, p. 59]

A typical organization of a 6th grade math textbook is often twelve chapters, starting with the first on whole number arithmetic and the second on decimals. Other chapter titles include measurement, data, fractions, plane geometry, and solid geometry, among other distinct, isolated topics. Achieving spiraling, integration, episodes, and coherence might be more feasible if textbooks were organized by themes such as sets, functions, proofs, counting (including multiplication principle, Venn Diagrams, and Cross Tabulations), and problem solving techniques (including drawing a picture, charting, listing, working backward, and solving a simpler problem).

These broad themes could be more creative—for example, invariance of quantities, such as each transformation of an equation, each simplified or expanded fraction, each equivalent row of a factorization, and each displaced volume. Jerome Bruner emphasized this concept when he quoted a participant at the Woods Hole Conference: "The most elementary forms of reasoning—whether logical, arithmetical, geometrical, or physical—rest on the principle of the invariance of quantities: that the whole remains, whatever may be the arrangement of its parts, the change of its form, or its displacement in space or time." [B21, p. 41]

15
Training Teachers, Changing Teaching

> *... the beginning teacher teaches all he knows and more;*
> *the experienced teacher teaches all he knows; but the master teacher*
> *selects, from what he knows, material appropriate to his students.*
> Arnold Ross [J7, p. 7]

"It all starts with the teachers" was the tag line of *Time* magazine's cover story "What Makes a School Great" by Amanda Ripley. [R12] Indeed, even if a math curriculum incorporates the ten features of the previous chapter, failure is possible because a strong math curriculum requires capable teachers. Inadequately trained teachers can destroy a great curriculum; poorly educated teachers can mislead a student's mind; and weakly prepared teachers can sabotage an innovative movement. Shamefully, in complete violation of common sense, America allows people who neither understand nor like math to teach math.

Martin Gross underscored a wise principle regarding teachers: "*It should be axiomatic that if we want students to be more scholarly, or at least appreciate scholarship as a goal, then we must have more scholarly teachers in public school.*" [G12, p. 52] Yet accomplishing that goal is challenging. While Chapter 11 covers in-field and out-of-field teachers, this chapter explores math teaching from a broader perspective by outlining fifteen successive, interlocking, pervasive postulates.

Postulate 1. A teacher's knowledge and love of math are all-important for successful teaching of the subject.

In his 1960 exploration of the Sputnik New Math, Jerome Bruner wrestled with "the production of a curriculum." He claimed: "A curriculum is more for teachers than it is for pupils. If it cannot change, move, perturb, inform teachers, it will have no effect on those whom they teach." Repeating that a curriculum must first influence teachers before it can affect students, Bruner boldly asserted: "The doctrine that a well-wrought curriculum is a way of 'teacher-proofing' a body of knowledge in order to get it to the student uncontaminated is nonsense." [B21, p. xv]

Bruner further developed his point: "Giving the material to them [children] in terms they understand, interestingly enough, turns out to involve knowing the mathematics oneself, and the better one knows it, the better it can be taught." [B21, p. 40] Moreover, Bruner emphasized *math* in math teaching: "Somebody who does not see anything beautiful or powerful about mathematics is not likely to ignite others with a sense of the intrinsic excitement of the subject. A teacher who will not or cannot give play to his own intuitiveness is not likely to be effective in encouraging intuition in his students." [B21, p. 90]

In the Foreword of the 1963 Cambridge Conference report, U.S. Commissioner of Education Francis Keppel confirmed that the teacher must know math to be effective: "But these ambitions [writing rigorous math curriculum] are immediately dampened by the awareness that serious limitations are imposed upon the student's ability to learn by the instructor's ability to teach. If the student is to be brought to the frontiers of knowledge, the teacher must know the whereabouts of those frontiers. If the student is to be encouraged to grope, the teacher must at least be able to suggest which of his roads are likely to be blind alleys." [C1, p. viii]

Postulate 2. A push-pull situation has driven math education—a push forward for strong curriculum and a pull back from weak teachers.

The push forward for strong curriculum was glaring, again by Keppel in the Cambridge Conference report: "The present report is a bold step . . . . It is characterized by a complete impatience with the present capacities of the educational system. It is not only that most teachers will be completely incapable of teaching much of the mathematics set forth in the curricula proposed here; [but also] most teachers would be hard put to comprehend it. No brief period of retraining will suffice. Even the first grade curriculum embodies notions with which the average teacher is totally unfamiliar. None the less, these are the curricula toward which the schools should be aiming . . . if we are ever to make real progress." [C1, pp. viii–ix]

Pullback was noted in 1980 by futurist Marilyn Ferguson: "Reform after reform, some no doubt promising, failed because too many teachers disliked the key concepts or misunderstood them." [F9, p. 310]

Postulate 3. Teaching math requires special skills—making connections beyond the textbook, directing discussion past the obvious, relating methods among the topics, and guiding students towards the goal.

In 1953 John Clark and Howard Fehr tied student growth to teacher skills: "The growth in mathematical knowledge by each individual student . . . calls for direction by a skillful teacher who has a balanced emphasis on the various phases of learning." [C9, p. 347]

In 1960 Jerome Bruner emphasized strong teacher techniques: "One of the least discussed ways of carrying a student through a hard unit of material is to challenge him with a chance to exercise his full powers, so that he may discover the pleasure of full and effective functioning. Good teachers know the power of this lure. Students should know what it feels like to be completely absorbed in a problem. They seldom experience this feeling in school." [B21, p. 50]

In 1985 Alan Schoenfeld described necessary math skills, needed for both teachers and students: "Heuristic strategies are rules of thumb for successful problem solving, general suggestions that help an individual to understand a problem better or to make progress toward its solution. Such strategies include exploiting analogies, introducing auxiliary elements in a problem or working auxiliary problems, arguing by contradiction, working forward from the data, decomposing and recombining, exploiting related problems, drawing figures, generalizing and using the 'inventor's paradox,' specializing, using reductio ad absurdum and indirect proof, varying the problem, and working backward." [S9, p. 23]

In 1992 Harold Stevenson and James Stigler, in writing about international math performance, stressed the deftness of teachers: "The reform of education in the United States requires a re-thinking of the profession of teaching. No other change is as basic as this one for, after all, any effort to reform the structure or organization of education depends on the skill with which it is carried out by teachers." [S25, p. 173]

In 1996 the National Commission on Teaching and America's Future confirmed with a research study what others knew intuitively: ". . . this kind of [desired, dynamic] teaching requires high levels of knowledge and skill. To be effective, teachers must know their subject matter so thoroughly that they can present it in a challenging, clear, and compelling way. They must also know how their students learn and how to make ideas accessible so that they can construct successful 'teachable moments.' Research confirms that teacher knowledge of subject matter, student learning, and teaching methods are all important elements of teacher effectiveness." [N12, p. 6]

Also in 1996 E. D. Hirsch described ideal lesson structure: "The only truly general principle that seems to emerge from process-outcome research on pedagogy is that focused and guided instruction is far more effective than naturalistic, discovery, learn-at-your-own-pace instruction." In that frame of reference, Hirsch described "dramatized instruction" in which the class resembles a play, "with a beginning, middle and end, well directed but not rigidly scripted by the teacher. The beginning sets up the question to be answered, the knowledge to be mastered, or the skill to be gained; the middle consists of a lot of back-and-forth between student and student, student and teacher; and the end consists of a feeling of closure and accomplishment." [H12, p. 174]

In 1999 Howard Gardner described the art of teaching: "The teacher's job resembles that of a master orchestrator, who keeps the whole score in mind and yet can home in on particular passages and players." Gardner's key adjective in describing a great teacher was "versatile." He or she should be capable of devising new questions, probing side topics, coordinating class discussions, relating supplementary material, fitting pieces together, engaging all students, and finding meaningful understandings. [G3, p. 209]

Also in 1999 James Stigler and James Hiebert discussed math reform recommendations that asked teachers to forgo controlled teacher demonstrations followed by practice worksheets and to embrace random student explorations followed by directed discussions, calling the latter "adventurous" and "ambitious." While acknowledging that such teaching can be "quite effective" when "well executed," they cautioned: "But unless one knows what to expect from students, it is a scary way to teach. Success depends on making split-second decisions about which student suggestions to follow up on and which to ignore. What is learned by students during the lesson seems to depend on whether students hit upon the solution methods that make for good class discussions. Teachers can feel that they have lost control of the lesson, but they are told to 'embrace the uncertainty,' because this is what better teaching is like." [S26, pp. 155–156]

In 2000 NCTM reiterated why a great math teacher needs to know more math than the immediate topic at hand: "At times, opportunities for mathematical investigations arise spontaneously in class." [N24, p. 203]

In 2013 Diane Ravitch expressed the frustration of finding master teachers: "Will three great teachers in a row close the achievement gap? It is possible, but there is no statistical method today that can accurately predict or identify which teachers are 'great' teachers." [R7, p. 113]

Postulate 4. Despite needing to know and love math, unqualified people choose to become non-math math teachers.

Summers off, vacations at holidays, and an early end to the formal work day—these are features that attract people with minimal comfort with numbers to the teaching profession. Certainly, some working parents desire having the same schedule as their children. Others enjoy coaching a sports team as part of the job. Openings often exist due to large numbers of math teachers needed nationwide. Moreover, some people consider math as little more than arithmetic. Others think they can explain how to add the same number to both sides of an equation as competently as their own math teachers did. Yet, comfort with balancing checkbooks does not equal skill with imparting mathematics. And many would-be math teachers don't fathom that great math teachers work in the evening grading homework and in the summer preparing lessons. American society even has a sad adage: *Those who can, do; those who can't, teach.*

Stigler and Hiebert echoed this sentiment: "Infused in society's view of education is the notion that teaching is not that difficult." [S26, p. xiv]

Postulate 5. These non-math math teachers receive scant training and then teach from inadequate textbooks, matching their low level of math understanding.

The 2010 report *Breaking the Cycle: An International Comparison of U.S. Mathematics Teacher Preparation* underscored the weakness of American elementary teachers: "The desire that these future [U.S.] elementary teachers would possess higher levels of mathematics knowledge is especially important as this nation confronts the international realities suggested by PISA and TIMSS detailing how far behind we are." The study expected but did not find stronger math preparation for middle school math teachers, who teach only math rather than all subjects: "The story for the United States is serious. Given that these are future teachers of mathematics, it is rather disconcerting that the future Taiwanese teachers scored over one and a half standard deviations higher on the mathematics content knowledge test." [C6, pp. 18–19, 27]

Postulate 6. Other non-math people evaluate these non-math math teachers.

Arthur Bestor commented on the flawed practice of the mathematically untrained evaluating the mathematically untrained: "Whether mathematical teaching is sound is a question for mathematicians to answer. ... The professor of education has no competence whatever in these matters, nor has the teacher who is trained exclusively in pedagogy." [B11, pp.183–184]

Postulate 7. Lacking intrinsic math ability, proper training, high-quality textbooks, and adequate supervision, these non-math math teachers revert to what they know—how they themselves learned math.

In 1999 James Stigler and James Hiebert explained the default—the perpetuation of bad math teaching: "The methods most teachers use are inherited from earlier generations of instructors, not invented when they reach the classroom. . . . Much of what happens in the classroom is determined by a cultural code . . . . That's why changing teachers will not automatically produce changes in teaching." [S26, p. xii]

Postulate 8. Students of non-math math teachers score poorly on local, state, national, and international tests. Raising test scores becomes a pressing issue, using any method including hiring even more unprepared non-math math teachers.

As if taken by surprise, society becomes upset when math test scores are low. But society has been perpetrating a hoax by calling these educators math teachers. Society then places a large share of the blame on existing math teachers as well as a disproportionate measure of the hope on new math teachers, who are often equally as unqualified. The system is nonsensical and unsustainable.

In 2010 Diane Ravitch summarized the situation: "The teacher was everything; that was the new mantra of economists and bottom-line school reformers. And not only was the teacher the key to closing the achievement gap, but the most effective teachers did not need to have any paper credentials or teacher education. There was no way to predict who would be a good teacher. So there was no reason to limit entry into teaching; anyone should be able to enter the profession and show whether she or he could raise test scores." [R6, p. 184]

As Ravitch explained, the best teachers became those who yielded test score gains year after year. But that success was only determined five years after the start of the teacher's career—two years to acquire experience and three years to show gains. She questioned whether a parent would want a child to be with a teacher who was an experiment. Moreover, the entire scoring structure could be misleading in evaluating both students and teachers: "And common sense suggests that any system of measurement that produces a top quartile will also produce three other quartiles." [R6, p. 219]

Postulate 9. Feeling threatened and worried about job security, non-math math teachers make important, far-reaching classroom decisions.

Teachers' comfort levels affect their decisions about content. In 1968 B. F. Skinner commented: "A teacher continues to teach those things he can teach effectively and he tends to discard others, and as a result the content of a course changes." [S17, p. 234]

Individual classroom determinations concerning topics can have serious consequences, as discussed by William Schmidt and Curtis McKnight in 2012: "This important decision [which math topics to teach, in what order, and for how long] seems to have become the domain of individual teachers. Since these teachers vary greatly in mathematics knowledge, it is not surprising to find large variation. . . . These practices fundamentally and arbitrarily compromise children's futures in significant ways. These practices seem impossible to defend as reasonable policy for how schools should be run." [S7, p. 142]

Postulate 10. Multiple approaches to improving math teaching have failed. Non-math math teachers remain in classrooms.

Inadequate approaches, because they give false hope and dissuade people from seeking real solutions, can be worse than no attempts. Moreover, most proposals have either been nonspecific or encountered the chicken-and-egg dilemma.

In 1960 Jerome Bruner suggested ideas still heard today and not accomplished, perhaps due to the size of the country, the stronghold of the system, or the absence of a plan—improvement in the areas of teacher recruitment, pre-job training, on-the-job training, summer in-service, teachers' salaries, and professional respect. [B21, p. 89]

In 1969 William Glasser proposed: "Only in a school where teacher and student are involved with each other and equally involved with the curriculum through thinking and problem solving does education flourish—an education that prepares students to live successfully in the world." [G7, p. 19]

In 1996 the report by the National Commission on Teaching and America's Future offered five admirable but vague major recommendations: "I. Get serious about standards, for both students and teachers. II. Reinvent teacher preparation and professional development. III. Fix teacher recruitment and put qualified teachers in every classroom. IV. Encourage and reward teacher knowledge and skill. V. Create schools that are organized for student and teacher success." [N12, p. 11]

In 1999 James Stigler and James Hiebert warned: "The most alarming aspect of classroom [math] teaching in the United States is not how we are teaching now but that we have no mechanism for getting better. Without such a mechanism, the teaching gap will continue to grow." They suggested building continuing education into math teachers' year-long schedules, as opposed to providing infrequent, bandage-approach in-service days: "We are convinced that the hard work of improving teaching cannot succeed without changes in our culture of teacher learning. . . . Effective teacher learning must be built into teachers' daily and weekly schedules. Schools must become the places where teachers, not just students, learn." These researchers suggested: "This path [forward] also moves away from viewing teaching as a solitary activity, owned personally by each instructor. It moves toward a view of teaching as a professional activity open to collective observations, study, and improvement." [S26, pp. xix, 191, xv]

Also in 1999 Howard Gardner offered five strategies for *"individually configured education."* One was: "Allow students to remain with the same teacher(s) for several years, so that they can get to know one another very well." That idea leads to more failure if the teacher is weak in math. Another was: "Assign teachers and students flexibly, so that more compatible matches can be made." [G4, pp. 151, 153]

In 2004 *Increasing the Odds: How Good Policies Can Yield Better Teachers* by the National Council on Teacher Quality debunked proposals for improvement in five categories. (1) *Master's Degrees*: "Advanced degrees do not make teachers more effective." (2) *Experience*: "A few years of experience makes a teacher more effective; after that it's unclear." (3) *Education Courses*: "Education courses taken before teaching have little impact on teacher effectiveness." (4) *Traditional Certification*: "Traditional routes into teaching do not appear to yield more effective teachers than alternative routes." (5) *Subject Area Knowledge*: "Strong preparation in a secondary teacher's intended subject area adds significant value. Less is known about the breadth and depth of subject matter needed for teaching elementary grades." [W2, pp. 2–5, 7]

In 2013 Diane Ravitch criticized the removal of teachers based on their students' high-stakes test scores, advocating not for "find and fire," but for locate and nurture. Yet her suggestions for growing "a highly skilled professional teacher corps," an educational "imperative," were familiarly general, including the improvement of recruitment, preparation, support, respect, and autonomy. [R7, p. 132]

Also in 2013 Amanda Ripley implied that the United States might try Finland's approach to improving math education: "The Finns decided that the only way to get serious about education was to select highly educated teachers, the best and the brightest of each generation, and train them rigorously. . . . It was a radically obvious strategy that few countries have attempted." However, the difference in size between Finland and the U.S. is a huge obstacle. [R13, p. 89]

Postulate 11. Math teaching is not now entirely a bona fide profession.

If physicians take the Hippocratic Oath and civil engineers pledge the Engineers' Creed, then why are educators allowed to teach incorrectly? In 1953 Arthur Bestor proposed elevating the profession, giving teachers professional freedom but holding them accountable: "Freedom, however, implies obligation. And freedom of teaching cannot be understood or defended without understanding and accepting the obligations that go with it. . . . in boldest terms, the teacher is not a mere private citizen but a public functionary, and those whom he addresses constitute, in a sense, a 'captive' audience." [B11, pp. 179–180]

In 1999 James Stigler and James Hiebert echoed the same theme: "We can see fashions and trends, ups and downs. But we cannot see the kind of gradual improvement that marks true professions. . . . In true professions, standard practices hold the wisdom of the profession. It is when the standard practices of teaching are improved that a profession begins to emerge. . . . And when teaching becomes a profession, teachers will inherit the professional badges that come from being members." Moreover, Stigler and Hiebert cited Albert Shanker's comparison to the field of medicine's "name for the failure to use standard practices—it's *malpractice*." [S26, pp. 127, 175–176]

Postulate 12. The power of great math teaching is an experience that all children should but don't share.

In 1960 Jerome Bruner remarked on the inequitable distribution of great math teachers: "There are many images [of positive, impactful teachers], and they are precious. Alas, there are also destructive images: the teachers who sapped confidence, the dream killers, and the rest of the cabinet of horrors. [Alfred] Whitehead once remarked that education should involve an exposure to greatness. Many of us have been fortunate. But there is no simple plan for attracting greatness to the teaching profession." [B21, p. 91]

In 2011, over a half-century later, Michael Greenstone and Adam Looney commented similarly, relating the lack of great math to economic impact: "In terms of delivering large potential gains, effective teaching is among the most important influences on student achievement. Research finds that teachers vary substantially in their effectiveness, even within the same school. These differences arise not just in the effect of teachers on test scores, but also in terms of their impact on the lives of children long after they leave the classroom—including impacts on their future employment prospects and earnings." [G10, p. xii]

In 2012 Schmidt and McKnight sounded an alarm about teacher-quality variation: "*. . . the greatest source of variation in opportunity to learn is not between local communities, or even schools, but between classrooms. . . .* To say that teachers are a major source of variation in opportunity to learn is not to blame teachers for educational inequality. Teachers are not the problem; putting them in such a situation and failing to give them the training and support they need *is*." [S7, p. xii]

Postulate 13. Great math teaching is complex.

In 1966 Jerome Bruner wrote: ". . . what the teacher must be, to be an effective competence model, is a day-to-day working model with whom to interact. It is not so much that the teacher provides a model to *imitate*. Rather, it is that the teacher can become a part of the student's internal dialogue—somebody whose respect he wants, someone whose standards he wishes to make his own. It is like becoming a speaker of a language one shares with somebody. The language of that interaction becomes a part of oneself, and the standards of style and clarity that one adopts for that interaction become a part of one's own standards." [B22, p. 124] I tutored many students who didn't respect their math teachers.

The 1996 publication by the National Commission on Teaching and America's Future stated: "Research has discovered . . . that expert teachers use knowledge about children and their learning to fashion lessons that connect ideas to students' experiences. They create a wide variety of learning opportunities that make subject matter come alive for young people who learn in very different ways. They know how to support students' continuing development and motivation to achieve while creating incremental steps that help students progress toward more complicated ideas and performances. They know how to diagnose sources of problems in students' learning and how to identify strengths on which to build. These skills make the difference between teaching that creates learning and teaching that just marks time." [N12, p. 6]

Postulate 14. Great math teaching needs constant refinement.

In 1972 in *Guidelines for Teaching Mathematics*, Donovan Johnson and Gerald Rising wrote: "Above all else, the continuing revolution in mathematics teaching makes it imperative that the classroom teacher keep abreast of current developments." [J7, p. 24] That statement remains relevant as new math teachers enter the profession.

In 1999 James Stigler and James Hiebert discussed the importance of continually improving math teaching, whether teachers learn from their students or their colleagues: ". . . becoming an expert teacher will require consistent opportunities over long periods of time for teachers to study and improve one's own teaching and the teaching of one's colleagues. Teaching the same old way is natural. Teaching in new ways is far more complicated than many think. Teachers must have knowledge of the domain (e.g. mathematics) and of how students think about and learn the domain. They must also have skills at implementing a variety of different methods that have been validated and incorporated into a growing knowledge base for teaching. Finally, they must have the skills to assess what students know and where they are in a learning trajectory, as well as the judgment to decide which of the methods in their repertoire to deploy when." [S26, pp. 192–193]

Postulate 15. Satisfying the previous postulates is virtually impossible when neither the meaning of a great math teacher nor an understanding about great math teaching exists.

In 2012 William Schmidt and Curtis McKnight identified this dilemma: "The definition of a high-quality mathematics teacher has never been standardized. Therefore, although improving the quality of teachers and teaching is a common cry when we seek to improve schools, there is little agreement and scant empirical evidence that indicates what characteristics define a high-quality mathematics teacher. Even an obvious definition, such as knowledge of mathematics, is problematic, since there is generally no agreement as to what specific mathematics knowledge is needed." [S7, p. 145] They continued: "In the case of mathematics, teacher quality also involves teachers' knowledge of mathematics as an academic or formal discipline and of the mathematics unique to the curriculum at the grade levels they teach. In combination, these types of knowledge define a teacher's professional competencies." [S7, p. 146]

Tinkering with the present state of math education—including retrying previously failed corrective approaches—will not remove teachers who neither know nor love math, will not advance a strong curriculum that ignores the level of existing teachers, will not find or train masterful teachers, will not prevent teachers from making unwise classroom decisions, will not deliver sound math equitably from all teachers, will not remove the complexities of great math teaching, and will not turn math teaching into a valued profession. Even if topics appear, for a good amount of time and in the proper sequence, instruction can still be shoddy—incorrect, ineffective, superficial, and/or time-wasting—due to the teachers. Improving the vast quantity of non-math math teachers via the usual ideas cannot happen—the present system lacks both the means to attract and the method to educate the countless replacements needed. While the current educational system endures, the country will never have the proper number of true math teachers and the resulting necessary amount of valuable, societal math talent. Radical change in math education is required for advancement.

16
Understanding Programmed Instruction

Teaching is the expediting of learning: a person who is taught learns more quickly than one who is not.
B. F. Skinner [S17, p. 5]

From Paul Saettler's 1990 historical analysis of computing devices and their inventors, *The Evolution of American Educational Technology*, I select three educators who helped to build the path needed for my plan.

First is Socrates (470–399 BC) who developed the Socratic method of instruction. Saettler wrote: "The inquiry was carried on through the give-and-take of conversation, which Socrates guided by a series of leading questions. In the Socratic method, the questioner used only those facts already known to the pupil." [S1, p. 26] The Socratic Method of learning still thrives in some private schools, colleges, and law schools.

Second is Maria Montessori (1870–1952) who "exerted a dynamic impact on educational technology through her development of graded materials designed to provide the proper sequencing of subject matter for each individual learner." [S1, p. 5] The Montessori Method still flourishes across the country in certified schools bearing her name.

Third is Edward Thorndike (1874–1949) who based his laws of learning on a "stimulus-response hypothesis." Saettler wrote: ". . . the instructional task of the teacher is guided by two broad rules: (1) to put together what should go together, and (2) to reward the expression of desirable connections . . . ." [S1, p. 55] Saettler named Thorndike's work as having the greatest influence on B. F. Skinner. Thorndike anticipated programmed instruction when he wrote in his 1912 book *Education*, "If, by a miracle of mechanical ingenuity, a book could be so arranged that only to him who had done what was directed on page one would page two become visible, and so on, much that now requires personal instruction could be managed by print." [G2, p. 31; S1, p. 56]

These visionaries—with their concepts of questioning by applying known facts, sequencing by using graded steps, and rewarding by connecting natural pairs—take us to psychologist B. F. Skinner (1904–1990), known for his Teaching Machine to execute his theory of Programmed Instruction. Skinner's work lives on today through the B. F. Skinner Foundation. [www16–1] In 1958 Skinner foresaw the necessity of machines to assist education. He wrote: "The demand [for education] cannot be met simply by building more schools and training more teachers. Education must become more efficient. To this end curricula must be revised and simplified, and textbooks and classroom techniques improved. ... Even in a small classroom the teacher usually knows that he is moving too slowly for some students and too fast for others. Those who could go faster are penalized, and those who should go slower are poorly taught and unnecessarily punished by criticism and failure. Machine instruction would permit each student to proceed at his own rate." [S16, p. 969]

In 1968 Skinner described quick feedback and positive reinforcement as essential components of programmed instruction. He criticized typical schooling as lacking those indispensable ingredients. While he stated that at some point, students might become able to provide their own feedback, the teacher is the usual source of corrections. Skinner declared: ". . . the lapse of only a few seconds between response and reinforcement destroys most of the effect." He criticized the system of the teacher moving among students to offer guidance as they worked because of the lapsed time "between the child's response and the teacher's reinforcement." And Skinner hammered an overnight delay: "In many cases—for example, when papers are taken home to be corrected—as much as 24 hours may intervene. It is surprising that this system has any effect whatsoever." [S17, p. 16]

Skinner continued: "Perhaps the most serious criticism of the current classroom is the relative infrequency of reinforcement. Since the pupil is usually dependent upon the teacher for being told that he is right, and since many pupils are usually dependent upon the same teacher, the total number of contingencies which may be arranged during, say, the first four years, is of the order of only a few thousand. But a very rough estimate suggests that efficient mathematical behavior at this level requires something of the order of 25,000 contingencies." [S17, p. 17]

Skinner also labeled the lack of quick feedback and positive reinforcement as a root cause of math anxiety. "The very subjects in which modern techniques are weakest are those in which failure is most conspicuous, and in the wake of an ever-growing incompetence come the anxieties, uncertainties, and aggressions which in their turn present other problems to the school. Most pupils soon claim the asylum of not being 'ready' for arithmetic . . . or, eventually, of not having a mathematical mind. Such explanations are readily seized upon by defensive teachers and parents. Few pupils ever reach the stage at which automatic reinforcements follow as natural consequences of mathematical behavior. On the contrary, the figures and symbols of mathematics have become standard emotional stimuli. The glimpse of a column of figures, not to say an algebraic symbol or an integral sign, is likely to set off, not mathematical behavior, but a reaction of anxiety, guilt, or fear." [S17, p. 18]

Yet Skinner insisted that these flaws in teaching could be corrected. He wrote: "There would be no point in urging these objections if improvement were impossible. . . . We can no longer allow the exigencies of a practical situation to suppress the tremendous improvements which are within reach." [S17, p. 19]

Moreover, Skinner argued that machines were necessary to improve education: "In the experimental study of learning it has been found that the contingencies of reinforcement which are most efficient in controlling the organism cannot be arranged through the personal mediation of the experimenter. An organism is affected by subtle details of contingencies which are beyond the capacity of the human organism to arrange. . . . Mechanical help is also demanded by the sheer number of contingencies which may be used efficiently in a single experimental session." [S17, p. 21]

Skinner contended that three components were mandatory for effective programmed instruction and teaching machines. The first was sequence: "The device [Skinner Teaching Machine] makes it possible to present carefully designed material in which one problem can depend upon the answer to the preceding problem and where, therefore, the most efficient progress to an eventually complex repertoire can be made." [S17, p. 24] The second was scale: "In acquiring complex behavior the student must pass through a carefully designed sequence of steps, often of considerable length. Each step must be so small that it can always be taken, yet in taking it the student moves somewhat closer to fully competent behavior." [S17, pp. 34–35] The third was feedback: ". . . the student always knew where he stood, without waiting for an hour test or final examination." [S17, p. 54]

Imagine learning mathematical tasks—from multiplying fractions to factoring a trinomial—in the Skinner method. A machine would present a carefully constructed sequence of information and questions, each tiny in breadth and depth, designed for the student to answer correctly, thereby providing positive feedback. The cumulative effect would be a magnificently revealed explanation of the skill with guaranteed learning.

Like other education reforms, Skinner's grand idea failed. Saettler continued his account: "By the late 1960s the decline of the programmed instruction movement was already evident. The high expectations and extravagant claims had led to disappointing outcomes." [S1, p. 303]

Perhaps Skinner's reference to children as *organisms* obstructed the acceptance of his idea. But the physical appearance of his Teaching Machine was no help either. Photos of Skinner's 1954 Teaching Machine showed a large wooden box, cranks, knobs, paper tape, and other rudimentary features. [S17, pp. 23, 25] Another objection focused around automation: the analysis of human intellectual achievement in mechanistic terms, the potential unemployment due to mechanization, and the dollar cost of mechanizing schools. [S17, pp. 26–27]

Moreover, Skinner's professional peers were not totally ready to accept his vision. Jerome Bruner, in his account of the 1959 Woods Hole Conference, provided meaningful, first-hand observations. He stated that Harvard Professor B. F. Skinner's demonstration of teaching machines "led to a lively, at times stormy, discussion." [B21, p. xxi] Bruner continued: "Virtually all of the participants agreed that not teaching devices but teachers were the principal agents of instruction, but there was a division of opinion on how the teacher was to be aided." [B21, p. 15] Perhaps inadequate technology caused these reactions.

Robert Gagné also described "a few of the many factors that contributed to the decline of the programmed instruction movement." He wrote: "By the late 1960s, the programmed instruction movement was coming to an end. . . . Research had shown that the instructional effectiveness of programmed materials often was no greater than the effectiveness of conventional instructional materials. . . . Furthermore, students often indicated that the programmed materials were uninteresting. . . . In addition, school administrators and teachers had difficulty adjusting to the new roles thrust upon them by the use of self-instructional materials in their classrooms." [G2, p. 32] I suggest that modern technology would negate these factors and that administrators and teachers should not have the option of blocking change if it is truly positive.

In 1977 Grace Burton offered a possible reason for the Teaching Machine's failure. She wrote: ". . . not all children find this type of learning congruent with their learning styles . . . ." [B25, p. 247] Today, children's love of modern technology would likely invalidate that argument.

Still, Skinner's ideas continued to surface as a model for later work. For example, in the *President's Report to the Harvard Board of Overseers for 1983–84*, Derek Bok wrote: "According to Skinner, the aim of designing programmed learning was to construct a series of questions that almost every student could answer correctly. The act of giving the correct answer and the reinforcement that followed served to plant the knowledge more firmly in the student's mind. The earliest computer-assisted instruction exemplified this method. The architects of CAI, however, soon broke with Skinner and sought to build programs that would be more challenging for the student. They stopped asking only questions that would elicit correct answers and began supplying text and helpful hints that would lead erring students to recognize their mistakes and figure out the correct answers." [B17, pp. 31–32]

In 1999 Howard Gardner offered another criticism of programmed instruction: "The epitome of this way of thinking [behavioral psychology] is represented by the teaching machine. Without the need for human intervention (except, of course, to program the machine), the student sits at a terminal, emits behaviors, and is continually shaped through positive (or negative) reinforcement until the correct stream of actions emerges. Nowadays, when the machine is likely to be a computer, some have dubbed such programs 'drill-and-kill.'" [G3, p. 64] However, Gardner's critique is debunked by using brilliantly designed software offering all of the curriculum features of Chapter 14 as well as employing master math teachers for other classroom experiences.

Note two important points in understanding Skinner's work. First, Skinner valued teachers: "Will machines replace teachers? . . . In assigning certain mechanizable functions to machines, the teacher emerges in his proper role as an indispensable human being." [S17, p. 55] I also value teachers; but I want poor math teachers removed and strong math teachers elevated. Second, Skinner valued his predecessors, writing about the earlier teaching machines of psychologist Sidney Pressey: " . . . the world of education was not ready for them." Moreover, Skinner quoted Pressey as saying that he hoped "enough may have been done to stimulate other workers, that this fascinating field may be developed." [S16, p. 969] I suggest the same applies to Skinner's work—society was not ready during his lifetime, but now we should build on his work.

Bringing programmed instruction full-circle, Saettler predicted encouragingly: "The educational technology of the next century may be totally different in terms of its methodology and outlook. Other exploration will be made in the years ahead. The possibilities seem endless." [S1, p. 15] We are now in that *next century*, with significantly more advanced educational technology. *From STEM To STEW* is the start of *other exploration*.

17
Shouting "Eureka!"

Revolutions shift into place suddenly, like the pattern in a kaleidoscope. They do not so much proceed as crystallize.
Marilyn Ferguson [F9, p. 38]

One evening several years ago, I had an Archimedes moment. No, I did not run from the bathtub screaming, "Eureka! I have found it!" But yes, my epiphany was more universal and consequential than understanding that the volume of displaced water equals the volume of the object causing the displacement. I believed I had discovered the solution to society's plaguing problem: inferior math education.

Psychologist Robert Sternberg wrote, "Contrary to popular myths, most creative insights do not happen in a flash. People require time to understand a problem, mull it over in their minds, and come up with a creative solution." [S24, p. 212] From that perspective, I had spent decades grappling with all aspects of poor math teaching. But my life's work united in a miraculous, surprising, instantaneous, and exciting flash of inspiration while viewing an Apple iPad commercial on television.

First, I had a flashback.

What my mind remembered from many decades ago was in itself astounding. I recalled my 5th grade experience with B. F. Skinner's programmed instruction in book form, not knowing what it was at the time. I adored the entire process—every small, pointed question and certain, correct answer as I progressed through learning about exponents. The experience was not only more exciting than the math classroom but also more thrilling than any other approach. I was fiercely disappointed, discovering that my precious workbook was experimental and temporary.

Second, I had a vision.

I saw the marriage of an old idea with new technology. I saw tablet technology as the missing hardware to Skinner's brilliant concept. Tablets today are in one respect what personal computers were in the 1980s—hardware desperately in need of appropriate software. The intersection of the three components—tablet hardware, rigorous math, and Skinner's programmed learning—was the key to finally fixing math education, I realized.

Third, I had a recollection.

From watching the 1957 film *A Dancer's World* one day in high school, I recalled Martha Graham's impactful statement: "It takes ten years, usually, to make a dancer. It takes ten years of handling the instrument, handling the material with which you are dealing, for you to know it completely." [www17–1] I wondered about taking ten years to teach children math in a coherent, unified fashion—training the mind for math just as training the body for dance. I also considered the British approach toward ballet, which accepts "dance for all," but recognizes "progress and achievement through taking examination." [www17–2] I wondered about a comparable assumption: math was for all children, with advancement not arbitrary at the end of each school year but rather determined by a series of carefully planned steps and appraisals.

Within my vision, children could learn at their own pace, whether below, on, or above grade level. Students' advancement of a school grade would be independent of their math progress. Perhaps most importantly, every student would have equal math content opportunity, a condition so explicitly and elegantly argued for by William Schmidt and Curtis McKnight [S7].

As Howard Gardner wrote, "An education based upon questions, understanding, in-depth probing, and mastery of disciplines is most likely to be realized if it is not simply described in the abstract." [G3, p. 229] Thus, in the next chapter, I explain the details of my solution.

18
Revealing the Plan

I have vision, and the rest of the world wears bifocals.
Butch Cassidy

Do I really want to transform the mold of today's math teacher? I say yes! Tinkering is inadequate. Instead, I propose radical change, based on the work of B. F. Skinner, but impractical prior to modern technology. I give my plan the working name PI-MATH for *Programmed Instruction Math*, with a play on the word *pi* for the famous irrational number.

While the main points of PI-MATH are inflexible—and must be to truly give children the math education they deserve—other aspects might change during development. Thus, *flexible rigidity* is the desired approach. The following is an outline of the overall strategy.

I. Advance Planning

1. Form a non-profit foundation to undertake a complete transformation of American math education, one school at a time on a voluntary basis.

As with all non-profits, a board would oversee the organization.

2. Apply for grant money to launch and support the project.

Capital could come from citizens, foundations, corporations, or government.

3. Create a website for the project.

Provide ongoing information from the start. Post sources of funding, members of the team, development scheduling and progress, job opportunities, workshop dates, and more.

4. Hire the most competent people to create PI-MATH software.

Assemble a team including: (1) school mathematics experts to design the curriculum, chart the integration, and write the millions of steps; (2) psychologists trained in Skinner's work to check the narrowness of steps; and (3) tablet programmers to write the software. In my opinion, those math experts with the necessary rigorous, creative math knowledge qualified to join the team currently fall into two groups: (1) math-question writers from premier competitions, as well as some former students (now adults) and coaches, if they earned recognition at the regional, state, or national levels; and (2) math professors who have successfully engaged non-math majors, having proven the breakdown of math into understandable components.

As Jerome Bruner wrote about SMSG and UICSM, "The experience of the past several years has taught at least one important lesson about the design of a curriculum that is true to the underlying structure of its subject matter. It is that the best minds in any particular discipline must be put to work on the task." [B21, p. 19] The precedent for participation by university professors dates back not only to the Sputnik era but also to the prior century. As reported in NCTM's compendium of historical math education documents, of the ten members of the mathematics subcommittee that issued the NEA's *Report of the Committee on Secondary School Studies* in 1893, six were university professors. "This committee, as well as others of the period, was dominated by college professors and school administrators. Only later [1923] were secondary teachers invited to participate in committee work . . . ." [B13, p. 127]

II. Software Development

5. Order and intertwine math into a continuous, logical structure.

This very act of sequence-creation is more empowering with programming than with writing. Skinner implied that the exercise alone could

Revealing the Plan

bring better math education: "This effect of the machine in confronting the programmer with the full scope of his task may in itself produce a considerable improvement in education." [S17, pp. 50]

6. Change the direction of the curriculum so that it is no longer one train speeding on a track toward calculus but a broader presentation of math with paths to number theory, discrete math, logic, and statistics.

I have observed too many bright math students take calculus at too young an age, only to lose their love of math.

7. Incorporate the richness of math into PI-MATH, with integrated strands rather than separate subjects, showing the fascinating connections among multiple areas.

In 1978 Stanley Kogelman and Joseph Warren warned: "Math is bound to be distasteful if it is experienced as rigid, judgmental, and inflexible." [K11, p. 26] PI-MATH would be elegant and fluid.

8. Engage parents who will permit their children to work with the team after school as the curriculum is written.

Jerome Bruner addressed this matter: ". . . a curriculum should be prepared jointly by the subject-matter expert, the teacher, and the psychologist, with due regard for the inherent structure of the material, its sequencing, the psychological pacing of reinforcement, and the building of maintaining of predispositions to problem solving. As the curriculum is being built, it must be tested in detail by close observational and experimental methods to assess not simply whether children are 'achieving' but rather what they are making of the material and how they are organizing it. It is on the basis of 'testing as you go' that revision is made. It is this process that puts the evaluation process at a time when and a place where its results can be used for correction while the curriculum is being constructed." [B22, pp. 70–71]

9. Create accompanying PI-MATH practice papers because ultimately math is done with paper and pencil.

These written assignments, done in-class to be sure that the student and only the student is doing them, would form part of the student's evaluation.

III. School Implementation

10. Purchase enough tablets in each school so that multiple math classes could occur concurrently throughout the school day.

Tablets would be the technology vehicle to deliver the math instruction using Skinner's methodology because they are more cost effective and less physically burdensome than laptop computers. They could include capabilities of a graphing calculator via an app. Moreover, they could be programmed for students' individual bookmarking capabilities. In Skinner's lifetime not only was fast, graphic-oriented technology non-existent, but also what could be built would only supply one per classroom or school, not one per student. Now, each student could have his/her own tablet in class, including one to borrow overnight if needed.

11. Begin PI-MATH in fourth grade (see step 30 in conjunction).

The work of Jean Piaget and Jerome Bruner support placing students in grades PK–3 with actual teachers. Piaget's concrete-operational stage is hands-on, thus not applicable to a tablet. Moreover, Piaget's exercises in conservation suggest that children can learn abstract math only when ready. Bruner postulated that a child learns math best when progressing through three stages: real objects (concrete), pictures of objects (iconic), and abstract representations of objects (symbolic). Again, the experience with real objects cannot occur on a tablet. And while programmed instruction is founded on Skinner's work on positive reinforcement by always getting the answer correct, PI-MATH cannot include the personal touch of smiles, praise, attention, and even stickers that young children enjoy and need. David Elkind's words offer support: "A child entering school does not need to be taught by a specialist in . . . math. This is true because teaching entry-level skills requires much more knowledge about the students being taught than it does specialization in the subject matter." [E1, p. 73]

However, in grades 4 and 5, often called the intermediate grades, math should be separated from the purview of the main teacher. As the authors of *The Educated Child* wrote, "At this level [grades 4–6], children should not have to rely on hands-on objects such as blocks, beans, cardboard cutouts, or fingers to perform basic skills and work most problems. Teachers may still use physical props to help illustrate some lessons, but as cognitive abilities develop, children should be required to do more abstract thinking. Simple manipulatives should be replaced by more advanced tools such as rulers, compasses, and protractors." [B10, p. 298] With PI-MATH, the tablet is one such *advanced tool*, providing spectacular graphics to illustrate many themes. And although grades 6–8 (middle school) is sometimes described as the blight of American math education, the weakness of the earlier grades was also noted by these same authors: "Be aware, however, that in some U.S. schools the math program is not as strong as it should be in the intermediate grades [fourth through sixth]. Lessons do not prepare children for work that lies ahead in junior high and high school." [B10, p. 298]

12. Replace existing math education with one hour of daily PI-MATH.

Because delivery would be so efficient, students might log in additional math at various times during the day, otherwise wasted.

13. Provide a mechanism for the PI-MATH software to be available to students on their home tablets.

14. Eliminate existing textbooks and curricula. Minimize state standards and exams.

The reason is obvious—they would be all inferior and inappropriate.

15. Remove the practice of making students repeat a grade in school due to a low grade on the state math exam.

As Skinner wrote: ". . . students may continue to be grouped in 'grades' or 'classes,' but it will be possible for each to proceed at his own level, advancing as rapidly as he can." [S17, pp. 55–56]

IV. Teacher Changes

16. Eliminate the current job called math teacher.

Note that removing an existing job is done in other industries to reorganize the workplace.

17. Create a new job called "PI-MATH Mentor."

Although the British meaning of "tutor" might work, unfortunately, the American meaning of the word associates it with remediation. And, as previously discussed, the term math coach is now used for school specialists who assist ill-prepared math teachers. The alliterative title "math mentor" seems appropriate.

18. Create three levels of PI-MATH Mentor Certification—1, 2, and 3.

Level 1 would encompass grades 4–6, Level 2 grades 7–9, and Level 3 grades 10–12. College Board Advanced Placement Courses such as Calculus and Statistics would remain distinct, not in Level 3.

19. Take applications to become a PI-MATH Mentor from anyone who wishes to apply.

Applicants could come from a variety of professions, including former math teachers, regardless of whether actively working or retired. Overall, the nervous fakes would flee, and the ecstatic stars would soar—elevating math educators into a true profession. Gone would be the system in which mathematically talented adults could not teach in a public school system because they lacked an education degree. A college major or minor in math would be helpful and likely but not mandatory. A candidate's aptitude and attitude would also be considered.

20. Administer a math aptitude test to all applicants.

Aptitude tests are mostly based on pattern recognition and not specific knowledge of math. However, demonstrated proficiency in solving general word problems would be included; otherwise candidates would have too much to learn. IBM developed such a test for prospective computer programmers five decades ago.

21. Continue the application process with a series of personal interviews, for those who show substantial math aptitude.

Gauge candidates' attitudes and experiences from their own K–12 math education and previous work. With a team of observers present, teach them math one-on-one to see how they respond. While the math aptitude test would likely remove all math-anxious candidates, determine their feelings about challenging students. As Marilyn Ferguson wrote, ". . . appropriate stress is essential. Teachers can fail to transform if they are afraid to upset the learner." [F9, p. 293]

22. Administer careful background checks as to character with regard to working with children, for those who pass the aptitude test and interview round.

Use local law enforcement to assist in screening candidates.

23. Send all ongoing candidates to an intensive, summer-long training program for Level 1.

For 8 weeks, 6 days a week, provide instruction for 3 hours in the morning, 4 hours in the afternoon, and 2 hours in the evening. During the first summer, only Level 1 certification would be offered; during the second summer, Levels 1 and 2 would be offered. For all summers thereafter, training in all three levels would be available. Candidates must become certified in a prior level before advancing.

As recently as 2016, E. D. Hirsch wrote: "It's true that in the United States, there has been a deep problem with teacher preparation for more than half a century. We have a system that, according to teachers themselves, does not prepare them adequately for . . . the substance of what they must teach." [H14, p. 36] PI-MATH candidates would receive thorough math training in every regard.

24. *Award those who successfully finish the summer training program the title "PI-MATH Mentor."*

Award those who pass this rigorous process not only with the title but also with the prestige and salary that they deserve.

25. *Allow PI-MATH Mentors flexibility in the use of the math hour for each individual student.*

Students would be working on the tablets, doing the practice papers, or studying with the mentors, on a rotating basis depending on their spot in lesson completion. Student groups would be fluid.

Time away from tablets is when students, now with solid background, might suggest original thoughts about math. As the authors of *The Learning Gap* wrote, teachers (now mentors) must feel secure "about the depth of their own mathematical training . . . to evaluate the validity of novel ideas that students inevitably propose." [S25, p. 191]

Time away from the tablets is also when students might make errors of varying degree, offering mentors teachable moments. Again, these authors wrote: ". . . American teachers place little emphasis on the constructive use of errors as a teaching technique. Learning about what is wrong may hasten understanding of why the correct procedures are appropriate . . . ." Errors should not "be interpreted as failure." [S25, p. 193] Gone would be non-math math teachers who would be frightened by this situation.

26. *Provide continuous, essential feedback to PI-MATH Mentors about their students' progress.*

As Skinner wrote, "Admittedly, a teacher cannot supervise 10,000 or 15,000 responses made by each pupil per year." [S17, pp. 41–42] But the tablet is a vehicle to monitor students' answers. He also wrote that this advantage of machine instruction is nonexistent for traditional professionals. [S17, p. 49] If students tried to fake learning by randomly answering the tiny, step-by-step questions presented, mentors would know immediately because the answers would be wrong. Mentors would have the option of handling the situation themselves or involving a school administrator or counselor. But the feedback would prevent an emotional or academic issue from festering.

27. Monitor the performance of all PI-MATH Mentors through data collection of their students' progress.

28. Provide annual continuing education for PI-MATH Mentors through in-person workshops, online newsletters, and conference-style or individual telephone consultations.

29. Add continuing education and collegial sharing to the summer session programs.

30. Enroll all K–3 teachers at PI-MATH schools in an intensive summer math workshop and provide school-year support.

Explain that the K–3 foundation is vital for future success. Discuss why K–3 teachers are an integral part of the team, correct their flawed notions about math, and work individually with those who have math anxiety.

31. Provide career counseling to previous math teachers who don't qualify as PI-MATH Mentors.

V. Continuing Operations

32. Employ tech experts, available by phone or online, to chat with PI-MATH schools in case of hardware or software problems.

A school district could also employ its own technology expert to help with technical problems that might arise.

33. Use the initial schools that enroll as field-test sites.

A wide range of schools might be interested at the start—those with low quality math instruction, those with excessively many out-of-field math teachers, those with difficulty in engaging students, those with bottom-ranking standardized test scores, those with trouble providing teacher continuing education, and those with inadequate programs for gifted students. Adoption would be voluntary, one independent school or public school system at a time. I believe that the free market would rule—that parents would want to join the movement when they heard of other children who came home happy from school, who did rigorous math easily, who needed math help neither from a parent nor a tutor, and who scored high on college admission math tests.

34. Provide the public with utmost transparency in data.

Once students begin participating, post on the PI-MATH website all data with compete transparency, including mean, median, mode, range, and outlier numbers for anonymous student progress in the lessons at each month of each school year. Also post statistics for school standardized test scores as well as SAT and ACT scores, whether for middle school talent identification or college admission.

35. Create a support group as part of the non-profit organization.

Part of changing the love-hate attitude that many Americans have toward math is engaging them in the PI-MATH movement.

~ ~ ~ ~ ~

A key aspect of this thirty-five point plan is that PI-MATH would remove the fifty obstacles to great math education detailed in Chapter 11.

Obstacle 1. In-field Teachers would no longer teach improper math improperly because they would all be removed at the outset.

Obstacle 2. Colleges of Education would become irrelevant for PI-MATH Mentors. Perhaps the loss of prospective teachers in math might motivate these schools to improve their offerings in other subjects.

Obstacle 3. Out-of-field Teachers in math would not exist in schools using PI-MATH—indeed, "math teachers" would not exist. Achieving the proper number of professionals in each classroom is attainable when fewer are needed and the pool of applicants is broader.

Obstacle 4. Math Teacher Pay would increase. With fewer PI-MATH Mentors needed than the previous number of math teachers, the same dollars could stretch further without impacting budgets.

Obstacle 5. The *Foundational Structure of Math*, implicit in the creation of PI-MATH, would be an internal strength rather than an external complication.

Obstacle 6. Vocabulary and Symbols would not only be correct in PI-MATH but also introduced early, developed carefully, reviewed regularly, and used appropriately.

Obstacle 7. Absences would no longer be a burden to students, parents, and teachers. Students ill at home or away on a trip could continue working on their tablets or postpone progress until their return without creating a gap in their knowledge. They would continue sessions with mentors once back at school.

Obstacle 8. Math Anxiety would be eliminated because tiny-step by tiny-step learning guarantees understanding as established by Skinner. Moreover, the negative effects of absences, parents, and math-phobic teachers—all also contributing to anxiety—would be gone.

Obstacle 9. Parents could stay away from their children's math education or re-learn math using the same software on their personal tablets. Mis-teaching their children or arguing with them would be eliminated.

Obstacle 10. Curriculum would be designed by true math experts, incorporating math's beauty and interconnectedness. Incomplete, convoluted standards would be ignored. Algebra and geometry could finally be learned side-by-side. Families could move from one neighborhood to another within a school system, from one city to another within a state, from one state to another within the country, and between public and private schools—without interrupting their children's math education.

Obstacle 11. Drill would be used appropriately in PI-MATH, as an effective tool and not a boring time-waster.

Obstacle 12. Fractions would be taught developmentally, thoroughly, and rigorously in PI-MATH. Their importance would be accepted once and for all.

Obstacle 13. Algebra would be rigorous because students would be prepared to learn the subject. It would include a wide variety of word problems that reinforce problem-solving techniques. Debate over whether to take the subject in grade 7, 8, or 9 would become meaningless.

Obstacle 14. Ability Grouping would be eliminated. All children could progress at their own pace, with mentors watching for healthy pacing—neither too slow nor too fast. The need for separate, gifted math classes would vanish. Formation of groups working with mentors would be fluid, based on weekly performance. Of course, schools could still form math clubs where students worked together as MATHCOUNTS or Mu Alpha Theta teams.

Obstacle 15. Inequality issues including tracking would be eradicated because all children, working at their own paces, would receive the same high quality PI-MATH, enhanced by comparably talented mentors. The quality of children's math education would no longer depend on the real estate value of homes or the placement within classrooms.

Obstacle 16. Textbook Publishers producing slanted, inaccurate, limited material full of distractions would be eliminated for schools using PI-MATH. UICSM and SMSG, with their self-written and self-published materials, have set the precedent.

Obstacle 17. State Policies would no longer establish or affect math curriculum. The role of state politicians who know nothing about math would be eliminated.

Obstacle 18. School Boards would no longer affect math education policy in a broad sense.

Obstacle 19. School Administrators would follow data from PI-MATH classes to check progress but would not have to intercede with poor teachers or inappropriate pacing.

Obstacle 20. Teacher Unions would have no control over the math education in PI-MATH classes, although mentors could be union members.

Obstacle 21. Classroom Structure would revolve around three activities—tablet time, written work based only on what was already learned via the PI-MATH tablet, and mentor interaction.

Obstacle 22. Time Management would become more effective. When special activities such as field trips, musical rehearsals, and special visitors interrupted math time, learning could still continue. For example, students could work quietly on the tablets in the auditorium while waiting for the drama teacher to call individuals to the stage to practice their parts in the school play.

Obstacle 23. Classroom Size would lose significance, replaced by an appropriate ratio of students to mentors. Schools could opt to have adults available to the classes as aides, but they would neither teach nor grade.

Obstacle 24. Cumulative Review would be built into PI-MATH.

Obstacle 25. Homework would become less important because students would learn more during the school day. However, students could continue with PI-MATH lessons at home, especially on interrupted days.

Obstacle 26. Summers would no longer be math wastelands. Children would continue learning math on their tablets during the summer, perhaps at a slower pace. They could stop by schools, which are open for summer school and administrative work, to pick up written practice papers as they reach benchmarks in the lessons. Inadequate, inappropriate summer workbooks would be eliminated.

Obstacle 27. Tutoring in classroom math would be essentially eliminated for PI-MATH students. Tutoring for SSAT independent school admission, ACT or SAT college admission, or AP Calculus would be for a different purpose—to gain a familiarity with the tests rather than to remediate math deficiencies.

Obstacle 28. Homeschooling families would have access to PI-MATH. Parents would no longer have to worry about teaching math themselves or hiring a quality math instructor at a high fee.

Obstacle 29. Charter, Independent, Magnet, Religious, and Virtual Schooling could all use PI-MATH. Seeking excellence in math education would no longer be a reason to leave a neighborhood school.

Obstacle 30. Grade Inflation would be eliminated in the programmed instruction work. Grades would essentially be the lesson numbers reached, combined with flexibility in reporting oral and written work.

Obstacle 31. Report Cards would be easy for the mentors to prepare as well as informative for the parents. Report cards would state the lesson number that a child had reached at the end of the grading period; included would be the mean and median lesson number for all students in that grade as well as the on-target lesson number. In fact, that data could go to parents monthly instead of quarterly. Report cards could also describe students' performance on the written work and in the mentor sessions.

Obstacle 32. Transparency would be a foundational principle of PI-MATH.

Obstacle 33. Standardized Testing—School Assessment would no longer waste huge sums of money with each state writing its own exams. Education dollars paid to testing companies for math exams could go back into education. Students would not have to repeat a grade due to low performance in math but rather, progressing solidly at their own paces, stay with their age-peers. Teachers would no longer skip around in texts, ruining flow to teach to the test.

Obstacle 34. Standardized Testing—University Admission might change as a result of PI-MATH. For example, the sixty math questions on the

ACT are straightforward. However, many students find the section challenging because they cannot remember math from middle school problem solving through beginning trigonometry. With cumulative review as an essential component of PI-MATH, students should start scoring higher on that test.

Obstacle 35. Associations of Math Education could continue to publish monthly journals or annual yearbooks full of interesting articles. But their plans produced each decade to change how math should be taught would be ignored by PI-MATH schools.

Obstacle 36. Education Organizations would continue with their wide range of work, not needing to solve the problem of inferior math education.

Obstacle 37. Research would no longer offer false hope for improvement. New research could study the implementation of PI-MATH.

Obstacle 38. Misguided Experts would be ignored.

Obstacle 39. Media would hopefully begin to cover the success of PI-MATH and to stop disparaging math as an obscure subject.

Obstacle 40. Technology would reign, with its valuable features, as discussed in Chapter 13, enhanced and its negative aspects removed.

Obstacle 41. Computer Science could be studied more completely because students would have the math background for authentic programming languages, not merely drag-and-drop ones.

Obstacle 42. Fads would become irrelevant.

Obstacle 43. Attitude would improve toward math—with rigorous content, engaged students, and satisfied parents—as well as toward mentors—with greater salary, more prestige, and higher training.

Obstacle 44. Motivation would improve naturally for students once understanding math increased and seeing its beauty developed.

Obstacle 45. Sports—for example, the ability to coach football—would no longer be a factor in hiring people to teach math.

Obstacle 46. The *Myth: Girls vs. Math* would end, with girls no longer negatively influenced by teachers, classmates, and parents.

Obstacle 47. The *United States Government* might optimistically stop funding constructivists' projects once positive results from PI-MATH were released.

Obstacle 48. The *United States Supreme Court* would hopefully no longer comment on pedagogy, especially as related to math.

Obstacle 49. Bandage Approaches would stop because the problem of poor math education would be fixed.

Obstacle 50. The *Individuality vs. Replication* argument would resolve when emphasis on replication yielded higher national and international test scores.

The existing system, which has not worked for over a century, requires countless people posing as math teachers. The number of out-of-field math teachers is already huge. People waiting to become certified math teachers do not exist. Education schools will not voluntarily teach more rigorous math—their enrollments would drop. Besides, how many people who select elementary or middle education truly treasure math? The re-training of math teachers is an impossible task. The use of math "experts" to coach teachers at schools will not work—the teachers would just balk. And what does teachers' needing coaches say about schools of education? After-school academic programs are resented by parents and students. Why should children waste time all day in school and then learn after school when they are supposed to be playing, exercising, or reading? National, inferior math education has propagated itself for too long. Approaching the problem of improving math education with the same strategies that have already failed will lead to further failure.

Current math teachers will not be revered by American society—the cultural shift is too broad.

Further, *scaling up*, as the educational term is known, is daunting. The existing number of isolated great math teachers cannot help the entire country. The Sputnik New Math, with enormous financial and mathematical support, tried and failed at massive retraining. *Scaling up* did not happen with any other past math education reform, and I deeply believe that *scaling up* cannot occur with any current or future reform except PI-MATH, which could create a new generation of students and mentors who know that they belong to something important.

The authors of *The Educated Child* recommended: "Support and respect good teachers." [B10, p. 642] But that advice is grueling when good math teachers are scarce. I have known students who scorned their math teachers—from taking notebook quizzes to memorizing geometry theorems—making the words of Martin Gross ring true: "The teachers are dumber than the students they're teaching. The system is virtually psychotic." [G12, p. 41] PI-MATH would improve not only intellectual content but also classroom morale.

As stated in *The Teaching Gap*, the "basic features" of most American math lessons on the TIMSS videos were: "the class reviewing previous material, the teacher presenting problems for the day, and students solving problems at their desks." [S26, p. 81] Thankfully, grading homework by "trading papers" was not mentioned. Such boring, uninspiring daily lessons would be gone with PI-MATH.

In 1902 E. H. Moore addressed the American Mathematical Society as its retiring president. Although he was a noted math researcher and a leader in higher mathematics, Moore's speech focused on the pedagogy of elementary math. "He . . . offered suggestions concerning the teaching of mathematics in the primary and secondary schools, where, he believed, the foundations of mathematics *could* be firmly established." [F3, p. 415]

In the same spirit, in 1960 Jerome Bruner wrote: "The early teaching of . . . mathematics . . . should be designed to teach . . . with scrupulous intellectual honesty." [B21, p. 13] Bruner formulated a list of necessary ingredients for "intellectual growth." Number four of six was: *Intellectual development depends upon a systematic and contingent interaction between a tutor and a learner*, the tutor already being equipped with a wide range of previously invented techniques that he teaches the child." [B22, p. 6] And thus, we return to the need for master teachers, namely PI-MATH Mentors.

In 1963 the Cambridge Conference participants noted that two mean levels would not change: native math ability of students and allotted math time of schools. Thus, their suggestion for affecting change included the transformation of curriculum organization. [C1, p. 7] PI-MATH would do exactly that by including all the features of a strong curriculum discussed in Chapter 14.

Unlike No Child Left Behind, PI-MATH would not steal time from art and music. NCLB's extra emphasis on math to the detriment of other subjects—with the objective of passing the mandated state exams—still resulted in weak math performance, underscoring the very premise of this book—that radical change is needed. Like the Sputnik New Math, what to teach and how to teach would be built into PI-MATH.

Like Benjamin Bloom's doctrine of Mastery Learning, PI-MATH believes that all children can learn with the right amount of time and attention. But with properly designed tiny steps of programmed learning, PI-MATH avoids Bloom's need to teach, test, progress if pass, and reteach-retest if fail. Unlike Bloom's Mastery Learning, PI-MATH will not lower the definition of success, not drop the entire class to the lowest common level, and not demand that the teacher operate on many different planes.

We could repeat the same approach for another century, try the same reforms with fresh names, and end in the same place with not only the children's opportunities squandered but also the nation's stability threatened—or we could create PI-MATH.

19
Demanding Improvement

Alice: "Would you tell me, please, which way I ought to go from here?"
Cheshire Cat: "That depends a good deal on where you want to get to."
Alice: "I don't much care where."
Cheshire Cat: "Then it doesn't matter which way you go."
Lewis Carroll [C4, Chapter 6]

Programmed Instruction Math is a serious, justified, detailed plan to finally fix math education. But society must demand improvement for PI-MATH to happen.

For over half a century, other authors have offered partial "solutions" to the ills of education. With due respect for the attempts, the words are futile. Create a new agency—but flaws and ineffectiveness are rampant. Improve textbooks—but profit overshadows learning. Copy a country the size of one U.S. state—but cultures do not transfer, and scaling-up is onerous. Retrain math teachers—but previous efforts have failed. Pay math teachers more—but money is scarce, and jealousy prevails. Fill children's tummies with healthy food—but teachers' brains still lack rigorous math. And thus, I label twelve solutions scant.

Scant Solution 1. In 1953 Arthur Bestor wrote: "The first step . . . must be for the learned world to create an agency entirely its own, through which it can state its views on public school policy independently and unitedly." [B11, p.124]

Scant Solution 2. In 1958 John Keats offered: "raise teacher salaries"; "try to find teachers who are masters of their subject matter"; "keep the school open all year"; "increase the qualitative performance of our present teachers . . . by allowing them to spend more time teaching and less time doing school housework" such as parking lot duty; "limit the school's job to the essentials"; "drive out of the schoolhouse a lot of dubious activity that has nothing to do with education" from sponsoring magazine contests to collecting for charities. [K2, pp. 154–158]

Scant Solution 3. In 1969 William Glasser suggested removing what he deemed causes of mediocre education: "grades"; "objective testing"; "the normal curve"; "closed-book examinations"; and "assignment of excessive, tedious, and often irrelevant homework." [G7, pp. 59–75]

Scant Solution 4. In 1991 the Carnegie Commission outlined some "assumptions" for steps in improving K–12 education.
"• Deep and effective change in the K–12 education system is needed if the goal is ever to be met.
• Student performance will not improve nationally until the teacher force is improved nationally.
• Reform strategies must be informed by the best available understanding of the education system and of teaching and learning practice.
• Effective educational innovations must be available to all schools.
• Specific reforms must also address what goes on inside the classroom, especially with regard to science and mathematics.
• All young people, including the non-college bound, can and should be competent in science and mathematics; in particular, efforts should be made to draw in women and minority men." [C2, pp. 20–24]

Scant Solution 5. In 1992 Harold Stevenson and James Stigler proposed: (1) "Free Teachers" by decreasing "the teaching load of American elementary school teachers" so that they "have adequate time to prepare lessons, work outside of class with individual students, and perfect their teaching practices by interacting with each other and with master teachers"; (2) "Improve Teacher Training" by giving teacher development "greater attention," shifting teacher training "from university lecture halls to school classrooms," and using the medical education model by creating something comparable to clinic and hospital time as well as requiring residency; (3) "Make Systematic Use of Learning Principles" by accepting rules of learning, not yet universally applied, on a broad scale; (4) "Teach to the Group" by spending "as much time as possible working with the whole class," thus avoiding lonely seat-work; (5) "Consider Increasing Class Size"; (6) "Revise Textbooks"; (7) "Free Children" by spending "more of the school day outside of the classroom"; and (8) "Eliminate Tracking." [S25, pp. 207–215]

Scant Solution 6. In 1999 Howard Gardner wrote: "Educators should be prepared to state publicly what they themselves wish for their students. . . . they must be willing to state what would count as evidence of success, and what they are prepared to do if success is not immediately achieved. In taking this courageous step, in seizing responsibility, educators would begin to establish that they are professionals, capable of monitoring their own calling." [G3, pp. 234–235]

Scant Solution 7. In 1999 James Stigler and James Hiebert wrote that Americans must adopt a "new path" that "moves away from viewing teaching as an inborn trait with little intellectual demand and toward viewing it as a complex skill that can be studied and learned over time." They added: ". . . we propose a program based squarely on the process of lesson study, . . . [which] will produce long-term steady improvements." Calling lessons the "most common form of teaching" in Japan and comparing lessons to "university courses" or "religious services," they cited the necessity of planning lessons as "complete experiences— as stories with a beginning, a middle, and an end." They stated that in successful lessons, parts must be connected and coherent. Students must partake in whole lessons. [S26, pp. xiv–xv, 137, 152, 95–96]

Stigler and Hiebert dismissed their critics who viewed lesson study as uncomplicated, unimaginative, and unappealing to U.S. math reformers: "'Wouldn't it take forever . . . to improve teaching one lesson at a time? . . . Our kids need help now, not ten years from now. . . . We need major restructuring, not modest improvements.' Yet despite our desperate rush to reform, the evidence shows that little has changed inside U.S. [math] classrooms." [S26, p. 129]

Scant Solution 8. In 1999 Martin Gross suggested upgrading weak curriculum, removing out-of-field teachers, instituting tracking, and paying teachers more who teach knowledge-based content. [G12, p. 209]

Scant Solution 9. In 2004 a publication by the NCTQ recommended using the teacher screening developed by Teach For America (TFA), praising the criteria as a "highly selective recruitment process (only one out of eight candidates is selected)" that ". . . identified seven personal attributes common to teachers who produced the greatest student learning gains," namely: (1) *High-Achieving*; (2) *Responsible*; (3) *Critical thinker*; (4) *Organized*; (5) *Motivating*; (6) *Respectful*; (7) *Shares the goal of the organization.* [W2, pp. 10–11] In refute, Diane Ravitch questioned TFA's procedure in 2013 when she wrote: "The medical profession would never permit a fresh college graduate to substitute for a doctor or even a nurse. Why, then, do American schools entrust vulnerable children to brand-new teachers with only five weeks of training?" [R7, p. 144] Moreover, Ravitch pointed out: "Most TFA teachers in urban districts leave after their two-year commitment ends, and 80 percent or more are gone after their third or fourth year." [R6, p. 190]

Scant Solution 10. In 2010 Diane Ravitch wrote: "The most durable way to improve schools is to improve curriculum and instruction and to improve the conditions in which teachers work and children learn . . . ." [R6, p. 225]

Scant Solution 11. In 2012 Schmidt and McKnight wrote: ". . . we need to develop and maintain the political will to do something about the hidden inequalities in content coverage in U.S. schools. [S7, pp. 212–213]

Scant Solution 12. In 2013 Amanda Ripley, having studied firsthand schools in Finland, Korea, and Poland, optimistically wrote: "Yet I also didn't see anything anywhere that I didn't think our parents, kids, and teachers could do just as well or better one day. . . . Despite politics, bureaucracy, antiquated union contracts and parental blind spots—the surprisingly universal plagues of all educational systems everywhere—it could be done. And other countries could help show us the way." [R13, p. 9] But copying other countries is not a new solution. The *1923 Report* stated: ". . . model curricula were offered, . . . [including] descriptions of experimental work in . . . foreign countries." [N17, p. 202]

Decades of reports, generations of politicians, and cohorts of educators have all called for math improvement with powerful words; but questions still linger. Do non-math math teachers want to know that math lessons are flawed, shaking blissful ignorance? Do parents want to hear that math textbooks are weak, upsetting comfortable satisfaction?

In 1992 Harold Stevenson and James Stigler asked similar questions: "Before the United States can begin meaningful educational reform, we Americans must decide what we expect of our students. Do we place a high value on academic achievement? Or do we give other goals, such as being popular or a good athlete, a higher priority?" [S25, p. 201]

Answering these questions presents seven contradictions.

Contradiction 1. Words speak greatness, but actions convey mediocrity.

In 1991 Robert Samuelson summarized the situation: "There's a real dilemma here. Our schools are giving us the mediocrity that we actually want as opposed to the excellence that we say we want. No reform can succeed unless it assaults and overcomes the contradiction." [S2]

Contradiction 2. Some parents recognize that American math education is seriously lacking, but they do not believe that the problem pertains to their own children.

In the same 1991 article Robert Samuelson claimed: "The evidence that Americans want demanding schools is meager. In a 1990 poll, only 8 percent of respondents picked 'poor curriculum/poor standards' as the schools' major problem. What parents really want from schools is to be told that their children are doing well. This relieves any guilt over not paying enough attention to their children's schoolwork and minimizes conflicts with children over their performance. Schools placate parents with easy course demands and lax grading." [S2]

In 1995 Charles Sykes stated, "Despite the mounting evidence of an educational crisis, most Americans do not think there is anything seriously wrong with their own children's schools or the education they are getting. However bad things might be elsewhere, most Americans are sure that the dumbing down of American education does not include their own children." [S29, p. 28]

In 2012 William Schmidt and Curtis McKnight wrote: "Equality of educational opportunity is not just a matter of economics. It is also a matter of fairness. It is hard to defend the status quo either legally or philosophically. ... The only reason there has been so little outcry about these matters is probably that the public and parents have been unaware of them." [S7, p. 55]

Contradiction 3. Some parents want their children to learn math, but they don't want their children to face defeat.

In 1992 Harold Stevenson and James Stigler discussed a parental worry: "If standards are too high, and more is expected of children than they are capable of, children's self-esteem could be damaged. To prevent this risk, Americans tend to adjust standards downward to a level considered to be appropriate for the child's level of ability." The authors continued: "Convincing parents that they can expect more of their children is difficult, however, for it quickly becomes confused with pushing children too early and too fast. We are not proposing that children should . . . be doing algebra in fifth grade. What we *are* saying is that lessons do not need to be repeated year after year if they are properly taught in the first place; that children can master school routines if someone takes the time to show them how; that children can comprehend far more complicated material than they learn now if it commands their interest and is explained clearly; and that most children are capable, given the proper instruction, of mastering the academic curriculum. Parents' reluctance to raise their expectations may be based on a fear that higher parental expectations lead to higher levels of stress in children. There is no evidence to support this fear." [S25, pp. 114, 218–219]

Contradiction 4. Some parents want great math education for their children, but they let their own math inadequacies interfere.

In 1995 Sykes wrote: ". . . [despite] the inadequacies of American schools, the dumbing down of American kids is also very much a family affair.... Our dilemma would be considerably eased if parents were clamoring for higher standards, more homework, and more rigorous grades. But this is hardly the case—teachers often have to adjust their expectations and standards downward because they cannot count on support from home for more demanding requirements." [S29, p. 295]

In 1999 Bennett, Finn, and Cribb stated: "That prospect [paying attention to math homework] alarms parents. ... Bring out the math problems, ... and some adults start to feel anxious." [B10, p. 335]

Contradiction 5. Some want great math education, but they lack the tools for proper evaluation.

In 1992 Stevenson and Stigler described how parents assume that all is fine academically with their children when they receive "smiley faces" on many papers and a promotion to the next grade. The authors wrote: "This clearly is not true." They stated that while American parents once lacked valid measures to assess their children's progress, the international exams now offer informative means of comparison. [S25, p. 218]

In 2012 Schmidt and McKnight wrote: "Parents concerned for their child's safety have often been asked, 'Do you know where your child is?' Modifying that phrase, parents should also be asked, 'Do you know what your child's learning opportunities are?' Or more specifically, 'Do you know what mathematics content your 4th-grade child is studying? Is that what she should be studying at that grade?'" [S7, p. 212]

Contradiction 6. The cost of a great math program may be high, but the consequences of an under-educated nation are far greater.

In 1953 Arthur Bestor described mere "warm-hearted benevolence": "We pay our school taxes, but we rarely conceive of ourselves as making thereby an investment in the intellectual advancement of the nation." [B11, p. 1]

Along the same theme, Derek Bok, former President of Harvard, once said: "If you think education is expensive, try ignorance."

In 2013 Diane Ravitch expressed: "Are all of these changes expensive? Yes, but not nearly as expensive as the social and economic costs of . . . wasted human talent." [R7, p. 299]

Contradiction 7. A belief exists that some children cannot learn math; however, most children can learn a reasonable amount of math with proper instruction.

In 1992 Harold Stevenson and James Stigler stated: "Because of the belief that not every child is capable of mastering the academic curriculum, and because of a commitment to provide schooling for all children, Americans find it hard to decide what it is they expect from the nation's schools. One reason they are unwilling to define the goal of education narrowly as academic excellence is that they believe that only some children are capable of achieving it." [S25, p. 111]

In 1996 E. D. Hirsch wrote: "No matter how much innate math ability a child has, he or she will not learn the multiplication table effectively by osmosis." Like music, he explained, math is a discipline that requires extensive practice as well as guidance from a teacher for successful learning. He called holding children "back by lack of such ability rather than lack of hard, directed work" an educational fallacy. [H12, p. 87]

In 2009 the National Research Council reported: ". . . although virtually all young children have the capability to learn and become competent in mathematics, for most the potential to learn mathematics in the early years of school is not currently realized." [N37, p. 1]

Incomplete solutions, pointing to unanswered questions and leading to contradictory positions, culminate in twelve realities—collectively what society must face in demanding improved math education.

Reality 1. Social change is difficult.

In 1952 sociologist Robert Hutchins wrote: "A program of social reform cannot be achieved through the educational system unless it is one that the society is prepared to accept. The educational system is the society's attempt to perpetuate itself and its own ideals. If a society wishes to improve, it will use the educational system for that purpose. . . . If a society does not wish to change, it cannot be reformed through the educational system." [H20, p. 11]

Also in 1977 Robert Laurer wrote: ". . . people . . . will resist change under three circumstances: when the change is perceived to be a threat to basic securities; when the change is not understood; and when the change is imposed upon them." [L1, p. 10]

In 1999 Howard Gardner expressed two indisputable considerations, seemingly contradictory but "actually complementary" for all citizens: (1) they "must become as comfortable as possible with change" despite wishes for consistency; and (2) they "must remain ever conscious of the constants in human experiences"—whether intrinsically or desirably permanent. [G3, p. 247]

Reality 2. Social change in education—breaking the status-quo—is arduous and uncomfortable.

In 1969 William Glasser attacked *business as usual*, writing that society was engaged in *foot-dragging* out of fear of *breaking with tradition*. He urged: "Today we have no choice but to make this break." He also wrote about the ambience he felt when visiting schools—a "resignation to the *status quo* and, despite some dissatisfaction with present practices, antagonism toward anyone who advocates change. . . . we have a complete circle in which teachers blame parents and administrators, administrators blame teachers and parents, and parents blame teachers and administrators." [G7, p. 11, 114]

In 1977 Jerome Bruner stated: "One cannot change education without affecting much else in the society as well—if the change takes, and it often fails to do so by virtue of running headlong into a contradictory set of cultural ideals." [B21, p. xi]

In 1999 Martin Gross wrote: "Breaking the status quo will require thought and determination." [G12, p. 67]

In 2012 William Schmidt and Curtis McKnight wrote: "The United States was founded on the idea that an unacceptable status quo presents, not a bar to progress, but a challenge to overcome. What we insist is that America live up to that tradition." [S7, p. 216]

Reality 3. Improving one piece of the interconnected education system affects little; improving all components is mandatory to affect change.

In 1999 Howard Gardner wrote about his "educational vision" with the "central goal" of "deep understanding." His construct had "two foundations" for educators: (1) the "need to recognize the difficulties students face in attaining genuine understanding of important topics and concepts"; and (2) the "need to take into account the differences among minds and . . . fashion an education that can reach the infinite variety of students." [G3, p. 186]

Also in 1999 Stigler and Hiebert expressed: "Teaching systems, like other complex systems, are composed of elements that interact and reinforce one another; the whole is greater than the sum of the parts. An immediate implication . . . is that it will be difficult, if not impossible, to improve teaching by changing individual elements or features. . . . If one feature is changed, the system will rush to 'repair the damage,' perhaps by modifying the new feature so it functions the way the old one did. . . . This point is missed in many popular attempts to reform teaching in the United States." They continued: "It has now been documented in several studies that teachers asked to change features of their teaching often modify the features to fit within their pre-existing system instead of changing the system itself. The system assimilates individual changes and swallows them up." [S26, pp. 97–98]

Moreover, Stigler and Hiebert stated: "Systems of teaching are much more than the things the teacher does. They include the physical setting of the classroom; the goals of the teacher; the materials, including textbooks and district or state objectives; the roles played by the students; the way the school day is scheduled; and other factors that influence how teachers teach. Changing any one of these individual features is unlikely to have the intended effect." [S26, p. 99]

Reality 4. Overall, math education now is random.

In 2012 William Schmidt and Curtis McKnight wrote: "Children find themselves in situations that are like games of chance, where ability, motivation, and effort are not the primary determinants of success. . . . Yet the outcome of the game is not the fun of winning a trivial contest, but obtaining the knowledge, skills, problem solving, and reasoning abilities necessary for success in today's complex and technologically oriented world. . . . Teachers define the parameters of the game by deciding what content will be covered in particular classrooms. This should not be determined by random and arbitrary factors such as the district in which they teach, the textbook . . . adopted, or the extent of the teacher's content knowledge provided in their teacher preparation program. The rules of the game should be the same for all students. The rules should be national, if not international, in scope because students will be playing against their peers in every country." [S7, pp. 2–3]

Reality 5. Local, state, and national politics interfere with quality education.

In 1996 E. D. Hirsch stated that the hostile attitude toward "the teaching of factual knowledge . . . also rallies Republicans and Democrats, parents and legislators, and . . . newspaper reporters as well." [H12, p. 106]

In 2005 Diane Ravitch wrote in an Op-Ed: "America will not begin to meet the challenge of developing the potential of our students until we have accurate reporting ["removed from the constraints of state and local politics"] about their educational progress. . . . We will be stuck with piecemeal and ineffective reforms until we agree as a nation that education . . . must be our highest domestic priority." [R4]

Reality 6. Many teachers have been and continue to be incapable of teaching math properly.

Cornerstone 7 of Chapter 5 encapsulated this reality. And as noted in Obstacle 3 of Chapter 11, Edwin Moise wrote that excellence in math teaching was neither the norm nor the foreseeable trend. [M6, p. 35]

In 1999 Bennett, Finn, and Cribb wrote: "There are many excellent math teachers in American schools. Unfortunately, there are also many elementary school teachers who do not have much mathematics education in their backgrounds, particularly in the lower grades. . . . Being afraid that your students will ask questions you can't answer does not make for a great teaching or learning experience." [B10, pp. 331–332]

Reality 7. People must feel as if they are part of an important, united mission for positive change to occur.

In 1953 Arthur Bestor expressed: "Teachers, . . . from the most elementary to the most advanced, must feel themselves bound together in a common endeavor. Unless they make substantially the same assumptions, there cannot be an educational *system* at all, but only a hodgepodge of schools. If teachers work at cross purposes to one another, they are bound to produce intellectual confusion instead of intellectual order." [B11, pp. 122–123]

In 1999 Howard Gardner stated: "Progress is more likely to occur within schools, or across networks of schools, and scaling up is more likely to become a reality, if the players feel that they belong to something important and if they secure the emotional rewards that come from engagement with a cause." [G3, p. 236]

In 2013 Amanda Ripley said: "All major shifts . . . require a feeling that spreads among people like a whispered oath, kitchen table by kitchen table, until enough . . . agree that something must be done." [R13, p. 199]

Reality 8. Time is of the essence for improving math education.

In 1991 the Carnegie Commission on Science, Technology, and Government outlined a list of "assumptions" for its strategy to improve math education. The first was: "There is no time to waste." [C2, p. 20]

In 2010 the *National Education Technology Plan*, heading one section with "The Time To Act Is Now," reported: "The NETP accepts that we do not have the luxury of time: We must act now and commit to fine-tuning and midcourse corrections as we go." [O2, p. xv]

Reality 9. Handing public schools to private, corporate interests is not the solution.

In 2010 Diane Ravitch explained: "What we need is not a marketplace, but a coherent curriculum that prepares all students. And our government should commit to providing a good school in every neighborhood . . . [similar to fire service] in every community. On our present course, we are disrupting communities, dumbing down our schools, giving students false reports of their progress, and creating a private sector that will undermine public education without improving it." [R5]

Reality 10. Improving math education is solitary and confrontational.

In 1999 Howard Gardner cautioned: "Reform can be a lonely undertaking, and the feeling that one is engaged in a solitary uphill fight can be discouraging, even devastating." [G3, p. 236] Also in 1999 Bennett, Finn, and Cribb listed twelve "points to keep in mind as you tread the path of education reform." Two of note are: "Don't be deterred" and "Be prepared to be called names. . . . This business is not for the faint of heart!" [B10, pp. 640–642]

And in 2017 I heard Geoffrey Canada, founder of Harlem Children's Zone, say that reforming education is "hard work" that "takes courage."

Reality 11. Citizens and businesses must unite in the desire to improve math education.

In 1991 the Carnegie Commission reported: "*The U.S. can succeed at educating and preparing our citizens when there is the national will and the leadership to do so.*" [C2, p. 25]

In 1992 the authors of *The Learning Gap* stated the uncertainty of citizens' belief in the value of good schools. Yet they affirmed: "Among the groups for whom education and education reform have become a strong concern, however, is American business." [S25, p. 220]

In 1995 the author of *Dumbing Down Our Kids* wrote: "Unless American parents raise those expectations, it is unlikely that America's school will ever raise them unilaterally." [S29, p. 297]

In 2012 the authors of *Inequality for All* asked: "Will Americans demand new policies to redistribute content learning opportunities to provide greater equality? Will they reverse this trend and reestablish schools as the level playing field that grants to all a chance at the American dream?" [S7, p. 208]

Reality 12. The next change in math education must be authentic and permanent. Then math education will be meaningful and pleasurable.

Diane Ravitch expressed: "Ultimately, it is imagination, joy, and disciplined inquiry that make education valuable, that distinguish real education from seat time, that constitute the difference between learning and a credential." [R7, pp. 180–181]

Amanda Ripley wrote: "All children must learn rigorous higher-order thinking to thrive in the modern world. The only way to do that is by creating a serious intellectual culture in schools, one that kids can sense is real and true." [R13, p. 199]

The parable *Who Moved My Cheese?* [J9] was a huge sensation, affecting primarily business. Almost twenty years later, the age of technological disruption is here—from wearable technology to driverless cars. Math education must now partake, yielding higher quality, broader access, steadier delivery, and truer accuracy. Century-old failed reforms are tiresome for citizens, hurtful for students, and wasteful with funding. Children's one chance at a math education must rich, comprehensive, and precise. I have seen parents, teachers, administrators, and politicians sporadically fearful when they confront math, but I have seen children consistently happy when they understand math. Clearly, PI-MATH moves math teachers' cheese; but I have confidence in the proposed system, eager students, and qualified mentors.

20

Speaking Personally

If I were again beginning my studies, I would follow the advice of Plato and start with mathematics.
Galileo Galilei

For decades, Miss America contestants answered *world peace* for the final Onstage Question, regardless of the topic. How I wish someone would have added *and all children understand math*.

Who am I to dare to write such a bold proposal?

My education did follow Plato's advice—I started with mathematics. My father was a math educator of significant accomplishment, and our home was full of math books that I joyfully perused. Before calculators, I checked the arithmetic on my father's IRS Form 1040 for fun.

The launching of Sputnik completely shaped the second decade of my life. My New Math experience and benefits were fourfold. First, my father was one of the initial math teachers in the nation chosen for training in the movement. After my father's maiden summer at the University of Illinois, in future summers I traveled with him when he taught other teachers. He allowed me to attend his lectures where I was like a child in a toy shop, marveling at set braces rather than doll houses. Second, both UICSM and SMSG math comprised my own education. Third, first as a student and then as a counselor, I was part of a remarkable summer Secondary Science Training Program funded by the NSF to expose high school students to university level mathematics. Fourth, I was awarded a graduate school National Science Foundation Traineeship, which, like the SSTP, was money made available during this period by the federal government to bolster math education. These NSF opportunities, requiring extensive study on my part, were life-changing. I have "paid it forward" first by educating hundreds of students who love math and use it in their careers, and now by writing this book.

Like many college math majors at that time, for graduate school and my first job I switched to a new field—now called Computer Science, but then placed under the umbrella of Applied Mathematics. After a short career as a computer programmer, I became a math educator—somewhat due to limited career opportunities in my new community and somewhat due to elevating my children in my priorities. But I quickly learned that teaching was indeed in my blood. I was fortunate to work at a private school that at the time had a headmaster who valued great math, students who overflowed with math talent, and parents who appreciated math rigor. I am grateful to all three.

Thus, my life is a circle with math education at the center. Important radii include not only growing up in a home full of math and experiencing Sputnik New Math firsthand, but also teaching math in FL, MA, MD, NC, and NY; writing my own teaching materials; publishing rigorous math workbooks; coaching students who won hundreds of math awards; owning and operating a private education center focused on math offerings; helping students earn high math scores on numerous standardized exams; and experiencing the full, interconnected range of math from consulting in the elementary grades to instructing at the university level.

People who are aware of my work know that my students have been extremely successful in math. Sometimes, focusing with deep intent, I ask, "Do you want to know my secret?" The excited reply is always, "Yes, of course." Then, with total seriousness I answer, "Teach math." When a quizzical gaze counteracts my advice, I explain that if correct math were taught correctly—if proper math were taught properly—then students would know math. Give a student great math, and the student will learn considerable math. Give a student weak math, and the student will learn minimal math.

As John Keats wrote, "What one educator calls education, another does not." [K2, p. 2] Unfortunately, what the majority of math teachers call math, I do not. I have seen truly great math teachers, but on the whole they are retired and not replaced. In my opinion, we now have only a small fraction of the number of great math teachers needed in this country—thus, the impetus for my writing. I have also seen children enjoy rigorous math. The formula is simple—as students gain knowledge and understanding, they gain competence and pleasure.

As a parent, I was vigilant for my own children; now I am deeply concerned about the math education of my grandchildren. John Keats described himself as a parent who studied public schooling and became an educated layman. The impetus for his extensive research and writing was an evening with friends at his home, an event which he called enjoyable until someone mentioned public schools, triggering the company to become very upset over ways schools were not preparing kids. Keats wrote: "A disinterested foreign observer [who] suddenly arrived in our living room might charitably have concluded that our public schools were engaged in a criminal conspiracy to subvert the nation." [K2, p. 1] I recall a similar evening at my home years ago with guests' rancor directed at both public and private schools.

This book is not intended for personal catharsis but for societal metamorphosis. My goal is not merely to analyze and synthesize my decades submersed in math, while unifying thoughts, principles, and experiences. My goal is not solely to stimulate conversation; other excellent books and reports have attempted that. My goal is to find and encourage like-minded people to join together to create rigorous, permanent school mathematics, using my realization of how to finally fix math education by turning it upside down. As the saying goes, one must break some eggs to make an omelette, and my plan breaks millions of dozens of eggs.

In a personal passage Diane Ravitch wrote: "I was increasingly skeptical about these reforms [testing, accountability, choice, and markets], reforms that I had supported enthusiastically. I was trying to see my way through the blinding assumptions of ideology and politics, including my own. I kept asking myself why I was losing confidence in these reforms. My answer: I have a right to change my mind." [R6, p. 2]

I had a parallel thought—I had lost faith in American math teachers. Reading Ravitch's words gave me the confidence and the *right* to change my mind. I used to believe that great math teachers could be trained—had to be trained—because I thought no other path forward existed. But in this book I offer a new, different route. I imagine my idea will be viewed as radical; however, my mission is to offer true math to all, opening career doors for the nation's children and fastening security windows for the children's nation.

Sheryl Sandberg wrote: "Early in her career, Arianna [Huffington] realized that the cost of speaking her mind was that she would inevitably offend someone." [S3, p. 49] Nevertheless, Ms. Sandberg encouraged women to *lean in*. If *From STEM To STEW* reaches the desired audience, I will offend not *someone* but *many*. I can't imagine leaning in any more than saving math education.

Moreover, as Diane Ravitch wrote about *A Nation At Risk*: "The report was an immediate sensation. Its conclusions were alarming, and its language was blunt to the point of being incendiary. . . . The report got what it wanted: the public's attention." [R6, pp. 24–25] Getting *the public's attention* to finally fix math education is exactly what I want. If my book is *incendiary*, so be it. Ironically, if this book becomes out-dated, then the problems of math education will have been solved—how perfect.

On October 4, 2017 the 60th anniversary of the launching of Sputnik passed, virtually unnoticed, except for recognition by the National Air and Space Museum. [www20–1] Reporters were busy with important news such as the hurricane devastation in Puerto Rico, the mass-shooting horror in Las Vegas, a news conference by the Chairman and Vice Chairman of the Senate Intelligence Committee, but also National Taco Day. All the while, U.S. math education remains severely inadequate.

The challenge is adding one more entry, like *typewriter repairman*, to the list of extinct job titles: *non-math math teacher*.

BIBLIOGRAPHY

A1   Aczel, Amir D. *The Artist and the Mathematician: The Story of Nicolas Bourbaki, the Genius Mathematician Who Never Existed*. Thunder's Mouth Press, 2006.

A2   Ahmann, J. Stanley. *How Much Are Our Young People Learning? The Story of the National Assessment*. The Phi Delta Kappa Educational Foundation, 1976.

A3   Aiken, Lewis. "Attitudes Towards Mathematics." *Review of Educational Research*, vol. 40, no. 4, Oct 1970, pp. 551–596.

A4   Alberts, Hana. "East Versus West." *Forbes*, May 11, 2009. https://www.forbes.com/free_forbes/2009/0511/024-opinions-science-psychology-ideas-opinions.html

A5   Allendoerfer, Carl B. "The Second Revolution in Mathematics." *Mathematics Teacher*. National Council of Teachers of Mathematics, vol. 58, Dec 1965, pp. 690–695.

A6   *American Mathematical Monthly*, vol. 101, no. 5, May 1994, p. 463.

A7   American Mathematical Society. "Report of the Committee of the Chicago Section of the American Mathematical Society." AMS, 1899. Reprinted in Bidwell and Clason.

A8   American Report of the International Commission on the Teaching of Mathematics. *Mathematics in the Public and Private Secondary Schools of the United States*. 1911. Reprinted in Bidwell and Clason.

A9   Archer, Jeff. "Out-of-Field Teaching Is Hard To Curb." *Education Week*, Mar 31, 1999. https://www.edweek.org/ew/articles/1999/03/31/29out.h18.html?qs=out-of-field+teaching

B1   Baker, Stephen. "Math Will Rock Your World." *BusinessWeek*, Jan 23, 2006, pp. 54–62.

B2   Barry, Dave. "Who can do the math?" *Miami Herald*, Aug 17, 2003; Aug 30, 2009. http://www.miamiherald.com/living/liv-columns-blogs/dave-barry/article1929910.html

Bibliography

B3   Bassler, Otto C. and John R. Kolb. *Learning to Teach Secondary School Mathematics*. Intext Educational Publishers, 1971.

B4   Beaumont, Thomas. Associated Press. "Education rising as issue among 2016 GOP class; standards now a metaphor for government reach." *U.S. News & World Report*, Apr 28, 2014. http://www.usnews.com/news/politics/articles/2014/04/28/education-a-new-defining-issue-for-2016-gop-class

B5   Beberman, Max. *An Emerging Program of Secondary School Mathematics*. Harvard University Press, 1958.

B6   Begle, Edward and Glenadine Gibb. "Why Do Research?" *Research in Mathematics Education*. Richard Shumway, ed. National Council of Teachers of Mathematics, 1980.

B7   Begley, Sharon. "Homework Doesn't Help." *Newsweek*, Mar 30, 1998, pp. 50–51.

B8   Benbow, Camilla P. and Julian C. Stanley. "Sex Differences in Mathematical Ability: Fact or Artifact?" *Science*. vol. 210, Dec 12, 1980.

B9   Bennett, William. *First lessons: A report on elementary education in America*. US ED, Sept, 1986. http://www.eric.ed.gov/?id=ED270236

B10   Bennett, William J., Chester E. Finn, Jr., and John T. E. Cribb, Jr. *The Educated Child: A Parent's Guide From Preschool Through Eighth Grade*. The Free Press, Simon & Schuster, 1999.

B11   Bestor, Arthur. *Educational Wastelands: The Retreat From Learning in Our Public Schools*. University of Illinois Press, 1953, 2nd ed. 1985.

B12   Betz, William. "Five Decades of Mathematical Reform—Evaluation and Challenge." *Mathematics Teacher*, vol. 60, Oct, 1967. pp. 600–610. (Reprinted from *Mathematics Teacher*, vol. 43, Dec, 1950, pp. 377–387.)

B13   Bidwell, James K. and Robert G. Clason, eds. *Readings in the History of Mathematics Education*. NCTM, 1970.

B14   Boaler, Jo. *What's Math Got to Do with It?* Viking, 2008.

B15 Boaler, Jo. "The Stereotypes That Distort How Americans Teach and Learn Math." *The Atlantic*, Nov 12, 2013.
http://www.theatlantic.com/education/archive/2013/11/the-stereotypes-that-distort-how-americans-teach-and-learn-math/281303/

B16 Bohannon, John. "Both Genders Think Women Are Bad at Basic Math." *Science*, Mar 10, 2014. http://www.sciencemag.org/news/2014/03/both-genders-think-women-are-bad-basic-math

B17 Bok, Derek. "Looking into education's high-tech future." President's Report to the Harvard Board of Overseers for 1983–84. *Harvard Magazine*, May–June 1985, pp. 29–38.

B18 Boksay, Istvan. "Grandparents Face Unusual Problems." Associated Press, Jan 14, 1998. http://www.apnewsarchive.com/1998/Grandparents-Face-Unusual-Problems/id-1e91c62c205b7705cfb-748858071f90e?SearchText=Homework;Display_

B19 *Boston Globe*. "Upgrading Teachers." Editorial. Sept 16, 1996. https://www.highbeam.com/doc/1P2-8389952.html

B20 Braams, Bas. "Critique of the New York State Regents Mathematics A Exam." June 2003.
http://www.math.nyu.edu/mfdd/braams/links/regents-0306.html

B21 Bruner, Jerome S. *The Process of Education*. Harvard University Press, 1960 (Preface pp. xvii–xxvi) and 2nd ed. 1977 (Preface pp. vii–xvi).

B22 Bruner, Jerome S. *Toward a Theory of Instruction*. Harvard University Press, 1966 and 2nd ed. 1971. Reprinted Belknap Press, 1974.

B23 Bruner, Jerome. "On Learning Mathematics," *Mathematics Teacher*, vol. 88, no. 4, 1995, pp. 330–335.

B24 Bulmahn, Barbara and David Young. "On the Transmission of Mathematics Anxiety." *Arithmetic Teacher*, vol. 30, no. 3, Nov 1982, pp. 55–56.

B25 Burton, Grace M. "Skinner, Piaget, Maslow, and the teachers of mathematics—strange companions?" *The Arithmetic Teacher*, vol. 24, no. 3, Mar 1977, pp. 246–250.

Bibliography

C1 Cambridge Conference on School Mathematics. *Goals for School Mathematics*. Houghton Mifflin, 1963.

C2 Carnegie Commission on Science, Technology, and Government. *In the National Interest: The Federal Government in the Reform of K–12 Math and Science Education*. Carnegie Corporation, Sept 1991.

C3 Carr, Sarah. "First-grade teacher dives into Common Core with cautious optimism." *The Hechinger Report*, Sept 2, 2013. http://www.hechingerreport.org/content/first-grade-teacher-dives-into-common-core-with-cautious-optimism_13033/

C4 Carroll, Lewis. *Alice in Wonderland*. Bantam Classics, 1984. Originally published 1865.

C5 Cavanagh, Sean. "Common-Core Testing Contracts Favor Big Vendors." *Education Week*, Sept 30, 2014. http://www.edweek.org/ew/articles/2014/10/01/06contract.h34.html

C6 Center for Research in Mathematics and Science Education. *Breaking the Cycle: An International Comparison of U.S. Mathematics Teacher Preparation*. Michigan State University, 2010. http://www.educ.msu.edu/content/sites/usteds/documents/Breaking-the-Cycle.pdf

C7 Cheney, Lynne. "Once Again, Basic Skills Fall Prey To a Fad." Op-Ed. *The New York Times*, Aug 11, 1997. http://www.nytimes.com/1997/08/11/opinion/once-again-basic-skills-fall-prey-to-a-fad.html

C8 Childress, Stacey. "Rethinking School." *Harvard Business Review*, Mar 2012, pp. 77–79.

C9 Clark, John and Howard Fehr. "Learning Theory and the Improvement of Instruction—A Balanced Program." *The Learning of Mathematics: Its Theory and Practice*. 21st Yearbook. NCTM, 1953.

C10 College Entrance Examination Board. *10 SATs*. 1st ed. CEEB, 1983.

C11 College Entrance Examination Board. *Academic Preparation in Mathematics*. CEEB, 1985.

C12 College Entrance Examination Board. *10 SATs*. 2nd ed. CEEB, 1986.

C13 College Entrance Examination Board. *10 SATs*. 3rd ed. CEEB, 1988.

C14 College Entrance Examination Board. "The New SAT." Winter, 1993–94, vol. 3, no. 2.

C15 College Entrance Examination Board. *Real SATs*. 1st ed. CEEB, 1995.

C16 Commission on Mathematics. *Program for College Preparatory Mathematics*. College Entrance Examination Board, 1959.

C17 Commission on Post-War Plans. "The Second Report of The Commission on Post-War Plans." *Mathematics Teacher*, vol. 38, May 1945, pp. 195–221. Reprinted in Bidwell and Clason.

C18 Committee on the Undergraduate Program in Mathematics. *A compendium of CUPM Recommendations*. Volume I. Mathematical Association of America, 1973.

C19 Cooper, Harris M. *The Battle over Homework: Common Ground for Administrators, Teachers and Parents*. Corwin Press, 2nd ed., 2001.

C20 Cooper, Harris, Barbara Nye, Kelly Charlton, James Lindsay, and Scott Greathouse. "The Effects of Summer Vacation on Achievement Test Scores: A Narrative and Meta-Analytic Review." *Review of Educational Research*, vol. 66, issue 3, Sept 1, 1996, pp. 227–268. http://journals.sagepub.com/doi/abs/10.3102/00346543066003227

C21 Crary, Alice and W. Stephen Wilson. "The Faulty Logic of the 'Math Wars'." Opinionator. *The New York Times*, June 16, 2013. https://opinionator.blogs.nytimes.com/2013/06/16/the-faulty-logic-of-the-math-wars/?_r=0

C22 Crone, Theodore M. "What Test Scores Can and Cannot Tell Us About the Quality of Our Schools." *Business Review*, Quarter 3, 2004, pp. 5–21.

C23 Crosswhite, Joe. "Better Teaching, Better Mathematics: Are They Enough?" *Mathematics Teacher*, vol. 79, Oct 1986, pp. 572–580.

D1 Davis, Robert B. *The Changing Curriculum: Mathematics*. Association for Supervision and Curriculum Development. National Education Association, 1967.

D2 Dee, Thomas S. "The Why Chromosome: How a teacher's gender affects boys and girls." *Education Next*, vol. 6, no. 4, Fall 2006. http://educationnext.org/the-why-chromosome/

D3 DeTurck, Dennis. "Down With Fractions!" The 60-Second Lectures. University of Pennsylvania, Sept 22, 2002. http://www.sas.upenn.edu/down-with-fractions

D4 De Witt, Karen. "Bush Pushes Education Goals At Math Educators' Meeting." *The New York Times*, Apr 25, 1991. http://www.nytimes.com/1991/04/25/us/bush-pushes-education-goals-at-math-educators-meeting.html

D5 Dienes, Z. P. *The Power of Mathematics*. Hutchinson Educational, 1964.

D6 Dolciani, Mary, William Wooton, Edwin Beckenbach, and William Chinn. *Modern School Mathematics Structure and Method Grade 7*. Houghton Mifflin, 1967.

D7 Donlan, Thomas G. "Stressing the System." Editorial Commentary. *Barron's*, July 21, 2003.

D8 Dow, Peter. "Sputnik Revisited: Historical Perspectives on Science Reform." http://www.nas.edu/sputnik/dow2.htm

D9 Duncan, Arne. Brookings Institution. "A Discussion With Secretary of Education Arne Duncan." Transcript. https://www.brookings.edu/wp-content/uploads/2012/04/20090511_education_transcript_corrected.pdf

D10 Duncan, Arne. "V. F. Portrait: Salman Kahn." *Vanity Fair*, Dec 2014, pp. 160–161. http://www.vanityfair.com/news/business/2014/12/salman-khan-arne-duncan

E1 Elkind, David. *The Hurried Child: Growing Up Too Fast Too Soon*. Perseus Publishing, 3rd ed., 2001.

E2 Ernest, John. "Is Mathematics A Sexist Discipline?" in *Women and the Mathematical Mystique*. Lynn Fox, Linda Brody, Dianne Tobin, eds. The Johns Hopkins University Press, 1980.

F1 FairTest. "Common Core Brings a New Chapter of High-Stakes Test Horrors." *FairTest Examiner*, Nov 2013. http://www.fairtest.org/Common-Core-Testing-Horror-Stories?utm_source=NOVEMBER+2013+EXAMINER&utm_campaign=new&utm_medium=email

F2 Farbman, David A., David J. Goldberg, and Tiffany D. Miller. "Redesigning and Expanding School Time to Support Common Core Implementation." Center for American Progress, Jan 31, 2014. http://www.americanprogress.org/issues/education/report/2014/01/31/81861/redesigning-and-expanding-school-time-to-support-common-core-implementation/

F3 Fawcett, Harold. "The Geometric Continuum." *Mathematics Teacher*, vol. 63, May 1970, pp. 411–420.

F4 Fehr, Howard F. "What Research Says to the Teacher." *Teaching High-School Mathematics*, no. 9. National Education Association, 1968.

F5 Feller, Ben. "Highly qualified teachers on the way—or are they?" Associated Press, Aug 22, 2005. http://www.teacherssupportnetwork.com/corporate/KnowledgeCenterArticle.do?id=1195

F6 Feller, Ben. "Review: Teacher-quality mandate a big hurdle for states." Associated Press, Aug 17, 2006. http://www.boston.com/news/nation/articles/2006/08/17/review_teacher_quality_mandate_a_big_hurdle_for_states/

F7 Feller, Ben. "Study: Teacher's Gender Affects Learning." Associated Press, Aug 27, 2006. http://www.washingtonpost.com/wp-dyn/content/article/2006/08/27/AR2006082700273.html

F8 Feller, Ben. "Study Says Teacher Training Is Chaotic." Associated Press, Sept 19, 2006. http://www.edschools.org/pdf/Associated_Press_091906.pdf

F9 Ferguson, Marilyn. *The Aquarian Conspiracy*. J. P. Tarcher, 1980.

F10 Fey, James T. "Mathematics Education Research on Curriculum and Instruction," in *Research in Mathematics Education*. Richard J. Shumway, ed. National Council of Teachers of Mathematics, 1980.

F11 Fox, Lynn H., Linda Brody, Dianne Tobin, eds. *Women and the Mathematical Mystique*. Proceedings of the 8th annual Hyman Blumberg Symposium. The Johns Hopkins University Press, 1980.

F12 Friedman, Thomas. "Still Eating Our Lunch." Op-Ed. *The New York Times*, Sept 16, 2005.
http://www.nytimes.com/2005/09/16/opinion/16friedman.html

G1 Gagné, Robert M. *The Conditions of Learning*. Holt, Rinehart, and Winston, 3rd ed., 1977.

G2 Gagné, Robert M., ed. *Instructional Technology: Foundations*. Lawrence Erlbaum Associates, 1987.

G3 Gardner, Howard. *The Disciplined Mind: What All Students Should Understand*. Simon & Schuster, 1999.

G4 Gardner, Howard. *Intelligence Reframed: Multiple Intelligences for the 21st Century*. Basic Books, 1999.

G5 Geary, David C., Mary K. Hoard, Lara Nugent, and Drew H. Bailey. "Adolescents' Functional Numeracy Is Predicted by Their School Entry Number System Knowledge." *PLOS ONE*, Jan 30, 2013.
http://journals.plos.org/plosone/article?id=10.1371/journal.pone.0054651

G6 Gillard, Julia. "The Path Forward for Improving Education." Brookings Institution, Dec 13, 2013.
https://www.brookings.edu/blog/education-plus-development/2013/12/13/the-path-forward-for-improving-education/

G7 Glasser, William. *Schools Without Failure*. Harper & Row, 1969.

G8 Golden, Daniel. "Initiative to Leave No Child Behind Leaves Out Gifted." *The Wall Street Journal*, Dec 29, 2003.
http://online.wsj.com/public/resources/documents/Polk_Gifted.htm

G9 Greenberg, Julie and Natalie Dugan. *Incoherent By Design: What You Should Know About Differences Between Undergraduate and Graduate Training of Elementary Teachers.* NCTQ, Feb 2015.

G10 Greenstone, Michael and Adam Looney. "Are We Short-Changing our Future? The Economic Imperative of Attracting Great Teachers." Brookings Opinion, Sept 22, 2011. http://www.brookings.edu/research/opinions/2011/09/22-teachers-greenstone-looney

G11 Gregorian, Vartan. "How to Train—and Retrain—Teachers." Op-Ed. *The New York Times*, July 6, 2001. http://www.nytimes.com/2001/07/06/opinion/how-to-train-and-retrain-teachers.html

G12 Gross, Martin. *The Conspiracy of Ignorance: The Failure of American Public Schools.* HarperCollins, 1999.

G13 Gustafsson, Jan-Eric. "Understanding Causal Influences on Educational Achievement through Analysis of Differences over Time within Countries." Chap. 3 in *Lessons Learned: What International Assessments Tell Us about Math Achievement.* Tom Loveless, ed. Brookings Institution Press, 2007, pp. 37–63.

H1 Hacker, Andrew. "Is Algebra Necessary?" Sunday Review Opinion. *The New York Times*, July 28, 2012. http://www.nytimes.com/2012/07/29/opinion/sunday/is-algebra-necessary.html

H2 Hamilton, Laura S. and José Felipe Martínez. "What Can TIMSS Surveys Tell Us about Mathematics Reforms in the United States during the 1990s?" Chap. 6 in *Lessons Learned: What International Assessments Tell Us about Math Achievement.* Tom Loveless, ed. Brookings Institution Press, 2007, pp. 127–174.

H3 Hanushek, Eric A. "Improving Student Achievement: Is Reducing Class Size the Answer?" Progressive Policy Institute, June, 1998.

H4 Hardy, G. H. *A Mathematician's Apology.* Cambridge University Press, 1941.

H5 Hart, Eric W. "Is Discrete Mathematics the New Math of the Eighties?" *Mathematics Teacher*. NCTM, vol. 78, no. 5, May 1985, pp. 334–338.

H6 Hechinger, John. "New Report Urges Return to Basics In Teaching Math." *The Wall Street Journal*, Sept 12, 2006, pp. A1, A16. http://www.wsj.com/articles/SB115802278519360136

H7 Hechinger, John. "Education Panel Lays Out Truce In Math Wars." *The Wall Street Journal*, Mar 5, 2008, pp. D1–D2. https://www.wsj.com/articles/SB120465579132610785

H8 Heitin, Liana. "Obama Touts Computer Science Education in Final State of the Union Address." *Education Week*, Jan 12, 2016. http://blogs.edweek.org/edweek/curriculum/2016/01/obama_touts_computer_science_state_of_the_union.html

H9 Hemel, Daniel J. "Summers' Comments on Women and Science Draw Ire." *The Harvard Crimson*, Jan 14, 2005. http://www.thecrimson.com/article/2005/1/14/summers-comments-on-women-and-science/

H10 Henkelman, James. *A Study of a Program Designed to Effect Mathematics Curriculum Change in the Saugus Massachusetts Secondary Schools*. Harvard University Graduate School of Education Ed.D. Thesis, 1965.

H11 Herold, Benjamin. "Why Ed Tech Is Not Transforming How Teachers Teach." *Education Week*, June 10, 2015. http://www.edweek.org/ew/articles/2015/06/11/why-ed-tech-is-not-transforming-how.html

H12 Hirsch, E. D. Jr. *The Schools We Need And Why We Don't Have Them*. Doubleday, 1996.

H13 Hirsch, E. D. Jr. *The Knowledge Deficit: Closing the Shocking Education Gap for American Children*. Houghton Mifflin Company, 2006.

H14 Hirsch, E. D. Jr. *Why Knowledge Matters: Rescuing Our Children From Failed Educational Theories*. Harvard Education Press, 2016.

H15 Hirstein, James J. "The Second National Assessment in Mathematics: Area and Volume." *Mathematics Teacher*, vol. 74, no. 9, Dec 1981, pp. 704–708.

H16 Hlavaty, Julius H. ed. *Mathematics for the Academically Talented Student*. NEA and NCTM, 1959.

H17 Hoff, David J. "Not All Agree on Meaning of NCLB Proficiency." *Education Week*, Apr 17, 2007. http://www.edweek.org/ew/articles/2007/04/18/33proficient.h26.html

H18 Hu, Winnie. "Making Math Lessons as Easy as 1, Pause, 2, Pause . . ." *The New York Times*, Sept 30, 2010. http://www.nytimes.com/2010/10/01/education/01math.html

H19 Hu, Winnie. "Many State Legislators Lack College Degrees." *The New York Times*, June 12, 2011. http://www.nytimes.com/2011/06/13/education/13legis.html?_r= 0

H20 Hutchins, Robert M. *The Great Conversation—The Substance of a Liberal Education*. Volume I, *Great Books of the Western World*. Encyclopedia Britannica, 1952.

H21 Hyde, Janet S., Sara M. Lindberg, Marcia C. Linn, Amy B. Ellis, and Caroline C. Williams. "Gender Similarities Characterize Math Performance." *Science*, vol. 321, issue 5888, July 25, 2008, pp. 494–495. http://science.sciencemag.org/content/321/5888/494

I1 Ingersoll, Richard M. "Putting Qualified Teachers in Every Classroom." *Education Week*, June 11, 1997. http://www.edweek.org/ew/articles/1997/06/11/37inger.h16.html?qs=out-of-field+teaching

I2 Ingersoll, Richard M. "The Problem of Out-of-Field Teaching." *Phi Delta Kappan*, June 1998, pp. 773–776. http://www.gse.upenn.edu/pdf/rmi/PDK-RMI-1998.pdf

I3 Ingersoll, Richard M. "Why So Many Under-qualified High School Teachers?" *Education Week*, Nov 4, 1998.

I4 Ingersoll, Richard M. "The Problem of Underqualified Teachers in American Secondary Schools." *Educational Researcher*, vol. 28, issue 2, Mar 1999, pp. 26–37. http://repository.upenn.edu/cgi/viewcontent.cgi?article=1139&context=gse_pubs

I5 Institute of Education Sciences. *U.S. Performance Across International Assessments of Student Achievement: Special Supplement to The Condition of Education 2009*. U.S. ED, NCES 2009-083, Aug 2009.

I6 International Society for Technology in Education. *Vision: TEST (Technologically Enriched Schools of Tomorrow)*. Executive Summary of the Final Report, 1990.

J1 Jennings, Marianne M. "To sum up new math, 2 + 2 = 4ish." *The Arizona Republic*, Dec 10, 1995, p. H3. http://www.azarchivesonline.org/xtf/view?docId=ead/asu/jenningsm.xml

J2 Jennings, Marianne M. "Rain Forest Algebra Course Teaches Everything but Algebra." *Christian Science Monitor*, Apr 2, 1996, p. 18.

J3 Jennings, Marianne M. "X + Y = F: Mesa's algebra textbooks flunk examination." *The Arizona Republic*, Oct 20, 1996, p. H1.

J4 Jennings, Marianne M. "Rain-Forest Algebra and MTV Geometry." *The Textbook Letter*, Nov–Dec, 1996, vol. 7, no. 5, pp. 4-6.

J5 Jennings, Marianne M. "MTV Math Doesn't Add Up." *The Wall Street Journal*, Dec 17, 1996, p. A22.

J6 Jennings, Marianne M. "Why Our Kids Can't Do Math." *The Wall Street Journal*, Dec 17, 1996, and *Reader's Digest*, Nov 1997, p. 181.

J7 Johnson, Donovan A. and Gerald R. Rising. *Guidelines for Teaching Mathematics*. Wadsworth Publishing, 2nd ed., 1972.

J8 Johnson, Eugene and Eugene Owen. *Linking the National Assessment of Educational Progress (NAEP) and the Third International Mathematics and Science Study (TIMSS): A Technical Report*. U.S. ED, NCES 98–499, Aug 1998.

J9 Johnson, Spencer. *Who Moved My Cheese?* Putnam, 1998.

K1 Kantrowitz, Barbara and Andrew Murr. "Subtracting the New Math." *Newsweek*, Dec 15, 1997, p. 62. http://www.newsweek.com/subtracting-new-math-170340

K2 Keats, John. *Schools Without Scholars*. Houghton Mifflin Company, 1958.

Bibliography

K3 Kilpatrick, Jeremy. "A Retrospective Account of the Past 25 Years of Research on Teaching Mathematical Problem Solving." *Teaching and Learning Mathematical Problem Solving: Multiple Research Perspectives*. Edward Silver, ed. Lawrence Erlaum Associates, 1985, pp. 1–15.

K4 Kilpatrick, Jeremy, Vilma Mesa, and Finbarr Sloane. "U.S. Algebra Performance in an International Context." Chap. 5 in *Lessons Learned*. Tom Loveless, ed. Brookings Institution Press, 2007, pp. 85–126.

K5 Kim, Mallie Jane. "The End Is Near for No Child Left Behind." *U.S. News & World Report*, Sept 23, 2011. http://www.usnews.com/news/articles/2011/09/23/the-end-is-near-for-no-child-left-behind

K6 Klein, David. "School math books, nonsense, and the National Science Foundation." *American Journal of Physics*, vol. 75, no. 2, Feb 2007, pp. 101–102. http://www.csun.edu/~vcmth00m/nsf.html

K7 Klein, Joel I., Julia C. Levy, and Condoleezza Rice. *U.S. Education Reform and National Security: Independent Task Force Report*. Council on Foreign Relations Press, 2012. http://www.cfr.org/united-states/us-education-reform-national-security/p27618

K8 Kline, Morris. *Why Johnny Can't Add*. St. Martin's Press, 1973.

K9 Kluttz, Marguerite and Harry L. Phillips. *Modern Mathematics and Your Child*. U.S. Dept of Health, Educ, Welfare. USGPO, 1963.

K10 Koebler, Jason. "Many STEM Teachers Don't Hold Certifications." *U.S. News & World Report*. June 8, 2011. https://www.usnews.com/education/blogs/high-school-notes/2011/06/08/many-stem-teachers-dont-hold-certifications

K11 Kogelman, Stanley and Joseph Warren. *Mind Over Math*. Dial Press, 1978.

K12 Kondracke, Morton. "A Better-Schools Deal: Pay Teachers More And Demand Results." *Roll Call*, July 12, 2006.

K13 Krieghbaum, Hillier and Hugh Rawson. *To Improve Secondary School Science and Mathematics Teaching: A Short History of the First Dozen Years of NSF's Summer Institutes Program, 1954–1965*. USGPO, 1968.

K14 Kristof, Nicholas D. "Our Greatest National Shame." Op-Ed. *The New York Times*, Feb 14, 2009. http://www.nytimes.com/2009/02/15/opinion/15kristof.html?_r=0

K15 Kurzweil, Ray. *The Singularity is Near*. Viking, 2005.

L1 Laurer, Robert. *Perspectives on Social Change*. Allyn and Bacon, 2nd ed., 1977.

L2 Lazarus, Mitchell. "Mathophobia: Some Personal Speculations." *National Elementary Principal*, vol. 53, no. 2, Jan/Feb, 1974, pp. 16–22.

L3 Lee, Traci G. "Holistic approach to education can close achievement gap." Mar 2, 2012. http://www.msnbc.com/morning-joe/holistic-approach-education-can-close

L4 Leino, Jarkko. "Knowledge and Learning in Mathematics." *Transforming Children's Mathematics Education: International Perspectives*. Leslie Steffe and Terry Wood, eds. Lawrence Erlbaum, 1990, pp. 41–46.

L5 Lester, Will. "Poll shows America's love-hate relationship with math." Associated Press, Aug 17, 2005. http://www2.ljworld.com/news/2005/aug/17/poll_shows_americas_lovehate_relationship_math/

L6 Lewis, Harry. "Reinventing the Classroom." *Harvard Magazine*, Sept–Oct, 2012, pp. 54–57.

L7 *Life*. "New Patterns in Mathematics." Vol. 44, Apr 14, 1958, pp. 124–125.

L8 *Life*. "Captivating Key to Math." Vol. 50, Feb 10, 1961, pp. 47–49.

L9 Liu, C. L. *Introduction to Combinatorial Mathematics*. McGraw-Hill, 1968.

L10 Lockhart, Paul. *A Mathematician's Lament*. Bellevue Literary Press, 2009.

L11 Loveless, Tom. *How Well Are American Students Learning? The 2007 Brown Center Report on American Education*. Brookings Institution, Dec 2007.

L12 Loveless, Tom. *The Misplaced Math Student: Lost in Eighth-Grade Algebra*. The 2008 Brown Center Report on American Education. Brookings Institution, Sept 2008.

L13 Loveless, Tom. *How Well Are American Students Learning?* The 2012 Brown Center Report on American Education. Brookings Institution, Feb 2012.

L14 Loveless, Tom. *How Well Are American Students Learning?* The 2013 Brown Center Report on American Education. Brookings Institution, Mar 2013.

L15 Loveless, Tom. *How Well Are American Students Learning?* The 2014 Brown Center Report on American Education. Brookings Institution, Mar 2014.

L16 Loveless, Tom. *How Well Are American Students Learning?* The 2016 Brown Center Report on American Education. Brookings Institution, Mar 2016.

L17 Loveless, Tom. *How Well Are American Students Learning?* The 2017 Brown Center Report on American Education. Brookings Institution, Mar 2017. https://www.brookings.edu/series/brown-center-report-on-american-education/

M1 Manegold, Catherine. "U.S. Schools Misuse Time, Study Asserts." *The New York Times*, May 5, 1994.

M2 Mann, Ted. "Down With Fractions." *Penn Arts & Sciences*. Spring 2005, pp. 12–14.
http://www.sas.upenn.edu/sasalum/newsltr/spring05/deturck.pdf

M3 MATHCOUNTS. *2002–2003 School Handbook*. MATHCOUNTS Foundation, 2002.

M4 Milford, Maureen. "Professor: Fractions should be scrapped." *USA Today*, Jan 23, 2008. http://usatoday30.usatoday.com/tech/science/math-science/2008-01-23-fractions_N.htm

M5 *Modern Healthcare*. "Q&A." Mar 28, 2016, pp. 30–31.

M6 Moise, Edwin. "Mathematics, Computation, and Psychic Intelligence." *Computers in Mathematics Education*. 1984 Yearbook. National Council of Teachers of Mathematics, 1984.

M7 Morgenstern, Anne. "Historical Survey of Grouping Practices in the Elementary School," in *Grouping in the Elementary School*. Anne Morgenstern, ed. Pitman Publishing, 1966, pp. 3–13.

M8 Mosteller, Frederick. "The Case for Smaller Classes." *Harvard Magazine*, May–June, 1999, pp. 34–35.

M9 Mueller, Francis J. "The Public Image of 'New Mathematics'." *Mathematics Teacher*. NCTM, vol. 59, Nov 1966, pp. 618–623.

M10 Mueller, Francis J. "The Revolution at Sputnik-Plus-Ten." *Mathematics Teacher*. NCTM, vol. 60, Nov 1967, pp. 696–706.

M11 Mullis, Ina V. S. and Michael O. Martin. "TIMSS in Perspective: Lessons Learned from IEA's Four Decades of International Mathematics Assessments." Chap. 2 in *Lessons Learned*. Tom Loveless, ed. Brookings Institution Press, 2007, pp. 9–36.

N1 National Academies Press. *Rising Above the Gathering Storm: Energizing and Employing America for a Brighter Economic Future*. 2007. www.nap.edu/read/11463/chapter/1#xix

N2 National Advisory Committee on Mathematics Education (NACOME), Conference Board of the Mathematical Sciences. *Overview and Analysis of School Mathematics, Grades K–12*. NCTM, 1975.

N3 National Center for Education Statistics. *Out-of-Field Teaching and Educational Equality*. U.S. ED, Oct 1996.

N4 National Center for Education Statistics. *Highlights From the TIMSS 1999 Video Study of Eighth-Grade Mathematics Teaching*. U.S. ED, Mar 2003. NCES 2003–011. https://nces.ed.gov/timss/video.asp

N5 National Center for Education Statistics. *Highlights From the Trends in International Mathematics and Science Study (TIMSS) 2003*. U.S. ED, Dec 2004. NCES 2005–005.

Bibliography 375

N6 National Center for Education Statistics. *The Nation's Report Card: An Introduction to The National Assessment of Educational Progress.* U.S. ED, Institute of Education Sciences, 2005. NCES 2005-454.

N7 National Center for Education Statistics. *The Nation's Report Card Mathematics 2005.* U.S. ED, Oct 2005. NCES 2006-453.

N8 National Center for Education Statistics. *Highlights From PISA 2006: Performance of U.S. 15-Year-Olds in Science and Mathematics Literacy in an International Context.* U.S. ED, Dec 2007. NCES 2008-016.

N9 National Center for Education Statistics. *Algebra I and Geometry Curricula: Results From the 2005 High School Transcript Mathematics Curriculum Study.* U.S. ED, Mar 2013. NCES 2013-451. https://nces.ed.gov/pubsearch/pubsinfo.asp?pubid=2013451

N10 National Center for Education Statistics. *The Condition of Education 2013.* U.S. ED, Institute of Education Sciences, 2013. NCES 2013-037. https://nces.ed.gov/pubs2013/2013037.pdf

N11 National Commission on Excellence in Education. *A Nation At Risk: The Imperative for Educational Reform.* USGPO, 1983. https://www2.ed.gov/pubs/NatAtRisk/index.html

N12 National Commission on Teaching and America's Future. *What Matters Most: Teaching for America's Future.* NCTAF, 1996. https://nctaf.org/wp-content/uploads/WhatMattersMost.pdf

N13 National Committee on Mathematical Requirements. *The Reorganization of Mathematics in Secondary Education.* MAA, 1923. https://books.google.com/books/about/The_Reorganization_of_Mathematics_in_Sec.html?id=XEM7AAAAIAAJ http://www.mathcurriculumcenter.org/PDFS/CCM/originals/reorg_of_math_report.pdf

N14 National Council of Teachers of Mathematics. *Curriculum Problems in Teaching Mathematics.* 2nd Yearbook. Teachers College Press, 1927.

N15 National Council of Teachers of Mathematics. *The Place of Mathematics in Secondary Education.* 15th Yearbook. NCTM, 1940.

N16 National Council of Teachers of Mathematics. *An Analysis of New Mathematics Programs*. NCTM, 1963.

N17 National Council of Teachers of Mathematics. *A History of Mathematics Education in the United States and Canada*. 32nd Yearbook. NCTM, 1970.

N18 National Council of Teachers of Mathematics. *An Agenda For Action: Recommendations for School Mathematics of the 1980s*. NCTM, 1980. http://www.nctm.org/flipbooks/standards/agendaforaction/index.html

N19 National Council of Teachers of Mathematics. *Priorities in School Mathematics (PRISM)*. NCTM, 1980. https://eric.ed.gov/?id=ED201476

N20 National Council of Teachers of Mathematics. *Curriculum and Evaluation Standards for School Mathematics*. NCTM, 1989.

N21 National Council of Teachers of Mathematics. *Professional Standards for Teaching Mathematics*. NCTM, 1991.

N22 National Council of Teachers of Mathematics. *Assessment Standards for School Mathematics*. NCTM, 1995.

N23 National Council of Teachers of Mathematics. "Who Should Determine What You Teach?" *Mathematics Education Dialogues*. NCTM, Apr 1999, vol. 2, issue 2.

N24 National Council of Teachers of Mathematics. *Principles and Standards for School Mathematics*. NCTM, 2000.

N25 National Council of Teachers of Mathematics. "Algebra? A Gate! A Barrier! A Mystery!" *Mathematics Education Dialogues*. NCTM, Apr 2000, vol. 3, issue 2.

N26 National Council of Teachers of Mathematics. *Curriculum Focal Points for Prekindergarten through Grade 8 Mathematics: A Quest for Coherence*. NCTM, 2006.

N27 National Council of Teachers of Mathematics. *Focus in High School Mathematics: Reasoning and Sense Making*. NCTM, 2009.

N28 National Council on Teacher Quality. *State Teacher Policy Yearbook 2007: Progress on Teacher Quality*. NCTQ, 2007.

N29 National Council on Teacher Quality. *State Teacher Policy Yearbook 2008: What States Can Do To Retain Effective New Teachers*. NCTQ, 2008.

N30 National Council on Teacher Quality. "Exit with Expertise: Do Ed Schools Prepare Elementary Teachers to Pass This Test?" Sample Test. June 2008. http://www.nctq.org/p/publications/docs/nctq_ttmath_test andanswerkey_20080626115952.pdf

N31 National Council on Teacher Quality. "Exit With Expertise: Are You Qualified To Teach Elementary School Math?" Sample Test. June 2008. http://www.nctq.org/p/docs/nctq_ttmath_testandanswerkey.pdf

N32 National Council on Teacher Quality. *2013 State Teacher Policy Yearbook: National Summary*. NCTQ, Jan 2014. http://www.nctq.org/dmsView/2013_State_Teacher_Policy_Yearbook_National_Summary_NCTQ_Report

N33 National Council on Teacher Quality. *2015 State Teacher Policy Yearbook*. NCTQ, Dec 2015. http://www.nctq.org/dmsView/2015_State_Teacher_Policy_Yearbook_National_Summary_NCTQ_Report

N34 National Council on Teacher Quality. *2016 State Teacher Policy Yearbook: National Summary*. NCTQ, Dec 2016. http://www.nctq.org/dmsView/2016_State_Teacher_Policy_Yearbook_National_Summary_NCTQ_Report

N35 National Education Commission on Time and Learning. *Prisoners of Time*. Apr 1994. http://www.ecs.org/clearinghouse/64/52/6452.pdf

N36 National Mathematics Advisory Panel. *Foundations for Success: The Final Report of the NMAP*. U.S. ED, 2008.

N37 National Research Council. *Mathematics Learning in Early Childhood: Paths Toward Excellence and Equity*. Christopher Cross, Taniesha Woods, and Heidi Schweingruber, eds. The National Academies Press, 2009. http://www.nap.edu/openbook.php?record_id=12519&page=R1

N38 National Science Board Commission on Precollege Education in Mathematics, Science, and Technology. *Educating Americans for the 21st Century: A plan of action for improving mathematics, science, and technology education for all American elementary and secondary students so that their achievement is the best in the world by 1995.* NSF, 1983. CPCE–NSF–04.

N39 *Newsweek.* "Digits and Dunces." Vol. 47, Apr 9, 1956, p. 78.

N40 *Newsweek.* "Can 'Math' Be Lively?" Vol. 53, Jan 5, 1959, p. 42.

N41 *Newsweek.* "Third R a Snap?" Vol. 54, Sept 21, 1959, p. 90.

N42 *Newsweek.* "Math Made Easy." Vol. 55, Feb 8, 1960, p. 91.

N43 *Newsweek.* "New Math—Does It Really Add Up?" Vol. 65, May 10, 1965, pp. 112–118.

O1 O'Daffer, Phares, Stanley Clemens, and Randall Charles. *Pre-Algebra: A Transition to Algebra.* Addison-Wesley, 1992.

O2 Office of Educational Technology. *Transforming American Education Learning Powered by Technology: National Education Technology Plan 2010.* U.S. ED, Nov 2010. https://www.ed.gov/sites/default/files/netp2010.pdf

O3 One-to-One Institute. "What's the future of iPads in schools?" June 26, 2015. http://www.one-to-oneinstitute.org/one-to-one-institute/what-s-the-future-of-ipads-in-schools

O4 Oxrieder, C. Ann and Janet P. Ray. *Your Number's Up: A Calculated Approach to Successful Math Study.* Addison Wesley, 1982.

P1 Paige, Rod. *The War Against Hope: How Teachers' Unions Hurt Children, Hinder Teachers, and Endanger Public Education.* Thomas Nelson, 2006.

P2 Papanastasiou, Elena and Efi Paparistodemou. "Examining Educational Technology and Achievement through Latent Variable Modeling." *Lessons Learned.* Tom Loveless, ed. Brookings Press, 2007, pp. 205–225.

Bibliography

P3 Papert, Seymour. *Mindstorms: Children, Computers, and Powerful Ideas*. Basic Books, 1980.

P4 Pappano, Laura. "The Algebra Problem: How to elicit algebraic thinking in students before eighth grade." *Harvard Education Letter*, vol. 28, no. 3, May/Jun 2012. www.hepg.org/hel-home/issues/28_3/helarticle/the-algebra- problem_533#home

P5 *Parade* Magazine. "Making a Profit Off Kids." *Intelligence Report*. Oct 28, 2007. http://4lakidsnews.blogspot.com/2007/11/making-profit-off-kids.html

P6 Park, Alice. "The Myth of the Math Gender Gap." *Time*, July 24, 2008. http://content.time.com/time/health/article/ 0,8599, 18263 99,00.html

P7 Perlstein, Linda. "Right Teacher, Wrong Class." *Washington Post*, Feb 15, 1999. http://www.washingtonpost.com/archive/politics/1999/02/15/right-teacher-wrong-class/e89ca357-a724-4b4f-b91a-05302edd892e/

P8 Peterson, Ivars. *The Mathematical Tourist: Snapshots of Modern Mathematics*. W. H. Freeman and Company, 1988.

P9 Pólya, G. *Mathematical Discovery*. Vol. II. John Wiley and Sons, 1965.

P10 Pólya, G. *How To Solve It*. Princeton University Press, 1st ed., 1945. Doubleday Anchor Books, 2nd ed., 1957.

R1 Ratnesar, Romesh. "This Is Math?" *Time*, Aug 25, 1997, pp. 66–67. http://content.time.com/time/magazine/article/0,9171,138201,00.html

R2 Ravitch, Diane. *The Language Police: How Pressure Groups Restrict What Students Learn*. Alfred A. Knopf, 2003.

R3 Ravitch, Diane. "Ethnomathematics." *The Wall Street Journal*, June 20, 2005. http://www.online.wsj.com/article/0,,SB111922877339463719-email,00.html

R4 Ravitch, Diane. "Every State Left Behind." Op-Ed. *The New York Times*, Nov 7, 2005. http://www.nytimes.com/2005/11/07/opinion/07ravitch.html?module=Search&mabReward=relbias%3As&_r=0

R5 Ravitch, Diane. "Why I Changed My Mind About School Reform." *The Wall Street Journal*, Mar 9, 2010. www.wsj.com/articles/SB10001424052748704869304575109443305343962

R6 Ravitch, Diane. *The Death and Life of the Great American School System: How Testing and Choice Are Undermining Education*. Basic Books, 2010.

R7 Ravitch, Diane. *Reign of Error: The Hoax of the Privatization Movement and the Danger to America's Public Schools*. Alfred A. Knopf, 2013.

R8 Reitz, Stephanie. "Many US schools adding iPads, trimming textbooks." Associated Press, Sept 3, 2011. http://www.nbcnews.com/id/44384057/ns/technology_and_science-tech_and_gadgets/t/many-us-schools-adding-ipads-trimming-textbooks/#.WFsFlTvyqCQ

R9 Richardson, Frank C. and Richard M. Suinn. "The Mathematics Anxiety Rating Scale: Psychometric Data." *Journal of Counseling Psychology*, vol. 19, no. 6, 1972, pp. 551–554.

R10 Richardson, Frank and Robert Woolfolk. "Mathematics Anxiety." *Test Anxiety: Theory, Research, and Applications*. Sarason, Irwin, ed. Lawrence Erlbaum Associates, 1980.

R11 Ripley, Amanda. "Who Says a Woman Can't be Einstein?" *Time*. Cover story: "The Math Myth: The real truth about women's brains and the gender gap in science." Mar 7, 2005. pp. 51–60. http://content.time.com/time/magazine/article/0,9171,1032332,00.html

R12 Ripley, Amanda. "A Call to Action for Public Schools." *Time*. "What Makes a School Great." Sept 20, 2010, pp. 32–42. https://docs.google.com/file/d/0BxpWi0-lt86sNTA3NGU4YWItYzdhMC00N2QwLWI1MWQtNjk3YTVlZjcwYTAx/edit

R13 Ripley, Amanda. *The Smartest Kids in the World and How They Got That Way*. Simon & Schuster, 2013.

R14 Rosemond, John. *Ending the Homework Hassle*. Andrews McMeel Publishing, 1990.

Bibliography

R15 Rosenberg, Merri. "When Homework Takes Over." *The New York Times*, Apr 18, 2004. http://www.nytimes.com/2004/04/18/nyregion/when-homework-takes-over.html?pagewanted=all&src=pm

R16 Rosenthal, Evelyn B. *Understanding the New Math*. Hawthorn Books, 1965.

R17 Rosenthal, Robert and Lenore Jacobson. *Pygmalion in the Classroom*. Holt, Rinehart, & Winston, 1968.

R18 Rothman, Robert. *Fewer, Clearer, Higher: How the Common Core State Standards Can Change Classroom Practice*. Harvard Education Press, 2013.

S1 Saettler, Paul. *The Evolution of American Educational Technology*. Libraries Unlimited, 1990.

S2 Samuelson, Robert J. "The School Reform Fraud." *Newsweek*, June 14, 1991, p. 44. http://www.newsweek.com/school-reform-fraud-204274

S3 Sandberg, Sheryl. *Lean In: Women, Work, and the Will to Lead*. Alfred A. Knopf, 2013.

S4 Sawyer, W. W. *Mathematician's Delight*. Penguin Books, 1959.

S5 Schmid, Randolph E. "Experts: Some women perform well in math." Associated Press, Oct 20, 2006. http://www.usatoday30.usatoday.com/tech/science/2006-10-20-math-women_x.htm

S6 Schmidt, William H. and Richard T. Houang. "Lack of Focus in the Mathematics Curriculum: Symptom or Cause?" Chap. 4 in *Lessons Learned*. Tom Loveless, ed. Brookings Institution Press, 2007, pp. 65–84.

S7 Schmidt, William H. and Curtis C. McKnight. *Inequality for All: The Challenge of Unequal Opportunity in American Schools*. Teachers College Press, 2012.

S8 Schneider, Mike. "Teenager stumps Bush with pop math quiz." Associated Press, July 6, 2004. www.jacksonville.com/tu-online/apnews/stories/070604/D83LFQD84.shtml

S9 Schoenfeld, Alan H. *Mathematical Problem Solving*. Academic Press, 1985.

S10 Schulz, Charles. "Peanuts." Apr 22, 1964 www.peanuts.com/search/?keyword=New%20Math&type=comic_strips#.VCCoM1ZOfoB

S11 Seelye, Katharine Q. "Group Seeks to Alter SAT to Raise Girls' Scores." *The New York Times*, Mar 14, 1997. www.nytimes.com/1997/03/14/us/group-seeks-to-alter-sat-to-raise-girls-scores.html

S12 Sells, Lucy. "Mathematics—A Critical Filter." *The Science Teacher*, vol. 45, no. 2, Feb 1978, pp. 28–29. https://eric.ed.gov/?id=EJ176337

S13 Shane, Harold G. "The School and Individual Differences." *Individualizing Instruction*: The Sixty-first Yearbook of the National Society for the Study of Education. Part I, pp. 44–61.

S14 Singmaster, David. *Notes On Rubik's Magic Cube*. Enslow, 1981.

S15 Skemp, Richard R. *The Psychology of Learning Mathematics*. Penguin Books. 1973.

S16 Skinner, B. F. "Teaching Machines," *Science*, vol. 128, no. 3330, Oct 24, 1958, pp. 969–977. http://www.sciencemag.org/content/128/3330/969.extract?sid=d8960820-1797-461d-a8df-a7be0738f258

S17 Skinner, B. F. *The Technology of Teaching*. Prentice-Hall Publishing. 1968.

S18 Sobel, Max. "Have Elementary Teachers Been Allowed to Muddle Through Math?" *Instructor*, vol. 91, no. 6, Feb 1982, pp. 84–85.

S19 Smink, Jeff. "This Is Your Brain on Summer." *The New York Times*, July 27, 2011. http://www.nytimes.com/2011/07/28/opinion/28smink.html

S20 Smith, Malbert III and Dee Brewer. "Stop Summer Academic Loss: An Education Policy Priority." White Paper. MetaMetrics, 2007. http://cdn.lexile.com/m/uploads/whitepapers/StopSummerAcademicLoss_MetaMetricsWhitepaper.pdf

S21 Smith, Susan. "Microcomputers in the Middle School," in *Computers in Mathematics Education*. 46th Yearbook. Hansen, Viggo and Zweng, Marilyn, eds. National Council of Teachers of Mathematics, 1984.

S22 Stalnaker, John M. "The Identification and Education of the Academically Talented Student in the American Secondary School." The Conference Report, James B. Conant, Chairman. National Education Association, 1958.

S23 Sternberg, Robert J. *The Triarchic Mind: A New Theory of Human Intelligence*. Viking Penguin, 1988.

S24 Sternberg, Robert J. *Successful Intelligence: How Practical and Creative Intelligence Determine Success In Life*. Simon & Schuster, 1996.

S25 Stevenson, Harold W. and James W. Stigler. *The Learning Gap: Why Our Schools Are Failing and What We Can Learn from Japanese and Chinese Education*. Simon & Schuster, 1992.

S26 Stigler, James W. and James Hiebert. *The Teaching Gap: Best Ideas From the World's Teachers for Improving Education in the Classroom*. Free Press, Simon & Schuster, 1999. (Paperback Preface pp. xi–xxii, Paperback Afterword pp. 181–194.)

S27 Summers, Lawrence. "Letter from President Summers on women and science." Jan 19, 2005. http://www.harvard.edu/president/speeches/summers_2005/womensci.php

S28 Supreme Court of the United States. Owasso Public Schools v. Falvo. 534 U.S. 426 (2002).
http://www.supreme.justia.com/cases/federal/us/534/426/case.html

S29 Sykes, Charles J. *Dumbing Down Our Kids: Why American Children Feel Good About Themselves But Can't Read, Write, or Add*. St. Martin's Press, 1995.

S30 Symonds, William C. "How To Fix America's Schools: Seven Ideas That Work." *Business Week*, Mar 19, 2001, pp. 66–80.
http://www.businessweek.com/stories/2001-03-18/how-to-fix-americas-schools

T1 *The New York Times*. "COMPANY NEWS: Mattel Says It Erred; Teen Talk Barbie Turns Silent on Math." Oct 21, 1992. http://www.nytimes.com/1992/10/21/business/company-news-mattel-says-it-erred-teen-talk-barbie-turns-silent-on-math.html

T2 *The New York Times*, Editorial Board. "Who Says Math Has to Be Boring?" Dec 7, 2013. http://www.nytimes.com/2013/12/08/opinion/sunday/who-says-math-has-to-be-boring.html

T3 *Time*. "Least Popular Subject." Vol. 67, June 18, 1956, p. 74.

T4 *Time*. "Math and Ticktacktoe." Vol. 68, July 23, 1956, pp. 78–80.

T5 *Time*. "The New Mathematics." Vol. 71, Feb 3 1958, p. 48.

T6 *Time*. "Math Is Fun." Vol. 76, July 25, 1960, pp. 44–46.

T7 *Time*. "Math Made Interesting." Vol. 78, Sept 22, 1961, p. 59. www.time.com/time/magazine/article/0,9171,873412,00.html

T8 *Time*. "What Makes a Good School." Oct 27, 1997. http://content.time.com/time/covers/0,16641,19971027,00.html

T9 Tobias, Sheila. *Overcoming Math Anxiety*. Houghton Mifflin Company, 1st ed., 1978.

T10 Tobias, Sheila. *Overcoming Math Anxiety*. W. W. Norton & Company, 2nd ed., 1993.

T11 Toch, Thomas. "Why Teachers Don't Teach." *U.S. News & World Report*, vol. 120, no. 8, Feb 26, 1996. www.landiss.com/teaching/why-teachers-dont-teach.htm

T12 Toppo, Greg. "A solution to how to teach math: Subtract." *USA Today*, Mar 12, 2008. www.usatoday30.usatoday.com/news/eduction/2008-03-13-math-panel_n. htm

T13 Trotter, Andrew. "Spellings Seeks Input on Technology's Role in Schools." *Education Week*, Apr 4, 2007 http://www.edweek.org/ew/articles/2007/04/04/31edtech.h26.html

Bibliography

T14 Twain, Mark. *Adventures of Huckleberry Finn*. Borders Classics, 2006. Originally published 1884.

U1 U.S. ED. *Helping Your Child with Homework*. 1995, 2002, and 2005. https://www.edpubs.gov/ProductCatalog.aspx?KeyWordSearch=&TypeofSearch=exact&searchterm=Helping%20Your%20Child%20With%20Homework

U2 U.S. ED. "What Do Student Grades Mean? Differences Across Schools." Office of Educational Research and Improvement, Jan 1994.

U3 U.S. ED. *Eisenhower Mathematics and Science State Curriculum Frameworks Projects: Final Evaluation Report*. Office of the Under Secretary of Education, 1997.

U4 U.S. ED. *Homeroom, The Official Blog.* https://blog.ed.gov/2011/03/national-security-through-quality-education/

U5 Usiskin, Zalman. "We Need Another Revolution in Secondary School Mathematics." *The Secondary School Mathematics Curriculum*. 1985 Yearbook. Hirsch and Zweng, eds. National Council of Teachers of Mathematics, 1985.

V1 Vascellaro, Jessica. "Sudoku: The Next Generation." *The Wall Street Journal*. Feb 9, 2006. http://www.wsj.com/articles/SB113944522393368929

V2 Vinovskis, Maris A. *The Road to Charlottesville: The 1989 Education Summit*. National Education Goals Panel, 1999. http://govinfo.library.unt.edu/negp/reports/negp30.pdf

W1 Walser, Nancy. "Assessing the New Common Core Tests—An Interview with Joan L. Herman." *Harvard Education Letter*, Harvard Education Publishing Group, vol. 29, no. 4, July/Aug 2013. www.hepg.org/hel-home/issues/29_4/helarticle/assessing-the-new-common-core-tests_572

W2 Walsh, Kate and Christopher O. Tracy. *Increasing the Odds: How Good Policies Can Yield Better Teachers*. NCTQ, Dec 2004. http://www.nctq.org/dmsView/Increasing_the_Odds_How_Good_Policies_Can_Yield_Better_Teachers_NCTQ_Report

W3 Walsh, Kate and Sandi Jacobs. *Alternative Certification Isn't Alternative*. Thomas B. Fordham Institute. National Council on Teacher Quality, Sept 2007.

W4 Walsh, Kate and Julie Greenberg. *No Common Denominator: The Preparation of Elementary Teachers in Mathematics by America's Education Schools*. National Council on Teacher Quality, June 2008. http://www.nctq.org/dmsView/No_Common_Denominator_Executive_Summary_pdf

W5 Walsh, Kate, Emily Cohen, and RiShawn Biddle. *Invisible Ink in Collective Bargaining: Why Key Issues Are Not Addressed*. National Council on Teacher Quality, July 2008.

W6 Weiss, Marla. *School Scandalle*. AuthorHouse, 2002.

W7 Wenglinsky, Harold. "Does It Compute? The Relationship Between Educational Technology and Student Achievement in Mathematics." Educational Testing Service, 1998. http://www.ets.org/Media/Research/pdf/PICTECHNOLOG.pdf

W8 Wheeler, Margariete and Stanley Bezuszka. "Middle Grade Mathematics: An Overview." *Mathematics for the Middle Grades*. 1982 Yearbook. Linda Silvery and James Smart, eds. National Council of Teachers of Mathematics, 1982.

W9 Wilhelms, Fred T. and Dorothy Westby-Gibson. "Grouping: Research Offers Leads." *Educational Leadership*, vol. 18, no. 7, Apr 1961, pp. 410–413, 476.

W10 Winerip, Michael. "Merit Scholarship Program Faces Sex Bias Complaint." *The New York Times*, Feb 16, 1994. http://www.nytimes.com/1994/02/16/us/merit-scholarship-program-faces-sex-bias-complaint.html

W11 Wooten, William. *SMSG—The Making of a Curriculum*. Yale University Press, 1965.

Y1 Young, J. W. A. *The Teaching of Mathematics in the Elementary and Secondary School*. Longmans, Green and Co., 1920.

BIBLIOGRAPHY—PAGE NUMBER CROSS REFERENCES

A1	80	B14	26, 27, 96, 98, 104, 133, 139, 159, 163, 167, 174, 202, 215, 216, 218, 248, 252, 258, 300	C6	306
A2	35			C7	92, 95, 230
A3	110			C8	283
A4	235			C9	110, 303
A5	57, 78			C10	1, 2, 3
A6	7			C11	27, 82, 132, 150, 265
A7	150, 155, 264	B15	106, 137		
A8	146	B16	258	C12	1
A9	127	B17	280, 320	C13	2, 3
B1	234	B18	198	C14	220
B2	234, 252	B19	126	C15	2
B3	276	B20	136	C16	28, 79, 110, 117, 149, 219, 265
B4	72, 99	B21	24, 30, 77, 79, 84, 86, 145, 152, 164, 213, 240, 248, 274, 277, 279, 289–292, 294, 299, 300, 302, 303, 308, 311, 319, 324, 340, 349	C17	119, 152, 299
B5	77, 87, 132, 152			C18	120
B6	272			C19	196, 198, 200
B7	200			C20	202
B8	254			C21	105, 175
B9	192			C22	213
B10	25, 86, 89, 91, 96, 106, 118, 119, 129, 131, 139–141, 153, 161, 162, 185, 193, 194, 200, 205, 242, 327, 339, 347, 352, 353			C23	9, 108
				D1	288
		B22	88, 89, 131, 132, 142, 218, 225, 231, 253, 276, 279, 288, 290, 291, 294, 312, 325, 340	D2	257
				D3	232
				D4	64, 144
				D5	271
				D6	175
				D7	213
B11	19, 22, 24, 29, 97, 117, 118, 121, 179, 212, 219, 242, 306, 310, 341, 347, 352	B23	290	D8	81, 82
		B24	266	D9	115, 129, 154
		B25	13, 319	D10	285
		C1	28, 146, 149, 152, 287, 293, 295, 296, 299, 302, 303, 340	E1	19, 21, 85, 141, 191, 216, 326
B12	75, 76			E2	138, 266
B13	24, 26, 27, 74, 76, 104, 119, 125, 128, 132, 145–150, 152, 155, 156, 172, 264, 265, 287, 299, 324			F1	214, 218
		C2	31, 81, 260, 342, 352, 353	F2	192
				F3	265, 339
		C3	106	F4	89, 148, 175
		C4	341	F5	67, 116
		C5	217	F6	68

Bibliography—Page Number Cross References

F7	257	H5	241	K1	95
F8	122	H6	97, 98	K2	47, 119, 123, 141, 162, 187, 208, 235, 342, 356, 357
F9	83, 303, 321, 329	H7	97		
F10	84, 295	H8	241		
F11	254	H9	256		
F12	249	H10	183	K3	275
G1	271	H11	238	K4	50, 146, 150, 156, 157, 160, 265, 296, 300
G2	316, 319	H12	21–23, 85, 90, 94, 121, 123, 145, 160, 196, 207, 210, 213, 216, 231, 272, 276, 292, 293, 304, 348, 351		
G3	87, 99, 133, 272, 274–276, 281, 304, 320, 322, 343, 349, 350, 352, 353			K5	72
				K6	106, 259
				K7	34
				K8	77, 97, 176
				K9	140, 259
G4	268, 278, 281, 309				
		H13	119, 191	K10	127
		H14	56, 167, 168, 240, 269, 270, 274, 329	K11	137, 325
G5	34			K12	128
G6	211, 284			K13	57, 58, 258
G7	20, 30, 82, 162, 197, 199, 208–211, 308, 342, 349			K14	19
		H15	36	K15	205
		H16	29	L1	82, 349
		H17	68	L2	136, 137
G8	165	H18	249	L3	14
G9	125	H19	179	L4	86, 90, 169, 231
G10	20, 34, 129, 311	H20	349	L5	234
G11	123, 129, 186	H21	257	L6	241
G12	19, 20, 23, 26, 32, 41, 65, 66, 95, 118, 119, 124, 125, 127, 129, 163, 165, 180, 183, 185, 187, 188, 194, 200, 206, 249, 268, 293, 301, 339, 343, 349	I1	126	L7	233
		I2	126	L8	233
		I3	126	L9	244
		I4	127, 129, 188	L10	16, 146, 151
		I5	45–47	L11	191, 201
		I6	280	L12	156
		J1	94	L13	56
		J2	94	L14	157
		J3	94	L15	201
		J4	94	L16	42, 43, 157, 166, 167
G13	195, 230	J5	94		
H1	160	J6	94		
H2	69, 96, 230	J7	15, 89, 301, 312	L17	45, 49
H3	193	J8	56	M1	191
H4	15, 250	J9	354	M2	231

Bibliography—Page Number Cross References

M3	225	N21	93, 132, 148, 151, 221, 223, 265	P4	160, 161
M4	232	N22	221	P5	217
M5	270	N23	269	P6	258
M6	125, 351	N24	26, 32, 101, 133, 146–148, 150, 151, 155, 221, 223–225, 264, 265, 281, 296, 305	P7	126
M7	161			P8	16
M8	194			P9	277
M9	233			P10	105
M10	75			R1	92, 96, 191
M11	50, 143			R2	170–172, 174, 255, 282
N1	32				
N2	83, 98	N25	155	R3	174
N3	126	N26	221, 225	R4	42, 214, 260, 351
N4	272, 273	N27	221, 225		
N5	50, 56	N28	124, 181	R5	69, 353
N6	35, 36	N29	124, 181	R6	20, 21, 23, 33, 42, 62, 64, 65, 68, 69, 73, 74, 85, 98, 100, 101, 116, 130, 142, 143, 170, 180, 184, 186, 196, 204, 214, 215, 217, 218, 230, 243, 253, 266, 307, 344, 357, 358
N7	36, 43	N30	124		
N8	51, 52, 54	N31	124		
N9	178	N32	124, 180, 181		
N10	36	N33	124, 181		
N11	24, 26, 30, 62, 63, 119, 150, 165, 176, 190, 199, 202, 219	N34	182		
		N35	191, 236, 280		
		N36	27, 32, 70, 102, 120, 154, 204, 267		
N12	18, 101, 110, 115, 120, 126, 304, 309, 312	N37	33, 120, 139, 147, 192, 348		
		N38	128, 150, 156, 236, 267	R7	14, 18, 22, 23, 38, 39, 42, 69, 71, 99, 100, 105, 111, 130, 141, 166, 180, 184, 186, 195, 215, 217, 229, 259, 283, 305, 310, 344, 348, 354
N13	24, 74, 125, 128, 149, 152, 155, 250				
		N39	233		
		N40	233		
N14	25, 76	N41	233		
N15	74, 250	N42	234		
N16	78, 79, 259	N43	83, 234		
N17	74, 76, 77, 119, 149, 164, 219, 250, 344	O1	175		
		O2	33, 237, 266, 282, 353		
N18	30, 148, 168, 221, 222, 251, 279	O3	284	R8	283
		O4	138	R9	136, 137
		P1	186, 212	R10	232
N19	221, 222	P2	237, 239, 282	R11	256
N20	91, 221, 248	P3	280	R12	301

Bibliography—Page Number Cross References

R13	18, 26, 34, 45, 55, 68, 124, 128, 131, 133, 138, 154, 158, 168, 172, 239, 252–254, 260, 310, 344, 352, 354	S16	316, 320	S30	127, 128, 236, 282
		S17	1, 17, 88, 172, 238, 308, 315–318, 320, 325, 327, 330	T1	255
				T2	235
				T3	114, 233
		S18	115	T4	81, 233
		S19	201, 202	T5	234
R14	198	S20	202	T6	233
R15	200	S21	109	T7	77, 233
R16	83, 233, 234	S22	78	T8	72
R17	254	S23	274	T9	80, 83, 136, 138, 141
R18	107	S24	178, 179, 210, 215, 219, 321		
S1	315, 316, 318, 320			T10	31, 93, 133, 134, 139, 140, 159, 160, 252, 255
		S25	19, 21, 25, 31, 65, 100, 117, 143, 148, 163, 169–171, 173, 177, 188–190, 193, 197, 202, 251, 264, 295, 297, 304, 330, 343, 345–348, 353		
S2	64, 199, 206, 345			T11	185
S3	358			T12	102
S4	138			T13	237
S5	257			T14	250
S6	226, 297			U1	198
S7	18, 23, 99, 111, 117, 125, 142, 143, 147, 155–158, 162, 165, 166, 168–170, 177, 178, 180, 192, 216, 218, 289, 298, 308, 311, 313, 322, 344, 346, 347, 350, 351, 354			U2	207
				U3	136, 142, 180, 260
		S26	12, 19, 22, 23, 25, 45, 50, 83, 107, 115, 135, 168, 189, 229, 242, 305–307, 309, 311, 313, 339, 343, 350	U4	33
				U5	28
				V1	245
				V2	64
				W1	215
				W2	116, 310, 344
				W3	243, 268
		S27	256	W4	120–123, 138
S8	214	S28	261	W5	184, 186, 187
S9	88, 134, 135, 151, 251, 303	S29	23, 25, 31, 54, 66, 84, 89–91, 94, 117, 161, 171, 199, 203, 204, 207, 212, 218, 229, 242, 249, 346, 347, 354	W6	187, 263
				W7	238
S10	83			W8	115
S11	255			W9	161
S12	11			W10	255
S13	164			W11	84
S14	245			Y1	148
S15	24, 137, 275				

WEBSITES ONLY

www6–1
http://www.occupationalinfo.org/appendxc_1.html

www6–2
http://listserv.ed.gov/cgi-bin/wa?A3=ind07&L=RURALED&E=quoted-printable&P=38801&B=-------_%3D_NextPart_001_01C7492C. C4C74D78&T=text%2Fhtml;%20charset=iso-8859-1
http://www.questia.com/magazine/1G1-169755255/web-sites-help-students-and-parents-with-math-and

www6–3
https://thejournal.com/articles/2007/05/14/does-technology-matter-in-schools-ed-wants-your-opinion.aspx

www6–4
https://www.brookings.edu/wp-content/uploads/2012/04/0912_stem_education_transcript.pdf

www7–1
https://nces.ed.gov/nationsreportcard/naepdata/dataset.aspx

www7–2
https://nces.ed.gov/nationsreportcard/mathematics/achieve.aspx

www7–3
https://www.nationsreportcard.gov/reading_math_2015/files/2015_Results_Appendix_Math.pdf
http://www.nationsreportcard.gov/reading_math_2015/#mathematics/state?grade=8

www7–4
https://nces.ed.gov/nationsreportcard/nqt/

www8–1
http://www.iea.nl/fims

www8–2
http://www.iea.nl/brief-history-iea-more

www8–3
http://www.iea.nl/timss-1995

www8–4
https://nces.ed.gov/timss/faq.asp

www8–5
https://nces.ed.gov/Timss/

www8–6
https://nces.ed.gov/timss/educators.asp

www8–7
https://nces.ed.gov/timss/timss2015/timss2015_table46.asp

www8–8
http://www.oecd.org/pisa/

www8–9
http://www.oecd.org/pisa/pisaproducts/pisa2012-2006-rel-items-maths-ENG.pdf

www8–10
http://www.oecd.org/pisa/keyfindings/PISA-2012-results-US.pdf

www8–11
https://nces.ed.gov/pubs2002/2002116.pdf
https://nces.ed.gov/pubs2005/2005003_1.pdf
https://nces.ed.gov/pubs2008/2008016_1.pdf
https://nces.ed.gov/pubs2011/2011004.pdf
https://nces.ed.gov/surveys/pisa/pisa2012/pisa2012highlights_3a.asp
https://nces.ed.gov/surveys/pisa/pisa2015/pisa2015highlights_5.asp

www8–12
http://nces.ed.gov/surveys/pisa/pisa2003highlights_2.asp

Websites Only

www8–13
https://nces.ed.gov/surveys/pisa/pisa2012/pisa2012highlights_8b_1.asp
https://nces.ed.gov/surveys/pisa/pisa2015/pisa2015highlights_5.asp

www8–14
https://www.brookings.edu/wp-content/uploads/2012/04/20080123.pdf

www9–1
http://www.hhs.gov/about/hhshist.html

www9–2
http://www2.ed.gov/about/overview/fed/role.html

www9–3
http://www.presidency.ucsb.edu/ws/?pid=8045

www9–4
http://www.presidency.ucsb.edu/ws/index.php?pid=9082

www9–5
http://www.presidency.ucsb.edu/ws/index.php?pid=9138

www9–6
http://eric.ed.gov/?id=ED018492

www9–7
http://nces.ed.gov/nationsreportcard/about/naephistory.aspx

www9–8
https://www.nagb.org/content/nagb/assets/documents/who-we-are/20-anniversary/bourque-achievement-levels-formatted.pdf

www9–9 and www9–11
http://learningmatters.tv/blog/web-series/discuss-who-was-americas-best-education-president/7879/

www9–10 (and www11–29)
http://www.eric.ed.gov/PDFS/ED193092.pdf

www9–12
http://mathcurriculumcenter.org/PDFS/CCM/summaries/NationAtRisk.pdf

www9–13
http://www2.ed.gov/about/bdscomm/list/com.html#nagb

www9–14
http://www.tecweb.org/eddevel/telecon/de99.html

www9–15
http://www.cnn.com/2005/ALLPOLITICS/01/31/sotu.clinton1997/

www9–16
http://www.washingtonpost.com/wp-srv/politics/special/states/docs/sou99.htm

www9–17
http://www2.ed.gov/policy/elsec/leg/esea02/beginning.html

www9–18
http://www2.ed.gov/nclb/methods/teachers/hqtflexibility.html

www9–19
http://www2.ed.gov/admins/lead/account/growthmodel/proficiency.html

www9–20
https://obamawhitehouse.archives.gov/the-press-office/remarks-president-educate-innovate-campaign-and-science-teaching-and-mentoring-awar

www9–21
https://obamawhitehouse.archives.gov/blog/2010/12/06/president-obama-north-carolina-our-generation-s-sputnik-moment-now

www9–22
https://obamawhitehouse.archives.gov/the-press-office/2011/02/19/weekly-address-win-future-america-must-win-global-competition-education

www9–23
https://obamawhitehouse.archives.gov/the-press-office/2012/07/17/president-obama-announces-plans-new-national-corps-recognize-and-reward-

www9–24
https://obamawhitehouse.archives.gov/the-press-office/2015/03/23/fact-sheet-president-obama-announces-over-240-million-new-stem-commitmen

www9–25
https://www.govtrack.us/congress/bills/113/s358

www9–26
http://www.nytimes.com/2012/07/06/education/no-child-left-behind-whittled-down-under-obama.html?_r=1&pagewanted=all

www9–27
https://www.ed.gov/essa?src=rn
https://obamawhitehouse.archives.gov/the-press-office/2015/12/10/remarks-president-every-student-succeeds-act-signing-ceremony

www9–28
https://www.whitehouse.gov/blog/2017/09/26/president-trump-signs-memorandum-stem-education-funding

www10–1
http://web.math.rochester.edu/people/faculty/rarm/ceeb_59.html

www10–2
https://www.brainyquote.com/quotes/quotes/j/johnwgard121287.html

www10–3
http://web.stanford.edu/~joboaler/

www10–4
http://www.corestandards.org/standards-in-your-state/

www10–5
http://www.corestandards.org/about-the-standards/development-process/

www10–6
http://achievethecore.org

www10–7
http://www.corestandards.org/other-resources/key-shifts-in-mathematics/

www10–8
http://www.corestandards.org/Math/Content/7/SP/

www10–9
https://www.hslda.org/commoncore/InTheNews.aspx

www10–10
http://www.oecd.org/pisa/keyfindings/PISA-2012-results-US.pdf

www11–1, www11–7, and www11–11
https://www.brookings.edu/wp-content/uploads/2012/04/20080123.pdf

www11–2
https://obamawhitehouse.archives.gov/the-press-office/remarks-president-arnold-missouri-town-hall

www11–3
http://www.tc.columbia.edu/articles/2009/october/arne-duncan-media-coverage/

www11–4
https://www.ets.org/s/praxis/pdf/5732.pdf

www11–5
https://www.ets.org/praxis/states

www11–6
http://www.washingtonpost.com/wp-srv/politics/special/states/docs/sou99.htm

www11-8, www11-9, and www11-10
https://www.brookings.edu/wp-content/uploads/2012/04/20081022_algebra.pdf

www11-12
http://old.mathleague.com

www11-13
http://www.ncsl.org/legislatures-elections/legisdata/legislator-occupations-national-data.aspx

www11-14
http://politicalticker.blogs.cnn.com/2012/05/24/romney-defends-class-size-stance-to-teachers/

www11-15
http://www.apnewsarchive.com/1987/Educator-Says-Homework-Not-An-Absolute-Good-/id-3c6c3c8af02e7ef1a42ed9e304179f9e?SearchText=Homework;Display_

www11-16
http://news.google.com/newspapers?nid=2199&dat=19921014&id=r-JEzAAAAIBAJ&sjid=IOcFAAAAIBAJ&pg=3702,4455137

www11-17
http://www.carnegiefoundation.org/developmental-math

www11-18
http://nces.ed.gov/pubs2009/2009030.pdf

www11-19
https://www2.ed.gov/about/offices/list/oii/nonpublic/statistics.html#homeschl

www11-20
http://fairtest.org/testoptional-admissions-list-tops-900-colleges-and

www11–21
http://articles.chicagotribune.com/1994-06-17/news/9406170113_1_re-centering-average-sat-score-verbal

www11–22
https://www.theatlantic.com/education/archive/2014/03/the-common-core-is-driving-the-changes-to-the-sat/284320/

www11–23
https://www.ada.org/~/media/ADA/Education%20and%20Careers/Files/dat_test_sampleitems.ashx

www11–24
http://www.corestandards.org/about-the-standards/

www11–25
http://mathdl.maa.org/mathDL/?pa=mathNews&sa=view&newsId=250

www11–26
http://transcripts.cnn.com/TRANSCRIPTS/1312/03/acl.01.html

www11–27
https://www.insidehighered.com/news/2006/03/03/engineers

www11–28
http://topics.nytimes.com/top/opinion/series/steven_strogatz_on_the_elements_of_math/index.html

www11–29 (and www9–10)
http://www.eric.ed.gov/PDFS/ED193092.pdf

www11–30
https://www.singaporemath.com

www11–31
http://www.singaporemath.com/v/PMSS_comparison.pdf

www11–32
http://www.cep-dc.org/displayDocument.cfm?DocumentID=405
http://files.eric.ed.gov/fulltext/ED532666.pdf

www11–33
http://www.youtube.com/watch?v=NO0cvqT1tAE

www11–34
http://www.unc.edu/news/clips/jan02/jan11.htm

www11–35
http://www.sciencemag.org/news/2008/07/girls-boys-math

www11–36
http://www.nbcnews.com/id/24882374/ns/us_news-education/t/gender-based-math-gap-missing-some-places/#.WLRC7zvyqCQ

www11–37
https://www.nsf.gov/about/budget/

www11–38
http://www.nsa.gov/research/math_research/index.shtml

www11–39
https://www.oyez.org/cases/2001/00-1073

www11–40
http://caselaw.findlaw.com/summary/opinion/us-supreme-court/2002/02/19/108313.html

www11–41
http://izonenyc.org/initiatives/school-of-one/

www11–42
https://www.oecd.org/pisa/pisaproducts/pisainfocus/48363440.pdf

www11–43
http://www.nctm.org/Standards-and-Positions/Position-Statements/The-Role-of-Elementary-Mathematics-Specialists-in-the-Teaching-and-Learning-of-Mathematics/

www11–44
http://content.time.com/time/covers/0,16641,19710920,00.html?iid=sr-link1

www13–1
http://www.educationdive.com/news/whats-the-future-of-ipads-in-schools/401354/

ww13–2
http://www.gatesfoundation.org/What-We-Do/US-Program/College-Ready-Education#OurStrategy

www13–3
www.nytimes.com/2014/01/28/science/salman-khan-turned-family-tutoring-into-khan-academy.html?_r=0

www13–4
https://www.khanacademy.org/talks-and-interviews/schools-using-khan-academy

www16–1
http://www.bfskinner.org

www17–1
http://www.youtube.com/watch?v=aFTNmGBKC2Y

www17–2
http://www.bbo.org.uk/training/student-training-and-exams.php

www20–1
https://airandspace.si.edu/stories/editorial/sputnik-and-space-age-60

INDEX (Not in CONTENTS or BIBLIOGRAPHY)

abstract, 31, 86, 90, 98, 118, 147, 157, 159–160, 164, 241, 286, 292, 295, 299, 322, 326–327
achievement tests, 68, 164, 166, 208
ACT, 10, 104, 219, 239, 245, 247, 332, 336–337
act it out, 105
Adams, President John, 57
AFT, 184
age problem, 13, 158, 292
Alexander, Lamar, 64, 206
algorithm, 7, 52, 87, 91–92, 104–105, 113, 150, 152, 175, 241, 246, 272, 275, 281, 283
Allen, Frank, 230
America 2000, 66
American Association of University Women, 255
AMS, 221
Andrews, George, 232
AP courses/exams, 167, 328, 336
Archimedes, 321
Aristotle, 35
Armed Forces, 33, 76, 160
art, 15–16, 69, 224, 247, 271, 278, 304, 340
average problem, 1–3, 10, 159, 220
Bacon, Roger, 17
Ball State Teachers College, 259
ballet, 131, 322
Barbie Doll, 255
Bell, Terrel H., 60–63
Bloom, Benjamin, 340
Boston College, 259
Bourbaki, Nicolas, 80
Bridges of Königsberg, 244
Bush, Jeb, 213–214
busywork, 197, 199
CAI, 319

calculator, 1, 8, 92, 97, 107, 124, 140, 219–220, 236, 239, 279, 286, 326, 355
calculus, 3, 10, 14, 31, 47, 106, 131, 157–158, 231, 241, 291, 299, 325, 328, 336
Canada, 53, 55, 256
Canada, Geoffrey, 353
Cantor, George, 271
Carnegie Corp, 17, 60, 123, 226
Carroll, Lewis, 341
Cassidy, Butch, 323
Caulkins, G. J., 7
Center for American Progress, 192
Center for Universal Education, 211, 227, 283
Center for Women Policy Studies, 227, 255
century, 11, 29, 32–33, 65, 73, 79–81, 116, 131, 144, 149, 155, 166, 198, 201, 205, 208, 220, 264, 267–268, 270, 274, 281, 287, 299, 311, 320, 329, 338, 340–341, 354
Charlottesville, 64, 100
charter school, 9, 23, 66, 205, 230, 336
charting, 105, 225, 273, 292, 300
cheating, 130, 198, 211, 217–218
Cheshire Cat, 84, 341
China, 48, 53, 172, 190, 235
circle, 44, 102–103, 111, 133, 140, 220
civil rights, 59–60, 84
cohort, 40–41, 50–51, 120, 344
coin problem, 13, 158
collective bargaining, 186
Columbia University Teachers College, 121–122
COM, 27, 78–79, 117, 149, 219

401

communication, 15, 93, 131, 188, 223–224
computer, 7, 9, 15, 26, 47, 57, 63, 69, 72, 150, 204, 220, 236–241, 255, 279–284, 286, 319–320, 322, 326, 329, 337, 356
computer adaptive, 283
congruence, 44, 96, 103, 136, 175
connection, 93, 133, 155, 169, 222–224, 234, 240, 245, 265, 295, 303, 315, 105, 146, 325
Cooper, Anderson, 232
cooperative learning, 92, 94, 248–249, 275, 283
corporate reform, 22–23, 69, 243, 283, 353
Council on Foreign Relations, 34
counting, 103, 262, 300
Couric, Katie, 261
critical thinking, 20, 98, 127, 293
Cross, Christopher, 61, 63
cross-cancel, 112, 134
cross-multiply, 134
cross tabulation, 300
Dance of the Lemons, 187
DAT, 10, 219–220
decimal, 13, 46, 76, 113, 124, 140, 153, 174, 286, 291, 300
deduction, 88, 98, 105
de facto curriculum, 100, 143, 170
delay, 59, 87, 91, 102–103, 154, 166–168, 187, 274, 316
Dewey, John, 73, 85, 229
dice, 103, 173, 245
Dictionary of Occupational Titles, 31
Diophantine equation, 244
discovery, 73, 85–90, 92, 98, 106, 132, 151, 251, 303–304
discrete math, 148–149, 241, 325
disruption, 354

division, 12–13, 46, 92, 97, 113, 153
DoDEA, 37
DPMA 113, 136, 234, 245
DRT, 13, 87, 158–159
DSM, 137
Duke University TIP, 158, 248, 299, 332
Einstein, Albert, 9, 256
engineer, 27, 55, 58–59, 61–62, 71, 81, 135, 214, 233, 235, 247, 310
equation, 3, 7, 16, 103, 105, 111–112, 114, 134, 146, 155–156, 197, 219–220, 225, 244, 246, 265, 273, 275, 286, 291–292, 300, 305
equivalence, 150, 239, 270
ESEA, 60, 67
ESSA, 72
ethnomath, 174
ETS, 124, 238–239
Euler, 244
exponents, 102, 114, 124, 134, 225, 321
expression (algebraic), 134, 152, 155–156, 224
ExxonMobil, 54
Falvo, Kristja, 261
FCAT, 68, 214
Fennell, Francis, 110
FERPA, 261, 263
FIMS, 46–47, 84
Finland, 46, 53, 123, 163, 252–253, 310, 344
Florida, 68, 213–214
FOIL, 113, 234, 245
Fordham, 67, 228
France, 46, 53, 56, 269–270
frequency, 103, 316
Friedman, Milton, 63
function, 47, 102, 120, 124, 148–149, 156, 174, 239, 241, 296, 299–

300, 320
fuzzy math, 91, 97
Galileo, 355
Gates Foundation, 227, 283–284
GED, 220
gender, 37, 174, 254–258
geometry, 14, 31, 34, 36, 46–47, 50, 76, 94, 109, 114, 120, 124, 136, 144–147, 151, 155, 157–158, 160, 175, 177–178, 181, 223–224, 288, 296, 300, 333, 339
Germany, 12, 46, 53, 55–56, 62
gifted, 78, 156, 162–165, 203, 249, 276, 283, 289, 332, 334
Gillard, Julia, 211, 283
GMAT, 10, 219
Goals 2000, 66, 101
Google, 240
Graham, Martha, 322
graphics, 54, 238, 280, 285, 327
graph theory, 149, 241, 244
GRE, 10, 219
Guthrie, Jim, 63
Harris-Perry, Melissa, 14
Harvard, 76, 107, 121, 159–160, 183, 194, 214, 241, 256, 280, 283, 319, 347
H-1B Visa, 71, 235
Haycock, Kati, 158
Hilbert, David, 45
Hong Kong, 48, 53, 272
Huffington, Arianna, 358
Hufstedler, Shirley, 61
IBM, 329
IEA, 46–47
imaginary number, 134
imitation, 138, 275
induction, 98, 148
inequality (math), 220, 234
integer, 50, 102, 124, 244

intermediate grades, 327
internet, 7, 49, 54, 66, 124, 205, 238, 240, 283
intuition, 89, 98, 132, 277–278, 302
iPad, 282, 284, 321
irrational number, 134, 323
isomorphism, 149
ISTE, 227, 235, 280
Japan, 12, 46, 48, 50, 53, 62, 115, 163, 168, 172, 189–190, 234, 272, 343
Jobs, Steve, 279
Johns Hopkins University, 254
Kansas, 43
Kennedy, Justice Anthony, 261–263
Keppel, Francis, 292, 302
Khan Academy, 284–285
Korea, 53, 252, 344
Langenberg, Donald, 61
Latin, 276
law enforcement, 10, 30, 329
Lehrer, Tom, 7, 153
lesson study, 343
Levine, Arthur, 122
Lincoln, Abraham, 5
logic, 10, 47, 86, 105, 133, 138, 149, 151, 224, 240–241, 325
LSAT, 10
MAA, 74, 78, 120, 221, 232, 265
MARS, 137
Maryland, 158, 259
Maslow, Abraham, 13
Massachusetts, vi, 42–43, 55, 101, 126, 135, 195, 356
Master Teacher Corps, 71
Mastery Learning, 340
MATHCOUNTS, 43, 111–112, 175, 225, 227, 324, 334
mathematician, 6–7, 14–16, 28, 57–58, 73, 75, 77–81, 86–88, 98, 106, 115, 133, 137, 153, 174, 177, 220,

224, 235, 244, 250–251, 259, 271, 273, 287, 290, 293, 306
Math League, 43, 172, 227, 324
math major, 67, 121, 126–127, 135, 260, 324, 328, 356
Mattel, 255
MCAT, 10
medicine, 10, 180, 185, 270, 311, 342, 344
memorization, 14, 75, 92–93, 106, 114, 132, 272, 275, 339
mental math, 12, 112, 239, 243, 245
merit pay, 130, 264
middle school, 11, 38, 47, 49–50, 103, 114, 117, 125, 131, 135, 146, 154, 163, 166, 169, 175, 183, 197, 200, 247, 291, 306, 327, 332, 337
mile wide/inch deep, 47, 101, 247
Milgram, James, 98
Minnesota, 43
Miss America, 355
mixture problems, 13, 158–159, 220, 273
mobility, 62, 144–145, 186
Montessori, Maria, 315
MSNBC, 14
Mu Alpha Theta, 334
multiplication, 46, 97, 112, 140, 154, 209, 224, 245, 250, 275, 285–286, 300, 348
multiplication principle, 300
NAGB, 35, 37, 43, 60, 64
National Conference of State Legislatures, 179
National Education Technology Plan, 33, 237, 266, 282, 352
National Institute of Child Health and Human Development, 34
National Merit Scholarship, 78, 255
National Museum of Mathematics, 228, 235
NCLB, 42, 67–69, 71–72, 165, 203, 212–214, 217–218, 230, 266, 340
NDEA, 58
NEA, 27, 145, 147–148, 155–156, 184
negative number, 113
New Hampshire, 43
new New Math, 91, 93–94, 101
non-math math teacher, 203, 305–308, 314, 330, 358
North Carolina, 70, 158, 256, 356
Northwestern University, 257–258
NSF, 57–58, 61, 81, 107, 149, 177, 247, 258–259, 294, 355
null set, 234
number line, 103, 246
number theory, 124–125, 225, 241, 294, 325
nutrition (hunger), 13–14, 26, 174
OECD, 51–54, 108, 266
Oklahoma, Owasso, 261
order of operations, 102, 245
osmosis, 274–275, 348
pattern recognition, 245, 277, 328
PCAT, 10
Peanuts, 83
pedagogy, 22, 73, 90, 118–121, 169, 175, 179, 184, 229, 263, 304, 306, 338–339
peer grading, 261, 263
Pennsylvania State University, 232
percent problem, 3, 10, 34, 38, 52, 77, 112, 124, 220, 225, 232, 275, 286, 291
Piaget, Jean, 230–231, 274, 326
picture, 133, 172–173, 176, 178, 326
Pick's Formula, 175
PI-MATH, 323–341, 354
place holder, 116

Index

place value, 13, 46, 150, 245, 275, 292
Plato, 27, 355
Poland, 53, 55, 168, 344
political correctness, 173
politics, 9, 11, 21, 32, 42, 45, 57, 63, 66, 68, 71–73, 84, 130, 150, 171, 173–174, 179–180, 183, 186, 193, 205, 218, 226, 233, 252, 287, 289, 334, 344, 351, 354, 357
poverty, 14, 20, 60, 84, 174, 206–207
Praxis, 124
pre-calculus, 10, 232, 299
Pressey, Sidney, 320
prime number, 13, 103, 134
PRISM, 221–222
private school, 3, 11–13, 55, 107, 111, 142, 164, 171, 183, 186, 188, 203, 230, 232, 280, 289, 295, 315, 332–333, 335, 356–357
probability, 36, 44, 47, 93, 109, 102–103, 112, 120, 124, 148–150, 209, 220, 223, 241, 291–292
problem solving, 1, 54, 93, 97–98, 104–107, 135, 142, 147–148, 164, 198, 219, 222–223, 241, 244, 251, 274–275, 277, 286, 300, 303, 308, 325, 337, 351
Progressive Education Association, 147, 149
proof, 15, 77, 80, 86, 95, 103, 134, 149–151, 223–224, 273, 300, 303
proportion, 10, 41, 44, 112, 134, 150, 275–276
Pythagorean Theorem, 34, 88, 94, 102, 133, 146
Race to the Top, 66, 70, 71, 99
radical change, 27–28, 222, 280, 286, 314, 323, 340
rain forest, 8, 91, 94

rate of change, 150
rational number, 231
real-life, 55, 86, 94, 108, 115, 137, 265, 273
real number, 124, 134, 149, 296
rectangle, 13, 35–36, 43, 113, 154, 224, 245–246, 275, 285, 293
reflection, 225, 275, 278
Regents Math Exam, 136, 213
representation, 15, 105, 131, 133, 146, 150–151, 174, 219, 223–225, 275, 277, 285, 326
revolution, 28–29, 57, 91, 118, 228, 236, 241, 282, 288, 312, 321
Rockefeller Foundation, 17
Romberg, Thomas, 144
Romney, Mitt, 195, 233
Ross, Arnold, 294, 301
rote learning, 92, 132, 152, 175, 212, 262, 264, 275
Rubik's Cube, 245
Russia (Soviet Union), 11, 51, 58, 62, 70–71, 73, 75, 78, 81
SAT, 1–4, 104, 175, 206, 219–220, 239, 247, 255, 285, 332, 336
Scalia, Justice Antonin, 263
scaling up, 339, 352
Schmid, Wilfried, 107
science, 6, 10, 14, 15, 17, 31–32, 47, 51, 58, 61–62, 64–66, 70–71, 81, 100, 115, 125–126, 129, 135, 149, 154, 181, 231, 233, 236, 247–248, 256, 259, 265, 273, 292, 342
seat-work, 189, 343
self-esteem, 20, 249, 346
set, 47, 79, 80, 96, 124, 140–141, 148–149, 175, 234, 241, 246, 293, 299–300
Shanker, Albert, 311
Shriver, Eunice Kennedy, 34

SIMS, 47
Singapore, 48, 49, 53, 55, 99, 108, 249–250
slope, 18, 112, 146, 156, 169, 177
Slovak Republic, 52
SMPY, 254
SMSG, 75, 77–78, 83–84, 176, 259, 271, 324, 334, 355
social change, 81, 348–349
Socrates, 315
solve a simpler problem, 1, 105, 300
SOTU, 59, 64, 66, 126
Spellings, Margaret, 32, 236
square root, 153, 220
SSAT, 43, 335
SSTP, 294, 355
stages of cognitive development, 274
Stanford University, 96, 230, 248, 259
statistics, 10, 14, 31, 36, 47, 54, 57, 93, 102, 120, 149–150, 194, 211, 224, 230, 232, 325, 328, 332
STEAM, 247
Steinem, Gloria, 109
STEM, 11, 33, 41, 61, 71–72, 205, 235, 247, 250, 260
Strogatz, Steven, 235
StudentsFirst, 54, 228
Sudoku, 245
Sweden, 46, 53, 56, 270
Syracuse University, 259
tablet, 237, 281, 283, 279, 286, 322–324, 326–327, 330, 333, 335
talent, 10, 59, 62, 129, 140, 157, 163, 165, 234, 254, 256, 268, 277, 290, 299, 314, 328, 332, 334, 348, 356
Teach for America, 228, 344
Teach to One, 265
teachable moment, 216, 304, 330
television, 11, 15, 54, 173, 216, 232–233, 245, 281, 321
tenure, 181, 184, 186
Thorndike, Edward, 315
TIMSS videos, 12, 22, 50, 107, 115, 189, 272, 339
trading papers, 261–263, 339
transfer, 12, 143–144, 184, 187, 266, 274, 276, 278, 295, 341
trigonometry, 14, 26, 109, 145, 149, 175, 214, 337
UICSM, vi, 75, 77, 82–83, 86–87, 176, 259, 324, 334, 355
University of California, 10, 257–258
University of Georgia, 126
University of Pennsylvania, 231
University of Wisconsin, 257–258
U.S. math teacher, 115, 265
U.S. math textbook, 170
validity, 67, 134, 151, 208, 215, 218, 234, 330
Venn Diagram, 4, 300
vision, 75–76, 88, 91, 142, 218, 223, 286, 316, 318, 322–323, 350
visitation, 187–188
voucher, 23, 63, 203, 266
Waterman, Alan, 58
whole number, 46, 84, 91, 104, 113, 147, 175, 209, 214, 245, 287, 300
Woods Hole Conference, 248, 300, 318
word problem, 11–13, 36, 52, 55, 139, 158–159, 174, 183, 220, 273, 329, 334
work backwards, 105
work problem, 13, 159
World War II, 57, 74, 77, 121
writing about math, 73, 93, 176, 248
Yale University, 77–78, 232
YouTube, 7, 284
zero, 80, 116, 140

Made in the USA
Middletown, DE
23 October 2017